T0239827

Software Essentials
Design and Construction

Chapman & Hall/CRC Innovations in Software Engineering and Software Development

Series Editor
Richard LeBlanc
Chair, Department of Computer Science and Software Engineering, Seattle University

AIMS AND SCOPE

This series covers all aspects of software engineering and software development. Books in the series will be innovative reference books, research monographs, and textbooks at the undergraduate and graduate level. Coverage will include traditional subject matter, cutting-edge research, and current industry practice, such as agile software development methods and service-oriented architectures. We also welcome proposals for books that capture the latest results on the domains and conditions in which practices are most effective.

PUBLISHED TITLES

Software Essentials: Design and Construction
Adair Dingle

Software Test Attacks to Break Mobile and Embedded Devices
Jon Duncan Hagar

Software Designers in Action: A Human-Centric Look at Design Work
André van der Hoek and Marian Petre

Fundamentals of Dependable Computing for Software Engineers
John Knight

Introduction to Combinatorial Testing
D. Richard Kuhn, Raghu N. Kacker, and Yu Lei

Building Enterprise Systems with ODP: An Introduction to Open Distributed Processing
Peter F. Linington, Zoran Milosevic, Akira Tanaka, and Antonio Vallecillo

Software Engineering: The Current Practice
Václav Rajlich

Software Development: An Open Source Approach
Allen Tucker, Ralph Morelli, and Chamindra de Silva

CHAPMAN & HALL/CRC INNOVATIONS IN
SOFTWARE ENGINEERING AND SOFTWARE DEVELOPMENT

Software Essentials
Design and Construction

Adair Dingle

Seattle University
Washington, USA

CRC Press
Taylor & Francis Group
Boca Raton London New York

CRC Press is an imprint of the
Taylor & Francis Group, an **informa** business
A CHAPMAN & HALL BOOK

CRC Press
Taylor & Francis Group
6000 Broken Sound Parkway NW, Suite 300
Boca Raton, FL 33487-2742

First issued in paperback 2020

© 2014 by Taylor & Francis Group, LLC
CRC Press is an imprint of Taylor & Francis Group, an Informa business

No claim to original U.S. Government works

ISBN-13: 978-1-4398-4120-4 (hbk)
ISBN-13: 978-0-367-65913-4 (pbk)

This book contains information obtained from authentic and highly regarded sources. Reasonable efforts have been made to publish reliable data and information, but the author and publisher cannot assume responsibility for the validity of all materials or the consequences of their use. The authors and publishers have attempted to trace the copyright holders of all material reproduced in this publication and apologize to copyright holders if permission to publish in this form has not been obtained. If any copyright material has not been acknowledged please write and let us know so we may rectify in any future reprint.

Except as permitted under U.S. Copyright Law, no part of this book may be reprinted, reproduced, transmitted, or utilized in any form by any electronic, mechanical, or other means, now known or hereafter invented, including photocopying, microfilming, and recording, or in any information storage or retrieval system, without written permission from the publishers.

For permission to photocopy or use material electronically from this work, please access www.copyright. com (http://www.copyright.com/) or contact the Copyright Clearance Center, Inc. (CCC), 222 Rosewood Drive, Danvers, MA 01923, 978-750-8400. CCC is a not-for-profit organization that provides licenses and registration for a variety of users. For organizations that have been granted a photocopy license by the CCC, a separate system of payment has been arranged.

Trademark Notice: Product or corporate names may be trademarks or registered trademarks, and are used only for identification and explanation without intent to infringe.

Library of Congress Cataloging-in-Publication Data

Dingle, Adair.
    Software essentials : design and construction / author, Adair Dingle.
        pages cm -- (Chapman & Hall/CRC innovations in software engineering and
        software development series)
    Includes bibliographical references and index.
    ISBN 978-1-4398-4120-4 (hardback)
    1. Software architecture. 2. Computer software--Development. I. Title.

QA76.76.D47D545 2014
005.1'2--dc23
                                                      2014008078

Visit the Taylor & Francis Web site at
http://www.taylorandfrancis.com

and the CRC Press Web site at
http://www.crcpress.com

Contents

SECTION III **SOFTWARE DESIGN**

Preface

WHY THIS BOOK?

Why should you read this book? The short answer is to study software design from a structured but hands-on perspective and to understand different models of control flow, memory, dynamic behavior, extensibility, etc. Software complexity and the growing impact of legacy systems motivate a renewed interest in software design and modeling. We emphasize design (and construction) in this text, using and contrasting C# and C++.

Many CS texts are "learn-to" books that focus on one programming language or tool. When perspective is so limited to a specific tool or programming language, high-level concepts are often slighted. Students may gain exposure to an idea via a "cookbook" implementation and thus fail to truly absorb essential concepts. Students and/or practitioners can understand and apply design principles more readily when such concepts are explicitly defined and illustrated. Design, not just syntax, must be stressed. The progression of programming languages, software process methodologies, and development tools continues to support abstraction: software developers should exploit this abstraction and solve problems (design) without being tied to a particular syntax or tool.

Software design and modeling are neither new nor trendy topics. Software development often focuses on immediate effect: implement, test (minimally), and deploy. Yet, the complexity, scale, and longevity of modern software require an intricate understanding of a software system as a whole—components and relationships, user interfaces, persistent data, etc. To accommodate existing use while preserving longevity, a software developer must look forward for extensibility and backward for compatibility. Hence, software developers must understand software design.

WHO SHOULD READ THIS BOOK?

Anyone who desires a stronger understanding of deliberate software design or more exposure to evaluating design options should read this book. Targeted readers include software developers, professionals, and students who seek a sustainable perspective on software construction. Aspiring software developers, or even experienced developers, who desire an emphasis on design and an understanding of long-term versus short-term analysis would benefit from the approach taken by this text.

Although a rudimentary understanding of software development is assumed, key terms and concepts are defined. Many different examples are given. Expertise with any particular language, platform, or IDE is not required. To assist those relatively new to programming, appendices are included to reinforce indirection and details relevant to C++ and C#. Moreover, an extensive glossary is included, defining over 200 common terms associated with software design and construction.

WHAT SHOULD READERS EXPECT TO GAIN FROM THIS TEXT?

By emphasizing software design and construction, this text may fill knowledge gaps by providing: a practical summary of object-oriented design (OOD), a succinct summary of memory management principles, an analysis of software design alongside knowledge of background processes, and comparative design options. Two immediate benefits are the recognition of structured, readable code as well as the effective use of dynamic memory without unintentional memory leaks and data corruption. Additionally, developers with backgrounds in either C++ or C#/Java, but not necessarily both, may benefit from explanations of language differences.

With respect to OOD (object-oriented design), this text examines specific motives for and consequences of design. Readers should learn: when to use inheritance and when not; how to design compact and extensible code; to avoid inheritance when composition suffices; how to simulate multiple inheritance; and when the overhead of polymorphism is not warranted. Overloading as a design option is also covered.

HOW IS THIS TEXT RELEVANT TO (PROFESSIONAL) SOFTWARE DEVELOPMENT?

In the rush to fill technical positions, the education of software developers often emphasizes skills over concepts: learn a new programming language, use a new tool, assess a user interface to add functionality to an existing system, etc. A high-level system perspective is lost. Without such a perspective, software development may yield applications that are feature-rich but not easily usable. Hence, this book strives to fill in knowledge gaps. To place design into context, we uncover background processes so that a software developer can gauge the impact of design.

Software design has evolved to a higher level of abstraction. Software tools, design, and testing methodologies as well as the construction of utilities and standard libraries, have decreased the complexity of producing software. Hardware and environmental dependencies have been abstracted away. Data storage and retrieval have been streamlined. Utilities provide functions for sorting, selection, and comparison. Standard algorithms have been encoded. Thus, this text emphasizes design choices. Although copious examples are given in C# and/or C++, often with redesigned alternatives, design (not syntax) remains the focal point.

WHO MIGHT NOT BENEFIT FROM READING THIS BOOK?

Developers with extensive software design and implementation experience may find this text too elementary, unless more exposure to deliberate software design or a transition to OOD is desired. Developers interested in examining real-time systems, event-handling software, or distributed systems should consult a different text.

Novice programmers may be overwhelmed. This book is not a "learn to program" book. It can be viewed as a "learn to program well" book, or a "software design" book. Although many code examples are given and supportive appendices provide specific C++ and C# language details, the book has a conceptual rather than a syntactic emphasis. Hence, a novice programmer who wishes to learn C++ or learn C# should consult another text or, as noted in the next section (detailed book outline), use this text in conjunction with an introductory programming text.

Acknowledgments

Many thanks are in order.

I have the good fortune to work with Richard LeBlanc, currently chair of the CSSE Department at Seattle University. Rich first suggested that I write this book, and he gave me the encouragement and support necessary to do so. Rich routinely strives to improve computer science education and endeavors to bring out the best in everyone. He truly is the role model of intelligence, competence, and humility.

For over a decade, I have been most fortunate to work with Michael Forrest Smith, a man of unparalleled wit and wisdom. Mike helped prepare several drafts of this text for different classes, gave me lots of advice, and regularly inquired about progress (in a jovial but persistent manner). A master of piquant kindness, Mike is simply exceptional. I also wish to thank other members of my department, all of whom are wonderful colleagues: Jeff Gilles, Eric Larson, Renny Philipose, Susan Reeder, Roshanak Roshandel, Ben Tribelhorn, and Yingwu Zhu.

Across a couple of courses on software design, dozens of students read drafts of this text, mastered this material, and gave valuable feedback. The text is better now because of their feedback as to what examples worked (and which did not) as well as what material proved useful in interviews and "real" work. Kudos to the many students who meticulously recorded errors and identified unclear passages.

In addition, several colleagues outside of Seattle University have been consistently supportive and helpful. Drawing on his vast knowledge and consulting experience, Robert Field has proffered many anecdotes, whether for technical detail, professional insight, or current design practices. Brian provided especially pertinent feedback—thanks for reading and editing every page! For general good humor and periodic reminders (including debates about perfectionism versus procrastination), I thank Gwen, Donald, and Eleanor.

This book has been prepared with the timely and professional assistance of the editorial staff of Taylor & Francis. Jennifer Stair, Amor Nanas, Samantha White, and Marsha Pronin all were very supportive and provided valuable assistance. Special thanks are due to my editor, Randi Cohen, for her patience, insight, and general oversight.

Lastly, and most importantly, thanks to Tom Hildebrandt. As a brilliant and broadly experienced professional, Tom is always an excellent source of knowledge as well as a touchstone for insightful conversation and analyses. His disassembler code (Chapter 7) is but one small example of his ongoing contributions to the professional software community.

Detailed Book Outline

I N THE NEXT FEW PAGES, we describe the format of the book and succinctly summarize each chapter and appendix. To accommodate readers from different backgrounds, we provide several sample reading paths
through the text. We conclude by outlining the general chapter format.

This book consists of ten chapters, separated into four sections. In
addition, four appendices supplement the text. These appendices isolate
implementation details that tend to be language dependent. Readers may
consult these appendices to reinforce details covered at the design level
in the text or to discern language dependencies. References are provided.
Another supplement provided is a glossary of over 200 common software
design and engineering terms.

Section I: Software Construction reviews characteristics of modern
software as well as software development. Both chapters are summative
in nature.

Chapter 1 seeks to motivate the effort expended for deliberate software
design. To establish a foundation for development, Chapter 1 defines software engineering and the software development life cycle and illustrates
the many modes of modeling. In short, Chapter 1 stresses that software
development must rest on design to produce usable and reusable code that
meets user expectations.

Chapter 2 traces the process of software execution, identifying tools that
support abstraction and ease the task of programming. The main stages of
a compiler are summarized. Programming language support for abstraction is discussed, as are key differences between structured and OO code.

Section II: Software Fundamentals summarizes fundamental elements
of software, providing many examples, analyses, design principles, and
guidelines.

Chapter 3 covers structured control flow, controlled interruption, and readability. Boolean logic, its application, and use are examined. Recursion and iteration are briefly contrasted, noting overhead.

Chapter 4 reviews memory management, an oft-neglected topic. Several distinctions are made: heap versus stack memory; C++ versus C# memory; explicit versus implicit allocation; and explicit versus implicit deallocation. The chapter closes by contrasting designs that emphasize storage versus computation.

Chapter 5 establishes the foundation of class design, noting essential differences between C# and C++. The chapter outlines contractual design—software written to fulfill a contract with the user. Design assumptions, conditions, and invariants are enumerated as contractual documentation.

Section III: Software Design provides an in-depth evaluation of software design using the object-oriented paradigm. The effect of design, rather than mechanics, is stressed. Again, many examples, analyses, and guidelines reinforce the prose.

Chapter 6 explores different ways in which to structure interdependent types and compares design alternatives. Inheritance as a design option is examined in detail, including the potential overuse of inheritance, its costs and benefits, and designs that simulate inheritance.

Chapter 7 examines the true benefit of OOD: language support for polymorphism. The design effects of polymorphism, with respect to both utility and longevity, are evaluated. As an example, code from an actual software product, a disassembler, is presented and dissected.

Chapter 8 takes the unusual step of comparing design alternatives, noting any impact of language choice. With multiple inheritance and its simulation as an example, the costs and benefits of different approaches are assessed. Different types of class design are also evaluated.

Section IV: Software Durability is summative in nature. The goal of its two chapters is to expose the reader to essential information and general software development goals. Both chapters are introductory: for a more detailed exposition, the reader is encouraged to consult additional texts.

Chapter 9 includes a brief review of the use of exceptions and provides an overview of software testing.

Chapter 10 explores software evolution and nonfunctional properties as characteristics of software longevity.

The appendices reinforce concepts covered in the text. Appendices A and B assist the C# or Java programmer who is transitioning to C++. Appendices C and D display the elegance of OOD by iteratively tracing design examples that exhibit the consistency and simplicity of well-designed code.

Appendix A covers the "pointer" type, a language construct broadly supported in C and C++, but not in C# or Java. Proper use as well as inappropriate handling are illustrated through pertinent examples.

Appendix B (Heap Memory and Aliases) extends the discussion of Appendix A by examining use of the "pointer" type to hold the address of a memory block allocated on the heap. Explicit allocation and deallocation are demonstrated. Examples and discussion enumerate class responsibilities when heap memory is allocated within a C++ object. Detailed examination of copy semantics closes the appendix.

Appendix C defines C++ function pointers, a programming language construct supported by C++ but not Java. C# provides the delegate construct, which is similar. This appendix mirrors programming language evolution, with respect to increasing support for polymorphism. An inventory design example is traced from a crude, and rigid, C-like design through refinements to a streamlined and extensible C++ solution using virtual functions.

Appendix D examines operator overloading as a design technique that enhances abstraction. C++ supports extensive operator overloading. Java supports none. C# supports a limited set of overloaded operators. Examples of intuitive and effective operator overloading, including type conversion, are provided. Language differences are summarized.

SAMPLE READING PATHS FOR THIS BOOK

This book provides an overview of software design, with emphases on underlying memory and control models, deliberate design, contractual expectations, and comparative analysis of design. The text thus should appeal to readers with different backgrounds. To accommodate different levels of experience, sample suggested readings are given below. Regardless of experience, Chapter 4 and Appendices A and B cover material highly recommended for readers without a C++ background.

Sample suggested paths for reading this book:

Intermediate programmers: the whole text is applicable	
As needed to fill in gaps:	Section I and Appendices A and B
Emphasize:	Sections II and III and Chapter 9
Optional:	Appendices C and D, Chapter 10

Engineers with rudimentary software knowledge:

Chapters 1 and 2, Appendix A, Chapter 3, Appendix B, Chapters 4, 5, 6, and 7

Experienced programmers who seek more exposure to deliberate software design:

As needed to fill in gaps:	Chapters 1 and 2, Appendices A
	Chapter 3 and Appendix B
Emphasize:	Chapters 4, 5, and 6, Appendix C
	Chapters 7 and 8
Optional:	Appendix D, Section IV

C programmers transitioning to OOD:

Emphasize:	Chapters 4, 5, and 6, Appendix C
	Chapters 7 and 8, Appendix D
Optional:	Section IV

C# or Java programmers familiar with OOD but transitioning to C++:

Transition:	Appendices A and B, Chapter 4
Review:	Chapters 5 and 6
Emphasize:	Appendix C, Chapters 7 and 8, Appendix D
Optional:	Section IV

Software engineers responsible for a large, OO (object-oriented) system:

Emphasize:	Sections I, III, and IV
Optional:	Section II, Appendices A and B

Professionals new to computer science (transitioning from a different field):

SUPPLEMENT with "LEARN TO PROGRAM" text

Emphasize:	Chapters 1 and 2, Appendix A
	Chapter 3, Appendix B, Chapters 4 and 5
	Chapters 9 and 10

Novice programmers:

SUPPLEMENT with "LEARN TO PROGRAM" text

Emphasize:	Chapters 1 and 2, Appendix A
	Chapter 3, Appendix B, Chapters 4 and 5

CHAPTER FORMAT

Each chapter begins with an introduction followed by a bulleted list of chapter objectives. Extensive code samples, design examples, figures, and summative tables augment the prose.

C++ code samples were compiled using g++ (version 4.6.3). C# code samples were compiled using Visual Studio 2012. Many code examples are open-ended (incomplete); hence, they were tested in a general framework. Since the text focuses on design rather than syntax, placeholders are often used for general initialization routines, common functionality (such as `action()` and `process()`), and relatively unrestricted user-defined types (such as `myType`, `Base`, and `Derived`). When assumptions are made, with respect to design, utility, memory management, maintainability, etc., such assumptions are noted. Code samples are distinguished according to source language (C++, C#) except when the distinction is not relevant.

Many figures are included to illustrate code structure, memory allocation, and type relationships. Tables summarize key concepts for quick review and reference. Many tables delineate complex material to reinforce understanding.

The text is partitioned into four sections: software construction, fundamentals, design, and durability. Each section has two or three chapters, explaining and applying foundational knowledge. To present a thorough overview, common software terms are used, even if such terms fall in the purview of the professional, rather than the academic. These terms are bolded and defined in the glossary. Italicized comments highlight design principles. Each chapter ends with a summary and conceptual questions intended to review major concepts. Many chapters list relevant design insights after the summary.

Four appendices follow the main text. The first two appendices are provided for readers with limited C and C++ exposure, in order to support a transition from a garbage-collected language (such as Java or C#) to C++. The material covered therein establishes a key difference between C++ and C#: the management of program memory. The third appendix traces a design example, from non-extensible code to a maintainable design that rests on the abstractions provided by modern programming languages. The fourth appendix examines operator overloading, a design technique that strives to reduce software complexity for the application programmer: examples are given in both C++ and C#.

A glossary of over 200 terms and a list of references close out the book.

PROGRAMMING LANGUAGE COMMENTS

This text strives to emphasize software design and to identify short- and long-term costs and benefits when evaluating design options. This text is not a programming language text. Many examples are given in C++ and C# in order to convey essential design ideas and to illustrate feasible implementation in a popular OOPL. For intricate language details, readers should consult a programming language manual, text, or blog.

Do note that most popular languages continue to offer refinements and improvements in order to facilitate use. Adhering to the C++ standards release, compilers are now becoming available for C++11. This latest release supplants C++98 but is backward-compatible with C++98, and thus, for the most part, C. Industry and academia are now beginning to integrate C++11 into development and education efforts.

New C++11 features enhance performance and improve support for multithreading and generics. To improve usability, C++11 supports lambda and regular expressions, moving the language into applications associated with Python. For a thorough discussion of C++11, please see Stroustrup (2013). Here, we briefly summarize C++11 features relevant to design topics covered in this text. The reader may wish to review these comments once the related portions of this text are read.

C++11 supports self-documenting code and design consistency. The provision of a `nullptr`, of type `nullptr _ t` (which is convertible to the Boolean type and any pointer type), clearly represents the notion of a null, or undefined, address. Inheritance design is also more evidently supported. As noted in Chapters 7 and 8, C# *requires* the use of the keyword "override" to tag redefined inherited functions in descendant classes, thus making design intent more apparent. C++11 provides a *special identifier* "override" that *may* be used in a similar manner. Similarly, C# *requires* the use of the keyword "sealed" to tag classes and methods that may not be redefined, again making design intent more apparent. C++11 provides a *special identifier* "final" that *may* be used in a similar manner.

C++11 defines "move semantics," expanding design options for copy semantics. As discussed in Chapter 4 and Appendix B, copy semantics require a conscious choice between deep and shallow copying in order to produce safe code and avoid data corruption. Move semantics provide a means to optimize deep copying. Please see Appendix B.

I

Software Construction

CHAPTER 1

Software Complexity and Modeling

W E BEGIN BY OUTLINING CHARACTERISTICS of modern software and general processes used in its development. We describe **software engineering** principles and their application. Our intent is to motivate explicit modeling and deliberate design with an understanding of required qualities and restrictions. Modern software is inherently complex and demands a formal approach to system construction and maintenance.

Using a "simple" problem to illustrate hidden expectations, we identify requirements of usable software. We summarize the different stages of software development and the emergence of software engineering as a field dedicated to the efficient and effective development of software. After examining the **software development life cycle** (SDLC), we note the emerging importance of **software integration**. The chapter closes with an emphasis on documentation. Throughout our discussion, software design and modeling are emphasized.

CHAPTER OBJECTIVES

- Motivate the deliberate design of software
- Establish the scope of modern software
  - Content, perspective, bounds, and targeted users
- Clarify the relevance of software engineering and its principles

- Identify the key stages of the SDLC
- Discuss common process methodologies
- Consider modeling for software architecture and code construction

1.1 MODERN SOFTWARE

The size and complexity of software systems has exploded in the last fifty years. Consider software systems deployed mid-20th century and their associated complexity. Systems designed to compute ballistic missile trajectories may be considered complex with respect to underlying mathematical computation. Business software designed to generate payroll checks and stubs, calculating taxes and vacation hours accrued, may be considered data intensive. However, early standalone systems did not support **user interfaces** (UIs) designed for the general user, gather and store data in multiple databases, support distributed processing, or provide extensive error handling. Moreover, several decades ago, software systems were designed from scratch, customized for a targeted platform and an audience of specialized users.

Fast forward to the 21st century. Tremendous growth in the use and application of software has driven dramatic advances in software development processes. Yet, despite all the improvements in design, implementation, and testing techniques, software development remains difficult. Why? Software systems are now intrinsically more complex, larger, and remain in service longer. *Modern software must provide more than basic functionality.* Consider the use and deployment of modern software. Security concerns exist for all software deployed on the Internet, as do expectations of data integrity and privacy. Software applications are often embedded, e.g., in cellphones and microwaves. Commercial software must provide a responsive user interface for a general audience, often augmented with user tutorials. E-**commerce** applications directly support online sales but may also depend on the **data mining** of customer histories to generate additional purchase suggestions and so forth.

The saturation of software use in mundane life tasks (e-commerce, medicine, education, banking, etc.) raises concerns not critical 40 years ago. How does software ensure privacy and data integrity? What are reasonable responses to erroneous user input? How does software guarantee **scalability** and ease of use? How can software be developed to run efficiently and on multiple platforms? How can software be designed to support current products as well as add-ons and variants?

Expectations increase as software use continues to expand. **Distributed systems** require efficient and secure data transmission. **Embedded systems** demand hardware and optimization expertise. This book strives to delineate major expectations of software and how design and modeling can support the development of complex software when longevity is anticipated.

1.1.1 Software Design

Most ideas start simply. Someone has an insight and pursues it. Software development is the same. One starts with an initial product, receives feedback and then expands the size, breadth, and/or complexity. Hence, we start with a simple example to underscore the need to explicitly model and design.

Say a programmer assumes the task of designing and implementing a simple math tutor for elementary school children. Without taking time for design, a developer may code a repetitive loop that controls a multistep query and response cycle: (1) generate a simple addition problem, (2) output problem, (3) prompt for solution, (4) accept input, (5) check input against expected answer, and (6) respond affirmatively or negatively. A flowchart models this simple feedback loop in Figure 1.1.

If implemented as the control flow model indicates, this software may be acceptable as a homework assignment for a novice programmer but is not an industrial-strength product. Why? Deficiencies abound. Looping never terminates, regardless of whether a given answer is correct or not. Error processing is missing—what happens if the student enters non-numeric data? The form and content of a sample problem is not defined— are negative numbers acceptable? User satisfaction is not considered: the same problem is repeated, over and over, until a correct answer is received. Overall, there is no specification of system design with respect to use, response, and repetition. The failure to design intentionally often yields narrowly scoped and brittle software. System design is prematurely

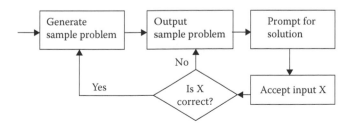

FIGURE 1.1   Query and respond loop.

constrained when the form and bounds of input and appropriate response are assumed but not specified.

Several design details remain unanswered in this math tutor example, primarily specification of functionality and use. Deciding what to model and build is a process of identifying missing or implicit assumptions. One can easily generate questions about content (domain knowledge of tutor), use (tutor response), limitations (constraints), and expected audience. The list in Figure 1.2 enumerates several design questions that serve to establish the scope of the math tutor software. Minimally, a designer should determine required domain knowledge, form and bounds of input, error processing, and output.

I. Consider *content* of the math tutor. What material is covered?
   a. What operations are drilled?
      i. Addition? Subtraction? Multiplication? Division?
      ii. Mixed-mode? If so, in what combination?
      iii. Negation? Reciprocals? Exponents?
   b. What type of numerical data is processed?
      i. Integers? Reals? Fractions? Decimals?
      ii. One digit? Multiple digits?
   c. What is the level of difficulty?
      i. One level? Variable?
      ii. Set by user (external)? Auto up or downgrade (internal)?
   d. Is there choice?
II. Evaluate *expected responses* from the tutor. What are the triggers?
   a. What if the answer is incorrect?
      i. Repeat problem? Show solution? Provide hints?
      ii. Replace with easier query? Walk through example?
   b. What if the data input is invalid?
      i. Ignore? Re-prompt?
      ii. Identify format errors? Attempt to interpret?
   c. What if user response is tardy?
      i. Timeout? Hints? Partial solution?
III. Quantify the *bounds* of the tutor. How is knowledge disseminated?
   a. How is content managed for a session?
      i. Bounds on repetition? All problems unique?
      ii. Patterned responses? Different tutorials?
   b. How is a session resumed?
      i. Automatic progression? Start over?
      ii. Review? Repeat?
IV. Who are the *users* of the system?
   a. Single user?
      i. Statistics tracked? Level of difficulty retained?
   b. Multiple users?
      i. User id? Licensed?
      ii. Grouped? Networked?

FIGURE 1.2　Math tutor: unspecified details.

To design intentionally, a software developer must state expectations and restrictions. Furthermore, if extensions are anticipated, design decisions must yield modifiable software. Will multiplication be incorporated into the design? How important is support for mixed-mode arithmetic? Might it be desirable to retain a history of problem sessions? In short, for a viable, commercial product, software developers should not just sit down at the keyboard and pound out code.

Perhaps it was misleading to describe our example application as a "simple" math tutor. See Figure 1.3 for a refinement that offers more detail for the design and implementation of a "simple" tutor. Yet, even this refinement illustrates a simple system without much of the complexity summarized in Figure 1.2. Although the undesirable feature of interminable guessing on an unsolved problem has been removed, termination of the whole process is not modeled. Error processing is nonexistent. Auxiliary support, via examples, tutorials, or hints, is not documented. Skill level, arithmetic operations, and domain of arithmetic values are still missing.

As shown in this math tutor example, software design is complicated. Why? In addition to the expected scenario of immediate and correct use, other scenarios must be considered. *Modern software must address broad expectations of use and longevity, as well as variety in targeted audiences and deployment.* We examine next the dimensions of software utility.

1.1.2 Software Utility

Software solutions for business and society abound since computational and data processing tasks are now automated. However, the expanded domain of automated tasks is not the sole reason for the complexity of

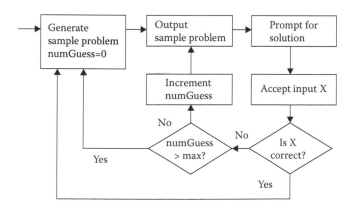

FIGURE 1.3   Modified query and respond loop.

modern software systems. Software use is no longer confined to experts. Software systems target a wide range of users, possibly multinational, with differing levels of expertise. Software systems are more likely to be distributed and consist of several components integrated together. Hence, design priorities shift from computer performance issues, such as data storage and processor clock cycles, to user expectations, such as responsive interfaces and meaningful error processing.

For example, an online reservation system must process requests to reserve an item, whether the item is a library book, a plane ticket, or a seat in a theater. Typically, a reservation system must be accessible in-house and/ or externally, often via different browsers. Software applications hosted on a LAN (local area network) or the web, rather than a dedicated machine, must service remote requests, handle distributed data and other background processes such as message passing, synchronization, recovery, traffic flow, etc. Fortunately, network software handles most background responsibilities for an application. Still, application software must be designed to work within the confines of network protocols. What works correctly on a single processor does not necessarily work well when distributed across a network.

Customers expect a responsive interface that is usable, secure, and robust. Vendors expect customer histories and retention of personal data. These expectations are not functional. That is, satisfying these expectations does not directly address the core functionality of the system: making a reservation. Software characteristics such as data persistence, usability, and security are considered **nonfunctional requirements** because their fulfillment does not immediately meet the strictly functional requirements of the software. Nonfunctional components include the user interface, error handling, storage of persistent data, performance tracking, security, and other requirements.

To support a broad customer base, multiple audiences with different degrees of experience and domain knowledge, software may be built in a generalized manner that enables customization. Ancillary files may be used for localization data, that is, data to customize the UI for a different language as well as default error messages and initialization data. Nonetheless, the end product must be correct and consistent. Hence, a commonality in design and implementation must be preserved.

The complexity of software design is also due to anticipated product longevity. Fiscal prudence, reinforced by perceptions of high replacement cost, encourages the retention of **legacy** software systems. A preference for integrating new features into existing systems entails a shift away from **clean-slate** design. Economic concerns aside, code often warrants retention. Why? Often, it is less disruptive to extend a stable code base than to begin anew. Users familiar with a system's form and functionality may be reluctant to migrate to an entirely new system.

The cost of upkeep (**software maintenance**) is justified when a software system has been used so extensively that its replacement would cause significant strife. An active customer base may not wish to work with a modified interface (or database). Professionals may be reluctant to migrate to new tools, whether the tools are word processors, compilers, or online tutors. In short, product identification may encourage retention of old software. Anything short of an immediate and exact replacement may be viewed as inferior or cause a service interruption.

When required to retain established functionality and/or form, developers do not have the luxury of designing from scratch. Developers must fit new features into an old system, possibly **refactoring** the legacy system to better absorb these new features. Software longevity and refactoring are subjects of increasing interest and warrant their own exposition.

1.1.3 Software Production

Modern software must meet expectations of responsive UIs, data retention, **portability**, and longevity. How then should software be produced? Methodically. Software construction is complex and thus expensive, requiring significant skill and experience. The cost of software development provides the incentive to maximize usage and extend lifetime. Software is thus typically decomposed into modules so that these components may be more easily reused and/or modified. Adherence to standards and convention, including design guidelines and patterns, supports reuse. Design for reuse drives development. After all, *it costs nothing to copy software.*

The preponderance of legacy systems encourages an emphasis on maintainability. **Software maintainability** refers to more than just bug fixes: it is the ability to update software to extend the UI, improve performance, expand error handling, migrate to a new platform, support a new localization release, and/or add new functionality. Many software professionals, concerned by the negative association of bug fixes with the term "software maintainability," prefer an alternate phrase: **software evolution**. Regardless of terminology, to properly maintain software, developers must understand the intent, design, and implementation of a legacy system as well as any new features. Hence, ideal software development stresses documented design and modeling.

TABLE 1.1   Software Documentation: Communicate Intent

Software Variants	Teams of Software Developers
Multiple platforms	Geographically dispersed
Different target audiences	Concurrent development
Multiple releases	Software evolution
Upgrades	Add new features
New platforms, etc.	Port to new platform, etc.
Compact, embedded versions	Unit and integrated testing

To maximize commercial gain, software is often developed for multiple platforms and many audiences. Documents, design artifacts, and models provide the means to communicate present as well as past requirements and assumptions to all stakeholders in product development. Table 1.1 summarizes why documentation is thus essential: *documentation provides a common foundation for design, implementation, and verification.* We examine business practices for such development next.

1.2 SOFTWARE ENGINEERING

Software engineering is the formalization of software project management and software development techniques. Software engineering brings a business orientation to the technical work of defining, modeling, designing, and constructing complex software. Software engineers manage projects, that is: define client expectations; solicit feedback from stakeholders (all those involved in the project); estimate resource requirements; construct design, development, and testing plans; create schedules for design, development, and testing; define benchmarks for progress and evaluation; and specify acceptance criteria. Different project methodologies exist yet every project methodology should be explicit and systematic.

Software engineering principles rest on conventions that imply the development of reliable and functional software. Characteristics of such software include **abstraction, modularity, functional decomposition, portability, scalability,** and **heterogeneity.** Few software characteristics can be measured directly. In fact, the chief challenge of software engineering is that *software is intangible.*

Academicians often compare software engineering to other engineering disciplines, such as civil engineering. Although there is merit in the analogy—both disciplines follow formal practices that are organized and strive to meet standards—software is not a bridge. Since software is not a physical entity, it is malleable; its execution depends on hardware configurations and user audiences (and their input). Software does not age, and it is essentially free to replicate. Yet, relative to testing and maintenance, software's lack of physical form is a liability: it is not easily examined.

Parallels exist between the maturation of other engineering disciplines and software engineering. A well-developed engineering discipline has standard procedures and formulae. Software engineering does also. Software professionals work in the many stages of software development, each stage focused on particular goals. In the next section, we briefly define these stages and subsequently consider each in turn. For more details, please consult a standard software engineering text.

1.2.1 The Software Development Life Cycle (SDLC)

The development of large, complex software systems depends on the efforts of many professionals. Project scope must be determined to construct a timeline and budget. Core software functionality must be defined, with all incompatibilities and constraints resolved. Software qualities, such as accessibility or efficiency, must be prioritized. Since the potential for code reuse may affect the high-level structure of a system (by determining component use and layout), anticipated longevity and product use should be estimated.

Initially, project scope and impact should be identified. Thereafter, specific processes for modeling, design, and development phases may be adopted. Regardless of the methodology used for project management, however, the different stages of software development are categorized formally as the SDLC.

SDLC falls under the purview of software engineering. Software engineering is the application of engineering principles to software development. As a formal discipline, software engineering encompasses the systematic processes used in the design, development, and deployment of software geared toward long-term use. Software engineering is not merely project management plus software development: it encompasses all stages of system construction and support, including software maintenance (evolution).

Table 1.2 outlines the classic stages of software development. Today, to emphasize the overlapping intent of some stages, one might refer to four stages: specification (requirements and specification), development (architecture, design, implementation), validation (testing), and evolution (maintenance). Software engineers use different process methodologies to manage the stages of the SDLC.

Regardless of the process model used for scheduling these stages, the design and development of software requires comprehensive and clear

TABLE 1.2 Software Development Life Cycle

Stage	Goal(s)	Details
Requirements	Contractual specifications Specify "what"	Functional properties Nonfunctional properties
Specifications	Properties enumerated Functionality delineated	How to satisfy requirements? Timing? Performance? Etc.
Architecture	Structural layout Connectors identified	Software elements Modules, interfaces
Design	Software form and function	Data types and algorithms
Implementation	Software development	Programming and integration
Testing	Verification	Unit and integrated
Maintenance	Update for longevity	Bug fixes and expansion

documentation. Systematic management of different versions of the software is also required. Hence, **configuration management** and quality assurance are essential engineering practices for large-scale software development.

Underlying software engineering is the business perspective of a producer satisfying consumer demands. This contractual emphasis can be seen in each stage of software development. Software engineers must meet with clients to identify user expectations and distinguish between "wants" and "needs." Knowledge of the skill sets and expectations of the target audience(s) is essential. Software may be marketed to different target groups, each of which may demand modified requirements, modeling, and/or design. Although UI differences may be intuitive and seem simple, slight differences in functionality may trigger significant deviations in design. Table 1.3 enumerates some sample applications and associated software characteristics.

TABLE 1.3 Software Applications with Different Requirements

Application	Deployment	Details	UI
Data processing	Desktop	General utility	General
E-commerce	Web	Financial interest	Customer
Control systems	Embedded	Constrained footprint Power consumption	Internalized
Games	Web or gamebox	Education, entertainment	Interactive
Simulation	Application specific	Computationally intensive	Specialized

Standalone systems, such as word processors, simple databases, and games, may be sold to any customer if designed with sufficient generality. Alternatively, such systems may be targeted toward more specialized communities such as education and medicine. Custom software typically requires specific contracts for product development. Common examples include embedded systems, aircraft, military, and government. Often such systems have enhanced requirements for security and/or preservation of proprietary information.

Perceived as an essential but costly stage of software development, software maintenance spans all stages of the SDLC and encompasses different types of modifications. When expanded functionality alters an existing system, changes may be pushed all the way back to the requirements stage. When improved quality is demanded, whether for performance, security, or usability, changes may be pushed back to the architectural level and so forth. Many professionals prefer the term **software evolution** because maintenance implies required cleanup rather than change for sustainability. *Software maintenance is not simply bug fixes.*

Each stage of the software development life cycle should be adaptive. What happens if expectations cannot be met, requirements change, or deadlines slip? Responses vary somewhat according to how each stage is managed, whether the stages overlap, the means and frequency of communication, etc. In the next section, we summarize common approaches to staging software development.

1.2.2 Software Process Methodologies

Software process methodologies model the organization of different stages of the software development life cycle. The classic methodology is the waterfall model, a strictly linear staging that fails to accommodate change. Other methodologies offer a more responsive progression. Table 1.4 summarizes some common software process methodologies. Incremental or iterative methodologies seek to improve upon the waterfall model by endorsing incremental development with feedback between requirements analysis and design. The most modern popular approach that uses this methodology is **agile software development** (Martin, 2009).

Extreme Programming (XP) is a well-known agile software development methodology. It relies on very short development cycles, with continuous customer feedback, so that requirements are identified and implemented incrementally. These short development cycles, or bursts, typically require code reviews and unit testing. Although effective,

TABLE 1.4   Software Process Methodologies

Approach	Emphasis	Characteristics	Details
Waterfall	Clean slate	Overly linear Dated	Independent stages
Incremental (iterative)	Intermediate versions Implicit prototyping	Concurrent activity for Specification Development Validation	=> RUP => Agile
Agile/scrum	Rapid development/ executable software	Evolving requirements	Self-organizing teams
RUP	Iterative/components Sanctity of requirements	Inception, elaboration, construction, transition Continuous integration	OOD, UML Elevated role of testing
Spiral	Prototyping Risk management	Augmented waterfall Top-down decomposition	Constraints Alternatives
Test-driven development	Tests Fine granularity	Tests written first Test drive code dev	Incremental

especially for many web applications, and popular, especially for its pair programming techniques in academia, XP has been criticized for insufficient modeling and documentation. Large software systems may need a more comprehensive, initial design specification along with a full disclosure of major functionality (Lakos, 1996).

Rational Unified Process (RUP) is a methodology built on top of object orientation: **object-oriented design** (OOD—Booch) and object modeling technology (OMT—Rumbaugh). It is a staged approach, like waterfall, but with continuous integration. Adaptation for different platforms and customization for localization and so forth can thus be accommodated. Another methodology that modifies the waterfall model is the "spiral" model. It focuses on prototyping and iterative development but includes risk management; that is, explicit specification of objectives, alternatives, and constraints. **Validation** is based on acceptance criteria.

With an emphasis on writing tests first, **test-driven development** (TDD) relies on a short development cycle just like XP. The initial step is to write (automated) test cases that define system requirements, or redefine functionality that warrants modification. Without an adequate code base, these initial tests will fail. The next step is to write code so that the test cases pass, followed by a step that **refactors** the code to sustain design principles and remove duplicate code. Each test must be designed and constructed to model the requirements well. A poorly designed test will not yield appropriate results, causing the code written in response to be insufficient for the desired functionality. Using TDD, features are tackled individually so that system functionality is developed incrementally. Hence, TDD may not work well for software systems highly dependent on generalized user interfaces, distributed processing, or databases.

How does one choose an appropriate software process model? Identify the essential characteristics of the software product and its intended audience. For example, web applications that serve a broad audience of users must support a variety of platforms and may be subject to volatile requirements. A process methodology with a short turnaround time looks like a promising candidate. In contrast, a customized large-scale system must fulfill substantial security requirements. A process methodology that emphasizes thorough specifications and extensive validation may be preferred.

Every process methodology attempts to deftly manage software product development. One must delineate the different stages of software development and then determine, via process methodology, how to schedule, staff, and coordinate each stage. Whether an iterative, linear, or cyclic process methodology is used, there must be communication between each stage of the SDLC. We next consider modeling as a means of communication that can be employed at any stage of the SDLC.

1.3 MODELS

What is a model? How is modeling related to design? What models are used for software development? Why should one bother modeling? We address these questions after some disclaimers. *Models do not solve problems; models represent solutions.* Models do not erase incompatibilities; models communicate intent and form. Models are not uniform, either in form or granularity. Models do not spring, fully formed, from tools; modeling tools assist in the representation of a constructed model. Selecting a modeling tool does not yield a model. One type of model does not span all software products or software development processes. Many types of models exist.

Hmmm, so many disclaimers! Why? Software models come in many different forms and are not consistently used or appreciated. Software modeling is not a new field but neither is it a mature field. Modeling efforts can focus on any stage of software development. Models can be recorded using software tools, yielding complex diagrams. Yet, to many professionals, a system description in a Word document is a model. No matter how a model is presented, a model satisfies the following definition.

Definition: A model is a conceptual description of a system that allows one to make predictions.

NOTE THAT A MODEL IS:

precise if it is exact or clearly bounded
accurate if it is correct, consistent, and represents factual observations
ambiguous if it supports more than one interpretation

An incomplete model may still yield utility if its limitations are known. Likewise, an imprecise model may still be usable if areas of imprecision are clearly identified. More troubling, however, is an ambiguous model: how does one know which interpretation applies or was used? Figure 1.4 illustrates a simple control model for recharging a cell phone. The model is precise, accurate, and unambiguous. Yet, even in this simple model, there are implicit assumptions: accurate cell phone display (green light represents recharging complete); power compatibility between power source (outlet) and phone; and connector (cord) available for recharging. Models are much more difficult to construct for lengthy and complex endeavors.

As a form of complexity management, a model should replace copious descriptions. A model replaces lengthy documentation of observed or desired behavior with a more succinct summary. Models thereby reduce space requirements for a system description. By representing complex systems, models provide a tool for comprehension, design, and maintenance. Regardless of form, models should communicate structure, design, and response. As a record of design, models compensate for the human brain's imperfect and bounded memory.

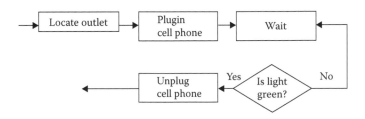

FIGURE 1.4   Recharge cell phone.

The complexity of a large software system is overwhelming: excessive and overlapping information can be disorienting, and the required details can be distracting. Since the brain has limited capacity for processing and retaining information, a readable form of documentation reduces the load on working memory. Much research has examined human capacity for absorbing and processing information (Torkel, 2009). Standard memory faults have been categorized (Schacter, 2003). Table 1.5 enumerates common memory omissions, when human memory has insufficient recall. Table 1.6 enumerates common memory faults, when human memory has inaccurate recall.

Models support both abstraction and generalization. Complex systems are typically reduced to a number of interacting subsystems. Understanding a large system requires an understanding of its constituent parts. Models of subsystems can then be viewed, as simply as possible, in isolation. To analyze subsystems, one must first assume that changes occur in isolation. **Emergent behavior** occurs when the subsystems are put back together and interactions enabled.

A model is a bridge between analysis and synthesis. Models permit a complex system to be specified, and system behavior understood before construction. To aid comprehension, models must distinguish between relevant and irrelevant details. Memory recall is supported by association, the ability to relate to the familiar. Thus, models should use a conventional

TABLE 1.5   Memory Omissions

Absent Mindedness	Blocking	Transience
Attention lapses	Repression	Forgetfulness curve
Poorly encoded information	Poor conceptual association	Poor encoding
Cognitive overload	Lack of context	Details short-term

Source: D. Schacter, *Seven Sins of Memory: How the Mind Forgets and Remembers,* Houghton Mifflin, 2003.

TABLE 1.6   Memory Faults

Bias	Misattribution	Persistence	Suggestibility
Rescripted memory	Déjà vu	Excessive Recall	False memory
Preservation of view	Poor association	Emotional affect	Misleading info
Distorted influence	Details missing	Failure response	External source

Source: D. Schacter, *Seven Sins of Memory: How the Mind Forgets and Remembers,* Houghton Mifflin, 2003.

form. Since reconstruction of experience is subject to bias, models must record essential assumptions and priorities so that recollection remains specific. Visual imagery helps.

Models abound. Many different types of models are used in software development, including domain models, architectural models, risk-driven models, deployment models, and design models. Specific representations of models include flowcharts, data flow models, decision tables, Petri nets, state charts, class diagrams, sequence diagrams, use cases, activity diagrams, and finite state machines. The wide variety of **UML** (**Unified Modeling Language**) constructs (see uml.org) illustrates the complexity of modeling and the many levels at which modeling may be used. Static models define structure at the component or class level as well as control flow. Dynamic (or execution) models illustrate interaction and response, often using a timeline.

Some conceptual models are neglected. For example, the instruction set, driver interfaces, and communication protocols of a particular computer are all models. Fundamental types and memory management within a particular programming language are also conceptual models. Many such representational models have some connection with the real world. For example, communication protocols usually include an acknowledgment of message receipt, which is typical of in-person or phone conversations. Usually, foundational models may be ignored because software development is far removed from low-level details. However, for optimality or consistency, one may need to re-examine models underlying a system.

Appropriate use of software modeling is often not obvious. The absence of a standard notion of modeling impedes decisions of when and how to model. The plethora of model types makes tool selection difficult: different modeling tools target different stages of the SDLC and even different applications. Nonetheless, models should be used across the software development life cycle. Why? *Models manage complexity and communicate design.*

As a record of design, models should be used throughout software development. Different texts cover different perspectives on the generation and use of models, such as Blaha and Rumbaugh (2005), Larman (2005) and Gomaa (2011). Much of this book emphasizes modeling expectations via contractual documentation. Section III promotes the modeling of software relationships by explicit design. Here, we peruse the stages of the SDLC, starting with requirements specifications.

1.3.1 Requirements Analysis and Specification

As the specification of user needs, the initial stage of the software development life cycle should establish project scope and software requirements. The primary goal is to define functionality: what does the user need the software to do? The task of defining requirements is more challenging than it might seem: users often do not know what should be required, may confuse wants with needs, cannot fully or accurately describe technical expectations or product characteristics, or may have unrealistic expectations. Even with concerted effort then, specifications may be ambiguous, inconsistent, and/or incomplete. Re-examination of requirements is often warranted, even in the midst of other stages of the SDLC. Figure 1.5 provides an initial response to defining characteristics of a math tutor, as previously explored in Figure 1.2.

The requirements document specifies system functionality and use, that is, the what (and maybe the why) but not the how. A requirements document serves as a touchstone for all subsequent stages; it is not static. Details may change as target audiences expand, technology changes, or budget allocations fluctuate. Nonetheless, core functionality, as well as interface and performance expectations, should be fairly stable. The requirements document should also specify system requirements such as compatibility with other packages and portability to a variety of platforms.

Well-specified functionality should accurately model (and, thus predict) the behavior of the system it emulates. Intuitive examples reflect real-world phenomena. Consider electronic bank transactions, online shopping, payroll systems, etc. Functionally, such systems can be viewed from either the front or the back end. The user most often considers only the front end: the automated bank teller, customer service representative, etc. The back-end database though is essential. This electronic store of account information and inventory replaces paper systems of the same and, more importantly, supports efficient data-intensive searches. Even computer games that simulate fantasy worlds may be viewed from the user interface, which includes video and gameplay, or from the back end where processing tracks player performance and handles object movement, state, and appearance. Both ends of a software system must be modeled, and the required functionality so specified.

Many different models may be used to reflect functional requirements. State machines, decision tables, state charts, and flowcharts are often used (Jorgenson, 2009). *The scale of a model affects its utility: a small scale may*

I. Functionality
   a. Generate arithmetic problems, appropriate to skill level
   b. Process user answers
      i. Verify correct response
      ii. Allow some number of guesses (retries) on a problem
   c. Provide tutorials
      i. explicitly by request
      ii. implicitly tied to skill regression
   d. Manage student skill level
      i. span from simple 1-digit addition up to 4-digit mixed mode
      ii. initially set by user
      iii. internally adjusted in response to user performance

II. Content knowledge of tutor
   a. Arithmetic operations: addition, subtraction, multiplication, division
   b. Mixed-mode supported (progressive, tied to level of difficulty)
   c. Legal values: integers, reals (decimal notation); negative and positive

III. Tutor response to user input
   a. Error processing
      i. Non-numeric entries discarded before re-prompt
      ii. Numeric data evaluated relative to pending problem
   b. Timed response
      i. Timeout on problem if user inactive for extended period
      ii. Logoff if user inactive for long extended period
   c. Problem repetition bounded
   d. Sessions
      i. Tied to skill level
      ii. Discreet; not resumed

IV. Users
   a. Student
      i. Tracked by id
      ii. Statistics on session retained
      iii. Associated with level of difficulty
   b. Teacher
      i. Tracked by id
      ii. Access to set of students
      iii. Read permission for student data

V. System requirements

FIGURE 1.5 Requirements for math tutor.

include relevant details but results in an unwieldy document; a large scale may omit critical details.

The process of defining and then refining system goals identifies critical functionality and desired properties. Thus, requirements and specifications overlap. Software engineers solicit client (stakeholder) requirements, taking care to differentiate between general criteria and customization details. The requirements document must define user requirements as specified and validated. A requirements document specifies system requirements such as integration expectations, compatibility constraints, and performance criteria. It details what the system should do; it is not a design document; it does not specify how the system works.

Nonfunctional properties (NFP) should be included as requirements, where a nonfunctional property is defined as a software characteristic that does not directly advance the goal of realizing core functionality. Also known as software qualities or nonfunctional requirements, NFPs embody software's appeal: usability, scalability, reliability, etc. NFPs are difficult to model, implement, and assess.

With an initial set of requirements, a feasibility study may be undertaken to determine costs and technical constraints. Cost may cause a reordering of project priorities and thus a revision of the functional and/or nonfunctional requirements. Thus, requirement specification is often not a one-step process. With reasonable requirements, one may sketch the system architecture. **Software architecture** is commonly associated with the topology of a system, and we examine it next.

1.3.2 Software Architecture

Software architecture came into prominence in the 1990s as a field of study. Why? The prevalence of large-scale software systems. Development costs and maintenance overhead emphasized the importance of sustainable design as well as the necessity of documenting and communicating design intent.

Intuition suggests that software architecture represents the structural form of a software system. Yet, many definitions abound (Shaw and Garlan, 1996; Gomaa, 2011). Elements of software architecture include components, **connectors**, interfaces, and the interactions between components and connectors. What is a connector? It is a piece of software that connects two or more components in a system. Connectors come in many forms: shared memory, message passing, function calls, wrappers, and adaptors. An architectural configuration is the set of components and the associations between those components as defined by connectors. From a static viewpoint then, the architectural configuration is the system's topology. Architecture so modeled must portray an overview of the system as well as its core functionality: developers should not depend on analysis of individual components to derive a sense of the system.

Figure 1.6 presents a high-level decomposition of an online math tutor, as consistent with the principle "**separation of concerns**"—a key tactic in software modeling and design. The critical components of a system are defined separately to isolate (separate) the primary tasks (concerns) of the

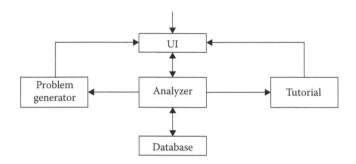

FIGURE 1.6   Conceptual design for math tutor.

system. In the math tutor model, the "analyzer" component determines whether the next action should be delegated to the "problem generator" or the "tutorial" component. This coarse model isolates both the UI (user interface) and the database: the "analyzer" is responsible for directing data selection and retention. Software components promote maintainability: upgrades and changes are confined to specific portions of a system so that software is easier to design, develop, test, and maintain.

Components may be distinguished by whether they request or provide services. This clear decoupling of request and response promotes consistency and maintainability. Moreover, the isolation of providers supports scalability as system load increases. Figure 1.6 models separation of the front end (UI) and the back end (database) of a system. Neither the UI nor the database provide critical computation for system core functionality. Both serve to support core functionality by displaying, filtering, and storing data. We next examine the **Model View Controller** (MVC), an architectural pattern that epitomizes this separation of request and service.

1.3.3 Model View Controller

The MVC is both a conceptual and an architectural model that serves to separate functionality from form. Figure 1.7 displays the three conceptual entities of the MVC: the model, the view, and the controller. The user sees the views and interacts with a controller. The model contains the functional software, that is, the **business logic** and the application data. A view is the presentation of data. A controller serves as a mediator, converting data to the view required and servicing requests. The functionality available to the user at any given point may be tied to the state of the model. Hence, the controller must observe the state of the model. MVC may

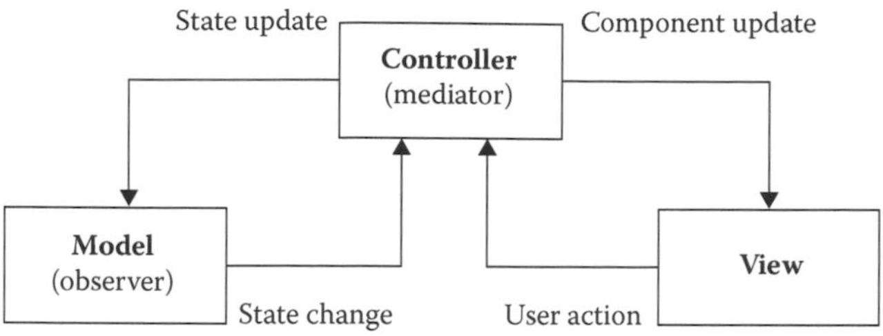

FIGURE 1.7   Model view controller.

support multiple views and multiple controllers and therein lies the power of the model.

How does the MVC work? A controller sends commands to a view when it is necessary to change the presentation of the model, e.g., when a bar graph is converted to a line graph. A controller also notifies the model to update state. Upon a state change, such as data modification, the model may notify the controller to update its views. A view requests data from the model to construct its presentation.

The MVC supports the clear decomposition of functionality. Components either request services or provide services. Expanding service to more users does not break the system: additional components are incorporated but the number of views is not increased. Thus, scalability is supported.

The MVC is adaptive. Different views may be developed for the same data (as generated and maintained by the model). Different controllers may also be developed for the same model. The MVC provides transparency while isolating clients from each other. A consistent model, MVC is maintainable and scalable: servers may be added as load increases.

Software architecture serves as the design template for both software construction and evolution. What then is the difference between architecture and design? It is primarily one of scope. Software architecture is a higher-level specification of elements (components) and their interactions (connectors) (Perry and Wolf, 1992). Software design is a lower-level specification of modules, interfaces, algorithms, and data structures. Design leads directly to implementation details. Architecture remains higher level with an emphasis on major design decisions that affect the system in totality.

1.3.4 Code Construction

Modern software requires easier access, more storage, broader compatibility, as well as support for nonfunctional properties. Requirements analysis, software architecture, and software design are thus more complex. We have seen some simple models for requirements and architecture. We devote Chapters 5 through 8 to structural, behavioral, and comparative design, using the object-oriented paradigm as a foundation. The question we address here is: May code be considered a model?

At a high level of abstraction, models focus on conceptual content and omit most implementation details. Code is the embodiment of implementation details, and should follow the modeled software design. Yet, can one consider code itself a model?

Let us consider the classic Fibonacci number generation problem, frequently used in introductory programming courses. The first two Fibonacci numbers are 1 and 1. Each subsequent number in the sequence is computed as the sum of the previous two numbers. Hence, the third Fibonacci number is 2 $(1 + 1 = 2)$, the fourth is 3 $(1 + 2 = 3)$, the fifth is 5 $(2 + 3 = 5)$, etc. Mathematically, the Fibonacci numbers are represented as

$$F_0 = 1, F_1 = 1$$
$$F_n = F_{n-1} + F_{n-2} \quad n >= 2$$

Two common approaches are used to generate the nth Fibonacci number. In one, storage trumps computation: the first n Fibonacci numbers are initially computed and then stored for all subsequent lookups. In the second, storage is minimized: only the last two numbers computed are stored, and upon request for the next Fibonacci number in the sequence, the smallest (oldest) value is replaced with the newly generated value. The latter model assumes that Fibonacci numbers will be requested only in sequence but can be easily modified to regenerate numbers from the sequence's initial values (see Example 1.1).

Example 1.1: Fibonacci Number Generation: Store versus Compute

```
//lookup:    F_i = f[i]; Fibonacci numbers stored //for lookup
int   f[n];
f[0] = f[1] = 1;
for (int j = 2; j < n; j++)
     f[j] = f[j-1] + f[j-2];
//compute F_i = computeF(i);
int   computeF(int i)
{
     int f1 = 1;
```

```
    int f2 = 1;
    int fN;
    int index = 1;
    while (index < i)
    {       fN = f1 + f2;
            f1 = f2;
            f2 = fN;
            index++;
    }
    return fN;
}
```

Software may represent a precise model of an external system. A model's state transitions are defined responses to input and thus effectively represent system response to input, whether the input is valid or invalid. Examples include cruise control, elevator control, and autonomous robots. For such software systems, there is a direct correspondence between software elements and those of the physical system. Yet, even with a strong association to a physical entity, software structure may not model all required elements of a software product. Recall that many software systems must include nonfunctional components, such as UI and security.

Graphical User Interfaces (GUIs) provide an example of software that itself is a model. Menus in a GUI represent a set of choices. Tiered dropdown menus order choices hierarchically, according to semantic content. In this manner, the GUI organizes the information presented to the user. The model of information thus presented affects user satisfaction and determines the usability of the system. Information organization and presentation are not trivial tasks, especially when one piece of software must accommodate a wide range of users.

Historically, software modeling was the high-level specification of requirements, statically or dynamically. Software modeling is no longer strictly associated with requirements. An architectural model views system components and their interactions, where each component consists of one or more software modules. The module level views data types and their interactions. The data type (class) level views data elements, their interactions, and functionality.

1.4 SOFTWARE INTEGRATION

Traditional software development starts with the specification of system functionality and form, via requirements gathering, followed by clean-slate software design and implementation. The key characteristic is that the system is built without existing dependencies on old software or without expectations of supporting a known product with a loyal user base. *Clean-slate software development is considered a luxury.*

Software development is typically taught to the novice as a standalone process: design and implementation are pursued without regard to other software components. Although a novice programmer may use utility software, such as libraries that support IO or provide random number generators, any design emphasis remains focused on building a system from scratch. However, in industry, the integration of existing software components and subsystems is now prevalent. Why has the form of software development shifted? Many reasons explain this shift, including (1) the success of modular design that promotes component reuse; (2) the size and longevity of software systems; and (3) the development of software product lines. Consider MS Office, a software product that embodies all three characteristics.

Once a commercial enterprise invests significant resources (time and money) to develop a software product, the incentive to reuse code is tremendous. Budgetary expenditures for maintenance are justified when software evolution promises expanded functionality, improved performance, updated standards, and a broader user base. Expansion by itself increases the complexity of software because any new functionality must be crafted for a broad user base. Different user audiences have different skills, expertise, and domain knowledge, and hence, different, often incompatible, expectations as to ease-of-use, error processing, performance, and reliability.

To justify development cost and maximize reuse potential, modern software systems are often multiplatform, and/or multipurpose. To maintain or replicate such a system, one must understand its requirements, architecture, design, constraints, etc. Even professionals with domain knowledge often face a steep learning curve. Explicit documentation is required of but not confined to API, modeling, localization, etc.

Software integration requires developers with broad knowledge and specific skills. To glue together existing pieces of software, software integration specialists must know how to resolve incompatible interfaces. To customize the appearance or augment functionality, software integration specialists must understand both reuse potential and limitations on such reuse. Hence, an understanding of interface design, database storage and access, and performance criteria is critical (Hammer and Timmerman, 2008). Moreover, testing drives verification of the configuration of integrated systems. Testing is necessarily more complex as one moves beyond unit or component testing and into system and integration testing.

With an emphasis on software architecture, software integration depends on knowledge of both structure and behavior. Does the integrated system need any quality improvements, such as better performance or increased security? Will any additional functionality be added? Software developers must identify current and targeted users of a legacy system, the feasibility of wrapping or migrating code, as well as performance and scalability details. For integration, both the front end (UI) and the back end (database, network) should be well known. Again, we return to the idea of having system documentation, or a model, that describes intent, restrictions, and form.

1.5 DOCUMENTATION

Software engineering stresses the need for high-quality documentation, at every stage of the SDLC. The complexity and longevity of software systems drive the need to record system requirements, structure, and functionality via models and documentation. Client expectations, vetted for feasibility and cost, turn into requirements. Goal prioritization drives the specification of functional and nonfunctional properties. The structure of a software system, its components and interactions, is recorded as the software architecture. Software design may be detailed from scratch using a modeling tool like UML.

Yet, to a novice, documentation suggests adding comments to code. Code should be self-documenting, that is, the naming protocol and structure of the code should reflect the immediate effect of code execution (review Example 1.1). Nonetheless, self-documenting code or comments do not typically contain a cohesive description of the overall system design or requirements. *Documentation scattered across hundreds of source files cannot effectively record system-level imperatives.* Thus, a system-level description is mandated.

Even an experienced professional may not think of documentation beyond a design document. After all, a design document delineates system structure and function, removing the dependency on code or inline comments. However, many forms of documentation record essential elements of a software system: requirements specify system functionality and software qualities; a software architecture model displays the structure and linkage of software components; a design document delineates elements of software construction; a testing document outlines testing plans, coverage and, possibly, essential test cases.

Whatever its form, documentation should provide an overview of the system as well as its core functionality: developers should not depend on a serial analysis of individual components to comprehend the form and effect of a system. Developers gain at best a module-level perspective if they must depend on perusing individual components for descriptions. A module-based perspective inhibits parallel development: programmer A cannot develop module X while programmer B develops module Y if module X is dependent on the design of module Y. Complex software systems require a "summary model."

Internal documentation should complement higher-level documentation, recording details such as valid ranges for inputs and outputs, error processing, etc. Essentially, *the developer must record assumptions made for correct execution of the software as well as anticipated software evolution.*

The cost of missing high-level design documentation is long-term and unbounded. Upgrades to a software system, such as UI enhancements or expanded error processing, can be needlessly protracted and expensive if developers must make educated guesses about the software's original functionality and constraints. New features may interfere with old, undocumented features, undermining integration testing. Maintenance is impeded if a developer, like a "hunt-and-peck" typist, must scan line by line through files looking for comments that describe functionality. Without a big-picture view of the system, inconsistent changes to the software are more likely.

Incomplete, inconsistent, or ambiguous specifications can be costly to a project: the end product may not meet the client's needs, even if it "works." Across the SDLC, insufficient documentation is problematic. Documentation serves to communicate and should compensate for personnel differences in location, background, experience, or assigned responsibility.

1.6 SUMMARY

Software is now more complex, not computationally but in terms of size, targeted audiences, supported platforms, UI responsiveness, longevity of code, quality of error processing, integration with existing code, distributed use, as well as breadth of automation. Software development is more complicated because software systems are larger, operational for longer, and embellished with more nonfunctional features. Communication between software developers on the same project is also complex: many software engineers and developers work on a product but not necessarily at the same time or in the same place.

To streamline the processes of software development, software engineering techniques formally delineate technical and business perspectives. Software development spans many phases: requirements specification for functionality; software architecture for structural layout of components and interactions; software design, implementation, and testing. Throughout these stages, documentation is critical. At a high level, models are a form of documentation that promote an understanding of form and function and support communication between developers.

Models may be employed at each level of the SDLC to aid conceptual understanding and to *communicate* intent and application. A model provides a more succinct description of the system than a list of empirical trials and their results. The value of a model is amplified when it is conveyed from one person to another. Several audiences must be satisfied: software developers responsible for design, implementation, testing, or maintenance; application programmers who use the developer's product to craft applications; and end users. Software should work as intended, that is, consistent with expectations for use and longevity. Hence, an effective model must specify not just the functional requirements but contextual use, interfaces, error processing, security, etc.

DESIGN INSIGHTS

SOFTWARE

Modern software must provide more than functionality
    Broad expectations of use, compatibility, and longevity
    User interface must be usable, robust, and secure
    Significant data retention (and analysis) expectations
Software is intangible = >
    Free to copy
    Difficult to test
Hard to discern software structure

MODELS

Communicate intent and design
Replace lengthy documents with succinct summaries
Provide a bridge between analysis and synthesis
Scale affects utility
    A large scale may omit critical details
    A small scale may include too many distracting details

SOFTWARE DESIGN

Clean-slate design is a luxury
Deliberate design for completeness and correctness
Software maintenance is more than just bug fixes
    Port to new platform
    Augment functionality
    Expand user interface
    Record system usage, etc.

DOCUMENTATION

Record assumptions
    Correct execution
    Software evolution
Common foundation for:
    Modeling
    Design
    Implementation
    Testing
    Maintenance

CONCEPTUAL QUESTIONS

1. Why is modern software complex?

2. When modeling interactive software, what details must be considered?

3. How are NFP distinguished from functional properties?

4. Why is software engineering different from other engineering disciplines?

5. Describe the drawbacks of using a strictly linear software process model (the waterfall model).

6. What are the key differences between requirements and design?

7. Identify different software process models and discuss their differentiated use.

8. What is a model? Where are models used? What do models provide?

9. Explain the difference(s) between static and dynamic models.

10. Why is the MVC architecture popular?

CHAPTER 2

Software Development

C ODING HAS EVOLVED from a tedious process mired in machine instruction addresses to a high-level description of executable tasks. At the lowest level, software execution may be viewed as fetching, evaluating, modifying, and storing data. To understand implementation and its costs, we first examine software execution at the machine level. Then we trace the progression of software development as it relies on operating systems, and software tools, primarily compilers. A short summary of the evolution of programming languages illustrates the importance of software design and the appropriate modeling of data through abstract structures. We provide a brief overview of a standard modeling tool, **Unified Modeling Language (UML)**, and close the chapter with a brief description of emerging standards for software construction.

Our discussion traces the transformation of the programmer's perspective from a microscopic level to a more abstract and macroscopic level. As tools and support for software development have advanced, the software designer's conceptual model of programming has shifted from isolated, concrete tasks to large, layered, intricate systems. Increasingly sophisticated, software development tools provide significant abstraction. Hence, modern software development should, but often does not, emphasize software architecture and design. We begin by examining software execution from the bottom up.

> **CHAPTER OBJECTIVES**
>
> - Outline the fundamentals of software execution
> - Identify general utility support provided by operating systems
> - Emphasize the abstraction afforded by high-level languages
> - Delineate key stages of compilation
> - Define abstract data type (ADT) and the class construct
> - Categorize UML constructs
> - Enumerate basic software construction tenets

2.1 SOFTWARE EXECUTION

Computers are electronic devices in which voltage states are used to represent 0 and 1. Running software then is essentially the evaluation of binary strings, sequences of zeroes and ones. A location storing a 0 or a 1 is called a **bit**. A **byte** is 8-bits. Computers store billions of bytes in their main memory and even more in external storage. Computers operate on collections of bytes called words. The arithmetic logic unit (ALU) operates on single or paired words. The bit-width of the ALU determines the "size" of the processor and the "size" of a word. A 64-bit processor has an ALU that is 64-bits wide. A computer program thus must be broken down into many, many words for execution.

At the lowest level, computer memory, including registers, is associated with absolute addresses. Binary string values are placed in and retrieved from these addresses. Actions are performed according to the value of the binary strings so stored. Although binary strings and addresses can be represented in **hexadecimal** code when debugging, this compact and more readable form does not add enough abstraction to make writing hexadecimal code enjoyable or safe! For the most part, software developers work in a **high-level language (HLL)** that is translated (typically, compiled) into machine level code.

Any particular binary string may be interpreted in different ways. Consider the string "01000001," which can be interpreted as the positive number 65 or as the ASCII letter "A." When a system is constructed, it establishes a consistent standard of interpretation. Thus, the binary string "1000001" is interpreted as 65 if it is associated with the integer type or as the letter "A" if it is associated with the character type. Critical here is the notion of interpretation. Often, the elegant simplicity of software derives from a flexible interpretation of type.

The notion of type is layered on the basic notion of storage. At the machine level, an executing program is unaware of types: it just shuffles bytes around. Type information is used in the translation of code written in a HLL. Consider the first two lines in Example 2.1. These lines represent code statements that declare four variables, where a variable is an abstract name for a memory location. The abstract names "a" and "b" represent **Boolean** values, values that can be true or false. True is denoted by any nonzero value and false is denoted by zero. The abstract names "x" and "y" represent integer values. The programmer need not know or track how much storage is allocated for a Boolean value, or for an integer value. The **compiler** does so.

Example 2.1: Type Affects Interpretation

```
bool a = 1, b = 1;
int        x = 1, y = 1;

//Boolean OR
a + b;                 =>            MOV     $tmp, a
                                    OR      $tmp, b
//integer addition
x + y;                 =>            MOV     $tmp, x
                                    ADD     $tmp, y
```

All four named values are initialized to 1. The same operation "+" is performed on each pair of values. However, the operator "+" is overloaded, that is, its meaning differs according to type. For integers, "+" is simply addition. For Boolean values, "+" is the disjunction (OR) of two Boolean values. Again, the programmer need not be concerned about different type implementations of "+" operation. The compiler tracks type and generates different instructions!

Most software developers no longer think in terms of binary strings. Likewise, they no longer deal with low-level hardware details, such as device drivers and memory disks. Instead, reliance on utility software predominates. We briefly review such software in the next section.

2.2 GENERAL PURPOSE UTILITY AND SUPPORT

Desktop computers and laptops are typically general purpose and thus are capable of running diverse software applications. High-performance computers are far more specialized but also run a variety of software. For any application, utility software must be present to start the system, load, execute, and reload multiple software programs. Utility modules provide basic functions of I/O, data storage and retrieval, and computation.

Advances in software development yielded the design and implementation of utility modules for extensive reuse.

Operating systems (OS) evolved from repositories of code that performed standard I/O operations. Abstraction hides differences between devices and thus supports higher-level perspectives of data and control. For example, the notion of volume control is standard even though sound cards differ from platform to platform. Programmers thus focus on computational tasks and software structure rather than low-level device details.

Operating systems automate the loading of computer programs into computer memory banks. An OS routine stores a software program into memory. During execution, program instructions are fetched (retrieved from memory) and executed on the processor. Operating systems manage different computer components (memory, device drives, processor) while supporting multiple processes (computer programs). Operating systems thus help streamline software development.

Operating systems consist of several modules to support seamless software execution. Figure 2.1 presents an abstract model of these services. The kernel comprises the core functionality of operating systems. Several software programs handle different components. Device drivers abstract away I/O and memory-mapped addresses, control messages, and data transfer protocols. Process scheduling (and threading) abstract away **CPU** assignment and process switching. Interrupt services abstract away device-specific and critical timing issues. Memory services abstract away memory to disk swapping and other virtual memory management

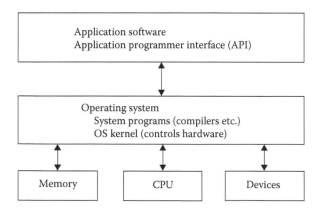

FIGURE 2.1   Operating system components.

details. Process independence is enforced by hardware and the operating system.

Operating systems have been so well integrated into modern development platforms their existence is usually assumed. Software designers, for the most part, do not consider I/O processing, linking, loading, and timing. By isolating the user and the developer from low-level hardware details, operating systems provide platform independence. That is, for the most part, one need not worry about the platform, or hardware configuration, on which software runs.

The study of operating systems no longer may be a cornerstone of an undergraduate education in computer science. Current software development often focuses on data management and front-end services such as user interfaces (UI). However, many back-end processes handled by operating systems, such as threading and memory management, impact software performance and maintainability.

Alongside operating systems, compilers and assemblers elevate the art of software development. By hiding processor-specific details, compilers sustain portability. For example, programmers use variable names to handle data; no longer must a programmer work with registers or specific machine addresses. A variable name is thus a symbolic address, abstractly representing a memory location that stores a data value. The substitution of symbolic addresses for machine addresses is fundamental in modern software.

Symbolic linkers resolve binary addresses when different components are merged together. In essence, assembly language code and symbolic linkers abstract away absolute addresses. How? Within each component, variable declarations (like the simple ones seen in Example 2.1) trigger the reservation of memory for data within that component. Each address so reserved may be considered a relative address, that is, its address is an offset to the base address of a component. A linker then links components together, translating relative addresses to absolute (specific) addresses.

To preserve integrity, and reduce human error, use of absolute addresses is discouraged. Absolute addresses in code compromise **relocatability** (the ability to load executable code into any arbitrary memory location). Why? Reference to an absolute address implies knowledge of where a program is loaded into memory, and the expectation that it be reloaded to the same location. Moreover, specific addresses are tied to specific representation of address length (platform dependent) and thus compromise portability.

2.3 PROGRAMMING LANGUAGE EVOLUTION

Programming languages and software tools elevate the low-level tedium of bit evaluation to a conceptual level. **Assembly language** is the first layer of abstraction, replacing command bit strings with pseudo-mnemonic code that directs the use of registers and memory locations. Thus, programmers work with coded locations rather than direct memory addresses. Instruction sets for an assembly language are tied to a specific processor family, yielding little or no portability.

Although an improvement over hard coding binary strings, assembly languages provided only limited portability due to direct association with specific processors. In the 1960s, research and industry efforts focused on streamlining the coding process. Shortly after the introduction of assembly language, HLLs such as Cobol and Fortran were developed. HLLs provide programmers with a set of reserved words, meant to be as readable as a restricted form of English. A programmer can then more easily and clearly write out instructions for manipulating and storing data.

2.3.1 Compilers

Example 2.2 presents a short C++ code example, computation of a Fibonacci number. Compare this HLL code with the *equivalent* assembly language code shown in Example 2.3. Which code would you rather write, read, modify? Compilers translate HLL code into assembly language code, and an assembler converts the assembly language into machine code. Some compilers produce machine code directly but can generate assembler for debugging purposes.

Example 2.2: High-Level Language Code: C++

```
//Compute and return the nth Fibonacci number.
int fib_loop(int n)
{
    int result = 0, last_result = 1;
    int i;
    if (n < 0) return -1;//error.
    for (i = 0; i < n; ++i)
    {
        int tmp = result + last_result;
        last_result = result;
        result = tmp;
    }
    return result;
}
#if UNIT_TEST
```

```
#include "stdio.h"
int main(int argc, char* argv[])
{
    printf("The zeroeth Fibonacci number is%d\n", fib_loop(0));
    printf("The first Fibonacci number is%d\n", fib_loop(1));
    printf("The second Fibonacci number is%d\n", fib_loop(2));
    printf("The third Fibonacci number is%d\n", fib_loop(3));
    printf("The tenth Fibonacci number is%d\n", fib_loop(10));
    return 0;//Success.
}
#endif
//Compile this program with the command:
//gcc -DUNIT_TEST -g -o fib_loop fib_loop.c
//Run this program with the commend:
//./fib_loop
```

Example 2.3: Assembly Language Produced for Example 2.2

```
//Obtain assembly listing using the commend:
//objdump -S fib_loop
//Obtained using the command "objdump -S fib_loop"
fib_loop: file format elf32-i386
Disassembly of section.text:
080483e4 <fib_loop>:
//Compute and return the nth Fibonacci number.
int fib_loop(int n)
{
80483e4: 55 push%ebp
80483e5: 89 e5 mov%esp,%ebp
80483e7: 83 ec 10 sub $0x10,%esp
int result = 0, last_result = 1;
80483ea: c7 45 f0 00 00 00 00 movl $0x0,-0x10(%ebp)
80483f1: c7 45 f4 01 00 00 00 movl $0x1,-0xc(%ebp)
int i;

if (n < 0) return -1;//error.
80483f8: 83 7d 08 00 cmpl $0x0,0x8(%ebp)
80483fc: 79 07 jns 8048405 <fib_loop+0x21>
80483fe: b8 ff ff ff ff mov $0xffffffff,%eax
8048403: eb 2f jmp 8048434 <fib_loop+0x50>

for (i = 0; i < n; ++i)
8048405: c7 45 f8 00 00 00 00 movl $0x0,-0x8(%ebp)
804840c: eb 1b jmp 8048429 <fib_loop+0x45>
{
int tmp = result + last_result;
804840e: 8b 45 f4 mov -0xc(%ebp),%eax
8048411: 8b 55 f0 mov -0x10(%ebp),%edx
8048414: 01 d0 add%edx,%eax
8048416: 89 45 fc mov%eax,-0x4(%ebp)
last_result = result;
8048419: 8b 45 f0 mov -0x10(%ebp),%eax
```

```
804841c: 89 45 f4 mov%eax,-0xc(%ebp)
result = tmp;
804841f: 8b 45 fc mov -0x4(%ebp),%eax
8048422: 89 45 f0 mov%eax,-0x10(%ebp)
int result = 0, last_result = 1;
int i;

if (n < 0) return -1;//error.

for (i = 0; i < n; ++i)
8048425: 83 45 f8 01 addl $0x1,-0x8(%ebp)
8048429: 8b 45 f8 mov -0x8(%ebp),%eax
804842c: 3b 45 08 cmp 0x8(%ebp),%eax
804842f: 7c dd jl 804840e <fib_loop+0x2a>
{
int tmp = result + last_result;
last_result = result;
result = tmp;
}
return result;
8048431: 8b 45 f0 mov -0x10(%ebp),%eax
}
8048434: c9 leave
8048435: c3 ret

08048436 <main>:

#if UNIT_TEST
#include "stdio.h"

int main(int argc, char* argv[])
{
8048436: 55 push%ebp
8048437: 89 e5 mov%esp,%ebp
8048439: 83 e4 f0 and $0xfffffff0,%esp
804843c: 83 ec 10 sub $0x10,%esp
printf("The zeroeth Fibonacci number is%d\n", fib_loop(0));
804843f: c7 04 24 00 00 00 00 movl $0x0,(%esp)
8048446: e8 99 ff ff ff call 80483e4 <fib_loop>
804844b: ba b0 85 04 08 mov $0x80485b0,%edx
8048450: 89 44 24 04 mov%eax,0x4(%esp)
8048454: 89 14 24 mov%edx,(%esp)
8048457: e8 a4 fe ff ff call 8048300 <printf@plt>
printf("The first Fibonacci number is%d\n", fib_loop(1));
804845c: c7 04 24 01 00 00 00 movl $0x1,(%esp)
8048463: e8 7c ff ff ff call 80483e4 <fib_loop>
8048468: ba d4 85 04 08 mov $0x80485d4,%edx
804846d: 89 44 24 04 mov%eax,0x4(%esp)
8048471: 89 14 24 mov%edx,(%esp)
8048474: e8 87 fe ff ff call 8048300 <printf@plt>
printf("The second Fibonacci number is%d\n", fib_loop(2));
```

```
8048479: c7 04 24 02 00 00 00 movl $0x2,(%esp)
8048480: e8 5f ff ff ff call 80483e4 <fib_loop>
8048485: ba f8 85 04 08 mov $0x80485f8,%edx
804848a: 89 44 24 04 mov%eax,0x4(%esp)
804848e: 89 14 24 mov%edx,(%esp)
8048491: e8 6a fe ff ff call 8048300 <printf@plt>
printf("The third Fibonacci number is%d\n", fib_loop(3));
8048496: c7 04 24 03 00 00 00 movl $0x3,(%esp)
804849d: e8 42 ff ff ff call 80483e4 <fib_loop>
80484a2: ba 1c 86 04 08 mov $0x804861c,%edx
80484a7: 89 44 24 04 mov%eax,0x4(%esp)
80484ab: 89 14 24 mov%edx,(%esp)
80484ae: e8 4d fe ff ff call 8048300 <printf@plt>
printf("The tenth Fibonacci number is%d\n", fib_loop(10));
80484b3: c7 04 24 0a 00 00 00 movl $0xa,(%esp)
80484ba: e8 25 ff ff ff call 80483e4 <fib_loop>
80484bf: ba 40 86 04 08 mov $0x8048640,%edx
80484c4: 89 44 24 04 mov%eax,0x4(%esp)
80484c8: 89 14 24 mov%edx,(%esp)
80484cb: e8 30 fe ff ff call 8048300 <printf@plt>
return 0;//Success.
80484d0: b8 00 00 00 00 mov $0x0,%eax
}
80484d5: c9 leave
80484d6: c3 ret
80484d7: 90 nop
80484d8: 90 nop
80484d9: 90 nop
80484da: 90 nop
80484db: 90 nop
80484dc: 90 nop
80484dd: 90 nop
80484de: 90 nop
80484df: 90 nop
```

HLLs abstract away instruction-set dependencies and thus provide portability; the same software code can run on different processors. Commands involving several small steps are replaced by logical representations. For example, setting a data value to 100 if its initial value is zero requires many low-level steps in assembly language:

LDA x	load register A with data value represented by x
CMP 0	compare x with zero
JMPZ labelA	skip next step if x is not zero
LDA 100	load register A with the value 100
STO x	store the value in register A in the memory associated with x

This instruction is clearly and compactly represented in a HLL by a statement such as

```
if (x == 0), x = 100
```

By translating HLL statements into the low-level steps required in assembly language, compilers made coding easier and more reusable.

Major actions performed by compilers are partitioned: a front end, an optimizer, and a back end, as shown in Figure 2.2. The front end is tied to the particular HLL being translated. It processes the HLL source code into intermediate code that is optimized and then passed to the back end. The back end translates the optimized code into machine code or an assembly language tied to a specific processor. The middle part is the optimizer. In Figure 2.2, to emphasize that front end is tied to a specific HLL, the initial input (source code) is bolded. Likewise, to emphasize that the back end is tied to a specific processor family, the final output (machine code) is also bolded.

The essential actions of each compilation stage are summarized in Table 2.1. Each stage advances the translation of source code from a high-level language into machine level code. The lexical scanner (analyzer) removes information not relevant to execution, such as comments and white space (tabs, punctuation, spaces). The scanner emits a stream of tokens, where each token represents the smallest meaningful unit. The parser analyzes tokens, verifying correct syntax, and ensuring that tokens are grouped together appropriately. For example, "a = b + c" is a statement composed of five tokens: a, =, b, +, and c. This single statement represents two operations: addition (b + c) and assignment (storage of sum "b + c").

	Input	=>	Output
Front end:			
Lexical scanner	**source code**		token stream
Parser	token stream		parse tree
Normalization	parse tree		standardized parse tree
Verification	parse tree		consistent parse tree
Middle:			
Optimizer	parse tree		optimized parse tree
Back end:			
Code generator	optimized parse tree		**machine/assembly code**

FIGURE 2.2   Compilation stages.

TABLE 2.1   Compilation Processes

Scanner	Remove comments and white space
	Track source code lines
	Tokenize
Parser	Syntactical analysis: report syntax errors
	Early semantic checks
Normalizer	Provide missing element
	Replace alternate forms with preferred forms
Verifier	Ensure consistent internal representation
Optimizer	Target agnostic optimizations
	Dead code removal; reduction in strength; hoisting;
	common subexpression elimination
	Target dependent optimizations
	Peephole optimization
Generator	Translation followed by dead or repeated instruction removal

During normalization, the parse tree is standardized. Statements are converted to a standard form that is meaningful to the compiler, but not necessarily a programmer. For example,

```
return;            // #A: return of no value implied
return void;       // #standardizedA

C     c = d;       // #B: object constructed and value
                   // copied
C     c(d);        // #standardardizedB: copy constructor
                   // invoked
```

The verifier checks semantic relevance. For example, a continue statement can exist only inside a loop.

Many optimizations occur automatically, unseen by software developers. Yet, software design impacts how often such optimizations may be applied. We review some optimizations, such as function **inlining**, in Chapter 3.

Compilers themselves support generality and abstraction! The same front end can be reused for multiple compiler versions, where each version supports a given HLL but targets a different, specific processor family. Likewise, the back end can be reused for multiple compiler versions, where each version processes the intermediate code from a specific HLL. *Compilers profoundly enhanced the productivity of software developers.*

With all the advances in programming languages and operating system support, why is software development still so complex? Why is software often hard to understand, sustain, or replicate? As noted in Chapter 1, much of modern software complexity is due to its longevity and scale. In the next sections, we briefly examine standard data structures used in HLLs to constrain software complexity.

2.3.2 Software Design

As software use became more embedded in society, software costs came under increasing scrutiny. Commercial expectations for correct and efficient software arose. Software development and code designs were analyzed. Concern developed over the proliferation of **spaghetti code**, code that had little inherent structure and no discernible control flow. *Software is difficult to understand, test, and modify when its control flow cannot be easily traced or predicted.*

When intense criticism of unstructured code surfaced, a focus on software design, specifically structured design, emerged. Pascal, a highly structured teaching language developed by Nicklaus Wirth, was used effectively to instill the tenets of **functional decomposition** (top-down design) as an alternative to **spaghetti code**. Software became more readable when a program's major responsibilities were thus decomposed at the high level first, with tasks assigned to lower-level functions. Example 2.4 displays a general `main()` routine used to demonstrate functional decomposition to novice programmers. Kernighan and Ritchie developed C, the successor of language B, at Bell Labs. C provided high-level language constructs but retained an emphasis on efficiency. Both Pascal and C promoted structured design, but Pascal enforced structured control flow more resolutely by prohibiting the **goto** statement.

Example 2.4: High-Level Functional Decomposition: C++

```
int main()           //delineate major tasks of program
{
   startUp();         //function handles intro/initializ
   while (!done())    //function tests if terminus reached
   { query();         //function acquires data and/or direction
     process();       //function processes data and/or action
   }
   cleanup();         //function releases resources, stores data
   return 0;
}
```

Structured programming supported clear control flow, functional decomposition, and the ability to clearly define composite types. Software so designed was more readable, and thus, more maintainable. However, structured programming provided little persistent connection between functions and data, using global data or passing parameters as the primary means to share data. Example 2.4 may not clearly illustrate the generation, sharing, or persistence of data, even though some data transfer likely exists between the query() and the process() functions. For greater consistency, software developers saw the benefit of associating data with its relevant functionality. Thus, the notion of an **abstract data type (ADT)** gained currency.

2.3.3 ADTs

Decades ago, **modular programming** proposed the isolation of functions that served the same purpose or addressed the same data. The intent was to better achieve the software engineering directives of low coupling and high cohesion. **Coupling** is a measure of the interdependency of two different software elements. The more tightly coupled, the more likely that a change in one element will force a change in the second. Hence, low coupling is associated with better **software maintainability**. **Cohesion** is a measure of how well the internals of a software element "stick together." High cohesion implies a significant degree of isolated functionality (or data) and thus confinement of a software change to a particular portion of the system.

A module is a set of procedures alongside with data needed for its functionality. By associating a module with specific functionality, modular programming yields design clarity and code readability. Cohesion further reduced software maintenance cost. Why? If change is mandated for a particular feature, and that feature is restricted to one module, change is isolated to one module. The cost of **cascading changes** is thus avoided.

For a defined type, modular programming led to a distinction between an **interface** (published set of available functions) and an **implementation** (internal selection of data structures and associated functionality). This **separation of concerns** (interface and implementation) promised reduced maintenance cost if the modules so designed were highly cohesive.

ADTs promote the separation of form from function by isolating the implementation of a data type from its interface declaration. A classic example is a queue data type: its use requires the availability of enQueue(), deQueue(), isEmpty(), isFull(), and clear() functions. Such functionality is independent of implementation: a queue data type could be implemented as a circular array or as a linked list. By separating interface from implementation, an ADT shifts the focus from implementation details to the functionality supported by the interface.

ADTs reinforced the **dual perspective** of utility software: external use by an application programmer, internal definition by a designer. This delineation between form and function supports the development of reusable, testable code since the application programmer is dependent only on the interface NOT the implementation. Internal changes need impact only the designer: no change should be required in application code when implementation changes. The application programmer codes only to the interface and thus must know only the form of function invocation, the data required to make a call, and any expected processing after the function terminates. We examine next the realization of an ADT via the class construct, which was greatly advanced by popular adoption of C++.

2.3.4 Class Construct

Bjarne Stroustrup developed C++ at Bell Labs. As an object-oriented programming language (OOPL), C++ was backward compatible with C. The name C++ played on the notion of shortcut increment via the "++" operator. C++ was an increment, an improvement, to C (although some pundits noted that post-increment implied use before the increment/improvement). C++ quickly became popular because it was built on and was interoperable with C. C++ retained the same top priority as C: efficiency! Enthusiasts for both languages appreciate the adage "pay only for what you use". C++ greatly advanced the concept of the ADT through its class construct.

Essentially an ADT, a C++ class is a type definition that can be separated into two files: an .h or header file and a .cpp or implementation file. Ideally, the header file should contain only the function prototypes specifying the public interface. However, since the compiler needs type information, to deduce size as needed for memory layout, the header file must contain the declarations of data members as well. Since the application programmer can thus look into the header file and see the private data members, the header file does not fully support **information hiding**. The .cpp or implementation file contains the function definitions. Example 2.5 illustrates the decoupling of interface and implementation, as implemented via the C++ class construct, for the classic stack data structure.

Example 2.5: Stack ADT: Form and Function Decoupled (C++)

```
//stack.h FILE: declare data members and function prototypes
class Stack
{    //class-wide global: often used for bookkeeping
     static int      countActive;
     //data members defined for each object instantiated
     int     top;
     int     size;
     int*    dataP;

     //suppress copying: see chapter 4
     void operator=(const Stack&);
     Stack(const Stack&);
public:
     //constructor and destructor
     Stack(unsigned dataSize = 100);
     ~Stack();

     //public utility
     bool    isEmpty();
     bool    isFull();
     int     pop();
     void    push(int);
     void    clear();

     //function to access static count
     static int numActive();
};

//stack .cpp FILE: implement functions; initialize static data
int  Stack::countActive = 0;

//constructor with provision for default size
Stack::Stack(unsigned dataSize)
{    top = 0;
     size = dataSize;
     dataP = new int[size];
}

//destructor
Stack::~Stack()            {    delete[]  dataP;         }
void   Stack::clear()      {    top = 0;      return;    }
bool   Stack::isEmpty()    {    return    top == 0;      }
bool   Stack::isFull()     {    return    top == size;   }

int  Stack::pop()
{    int     localValue = dataP[top];
     top--;
     return  localValue;
}
```

```
void Stack::push(int value)
{     dataP[top] = value;
      top++;
}


int  Stack::numActive()      {    return countActive;  }
```

As a type definition, the class construct is similar in other languages. Typically, data is **encapsulated** and tagged as **private**, that is, not directly accessible outside the class definition. Functionality can be either **public** (directly accessible outside the class), or private. These different accessibility rights allow elements of a class definition to be viewed as private (internal) or public (external) details.

Since the class construct is a type definition, no memory is allocated until a variable declaration triggers such an allocation. Object declarations are also known as object **instantiations** because an object is synonymous with an instance of the class. Object instantiation is more than memory allocation. Special functions, called **constructors**, are implicitly invoked by the compiler to initialize the object so instantiated, and usually bear the name of the class. See Chapter 5 for more detail.

An application programmer manipulates instantiated objects. However, object manipulation is restricted to the public interface of the class. As seen above, a stack object may be used but only for the public functions of push, pop, etc. To advance the notion of security via encapsulation, class data and member functions are private, by default. For additional accessibility definitions and detail, see Chapter 5.

A class definition specifies data members along with associated functionality. Each class method (member function) is a function declared in the scope of that class. An instance of a class is an actual data realization (memory allocation) of that class definition. Since every class member function must be able to distinguish between multiple instances of the class, the notion of the **this** pointer emerged. The this pointer holds the address of the active object and is an implicit parameter passed with each member function invocation, as seen in Example 2.6. For more details, see Appendix A.

Example 2.6: OO Code (C++): Implicit **this** Pointer

```
//sample object allocation
Stack          s1;    //s1 allocated at memory location B404
Stack          s2;    //s2 allocated at memory location B442
s1.push(42);          //Stack::push(B404, 42)
s2.push(17);          //Stack::push(B442, 17)
```

FIGURE 2.3   Memory layout for Example 2.6 objects => this pointers.

Every object has its own data fields (that is, a copy of each defined data member), except for class-wide globals (static data members). To track object instantiation and destruction, one can define a static count in a class: this count can be incremented in each constructor and decremented in the destructor. countActive is a static data member for our stack class. One copy of a static data field is allocated for the ENTIRE class, independent of the number of objects instantiated. Frequently, static data fields are used to track class usage, such as the number of objects instantiated, or the number of calls to a specific function. However, in general, the use of global data and class statics is discouraged.

Consider the two stack objects, s1 and s2, in Example 2.6. The statement s1.push(42) is an invocation of the Stack::push() method that passes in the address of s1 (received as the this pointer) alongside the integer value to be stored in the stack object s1, i.e., Stack::push(&s1,42). Similarly, s2.push(17) is an invocation of the Stack::push() method that passes in the address of s2 alongside the integer value to be stored in the stack object s2, i.e., Stack::push(&s2,17). Figure 2.3 illustrates sample memory allocation for the code that declares and manipulates stack objects in Example 2.6. Using this sample memory assignment, the comments in Example 2.6 indicates what method invocations look like from the compiler's perspective.

2.3.5 Object-Oriented Programming Languages

In the mid-1990s, Java was developed at Sun Microsystems with James Gosling as the chief architect. Java met the burgeoning web's need for an OOPL that provided portability. Java is similar to C++ but prioritizes portability and security in contrast to C++'s emphasis on efficiency. Java stressed object orientation by imposing the syntactical restriction that all code must be defined in a class construct. Thus, even a structured driver had to be declared in the form of an object.

Java became immediately popular for a few reasons. In Java, each primitive type is associated with a specific size. Regardless of platform then, an int will always require the same amount of memory. If a Boolean requires one byte on platformA, it will require one byte on platformB and so forth.

Data declarations, and stack frame layouts, are thus consistent across platforms, supporting the portability of Java code. Java also provided an easier development environment: programmers did not have to track memory management as closely as in C++. The learning curve for coding in Java is thus shorter and shallower. For more detail on memory management within a program, see Chapter 4.

OOPLs, such as C++, Java, and C#, emphasize the notion of **encapsulation** as well as abstraction. A type definition is wrapped up in one class (capsule), and hence, its data is protected. To further the concept of an independent capsule, design principles stress that a class definition should contain all the functionality needed to manipulate instances of the class (that is, objects) and no more. Classes so designed achieve high cohesion since there is no extraneous functionality or data. Classes so designed also achieve low coupling because all needed data AND functionality are contained within the type definition: external dependencies are minimized. Encapsulation affords design control over the external interface and the internal implementation of data. Well-designed classes are better able to preserve type properties and thus support software maintainability.

Beyond providing language constructs that support abstraction and encapsulation, OO languages impacted software design. Encapsulation led directly to the notion of an object having an internal state, where the state of an object is the value of all its data members at a particular point. The emphasis on internal control further advanced a dual perspective. That is, functionality is grossly delineated into two categories: public type behavior that is available to the application programmer (such as pop(), clear(), etc. for a stack) and private internal functionality that provides common utility (e.g., copying) and is of interest to the class designer.

Only certain states may be significant. For a stack object, in fact for any container, empty and non-empty are distinct states. *A state transition is the change in an object state that bears significance.* Consider a stack data type that internally resizes and thus does not have the notion of "full." Upon a pop() operation, a stack object may transition from a non-empty to an empty state. Similarly, on a push() operation, a stack object may transition from an empty to a non-empty state. In contrast, a push() operation on a non-empty stack does not trigger a state change. For data integrity, the class should control state and disallow unregulated public functions, such as unconditional **mutator** operations, that open a class up to unreserved modification. The class designer should structure the class definition so that all state transitions are legal and consistent. Chapter 5 examines class design in greater detail.

Customized data types, defined with the class construct, should be easy to use safely and consistently. Ideally, their use should be as intuitive as manipulating built-in types provided a programming language. Also, to ease software development, software designers may use explicit models. We examine a common modeling tool, UML, next.

2.4 UML

Developed by the Object Management Group (OMG), UML is freely available at uml.org. UML provides standard diagrams to represent design, and to a limited extent, to document software architecture. Awareness of UML is fairly ubiquitous. Although UML defines a plethora of modeling constructs, it is just a tool. It does not make modeling any easier; it often makes the representation of models easier.

UML is the de facto standard for representing software structures and functionality. A UML approach comprises several views: classes with attributes (data), operations, and relationships; specific realizations (instantiations) of these classes, commonly referred to as objects; packages of classes, alongside their dependencies; states and behavior of individual classes; example scenarios of system usage; scenarios of interacting instances; and distributed component communication.

UML defines three types of diagrams: structural, behavioral, and interaction. We provide only a broad overview. For more details, please see uml.org. Structural diagrams document the static structure of the software system and how different portions relate to each other. At a low level, software architecture models classes, objects, interfaces, components, relationships, and dependencies between elements. UML defines several different types of structure diagrams, as enumerated in Table 2.2. We use the class construct in subsequent chapters.

Behavioral Modeling Diagrams capture interactions within a model as well as system states and state transitions. By modeling dynamic behavior, one can track system use and response under both normal and abnormal conditions. Behavioral diagrams record the effects of an operation or event and thus define functionality and identify error conditions and responses. Table 2.3 summarizes three types of behavioral diagrams: use case, activity, and state machine.

Interaction diagrams are a subset of behavior diagrams and model interactions between components, system, and environment. Table 2.4

TABLE 2.2   UML Structure Diagrams

Diagram	Relevance	Intent	Details
Class	Basic building blocks of a model	Define type, interface, attributes	Cardinality Relationships
Object	Instantiation of class	Sample data	Runtime use
Composite	Layering of structure	Focus on construction and relationships	Collaborations supported
Component	Provide well defined interface	Model higher level, complex structures	Built from one or more classes
Package	System decomposition	Identify logical groupings	Identify high-level interactions and dependencies
Deployment	Note execution environment	Provide hardware details	Identify dependencies

TABLE 2.3   UML Behavioral Diagrams

Diagram	Relevance	Intent	Details
Use case	Model user/system interactions	Define behavior, requirements, and constraints	Actors, associated goals (use cases), and dependencies
Activity	Operational	Workflows of components	Note decision points and actions
State machine	Reaction to external and internal input	States and state transitions Illustrate "run state" of a model	Model event-response, functionality, error conditions

TABLE 2.4   UML Interaction Diagrams

Diagram	Relevance	Intent	Details
Communication	Describe static structure and dynamic behavior	Show sequence of messages at runtime	Interactions between objects
Sequence diagram	Progressive timeline	Sequenced messages	Vertical timeline
Timing	View of object's state over time	Identify what modifies state	Timing constraints

lists several types of interaction diagrams. Behavioral diagrams communicate system response and sketch accommodation of different scenarios. Use cases, state machines, and sequence diagrams are often use in analysis and design. In this text, we focus on structural design and reuse; in this context, the class construct is most useful.

UML provides the means to visually model a software system's structure and design, independent of any particular programming language or development process. UML provides modeling notations for typical software projects. As a documentation tool, UML communicates assumptions, restrictions, and design intent. Although focused on design, UML delineates essential components of a system and can document software architecture. Nonetheless, it is most often used to represent the design of OO software systems, patterns, and components.

With over a dozen different types of diagrams, some overlapping in effect, UML has been called the "Swiss Army knife" of notations. With multiple constructs to model a given design or architecture, it is often difficult, or at least confusing, to determine the potential equivalence of different diagrams. *Ambiguity is not a friend of modeling.* Although UML does enforce specification of interface detail, it lacks precision and does not provide an easy means to incorporate custom information or features.

Any technique for modeling and designing large complex systems yields lengthy and cumbersome documentation. UML is no exception. Highly descriptive documentation is unavoidable because large and complex systems must be detailed at both macro and micro levels. Hence, it is difficult in UML, as it is likely to be in any representational schema, to succinctly note software evolution whether modification is viewed through the perspective of time, space, or product variant.

2.5 LIBRARIES AND FRAMEWORKS

Central to modern software development is the reuse of utilities so that the same routines for I/O and data manipulation, for example, do not have to be rewritten repeatedly. To use a cliché, no need to reinvent the wheel. A library is a collection of functions and data types. Software developers import the file containing a library to access the library's functionality. Developers must learn the interface to library routines but otherwise can focus on defining their own program. For example, with its extensive provision of algorithms, and standard data types (such as stacks, queues, sets, etc.), the **Standard Template Library (STL)** supports C++ software development.

Frameworks also support reuse, and relieve programmers from routine, tedious, repetitive software construction. Designed to ease the task of developing applications, **frameworks** are more structured than libraries. A framework defines the underlying structure of an application; the application programmer may extend or redefine some of the built-in functionality but must adhere to the overall structure of the framework. By simplifying the specification of an interface, and by handling the details of I/O, a framework can accelerate application development. Caveat: your application should fit conceptually into the framework used. Sample frameworks include media authoring tools, web applications, .NET platform, Linux, etc.

2.6 SOFTWARE CONSTRUCTION FUNDAMENTALS

As the premier professional organization for software engineering, the IEEE Computer Society strives to develop standards for and advance knowledge of software development. SoftWare Engineering Body of Knowledge (SWEBOK) is an endeavor to summarize current best practices of and tool usage within software development. Software construction is one area of focus and covers the concepts reviewed in this chapter. The essential details of software construction, as outlined by SWEBOK, are summarized in Table 2.5. For more details, see http://www.computer.org/portal/web/swebok.

Software construction suggests code development but spans verification of functionality via unit and integration testing as well as debugging. Although the four fundamentals listed in Table 2.5 apply also to the modeling and design phases of software development, we examine them here in the context of coding.

SWEBOK's fundamental to minimize code complexity seeks to produce clear and readable code. Constraining **software complexity** eases the tasks of modeling, documentation, and testing. To limit the software complexity of a code base, good programming practices should be followed, including functional decomposition, encapsulation, appropriate use of control structures, **self-documenting code** using mnemonic names and constants, conscious design and implementation of error processing

TABLE 2.5   SWEBOK Software Construction Essentials

	Fundamentals	Management Approach	Practical Details
1	Minimize complexity	Model	Design
2	Anticipate change	Plan	Programming languages Coding Reuse
3	Construct for verification	Measure	Testing
4	Standards	Communicate	Quality Integration

strategies, effective and responsive resource management, and, of course, documentation.

SWEBOK's fundamental to anticipate change recognizes the prominence of legacy systems, and the drive to retain them. Good programming techniques should yield maintainable software, especially if sufficient documentation records model and design assumptions. Programming language selection should be undertaken with the understanding that software evolution is likely.

Construction for **verification**, SWEBOK's third fundamental, elevates the critical importance of testing especially when reuse is anticipated. Code must be designed and implemented with an explicit plan to verify functionality, through both code reviews and testing. Unit and integration testing should be integrated in the development cycle. As much as possible, testing should be automated.

The fundamental to use and adhere to standards reflects the drive to develop software systems consistently and correctly, much like any engineering product. In particular, an emphasis on standards in communication and in interfaces eases software integration and supports software evolution.

TABLE 2.6   Abstractions and Effects

Advance	Abstraction	Benefits	Costs
Symbolic address	Absolute address where data stored	Data not tied to specific location Postpone data layout	Less control over locality
Re-locatable address	Symbol location relative to component	Variable load address Linker map => optimize memory	Harder to debug Load address less predictable
Typing	Data type	Automatic association with functionality Compiler verification	Constrained manipulation
Functions	Named set of instructions	Clear control flow Readability Reuse	Call overhead Return overhead Parameters
Class construct	Encapsulated ADT	Data integrity Controlled access Separated interface and implementation	Design responsibility
Dynamic binding (see Chapter 8)	Runtime function selection	Flexibility Extensibility Heterogeneity	Runtime overhead Constrained inlining

Each advance in software development may be viewed as the introduction of another abstraction. The layering of abstractions serves to isolate software developers from "incidental" or arbitrary details, such as hardware specifics. In this manner, computing is truly general purpose and software has becomes more portable. Although each programming advance is an improvement, we show the net effects of some cornerstone abstractions, in Table 2.6. Each layer of software development (compiler, assembler, linker) presents a more abstract view than the one above it but at the same time refines a software solution.

2.7 SUMMARY

As the influence of software expanded, professional interest in code reuse increased. Access to standardized utility functions for mundane tasks, such as I/O, decreased development time, and cost. At this same time, operating systems grew in size and complexity, offering system support for background tasks, such as memory management and I/O. Consequently, it became feasible to rest on the advances of operating systems and build standard functions for reuse.

To place modern software in the context of reuse and high-level abstraction, this chapter examined the foundations of software development. Key abstractions reviewed include abstract data types and the modeling tool, UML. To stress the emergence of software development as a discipline, we ended the chapter with a review of standards for software construction.

DESIGN INSIGHTS

SOFTWARE

Low-level details (hardware) abstracted away
Typing supports multiple interpretations of binary values
High-level languages streamline software development
    Compilers translate code into assembly (or executable)
    Code is more portable with hardware dependencies removed
Operating systems absorbed much responsibility, including:
    Loading and executing software
    I/O, data storage and retrieval

MODELS

Ambiguous models are of limited utility
    Models should precisely represent design

Software development rests on many types of models
UML provides standard forms for representing design solutions

SOFTWARE DESIGN

Abstraction elevates the art of programming
Structured programming promotes software maintainability
    Control constructs
    Functional decomposition
    Composite types
ADTs wrap functionality with associated data
    Promote cohesion
    Support maintainability
Class construct is ADT + encapsulation
    Interface provides external face of type definition
    Implementation hides internal details
Constrain software complexity for maintainability

DOCUMENTATION

Must be accurate and available

CONCEPTUAL QUESTIONS

1. Why is abstraction important?

2. How does the notion of type support abstraction?

3. What does the operating system do?

4. How did HLLs advance software development?

5. What do compilers do?

6. Why is functional decomposition preferred to spaghetti code?

7. Define an ADT and describe its structure.

8. Identify the key difference(s) between an ADT and the class construct.

9. How do ADTs and classes support the dual perspective?

10. List some common best practices.

II

Software Fundamentals

CHAPTER 3

Functionality

S OFTWARE IS USEFUL WHEN it satisfies user demand or provides commercial value. One chooses an editor (word processor) to store and
format words (data), a calculator to compute numeric results and graph
functions, and a database to store and retrieve tagged data (customer
records...), etc. The use, development, and retention of software is thus
tightly bound to its functionality. The high-level specification of functionality via software requirements was summarized in Chapter 1. In this
chapter, we examine lower-level modeling of functionality, with a focus on
execution control.

The execution or control path of software is the order in which statements are executed. This order does not usually correlate directly to the
sequential listing of statements in source code files. One must understand
different control structures to track the logic of running software. This
chapter begins by defining and illustrating the conceptual types of control,
structured **control flow**, and deliberate interruption of structured control.
Boolean logic in controlling flow is illustrated. Recursion is explained
and contrasted to iteration. The chapter closes by evaluating important
but often considered tangential details, such as side effects and common
optimizations.

CHAPTER OBJECTIVES
- Identify primary control structures
- Emphasize preference for controlled interruption
- Illustrate design imperative for readability

- Summarize Boolean logic and associated laws
- Contrast recursion and sequential execution
- Discuss optimization

3.1 CONTROL FLOW

Control refers to the execution order of code statements consecutively listed in a source code file. Three types of control flow—sequential, conditional, and repetitive—determine the order in which consecutively listed statements fire. The sequential execution model is the traditional conceptual perspective: statements are executed in the exact order (sequence) specified. The state of data in the system is easy to infer at each statement boundary. Likewise, the response to a given input in a particular state should be evident. Interruptions to sequential execution may be problematic, both for data consistency and for logical comprehension.

Say we are given consecutive statements: *A*; *B*; *C*;. Sequential execution processes the statements in the order specified, i.e., *A*, *B*, *C*. Conditional execution may cause one or more statements to be skipped. If statement A is a true/false test and the result of the Boolean test is true, statement B is executed; otherwise statement B is skipped. Repetitive execution is essentially shorthand notation for the repeated execution of a statement for a specific number of executions or until a terminating condition is reached. See Example 3.1 for sample code segments, Figure 3.1 for their corresponding flowcharts and Table 3.1 for a short summary of possible execution paths for arbitrary statements A, B, and C.

Example 3.1: Sample Code Structures

```
//SEQUENTIAL:        A1, B1, C1 executed in order specified
x = 100;             //statement A1
y = 10*x - 4;        //statement B1
z = GetInput();      //statement C1

//CONDITIONAL:        A2 executes test condition
                     B2 executes if A2 is true
                     C2 executes, whether or not A2 is true

if (x < z)           //statement A2
    x = 100;         //statement B2
y = x*2 - 100;       //statement C2

//REPETITIVE:         B3 repeats for some number of passes
x = 10;              //statement A3
```

```
for (int k = 0; k < limit; k++)
    x = x*2 + 10;              //statement B3
y = 100;                       //statement C3
```

One can model control flow using flowcharts. As is standard, arrows represent the flow of execution, boxes represent actions taken, diamonds represent a test (conditional evaluation) with two outcomes: a response associated with a true result and another response associated with a false result. Returning to the simple math tutor from Chapter 1, we replicate Figure 1.3 here as Figure 3.2.

Hmmm. The repetitive process for math drills has been modeled but without termination. Even the most diligent elementary school student does not want to add digits interminably. Few students benefit from repeating the same problem without assistance. How is termination supported? What responses are appropriate for an incorrect answer? No detail is given as to whether "numGuess" is an internal evaluation (up to three attempts

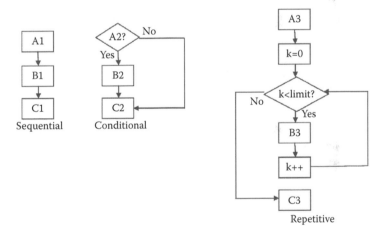

FIGURE 3.1   Flowcharts for Example 3.1.

TABLE 3.1   Possible Execution Paths for Example 3.1

Sequential	Conditional	Repetitive
A, B, C	A, B, C	A, C
	A, C	A, B, C
		A, B, B, C
		A, B, B, B, C
		A, B,…, B, C

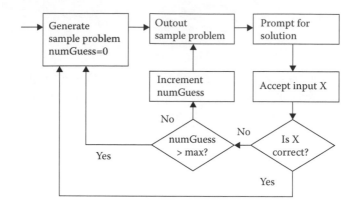

FIGURE 3.2   Flowchart for simple math tutor.

permitted) or a response to an external query ("how many guesses do you want?"). Alternatively, each incorrect response could be met with a query asking the user's preference for trying again.

Figures 3.1 and 3.2 illustrate two key points:

1. Control flow models translate directly to code.

2. Control flow models communicate solutions, after their design.

A model illustrates a solution to a design problem, such as how to structure the query/answer exchange in a tutoring session. The model designer must answer several questions and then model the determined response. Domain knowledge is essential. Consider just one question for a math tutor design: what termination criteria are valid for the math tutor? One cannot answer this question without knowing what audience is targeted, the level of expertise expected, etc.

Familiarity with control structures alone is not sufficient for modeling repetition and termination effectively. *A software developer must know when to interrupt control flow, how to interrupt control flow while preserving readability, and how to use control flow to incorporate error processing.*

3.1.1 Structured Control Flow

Control flow can be categorized into the three basic constructs of sequential, conditional, and repetitive, whether one considers blocks of code or statements. A code block or compound statement is a sequence of simple and (nested) compound statements that are executed in lexical order. Statements within the block can be sequential, conditional, or repetitive. Control enters at the top of the block and usually exits from the bottom. This assumption of single entry and single exit supports static analysis and intuition. At any point within a given block, all unconditional statements above that point—most notably data allocation and initialization—can be assumed to have been executed.

Code can be represented as sequences of statements or blocks, with control statements altering the flow of control in a predictable way, depending on whether the construct is conditional or repetitive. Direct jumps, such as the goto statement compromise the linearity of control flow and hence code readability. Most design guidelines proscribe the use of gotos. In contrast, indirect jumps via function calls isolate functionality and hence promote top-down decomposition and readability.

Conditional execution is effected using the *if/else* construct or the *switch* statement. If the condition associated with an *if* statement is true, then the following statement (block) is executed. If the condition is not true, and there is a corresponding *else* statement, the statement block following the *else* is executed. Regardless of the outcome of the conditional evaluation, flow continues with the statement following the if-else construct. Example 3.2 provides sample conditional code segments using the *if* construct, ranging from a simple if in statement #A to a long, chained if/else in statement #D.

Example 3.2: Conditional Evaluation: If/Else

```
if (size < 1)        size = 100;    //#A simple if

if (action == 1)     z = x*y;       //#B simple if/else
else                 z = x + y;

if (magnitude == 0)           inflate = 0; //#C 3-way branch
else if (magnitude < 1)       inflate/= 2; //chained if/else
else                          inflate *= 2;

if (command == 1)        { ... }   //#D long chained if/else
else if (command == 2)   { ... }
else if (command == 3)   { ... }
...
else if (command == 20)  { ... }
else                     { ... }
```

Control flow should be evident from software structure. Although simple, the if/else construct may impede code analysis. It is difficult to track the state of values or the outcome of evaluations when Boolean expressions are overly complex or too many if/else statements are chained. Software developers should also be aware of the dangling-else problem: when a chained if statement contains fewer elses than ifs, it may be unclear how to match the else statements to the if statements.

Code segments #A and #B in Example 3.3 are equivalent even though the format (indentation) implies different control flows. However, indentation does not matter in C-like languages. C-like languages are "free format": white space such as blanks and tabs are discarded by the compiler; the semicolon (";") is used to separate statements so that the compiler can identify statements independent of placement. Hence, format is stylistic and does not affect compilation. (In contrast, Python is a "fixed format" language: indentation implies scope.)

Example 3.3: Dangling Else

```
//#A form implies action2() fires when !conditionA (BUT not so!)
if (conditionA)
      if (conditionB)
            action1();
else
      action2();


//#B form implies action2() fires when !conditionA && !conditionB
if (conditionA)
      if (conditionB)
            action1();
      else
            action2();


//#C parentheses override default association
//    action2() fires when !conditionA
if (conditionA)
{     if (conditionB)
            action1();
}
else
      action2();
```

In Example 3.3, action2() fires when !conditionA && !conditionB, for both code segments #A and #B. Why? The compiler follows the rule "match an else to the closest preceding unmatched if." Thus, "else action2()" is matched to "if (conditionB)" in both code segments because the closest if is the same regardless of the indentation. Some languages enforce a syntactical solution to the dangling-else problem. For example, Ada requires an "END IF" terminator for each "IF" statement. Placing an "END IF" after "action1()" informs the compiler that there is no else to execute when conditionB is false, and so action2() fires when !conditionA (and conditionB) is not evaluated. C-like languages do not offer such definitive control flow; programmers must override the compiler's resolution of the dangling-else by using parentheses, as illustrated by code segment #C.

When many alternative conditions must be tested in sequence, the resulting if/else statement may be long and difficult to read. *Code that is difficult to read is hard to maintain.* Often, switch or case statements are preferred. A switch statement is a block with several alternatives for execution. Each alternative case is labeled with a value that resolves to an integer. Upon entry to a switch statement, the control variable evaluates to an integer value. The case statement with a matching integer value is then executed. If no matching case statement is found, then the default case is executed. If the default case also does not exist, then no action is taken. Example 3.4 provides some sample conditional C-style code segments using the switch construct. In terms of effect, the statements labeled #B in Example 3.2 (*if*) and Example 3.4 (*switch*) are equivalent.

Example 3.4: Conditional Evaluation (C++): SWITCH

```
switch (action)       //#B simple switch
{    case 1:          z = x*y;
                      break;
     default:         z = x + y;
}

int value = 100;
//break statement needed for each case
//if break missing, execution falls through to next case
//    e.g., if command == 10, value will be incremented by 300
switch(command)
{    case    1:       value++;
                      break;
     case    2:       value += 10;
                      break;
     case    10:      value += 100;
     case    20:      value += 200;
                      break;
```

```
        default:          value--;
}

//readability improved with enumeration literals
enum          laserOrient {up, down, left, right};
laserOrient  myLaserPts;
...
switch(myLaserPts)
{     case   up:      ...
                      break;
      case   down:    ...
                      break;
      case   left:    ...
                      break;
      case   right:   ...
                      break;
      default:        ...
}
```

The syntax for switch statements varies from language to language, as do some finer details. Some languages provide ranges as a viable case statement option. C-like languages require a break statement at the end of each case statement. Without a break, the case statement that matches the control variable will execute and then fall through to the next case statement. Fall-through can be used to drive execution of more than one consecutive case statement. However, fall-through compromises readability and maintainability and is thus discouraged.

The switch statement compares the control variable to the case statements, one by one, in the order specified. Efficiency is obtained when the fewest number of comparisons are made, on average. Hence, programmers often order the case statements in decreasing order of the likelihood of producing a match with the control variable. For clarity, switch statements are best used in place of lengthy if/else statements. For increased readability, enumeration literals (the enum construct in C-like languages) can replace case labels. If designed in a streamlined fashion, switch statements should be fairly easy to extend.

Repetition comes in two flavors: iterative and conditional. Iterative repetition repeats a statement (block) a specified number of times. Such enumerated (counted) repetition is implemented via for-loops. Conditional repetition repeats a statement (block) as long as a condition holds true. Both conditional and iterative loops test termination criteria with each pass of the loop: Is the specified number of iterations met? Or is the condition still true?

Conditional repetition is typically achieved via *while/do* or *do/while* loop constructs. These constructs are not strictly equivalent. If the specified condition is initially false, the *while/do* statement (block) is not executed at all; for the *do/while* loop, it would execute once. Some languages offer a *repeat/until* construct that drives execution until a specific condition becomes true. Equivalent to *do/while*, the *repeat/until* construct also executes its associated statement (block) at least once.

Loop statements execute the controlled statement block repeatedly as long as the control condition is true. The while-statement tests the condition at the top of the loop. What does this pretest imply? On each iteration, before the controlled statement is entered, the test condition is evaluated. Only if the test condition holds will the loop body be executed. Thus, the body of the while loop may not be executed at all, e.g., when the test condition fails initially. The do/while statement tests the loop condition at the bottom of the loop, and thus employs a post-test. After each iteration or execution of the controlled statement, the test condition is evaluated. Hence, the body of a do/while loop always execute at least once.

The *for*-loop is shorthand for a while loop with a built-in loop index that is initialized, as specified, before the loop is entered. The for-loop construct also specifies the terminating condition and update action executed upon the end of each loop pass. In the for-loop of Example 3.5, "int index = 0;" is the loop index initialization; "index < 100" is the terminating condition and "index++" is the index update operation (commonly a simple increment, as it is here).

Example 3.5: Use For-Loop for Counting: C++

```
int   dB[100];
for (int index = 0; index < 100; index++)    //simple for loop
dB[index] = 1 + 10*index;                     //array initialization

//while loop equivalent to preceding for loop
//NOT preferred: programmer responsible for index
int index = 0;
while (index < 100)
{     dB[index] = 1 + 10*index;
      index++;
}
```

Since any for-loop can be written as a while loop, why bother with for-loops? Safe code and readability are two immediate answers. The for-loop automatically updates and tests the counter or loop index (index in Example 3.5), thus removing responsibility for counting from the programmer. A common error within a while-loop occurs when the programmer fails to correctly test or update the index. For readability, loop constructs should be used as intended: for-loops for counted repetition; while-loop for conditional repetition (of unknown duration). Example 3.6 shows reasonable uses of the while-loop construct, alongside a couple of poorly designed for-loops.

Example 3.6: Use While-Loop for Conditional Repetition: C++

```
//Boolean function: returns status (true or false)
bool done()
{     char    userChoice;
      cout << "Enter a "q" or "Q" to quit" << endl;
cin >> userChoice;
return (userChoice == "q" || userChoice == "Q");
|

//truly conditional loop: number of iterations unknown
while (!done())
{     ...         }


//indefinite loop: exit may be possible via exception or break
while (true)
{     ...         }


//also indefinite loop: no termination criteria specified
//works but NOT preferred design
for (; ;)


//counting loop used as conditional loop: poor design; not readable
//    more intuitive and consistent to use first while loop above
for (bool doneV = false; !doneV;)
{     ...
      doneV = done();
}
```

3.1.2 Controlled Interruption to Sequential Execution

Control flow affects readability and, possibly, efficiency. Functional decomposition supports a high-level perspective of control flow. A function is a named code block that is associated with an address. A programmer can thus call, or invoke, a function without a direct dependency on an address. The compiler does the background work to support such a call. A function call is processed as a jump statement: the compiler resolves the function address, and stores the value of the program counter at the point of call (so that the function return can execute correctly). Functions may have local data: the compiler lays out memory for such data. Statement #1 in each function in Example 3.7 illustrates the allocation of local data (the pointer db) as does the passed parameter n in Example 3.14. The **program counter** and local data are laid out in a **stack frame** associated with the function.

Example 3.7: Premature vs. Timely Return: C++

```cpp
//return may be executed before resource released => memory leak
void misManagedResources()
{    int*    db = new int[100];    //#1 resource (memory) allocated

     if (done())      return;      //#2 avoid work if not needed
                                   //resource not released => leak
     for (int j = 0; j < 100; j++) //j is loop index
            db[j] = process(j);
     someAction();
     delete[] db;                  //#3 resource (memory) released
     return;                       //#4
}


void returnWithoutLeak()
{    int*    db = new int[100];    //#1 resource (memory) allocated

     if (!done())                  //#2 avoid work if not needed
     { for (int j = 0; j < 100; j++)
            db[j] = process(j);
       someAction();
     }
     delete[] db;                  //#3 all paths release resource
     return;                       //#4
}
```

Functions, and code blocks, promote the notion of scope: the context or locality within which an identifier (variable name) is valid. C-like languages have block scope. Within a set of brackets, {}, identifiers may be declared and then used. In Example 3.7, the loop index j is in scope only within the for-loop; it cannot be accessed outside the for-loop. The integer pointer db is in function scope; it is considered a variable local to the function and thus cannot be accessed outside the function. A function may have multiple exit points, including interruptions to normal flow, such as an exception. We consider here nonstandard entry and exit points (as commonly denoted by break, continue, return, and goto statements within procedural languages).

A **break** statement may occur within the controlled (compound) state-ment of a switch or loop and behaves differently in each. In a C/C++ switch statement, by default control "falls through" from one case to the next one in lexical order. A break statement is typically used to exit the switch at the end of the case statement. Sequencing code in consecutive case labels without an intervening break statement is discouraged. Although possible to leverage this fall-through behavior, such usage is difficult to under-stand, and makes the code less robust. The accepted practice of using break statements allows case labels and statements to be moved around as a unit without changing the behavior of the switch statement as a whole. If break does not follow every case statement, then the correctness of this rewriting rule cannot be guaranteed.

Example 3.8 modifies the second switch statement from Example 3.4 to demonstrate fall-through. Clarity is lost. It is difficult to discern the value of the integer value at a glance. When command is "1", control will fall through all switch cases, yielding a value of 410 (100 + 1 + 10 + 100 + 200 –1). When command is "2", case 2 will be executed first, followed by all remaining cases, yielding a value of 409 (100 + 10 + 100 + 200 –1), etc.

Example 3.8: Conditional Evaluation: SWITCH

```
int value = 100;
switch(command)          //switch statement fall-through
{     case    1:         value++;
      case    2:         value += 10;
      case    10:        value += 100;
      case    20:        value += 200;
      default:           value--;
}
```

Within a loop, a break statement causes the loop to be exited immediately. Allocated resources must be released whether or not the break statement is executed. Termination via a break should be similar to exiting a function body via the return statement. Example 3.9 displays two loops (a for-loop with a break statement and a while-loop) that produce the same effect: ter-minate scan of num array upon encountering the first even number.

Example 3.9: Use of Break Statement in Loop

```
//counting loop with conditional break (exit from loop)
for (int j = 0; j < n; j++)
```

```
{     if (!(num[j]% 2))       break;   //exit loop on first even number
      process(num[j]);
}


//equivalent conditional loop
int  j = 0;
bool done = false;
while (!done && j < n)
{     done = num[j]% 2;                //exit loop on first even number
      if       (!done)
      {       process(num[j]);       j++;     }
}
```

A **continue** statement may be used only within the controlled statement of a loop statement. It causes the next iteration of the enclosing loop (for or while) to begin. That is, it causes an immediate transfer of control to the end of the loop. In a for-loop, the loop update statement is still executed. In a while (or do) loop, the control conditional is executed in the normal fashion, and the controlled statement is re-entered from the top if it evaluates to true (see Example 3.10). With an appropriate use of conditional evaluations, most loops with continue statements can be rewritten without them. Code readability is sustained when language constructs, such as counting and conditional loops, are used as intended.

Example 3.10: Use of Continue Statement

```
//continue in counting loop
for (int j = 0; j < n; j++)
{     if (!(num[j]% 2))    continue;        //skip even numbers
      process(num[j]);
}


//equivalent for-loop without continue;
for (int j = 0; j < n; j++)
      if (num[j]% 2)       process(num[j]); //process odd numbers


//continue in conditional loop
while (!done())
{     bool filtered = action1();
      if (filtered)         continue;        //skip if filtered

      action2();
      action3();
}


//equivalent conditional loop without continue
while (!done())
```

```
{    bool filtered = action1();
     if (!filtered)                          //process if not filtered
     {        action2();
              action3();
     }
}
```

The **goto** statement transfers control to the statement in the same function that follows the label matching the goto. Goto statements have been
vilified for decades because their use easily produces "spaghetti code."
With unstructured jumps (gotos), control flow is hard to follow: *jumps
interfere with a clear understanding of logical progression.* Spaghetti code
thus undermines software readability and maintainability. Software
design guidelines strongly discouraged use of the goto. Modern programming languages often do not provide the construct. Initially, the goto
statement was retained in C++ to support backward compatibility with C.

Structured programming is accepted practice and is supported by
modern programming languages. Careful use of nonstandard entry and
exit points as well as exceptions is warranted, especially if the meaning of
the code is muddied by their absence, but *no one needs a goto.* The stric-
ture against using goto is unequivocal. Java and C# both disallow the use
of goto by omitting it from the language. Their inclusion of the finally
statement simplifies the release of resources in case of exceptions or quick
returns. How? Any code in a finally clause is executed before leaving scope,
regardless of the means of exit.

Conceptually, a goto statement makes sense only if the target label is
not in a context in which additional initialization must be performed.
Thus, the goto jump to INNER_LABEL in Example 3.11 is not permitted;
how would the Boolean variable flag1, for example, be initialized? A
goto that jumps out of nested statement blocks (even looping and conditional code blocks) is permitted. Thus, the goto jump to OUTER_LABEL
in Example 3.11 is permitted; the local variables simply go out of scope.
If a goto causes a block with an associated finally clause to be exited, the
finally clause is executed, in a manner similar to the return statement.
Gotos are discouraged because their use compromises readability, and
thus, maintainability.

Example 3.11: Goto and Scope (C++)

```
//ILLEGAL goto: jumping into nested scope - variables not
//  initialized
```

```
goto INNER_LABEL;
...
{    //allocate block variables
     int     db[100];
     bool    flag1 = false;
INNER_LABEL:
     action1();
     ...
}

//permissible goto, although preferable to write structured
//  code
OUTER_LABEL:
x++;
{    //block variables come into scope
     int     db[100];
     bool    flag1 = false;


     ...
     goto OUTER_LABEL;      //exit scope
}
```

3.1.3 Readability

Control flow constructs affect the state of an executing program: one or more execution frames may be exited, and the objects allocated within those frames released. Expressions determine control flow, whether conditional or repetitive, and so should be easily understood. We have seen simple examples of Boolean expressions: control of while loops, Boolean functions, and parity checks.

When Boolean expressions are complex, it is often necessary to document meaning. If a conditional expression exceeds one or two lines of code, consider moving the expression into a predicate function. The name of the predicate can be chosen to suggest the condition(s) being tested. Modern compilers will inline predicate code as appropriate, so the run-time consequences of this rewriting are typically nil.

At any given point in the code, a software developer should be able to evaluate any variable. Well-designed software puts data in valid, initial states and allows only those data manipulations that preserve data integrity. Note language differences: C++ does not initialize variables of built-in types to a default value upon declaration; C# does. Hence, C++ programmers must take care to initialize variables upon declaration; if applicable, C# programmers can rely on default values (typically, zero). In general, initialization code should run before code block entry so that locally defined variables are in a known state upon entry.

TABLE 3.2   Cluttered versus Readable Control Flow

Cluttered Code	Equivalent Streamlined Statement
| ```
if (boolX)  return true;
else        return false;
``` | ```
return (boolX);
``` |
| ```
if (boolY){
    A;
    B;
}
else if (boolZ){
    A;
    C;
}
else A;
``` | ```
A;
if (boolY)        B;
else if (boolZ)   C;
}
``` |

With properly defined control flow, static analysis can verify that variables are in a known state during execution. Optimizations such as dead code removal or memory reuse can then be applied. One may also factor out duplicate code into a helper routine.

Even with appropriate use of control structures, readability may be compromised. Redundant evaluation and code repetition clutter code. Reworking conditional evaluations or the order in which they are applied can eliminate repeated clauses, as shown in Table 3.2. A clear understanding of Boolean logic supports a clear coding style. We next examine the tenets of Boolean logic.

3.2 BOOLEAN LOGIC

Boolean logic rests on two values, $\{0,1\}$. Commonly, 0 is equated with false (or test failure), and 1 with true (or test success). Boolean sentences may be rewritten according to many rules; techniques of simplification and logical equivalences permit transformations that retain the truth value of a Boolean expression. A clear understanding of Boolean expressions helps one to write and read code, especially relative to the design of control structures.

Boolean values are commonly manipulated with two binary operators: AND, commonly denoted by "∧" or "&&", and OR, denoted by "+" or "||". The AND operation is known as conjunction and represents the combination of two Boolean values such that the result is true if and only if both values are true. The OR operation is known as disjunction and represents the combination of two Boolean values such that the result is false if and only if both values are false.

The logical OR differs from common usage of "or" in the English language. The colloquial question "would you prefer vanilla or chocolate ice cream?" implies a choice between two alternatives and usually would be answered with "vanilla" or "chocolate." However, as a logical question, the answer would be true (affirmative) if one wanted either or both flavors and false if neither flavor would suffice.

The logical operation EXCLUSIVE-OR or XOR denotes an evaluation more consistent with the use of "or" in the English language: p XOR q is true if and only if exactly one of the Boolean values is true. Thus, one chooses exactly one flavor, chocolate or vanilla, of ice cream. A single Boolean value or variable may be negated; negation is denoted by "!". Table 3.3 is the classic truth table displaying the value of simple Boolean sentences.

Many useful identities can be used to rewrite Boolean expressions. The important axioms in Boolean Logic are reductions, identities, and distributions (see Table 3.4). A most useful theorem for simplifying logical expressions is DeMorgan's theorem:

$$!(P \mid\mid Q) = !P \&\& !Q$$
$$!(P \&\& Q) = !P \mid\mid !Q$$

Both forms noted above can be derived from the distribution axioms. See Table 3.5 for verification of the equivalences so noted.

Boolean logic may be overused or poorly designed in programming. Conditionals can be used to partition input values into cases to be handled separately. After an implementation is so written, cases containing the same action should be coalesced, not only to remove redundant

TABLE 3.3 Truth Table

P	Q	P && Q	P || Q	P XOR Q	!P
T	T	T	T	F	F
T	F	F	T	T	F
F	T	F	T	T	T
F	F	F	F	F	T

TABLE 3.4 Boolean Simplifications

Reductions	Identities	Distributions
P && 0 = 0	P && 1 = P	P || (Q && R) = (P || Q) && (P || R)
P || 1 = 1	P || 0 = P	P && (Q || R) = (P && Q) || (P && R)
!!P = P		

TABLE 3.5   DeMorgan's Law Verified

P	Q	!(P || Q)	!P && !Q	!(P && Q)	!P || !Q
T	T	F	F	F	F
T	F	F	F	T	T
F	T	F	F	T	T
F	F	T	T	T	T

action code but also to reduce the number of conditionals that must be evaluated (see Examples 3.12 and 3.13). DeMorgan's laws and the properties of Booleans can be used to simplify expressions. When in doubt, one can build and check a truth table to verify that a simplification is, in fact, equivalent to the original expression.

Example 3.12: Simplifying Boolean Expressions

```
//simplify expressions => more efficient and readable
if ((a || b) && (a || c) && (a || d))        actionA();

//equivalent expression (distributive law), check via truth table
if (a || (b && c && d))                      actionA();
```

Example 3.13: Decreasing the Number of Boolean Conditionals

```
//excessive evaluations: actionA executed in all cases
if (a)          actionA();
else if (a || b)                 //silly, only get here if
{     actionA();                 //a false b TRUE
      actionB();
}
else if (a || b || c)            //now both a and b false
{     actionA();                 //c TRUE
      actionB();
      actionC();
}

if (a || b || c)    actionA();   //equivalent to above
if (!a)
{     if (b || c)                actionB();
      if (!b && c)               actionC();
}
```

The complexity of a logical expression correlates to the number of inputs (variables) evaluated. From a software perspective, the number of variables evaluated is an expense, both conceptually and in terms of memory storage (and the corresponding required fetches to retrieve values from memory). *Conditionals are costly because they cause a break in the linear flow of the code.* Hence, for both clarity and efficiency, it is desirable to simplify logical tests.

Algebraic solutions are almost always faster than those based on Boolean logic. Suppose that Boolean false can be converted into the integer 0 and Boolean true is converted to integer 1. Consider

```
if (testTF)        b = 5;        //5 = 7 - 2
else               b = 7;        //7 = 7 - 0
```

as compared with b = 7 - 2 * testTF;. The latter is more compact and will run faster.

3.2.1 Short-Circuit Evaluation

Short-circuit evaluation provides efficient evaluation of compound Boolean expressions. If the first portion of a compound Boolean expression determines the value of the entire expression, why bother evaluating the remainder? For example, the conjunction a AND b is true if and only if both a and b are true. Thus, if a is false, the value of b does not matter; the conjunction will be false regardless. Likewise, the disjunction a OR b is false if and only if both a and b are false. Thus, if a is true, the value of b does not matter; the disjunction will be true regardless.

C-like languages use short-circuit evaluation. Ada provides both full evaluation and short-circuit evaluation by defining distinguishing terms "AND" and "AND THEN". Pascal does not provide short-circuit evaluation, with some interesting effects. Consider the following loop, a classic walk through a linked list:

```
while (ptr != null && ptr->data != searchItem)
        ptr = ptr->next;
```

If the pointer value is null (due to the list being empty or to the complete traversal of the list without finding the desired item), there is no valid data to examine. Hence, ptr->data should not be examined. Short-circuit evaluation prevents the dereferencing of the pointer variable ptr when it is null: the loop terminates because the null (zero) pointer forces the conjunction to be false. Short-circuit evaluation thus promotes safety since dereferencing a null pointer would trigger a runtime error.

If written in Pascal, the above code would yield a runtime error if searchItem is not found. Why? Without short-circuit evaluation, both portions of the conjunction are evaluated so ptr->data is processed even when ptr holds zero as an address, resulting in a runtime error. Without short-circuit evaluation, the classic linked list traversal would have to be written in a clunky manner:

```
boolean     search = true;
while (ptr != null)
      if (search)
            if (ptr->data != searchItem)
                  ptr = ptr->next;
            else  search = false;
```

When a condition is costly to evaluate, conditionals can be structured to avoid repeated evaluation, or stored in a Boolean variable. Also, Boolean expressions often can be reduced and simplified. Recalling the actions of short-circuit evaluation may help one simplify correctly. Consider a compound Boolean expression used in an if/else construct. The else clause may be reached if the first term evaluates to false for conjunction, or true for disjunction. Table 3.6 illustrates both correct and incorrect simplifications that avoid the repeated evaluation of predicate P.

Care must be practiced when simplifying expressions. Without verification, one can alter intended control flow by erroneously simplifying Boolean expressions, as is also illustrated in Table 3.6. It is worth noting that negations are often counterintuitive and thus difficult to interpret consistently.

TABLE 3.6 Simplifying Boolean Expressions

Inefficient Compound		Incorrect Simplification	
//actionB() when (!P && Q)		//actionB() when Q	
if (!P && !Q)	actionA();	if (!P && !Q)	actionA();
else if (!P)	actionB();	else if (Q)	actionB();
Correct Simplification		**Correct Simplification**	
if (!P){		if (!P){	
if (!Q)	actionA();	if (Q)	actionB();
else	actionB();	else	actionA();
}		}	

3.3 RECURSION

Repetition may be implemented through recursion, an *elegant but over-used construct*. Recursion is the definition of a function, or structure, in terms of itself. Hallmarks of well-designed recursion require the clear specification of terminating or base cases and well-defined means to reach such terminating conditions.

Elementary examples of recursion include the calculation of mathematical terms that are themselves defined recursively. Classic examples are calculating the Fibonacci numbers as well as factorial values. See Example 3.14 for simple code solutions to these two problems that correspond directly to their mathematical definitions. Both examples demonstrate clearly defined recursion as well as reachable base cases.

Example 3.14: Recursive Fibonacci and Factorial

```
//Fibonacci          F_n = F_{n-1} + F_{n-2}; F_2 = 1; F_1 = 1
int   recurseFib(int n)
{     if (n < 3)       return 1;
      return recurseFib(n-1) + recurseFib(n-2);
}

//Factorial          F_n = F_n * (F_{n-1})!; F_1 = 1; F_2 = 2
int   recurseFactorial(int n)
{     if (n < 3)       return n;
      return n * recurseFactorial(n-1);
}
```

Why complain about these recursive functions? After all, many introductory CS textbooks use them. Recursion requires more overhead than iteration. Each recursive call requires the layout and initialization of memory for a distinct function call (see Chapter 4). A good compiler can convert a tail-recursive function, such as the Factorial example, into a loop. A tail-recursive function is a function that has one recursive call and that call is the last statement in the function.

The Fibonacci recursive function is not tail-recursive because it has two recursive calls. This recursive function is grossly inefficient, computing many of the same values over and over again. As shown in Table 3.7, calculation of F_8 recursively requires, in total: one call for F_7; two calls for F_6; three calls for F_5; five calls for F_4; eight calls for F_3; thirteen calls for F_2; and ten calls for F_1. The iterative solution, shown in Example 3.15,

TABLE 3.7 Layout of Recursive Calls Needed to Compute F_8

Recursive Calls, Enumerated by Level: Initial Call Is to F_8						
Level1	Level2	Level3	Level4	Level5	Level6	Level7
F_8	F_7	F_6	F_5	F_4	F_3	F_2
						F_1
					F_2	
				F_3	F_2	
					F_1	
			F_4	F_3	F_2	
					F_1	
				F_2		
		F_5	F_4	F_3	F_2	
					F_1	
				F_2		
			F_3	F_2		
				F_1		
	F_6	F_5	F_4	F_3	F_2	
					F_1	
				F_2		
			F_3	F_2		
				F_1		
		F_4	F_3	F_2		
				F_1		
			F_2			

uses a loop construct instead and does not perform redundant calculations. Recursive solutions may be grossly efficient if they calculate many redundant values.

Example 3.15: Iterative Fibonacci and Factorial

```
//Fibonacci          F_n = F_{n-1} + F_{n-2}; F_2 = 1; F_1 = 1
int  iterativeFib(int n)
{    if (n < 3)       return 1;
     int f1 = 1;
     int f2 = 1;
     int sum;
     while (n > 2)
     {       sum = f1 + f2;
             f1 = f2;
             f2 = sum;
             n--;
     }
```

```
        return sum;
}

//Factorial           Fₙ = Fₙ * (Fₙ₋₁)!; F₁ = 1; F₂ = 2
int  iterativeFactorial(int n)
{     int sum = n;
      while (n > 1)
      {      n--;
             sum = sum * n;
      }
      return sum;
}
```

Valid applications exist for recursion, as evident in standard CS data structures courses and textbooks. Tree structures are recursive in nature and thus recursive functions for tree traversals are a natural fit. Although local stack variables allow one to mimic recursion, and thus write iterative tree traversals, these solutions are often dense and hard to read. The corresponding recursive form is typically easier to understand.

Example 3.16 contrasts an iterative version of an in-order traversal of a binary search tree (BST) with its intuitive recursive form. With a little effort, one can see the correspondence: each recursive call to the left child of an interior BST node is mimicked by pushing the parent node address on the stack; when the leftward progression of a (sub)tree terminates, the parent node is popped off the stack, examined, and the traversal moves right. Not all recursive algorithms can be mimicked by readable iterative versions. Despite the simplicity of a recursive post-order traversal, its iterative counterpart is difficult to understand (possibly because two local stacks must be used). For more details, consult a good data structures text. Nonetheless, software developers should understand how local stacks can hold values normally embedded in recursive function calls.

Example 3.16: Iterative versus Recursive InOrder Tree Traversal

```
//recursive version of an inorder BST traversal
void inorder(BST* root)
{                                  //base condition:
     if (!root)       return;     //empty (sub)tree, terminate

     inorder(root->left);
     process(root->data);
     inorder(root->right);
}
```

```
//iterative inorder BST traversal
//local stack variable used to mimic recursion
void inorder_iter(BST* root)
{      stack<BST*>    s;       //holds local data
       BST*           current = root;
       bool           done = false;

       while (!done)
       {       if (current)
               {   s.push(current);
                   current = current->left;
               }
               else
               {   if (s.empty())       done = true;
                   else
                   {    current = s.top();
                        s.pop();
                        process(current);
                        current = current->right;
                   }
               }
       }
}
```

At a system-level perspective, it should not matter whether recursion or iteration is used. Control flow though matters at design, implementation, and testing levels. If code readability is a priority and an algorithm is more clearly defined recursively (as is a postorder tree traversal), then recursion would be preferred. If performance criteria demand efficiency, then iteration may be preferred. When using recursion, one must ensure that the recursion is well-defined with clearly defined and reachable terminating conditions.

3.4 SEQUENTIAL EXECUTION

A computer program consists of instructions and data, both of which are stored in memory and retrieved when needed. The computer bus transfers information (memory content that is data or instructions) in blocks, where block size usually exceeds the size of a data item or single instruction. Thus, there is an inherent reduction in overhead when accessing sequential instructions or contiguous data: the address of the next instruction (or data item) may have already been transferred with the previous instruction (or data item). Since the address of the next instruction (or data item) can be inferred from the current one, code space is saved. Moreover, sequential execution is favored because linear paths are easier to read and comprehend.

Pipelined staging of CPU computations favors sequential execution. Instruction execution can be decomposed into fetch, decode, and execute stages. Additional stages include memory references and writing back values to registers. Low-level parallelism is achieved by overlapping these stages in the instruction pipeline. Consider the instruction-level parallelism of five stages of an instruction: instruction fetch #1 (F), instruction decode #2 (D), execute #3 (E), memory reference #4 (M), and register write back #5 (W). Each instruction advances one stage at the end of each clock cycle. Table 3.8 illustrates this staged parallelism. The instruction pipeline stalls when data is not readily available, possibly due to the differing speeds of accessing memory in a cache, main memory, or secondary store. The instruction pipeline is flushed when sequential execution is interrupted, causing an immediate loss of efficiency.

The benefit of low-level parallelism is lost when the instruction pipeline is flushed or stalled. To avoid interrupted sequential execution, software design may strive to achieve **temporal locality** and/or **spatial locality**. Temporal locality suggests that items recently referenced will likely be referenced again. If a word is to be read (or written) n times in a short interval, one slow access retrieves it from (main) memory and the remaining n-1 accesses are fast cache accesses. Spatial locality suggests that items referenced are likely to be located near other referenced items. Since memory accesses are processed in blocks, neighboring words may be brought into the cache together. Temporal and spatial locality both depend on the cache to enhance performance by avoiding slow memory fetches. Matrix multiplication is a classic example of data access satisfying both these principles.

TABLE 3.8   Pipelined Instructions

Instr#	Pipeline Stage								
1	F	D	E	M	W				
2		F	D	E	M	W			
3			F	D	E	M	W		
4				F	D	E	M	W	
5					F	D	E	M	W
6						F	D	E	M
clock	1	2	3	4	5	6	7	8	9

3.4.1 Optimization

Optimization covers hardware and software changes that yield faster running code and/or code that uses less space. Significant advances in computing are due to hardware optimizations. Fast processing is supported by special registers, multiple levels of on-chip caches, and continued breakthroughs in supercomputing. Software optimizations include the customization of algorithms and data structures, data compression, software design, memory management, and automatic code refinement via compilation.

Most software is developed without much attention paid to hardware. As noted in Chapter 2, this attitude is not the by-product of advances in software development but its intent. Design that is independent of hardware is reusable and portable. *Software design thus rests on high levels of abstraction as well as an idealized view of a computing system.* As summarized in Table 3.9, unchecked assumptions include infinite memory, uniform (and relatively cheap) access to memory, and a dedicated CPU. Nonetheless, memory is costly and some optimizations strive to reduce memory access.

Since the computer bus transfers information (memory content that is data or instructions) in blocks, there is an inherent reduction in overhead when accessing sequential instructions or contiguous data. We covered the various ways in which sequential execution was altered by branching in the first portion of this chapter. In Chapters 5 to 8, we discuss software design. We look at memory management in Chapter 4. Here, we note some compiler optimizations.

When the compiler resolves a type or a function call, it is called "static" because that resolution does not change at runtime. Static resolution of function calls (static binding) and type determination (static typing) yield more efficient code because no runtime evaluation must be made. Runtime overhead is reduced whenever a runtime evaluation can be resolved instead by the compiler. Compiler work is considered to

TABLE 3.9   Computing System Views

Ideal	Reality	Masking Construct	Cost
Infinite memory	Memory bounded	Virtual memory	Paging
Uniform memory access	Memory Hierarchy	HLL code access not differentiated	Secondary store slower and more expensive
Dedicated CPU	Time-sliced	Parallel threads	Context switch

TABLE 3.10   Design Techniques for Efficiency

Expensive Construct	Cost	Response
I/O	Memory access	Minimize
Function call	Call and return overhead	Inline function call
	Loss of spatial locality	Statically resolve function calls
Copying data	Time and space overhead	Aliases and Pass by Reference
Temporary data	Allocation/deallocation overhead	Avoid generation of temporaries
	Fragmented heap	

be mostly "free." This efficiency, however, produces less flexible code. If a function call is resolved at compile-time, function selection cannot be modified at runtime. Chapter 7 provides extensive coverage of dynamic function invocation.

Software optimizations refine or restructure existing code to run more efficiently or use less space. Most application-specific optimizations are developed after working code has been evaluated: it is futile to optimize code that does not run effectively or reliably. Moreover, as noted by renowned computer scientist, Donald Knuth, "premature optimization is the root of all evil." Table 3.10 notes general software design principles for efficiency: minimizing I/O, judiciously inlining functions, avoiding the copying of data, and using constants where appropriate.

Typical optimizations either reduce computation or memory accesses. Computing values at compile-time or reusing values to avoid recomputation reduces processing at runtime. Simple coding practices can support such optimizations. Consider the use of constants. With a constant, the compiler makes a textual substitution of the actual value for the identifier, thus removing the need for a memory fetch at runtime. Constants also permit the compiler to replace a runtime computation with an actual value. Consider Example 3.17. If the constant value pi were stored in a real variable rather than as a constant, both a runtime memory fetch of pi's value and a runtime computation of (4.0 * pi) would be required.

Example 3.17: Code Optimization by Design: Use Constants

```
const      double  pi = 3.14159;
double     r;
...
double     area = 4.0 * pi * r * r;
//compiler: area = 12.56636 * r * r;
```

Many optimizations strive to reduce space used, whether for data or code. The elimination of local temporaries, loop invariant code, useless variables, dead code, and/or useless code all reduce the footprint of a program and thus decrease space requirements. Compiler response may differ by language. The useless statement "x;", where x is, say, a simple integer, is discarded as useless code without a response by the compiler in C-like languages. In Ada, a compiler error is generated.

Optimization may be achieved through careful software design. To avoid repetitive data accesses or CPU-intensive calculations, **caching** stores the result of frequent or costly computations. To remove an expensive computation from a time-critical or frequently traversed control path, values may be precomputed and stored. Deferring object instantiation may be beneficial if an object ends up not being used. Such optimizations rest on the Pareto principle that 20% of software's code is executed 80% of the time and determining, with a **profiler**, what code that is.

Data alignment is a rather specific optimization geared toward maximizing use of the cache. Table 3.11 lists some design recommendations for data declarations and use. Data compression is a huge field, primarily because of the need for efficiently transmitting data across networks. Note that data compression is not necessarily an effective optimization, especially if cost of data compression and decompression exceed the temporary benefit of reducing space requirements.

Optimizations may be misapplied. Good software design strives to minimize I/O, use constants where appropriate, avoid unneeded copying, and, thus, will yield more efficient code. **Inlining** is another optimization that can be effective. Often it is left to the compiler to do so. We examine function inlining next.

3.4.2 Inlining

Functional decomposition supports intentional software design through code reuse, isolation of functionality, and improved readability. When

TABLE 3.11　Data Alignment

Data Declarations in Scope	Why?
Large items first	Large blocks reduce fragmentation
Arrays before scalars	Large blocks reduce fragmentation
Data accessed together	Achieve locality of reference
Data referenced together	Achieve locality of reference
Static variables preferred	Avoid runtime overhead

designed well, functions improve software maintainability, an increasingly important software endeavor. However, function calls are not free. Just like any branch statement, a function call breaks sequential processing—twice, in fact: a jump to the function and then a return. Moreover, function calls require the preparation and storage of activation records (also known as stack frames).

Function inlining is an optimization technique that replaces the function invocation with the body (code) of the function itself. Although it may appear to be as simple as copying the block of the inlined method at the point of call, inlining must also allocate local variables and translate (multiple) return statements into jumps to the end of the inlined block of code. Small functions are less likely to have many local variables or multiple returns and thus are easier to inline.

Function inlining trades code size for performance. Inlining can yield **code bloat** and thereby reduce rather than increase the speed of an executing program due to expanded memory requirements. Compilers often inline only small functions. Why? With small functions, the overhead of the function call most likely exceeds the execution cost of the function. Thus, a performance improvement is more likely when inlining a small function. Call, return, and stack frame setup are all avoided with inlining. Example 3.18 shows a sample inlining: function parameters are evaluated only once when copied into temporary (compiler tracked) memory.

Example 3.18: Inlining (C++)

```
int min(int x, int y)
{    if (x < y)      return x;
     return y;
}


....
int   smallValue;
...
smallValue = min(db[i], db[j]);


//when inlined, function call replaced by
int   temp1 = db[i];
int   temp2 = db[j];

if (temp1 < temp2)  smallValue = temp1;
else                smallValue = temp2;
```

TABLE 3.12   Common Side Effects of Function Calls

Data Modification	Control Flow	External
Global or static variable	Raising exception	File IO
Parameter passed by reference	Calling another function	State change (embedded)
Allocating heap memory	Event notification	Signal

The keyword "inline" is only a suggestion to the compiler. Caution should be observed when contemplating "manual" inlining. Writing code in place of a function call alters the software structure. This customization may be harder to maintain. If a manually inlined function is subsequently modified, then the process of updating the software is akin to a search and replace endeavor—an error-prone and tedious process. Every code location where the function call was replaced with manually inlined code must be updated. In general, manual inlining reduces software readability and maintainability.

Side effects often make it more difficult to inline functions. A function or expression produces a side effect when it modifies state or some data value(s) other than the value returned from the function call. Table 3.12 delineates common side effects in terms of data modification, control flow, and external access.

Optimization is not intended to modify the functionality of software, but it may alter the means by which solutions are generated or stored. Software developers must first construct functional and usable software. *Compilers will optimize code only if it is safe to do so.* Compiler optimization directives are treated as mere suggestions. Compilers must guarantee that a code transformation does not alter functionality. It is much easier to verify that a transformation preserves correctness if it is confined to a single code block. Data dependencies tend to span more than one code block. Consequently, optimizations may be more extensive if function inlining draws data dependencies into one block.

3.5 SUMMARY

In this chapter, we examined control flow and its effect on software design and efficiency. We contrasted different control constructs, as well as recursion and iteration, and discussed Boolean logic. Tracing execution paths is often not easy, even with the assistance of debugging tools and profilers. Clear control flow, alongside functional decomposition and self-documenting code, should make that task easier. For efficient software maintenance and effective placement of error processing, software developers should understand the logic that controls the execution path of running software. By examining the impact of software design on readability and execution control, one determines the costs and benefits of structure and possibilities for optimization.

DESIGN INSIGHTS

SOFTWARE

Compilers will optimize code only if it is safe to do so
There is no point in optimizing code unless it is correct

MODELS

Software development rests on abstraction
Idealized view of computer
    Infinite memory
    Uniform cost
Control flow
    Sequential, conditional, repetitive
    Conditional and iterative loop constructs
Recursion
    Elegant but often overused
    Expresses intuitive decomposition
    Often inefficient, especially when computing redundant values
    Can be simulated with local stack variables

SOFTWARE DESIGN

For maintainability, construct readable software
Design clearly using appropriate control structures
    Gotos disrupt structured control flow
      Do NOT use
    Use while loops for conditional repetition
    Use for loops for iterative repetition
    Simplify Boolean expressions
Optimize by design
    Minimize I/O
    Avoid copying data
    Use constants
    Promote inlining

Declare data efficiently
    Large and contiguous items first
Functional decomposition
  Affords code reuse
  Isolates functionality
    Enhances readability
    Promotes software maintainability

DOCUMENTATION
Code should be as self-documenting as possible

CONCEPTUAL QUESTIONS

1. When are conditional statements hard to read?

2. When are repetitive loops hard to read?

3. Why is use of the GOTO discouraged? What constructs replace the GOTO?

4. What advantage(s) does design with only single entry and single exit points provide?

5. How can the validity of a simplified Boolean expression be verified?

6. What drawbacks are associated with recursion?

7. When would recursion be preferred to iteration?

8. What does function inlining do? What is its effect?

9. When is a function call too costly? Why?

10. List some common best practices for design and data declarations.

CHAPTER 4

Memory

M EMORY USAGE DIRECTLY IMPACTS software correctness and performance. In this chapter, we consider memory management within a program. We begin with an overview of memory used for running programs, differentiating between program stack and heap memory. We examine the task of copying data, when that data is stored in heap memory, noting differences inherent in programming languages. We briefly discuss memory allocation and deallocation schemes, including explicit deallocation, garbage collection, and reference counting.

Most importantly, we identify memory management details that impact software design. Although memory manipulation remains abstract, a competent software developer should understand the underlying mechanism for managing memory as a resource. Reinforcing details and examples are provided in Appendices A and B. Those who are unfamiliar with both C and C++ should consult Appendix A before reading this chapter.

CHAPTER OBJECTIVES

- Outline memory organization
- Discuss program memory usage
- Identify programming language differences with respect to memory
- Illustrate allocation process
- Contrast deallocation processes
- Summarize garbage collection
- Evaluate design choices: storage versus computation

4.1 ABSTRACTION OF MEMORY

Logically, memory is a physical resource that is 'owned' when it is allocated to a process. Memory is available for use or assignment when it is not so allocated. Competition exists for memory, even within one single program. For example, independent of core functionality, the user interface requires memory as do backup utilities and databases. Operating system utilities are needed to manage the assignment (allocation) and release (deallocation) of memory while preserving data integrity. At a given time, only one process can use (own) a given memory block. This basic model is simple: behavior is much more 'interesting' when memory is shared. The sharing of memory should be explicit and tracked.

The operating system manages computer memory when software executes. Control of memory allocation and deallocation processes typically resides within the runtime environment (OS and runtime library). Entire books have been devoted to operating systems and resource management. Here, we provide only a brief overview of how memory is allocated and used by a running program. For more information, please consult a standard operating system text.

There are many different physical types of memory (registers, cache, secondary store, etc.). Each type has different costs and performance characteristics. For example, main memory is memory directly accessible by the CPU. Co-located with the processing core, the cache is a smaller, faster memory store that holds data from main memory to reduce access time. Nonetheless, *as far as an executing program is concerned, all memory is simply a means of storage*. Adhering to the tenets of abstraction, we view memory as a uniform resource and leave the technical details of hardware to the operating system. At a superficial level, we can consider memory to be an unlimited resource, again leaving the technical details of mapping a memory address to an actual memory location to the operating system. This abstract view supports the design and implementation of portable code.

The operating system treats memory as blocks of contiguous memory cells. How a running program uses this memory does not concern the allocator. Each memory request will be filled or rejected based solely on whether memory is available or not. Likewise, a running program (process) does not care how the allocator finds free blocks or maintains bookkeeping details for managing memory. Processes make only the fundamental assumption that each memory block is uniquely allocated; that is, if a request for memory is satisfied, the requestor assumes sole ownership.

Conceptually then, we view memory as a uniform resource whose management is remote. Defined as imaginary or alternate memory addresses that simulate real, physical memory, virtual memory embodies this abstract view of memory. Virtual memory is the perception of memory as a set of uniform, addressed locations without artificial size or boundary limitations. Virtual memory abstracts away consideration of the actual address ranges occupied by physical memory. Hardware support and operating system utilities are thus needed to map a virtual address to an actual, physical address. Processors have memory management units to provide this support for virtual memory. Although some virtual memory blocks can be locked, most virtual memory space may be mapped to any available block of physical memory.

The operating system manages blocks of memory of uniform size, called pages. By overlaying, that is, replacing one page of memory with another, the operating system may manipulate programs (and their associated data) that are larger than the main memory of a computer. Thus, the size of allocated virtual memory may exceed that of physical memory.

A process can only access two or three memory locations at a time, so virtual memory pages resident in physical memory sit idle most of the time. If referenced data is not loaded into actual memory, a page fault occurs and the needed page is then swapped with a resident page. When needed, data can be written out to secondary storage (usually a hard drive). Since secondary memory is much slower than main memory (RAM), there is a significant cost involved in swapping out one virtual memory page so that another can take its place. Caching uses a similar mechanism to share the limited physical high-end cache memory.

System performance can degrade dramatically if too many memory references cause page faults. When memory references are confined to a certain locality, a set of relatively contiguous blocks of memory, a minimal number of virtual memory pages need to access physical memory. This principle of 'locality of reference' can be used to enhance the performance of an algorithm, database, or application.

4.2 HEAP MEMORY

In architectures traditionally called 'Von Neumann'—typical of modern desktop systems—code and data share the same memory space. The executable image for the process and any modules loaded dynamically by that process must be assigned blocks within the process' memory pool, thus reducing the amount of virtual memory available for storing data objects. When the executable image of a program is loaded into memory, its layout can be viewed as a partition between the code section and the data section. The code section contains the software instructions while the data section is memory reserved for data used and generated by the running software.

Two portions of memory comprise the data section of a running program: the heap and the runtime stack. The **heap** consists of blocks of memory allocated for program use when explicitly requested by a process as the program runs. Memory so allocated is called 'dynamic' because its address is not known or allocated until runtime. The **runtime stack** holds the activation records (**stack frames**) that record essential information, such as the program counter and local variables, for function calls. Since the size of a stack frame is known at compile-time, it is laid out statically.

The primary (heap) and stack allocators share the same initial pool of memory; each allocator starts at opposite ends of this chunk of memory and as each allocates memory, they 'grow' toward each other. In a typical implementation, the allocation limit for the primary allocator starts at low memory addresses and grows upward, while the allocation limit for the stack starts at a high address and grows downward (see Figure 4.1). Obviously, these two limits must not cross.

Processes request memory blocks of a specified size. In C, using the malloc or calloc calls, the caller passes in the size of data requested,

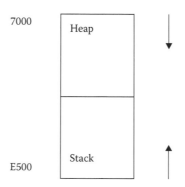

FIGURE 4.1   Program heap-and-stack memory.

usually using the sizeof operator. In C++, C#, and Java, the new operator is invoked with a typed pointer or reference: the size of memory requested can be inferred from the type. Example 4.1 gives sample C++ allocations; Figure 4.2 illustrates the corresponding memory diagrams. The allocator processes memory requests: it does not track address values held in pointer (or reference) variables. Consequently, the application programmer MUST be responsible for nulling out pointers (or references) when ownership of heap memory has been released!

Example 4.1: C++ Allocation of (Heap) Memory at Runtime

```
// C++ allocation of heap memory
//    "ptr" is a pointer variable allocated on the stack
//    "ptr" holds the address of the heap object return by new

MyType*      ptr = new MyType;        //#A: MyType object allocated

// deallocate heap memory via call to delete operator
delete ptr;                 //#B: MyType object deallocated

// null out pointer to indicate it 'points to nothing'
ptr = 0;                    //#C: programmer must reset pointer

// pointers can also hold the address of an array
ptr = new MyType[10];       //#D: 10 MyType objects allocated
...
// must use delete[] when deallocating an array on heap
delete[]     ptr;           //#E: 10 MyType objects deallocated
```

The type of a pointer is an implicit size parameter, an int requires 4 bytes of memory, a char requires 2, etc. In response to a call, the allocator finds and returns the starting address of a memory block large enough to hold the requested amount of memory. This block is guaranteed to be distinct from memory actively allocated to any other execution context (thread, stack frame, etc.). Later, when this memory is released, the block is returned to the pool and is available once again to be allocated.

For all satisfied memory requests, the allocator returns the base address of the block just allocated. The caller knows the size of the block it requested, so there is no need for the allocator to return this information. The allocator maintains information about memory available for allocation in a 'free' list. Likewise, the addresses of allocated blocks are stored in an 'allocated' list. The allocator records the size of each block allocated, so that the correct amount of memory can be returned to the pool of available memory when blocks are deallocated.

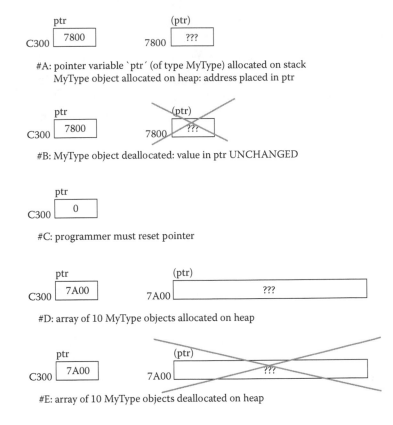

FIGURE 4.2 Heap allocation at runtime.

Memory requests may fail and obviously will do so when the amount of memory requested exceeds that available. When the amount of memory requested is available but is not contiguously located, that is, when there is no one block big enough to satisfy the request, a memory request will also fail. This state of memory is called **fragmented** memory. Consider a request to allocate an array of 500 reals (double variable type). If a double is of size 8 bytes, 4000 bytes are needed. If 30,000 bytes are available but all blocks are of size 3200 or smaller, the memory request will fail. To indicate an unsatisfied memory request, the allocator may throw an OutOfMemory exception.

To release memory in C++, one passes the address of the memory to be returned by calling the delete operator with a pointer variable. Normally, there is no response to the explicit release of a memory block. However, if an invalid pointer is supplied as the base address of the block, the allocator may throw an exception. Java and C# do not use explicit deallocation.

4.2.1 C++ Deallocation

In C and C++, deallocation of heap memory is explicit: the programmer must call free in C or delete (or delete[] for arrays) in C++. The freed memory block is then taken off the allocated list and returned to the free list. Failure to release memory yields a memory leak. Why? Once a handle (pointer) goes out of scope, the memory so referenced is no longer accessible: the memory remains allocated on the heap even though it can no longer be accessed (and thus used). The allocator does not know that this memory block is inaccessible. To the allocator, the block is still in use because no explicit request for release was received.

A common mantra for C++ programmers is 'match every new with a delete.' If only design could be so simple! Due to aliasing and transfer of ownership, matching each new with a delete is not a trivial endeavor.

Example 4.2 presents three functions. The first function leaks memory because there is no call to the delete operator before the pointer holding the address of the heap memory goes out of scope. The second function does not leak memory because there is a call to the delete operator before the pointer goes out of scope. The third function does not leak memory because it passes out ownership of the heap memory. Heap memory must be deallocated, via the delete operator, or transferred to another owner, before the pointer or reference to that heap memory goes out of scope. Otherwise, access to that heap memory is lost and cannot be reclaimed.

Example 4.2: C++ Primitives: Allocation/Deallocation Clear

```
// function code: primitives used, no class objects
// application programmer ERROR: NEW not matched with DELETE
void leakMemory()
{    int*    heapData;
     heapData = new int[100];
     ...
     return;
}    // memory leak obvious: no explicit deallocation

// function code ok: NEW matched with DELETE
void noMemoryLeak()
{    int*    heapData;
     heapData = new int[100];
     ...
     // heap memory explicitly deallocated: delete matches new
     delete[] heapData;
     return;
}
```

```
// function code ok: access to heap memory passed back to callee
//CALLEE MUST ASSUME RESPONSIBILITY (ownership) FOR HEAP MEMORY
int* passMemory()
{    int*    heapData;
     heapData = new int[100];
     ...
     return heapData;
}
```

Explicit deallocation, as demanded by C and C++, requires that a programmer retain responsibility for both allocation and deallocation of heap memory. Correct memory management rapidly becomes complex: **aliases**, transfer of ownership, call by reference, and shared use all complicate the task of tracking ownership. *It is a challenge to reliably ensure appropriate deallocation of memory.* See Dingle (2006).

In the 1970s, C programming dominated software development. The need to manage memory was overt and (often reluctantly) addressed. When C++ became popular in the 1990s, the object-oriented paradigm came into vogue. *Objects encapsulated dynamic memory allocation and obscured the need for directly managing memory.* If class designers failed to manage memory correctly, memory leaks occurred even when application programmers 'followed the rules.' We illustrate such insufficient C++ class designs in a few examples. Please see Appendix B for more detail.

Example 4.3 displays function definitions that contain object allocation(s) that should not result in memory leaks. (To review parameter passing, please see Appendix A.) How do these functions leak memory? The leakMemory function in Example 4.2 failed to either deallocate (via a call to the delete[] operator) or to transfer ownership. These deficiencies are not evident in Example 4.3. Each function in Example 4.3 looks correctly written, and seems to follow standard design guidelines. The first function invokes the delete operator to match the call to new. The second function only allocates a local object via pass by value. The third function simply assigns one object to another. If the fault is not in the application code, examination of the hiddenLeak class definition is warranted.

Example 4.3: C++: Why Memory Leaks?

```
// function code looks correct
void whyLeakMemory1()
{    hiddenLeak*    naive;
     naive = new hiddenLeak[100];
     ...
```

```
        delete[] naive; //delete[] matches new[]
}

void whyLeakMemory2(hiddenLeak localVar)
{    ...    }

void whyLeakMemory3()
{    hiddenLeak        steal;
     hiddenLeak        share;
     ...
     steal = share;
     return;
}
```

The first function, whyLeakMemory1(), in Example 4.3 looks like the second function, noMemoryLeak(), defined in Example 4.2. The call to the new[] operator is matched with a call to the delete[] operator. The application programmer has followed the memory management mantra: every new is matched with a delete. How does memory leak then? What is missing?

The second function, whyLeakMemory2(), in Example 4.3, also looks innocuous. The only code evident is the definition of the formal parameter, which is passed by value. If there is a memory leak then, it must be associated with the copy constructor. The third function, whyLeakMemory3(), in Example 4.3, merely assigns one locally allocated (stack) object to another. Again, no action appears to be missing. If there is a memory leak then, it must be associated with the assignment operator.

Example 4.3 differs from Example 4.2 in that it uses objects not the built-in integer type for its data variables. If a leak occurs, it is due to the internal design of the hiddenLeak class. A class without any internally allocated heap memory will not yield memory leaks. However, a class that internally allocates heap memory will yield memory leaks unless it is carefully designed. Such errors may be deadly. Application programmers will be unable to easily detect the source, or to correct it.

Analysis of the Example 4.3 leaks indicate that the class design for hiddenLeak does not have proper deallocation, support for call by value or for assignment. In other words, the hiddenLeak class is missing a **destructor**, a **copy constructor**, and an overloaded assignment operator. Example 4.4 shows the inferred inadequate design of class hiddenLeak. In Example 4.5, we revise this class design by defining the missing functions. We describe them briefly below. For more details, please see Appendix B.

Example 4.4: C++ Class without Proper Memory Management

```cpp
// IMPROPERLY DESIGNED: heap memory allocated in constructor
//    MISSING: destructor, copy constructor, overloaded =
class hiddenLeak{
    private:
            int*    heapData;
            int     size;
    public:
            hiddenLeak(unsigned s = 100)
            { size = s;     heapData = new int[size]; }
            ...
};
```

Example 4.5: C++ Class with Proper Memory Management

```cpp
// class definition,.h file, memory managed properly
class noLeak{
private:
    int*    heapData;
    int     size;
public:
    noLeak(unsigned s = 100)
    { size = s;     heapData = new int[size]; }
    // copy constructor supports call by value
    noLeak(const noLeak&);
    // overloaded = supports deep copying
    void operator=(const noLeak&);
    // destructor deallocates heapData
    ~noLeak() {delete[] heapData;}
    ...
};

// .cpp, implementation file
// copy constructor
noLeak::noLeak(const noLeak& source)
{    size = source.size;
     heapData = new int[size];
     for (int j = 0; j < size; j++)
            heapData[j] = source.heapData[j];
}

// overloaded = supports deep copying
void noLeak::operator=(const noLeak& rhs)
{    if (this != &rhs)       //avoid self-assignment
    {        delete[] heapData;     //dellocate 'old' memory
             size = rhs.size;
             heapData = new int[size];
             for (int j=0; j < size; j++)
                    heapData[j] = rhs.heapData[j];
    }
    return;
}
```

C++ classes must define a destructor when any class method (usually the constructor) allocates heap memory that is retained by an object. The destructor is a special function that has no return type (not even void) and bears the same name as the class, preceded by '~'. The compiler implicitly invokes the destructor when objects go out of scope or when the delete operator is called. Thus, the class destructor is poised to deallocate any heap memory before its handle (an object data member) goes out of scope. A destructor is appropriately defined in Example 4.5.

Classes must also define a copy constructor when objects allocate heap memory. Why? The compiler automatically provides a default copy constructor that simply copies each field value directly. After copying, two objects will contain exactly the same data values. Pointer values (addresses) are treated no differently than other data members. This standard (bitwise) copy yields a **shallow** (aliased) copy, whenever an object contains a pointer data field that holds the address of heap memory. After copying data fields from one object to another, the two different objects will have the same value in their pointer fields and thus will point to the same memory.

Consider the three diagrams of variables a and b in Figure 4.3. One can view these diagrams as representations of pass by value: a is the formal parameter and b is the actual argument passed in at the point of call. If the class designer does not define a copy constructor, the compiler provides the default bitwise copy constructor. With shallow copying, the formal parameter a now accesses the heap memory allocated to the actual parameter b, as seen in the first diagram, violating the security of pass by value. Moreover, when the function terminates, a goes out of scope. If a destructor is defined, as it should be, the destructor deallocates the heap memory that a 'points to.' But this memory is the heap memory 'owned' by b! Moreover, b does not know that its heap memory has been released and can thus be reassigned to another 'owner.' Data corruption is now possible, if b, under the impression of continued ownership, alters 'its' heap memory. The desired **deep** (true) copy, as displayed by the third diagram in Figure 4.3, results when the class designer defines the copy constructor appropriately.

The copy constructor is a special function that has no return type (not even void), bears the same name as the class, and takes one passed parameter that is an object of the same type. An appropriate copy constructor is defined in Example 4.5. This copy constructor copies all nonpointer fields directly. For the newly constructed object, additional heap memory

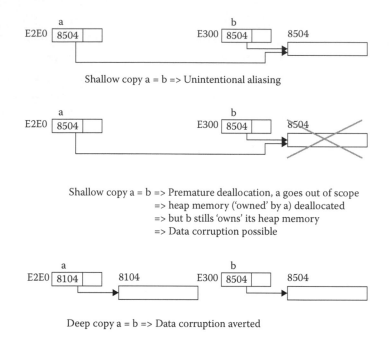

FIGURE 4.3   Shallow copy versus deep copy.

is allocated, of the same size as the source object, and then the data values from the source object's heap memory are copied to the new object's heap memory.

If an overloaded assignment operator is not defined, the compiler automatically generates an assignment operator that merely performs a bitwise copy. Assignment, a = b, would then result in unintentional aliasing, as illustrated by the memory diagrams in Figure 4.3. While the copy constructor is invoked to construct a new object, the assignment operator is invoked through an existing object. Thus, a = b translates to the function invocation noLeak::operator=(&a, b). Like the copy constructor, the assignment operator must allocate new heap memory and then copy data values resident in the source heap memory. Before doing so, however, the assignment operator has the additional responsibility of deallocating heap memory owned by a before a's values are overwritten with a copy of b's values. Memory leaks if such deallocation does not occur. For more discussion, please see Appendix B.

If copying is not desired, as it is not for large collections such as hash tables, a C++ class designer may simply suppress copying, that is, do not support assignment or call by value. Example 4.6 modifies the class design of Example 4.5 to do so. The copy constructor and the overloaded assignment operator are declared via function headers in the private section of the class alongside a comment 'copying suppressed.' There is no need to define these suppressed methods since there is no intent to use them. As private functions then, they cannot be invoked. Thus, if any application code attempts to assign one noCopy object to another, pass by value a noCopy object into a function, or return by value a noCopy object from a function, the compiler will generate an error.

Example 4.6: C++ Class Design with Copying Suppressed

```
class noCopy{
private:
     int*    heapData;
     int     size;
     // copying suppressed!
     noCopy(const noCopy&);
     void operator=(const noCopy&);
public:
     noCopy(unsigned s = 100)
     { size = s;    heapData = new int[size]; }

     //destructor deallocates heapData
     ~noCopy () {delete[] heapData;}
     ...
};
```

If copying is not desired, why declare the copy constructor or overloaded assignment operator at all? If not defined, the compiler will provide default versions, which provide bitwise copying and thus produce the errors discussed above. *Declaration of the copy constructor and the overloaded assignment operator as private suppresses the compiler's provision of default versions.*

Scott Meyers has written definitive guidelines on C++ class design, including thorough coverage of C++ memory management. Please consult the classic work of Meyers (1998) or a more recent version. His guidelines cover memory management within a class. Appendix B further illustrates a class design with internal heap memory and provides relevant C++11 details.

4.2.2 C#/Java Heap Memory Management

Java and C# offer a different memory management model. Like C++, heap memory is allocated via the new operator. In fact, the heap is used much more extensively in Java and C# because all objects are allocated on the heap. However, C# and Java programmers labor under no requirement to deallocate memory. Memory usage and availability is tracked on a system level and, when necessary, a broad reclamation is triggered. We examine garbage collection in more detail in a subsequent section.

Java and C# code produces fewer memory leaks than C++ but incurs greater, and less predictable, overhead. We examine reasons why memory leaks cannot be completely prevented in a later section. At the moment, look at Example 4.7, which presents the C# version of the class designed in Example 4.4. Since explicit deallocation is not necessary in C#/Java, there is no need for a destructor. What about copying?

Example 4.7: C# Heap Memory Internal to a Class

```
// C# class allocates heap memory of variable size
// no need to deallocate => no destructor needed
class noLeak{
        private      int[]   heapData;
        private      uint    size;

        public noLeak(uint s = 100)
        { size = s;  heapData = new int[size]; }
        ...
}
```

By default, copying is shallow, also known as bitwise copying. A bitwise copy simply copies the bit string resident in the source to the destination. *The distinction between shallow and deep copying is often not obvious in programming languages.* Shallow copies may lead to unintentional aliasing, and thus, errors. When two objects point to the same heap memory and both objects assume ownership, there is potential for data corruption, in any language. In C++, there is also potential for premature deallocation (via destructor invocation). Deep copies are safer because each object points to and owns distinct heap memory.

In C# and Java, the default bitwise copying works well for simple objects since objects in these languages are just references. Copying in C# and Java thus establishes aliases. To acquire a deep copy, the C# (or Java) class designer must implement the Cloneable interface and define a Clone() method. Additionally, application programmers must clone objects. Example 4.8 outlines C# copy semantics with corresponding memory diagrams in Figure 4.4. Cloning in C# shifts responsibility to the application programmer. The Clone() method returns an object of type

`Object` so the caller must cast the return value back to the desired type. This type reclamation for copying is not intuitive. In contrast, copying in C++ is more onerous for the class designer but less so for the application programmer.

Example 4.8: C# Cloning

```
public class uCopy: ICloneable
{       private anotherClass    refd;

        // 'anotherClass' instance allocated on heap
        //       address of subobject held in reference 'ref'
        public uCopy()
        {       refd = new anotherClass();      }
        ...

        // deep copy: more heap memory allocated via clone
        //       subobject copied into new memory
        public object Clone()
        {       uCopy   local = this.MemberwiseClone() as uCopy;
                local.refd = this.refd.Clone() as anotherClass;
                return local;
        }
        ...

}
...
// application code
uCopy    u1 = new uCopy();        // #A: uCopy object allocated

// intuitive but yields shallow copy
uCopy    u2 = u1;         // #B: shallow copy of uCopy object

// deep copy: must cast to retrieve type information
u2 = u1.Clone() as uCopy; // #C: clone of uCopy object
```

Data corruption arises from inappropriate aliasing. Data corruption may be immediate or delayed. If two objects hold the address of the same heap memory, either can alter the memory contents, thus 'corrupting' that data for the other object. Hence, in any programming language, the class designer must determine whether or not copying should be supported, and if so, whether deep or shallow copying is appropriate.

4.3 MEMORY OVERHEAD

For an executing program, *heap memory is more expensive than stack allocated memory*. Why? Stack memory is laid out at compile-time when

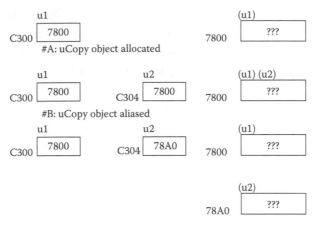

FIGURE 4.4   C# cloning.

compiler determines the size of stack frames. At runtime then, there is no overhead for computing the location of allocated memory. Dedicated hardware, such as the stack register, supports fast updates to stack memory references. In contrast, heap memory is controlled through the allocator (and deallocator), incurring runtime overhead.

4.3.1 Allocation

Efficient memory allocation is not a trivial endeavor. Standard approaches include first-fit and best-fit. First-fit allocates the first block found on the free list that is large enough to satisfy the memory request; best-fit finds the smallest block that satisfies the memory request, and in so doing, minimizes possible fragmentation. The efficacy of different algorithms depends on the order and size of memory requests. Profiling tools may identify time spent in memory allocation and reclamation.

A memory block cannot be allocated more than once so individual addresses uniquely identify (the first byte of) specific allocated blocks. Typically, the allocated size is retained in a block header so that the last byte allocated can be determined from the block address. When a block is released (deallocated), through a call to free (C) or delete (C++), the address of the allocated memory is passed to the allocator via a pointer. The allocator can thus easily determine how much memory should be released.

Memory allocation requires both computational and space overhead. Block size must be stored (in a block header) for each allocated block.

Physical memory has a cost associated with it, and programs tend to use large amounts of it. Therefore, it is still necessary to reclaim and reuse memory as the program is running. Even virtual memory has its limits: memory is a resource that must be conserved or at least recycled.

4.3.2 Memory Reclamation

Two primary methods used for memory reclamation are explicit deallocation and **implicit deallocation**. **Garbage collection** and **reference counting** are implicit deallocation methods. As the name implies, explicit deallocation relies on code statements (calls to delete or free) to explicitly release a block of memory when it is no longer needed. In contrast, as an internal process, garbage collection periodically reviews the state of all allocated blocks, reclaiming those that are no longer reachable (an unreachable block of memory cannot be used). Data is considered reachable if it can be directly addressed by a variable in the set of variables currently active, or indirectly addressed via a pointer (reference) embedded in an active variable (or in a variable referenced by an active variable, etc.).

Garbage collection typically runs as a background process; it is invoked when insufficient heap memory is available or the heap is too fragmented. The time between when a memory block is no longer needed and when it is reclaimed may be large since no explicit request for reclamation is recognized. For example, in Java, the call System.gc() is only a suggestion, not a directive. Memory tends to stay allocated, resulting in more physical memory remaining claimed than under explicit deallocation.

Modern programs often prioritize data manipulation. Memory allocation and reclamation impacts the overall performance of an application. The computational overhead of locating a block, marking it as allocated, storing its size, and returning its base address to the caller should be as efficient as possible. Allocation, and its overhead, is consistent across languages whether a language supports explicit deallocation or relies on garbage collection. The *overhead of explicit deallocation is borne incrementally*, as each deallocation request is processed. In contrast, the *overhead of garbage collection occurs in a pause, when the program must stop running*. However, with implicit deallocation, the heap is more likely to become fragmented, resulting in a more costly search for free blocks during allocation and thus degraded performance.

C++ lead the growth of large-scale software development, with a concomitant increase in the number of software developers, many without extensive knowledge of software design or experience with machine hardware. Hence, the reliability of programmer-managed memory became a significant concern. Experienced professionals summarized coding principles to reduce bugs due to memory errors. Figure 4.5 enumerates common C++ recommendations with respect to managing memory. However, *design guidelines cannot be enforced by any compiler and thus are always insufficient.* The popularity of garbage collected languages such as Java and C# is somewhat due to reduced memory management responsibilities.

Since garbage collection is not a perfect process, C#/Java professionals should track memory ownership. Why? Effective garbage collection depends on appropriate values in references, that is, nonzero for valid addresses and zero for inactive references. Both C# and Java provide auxiliary constructs, such as **weak references** and 'finalize()' methods, to assist the garbage collection process. For more details, see sun.com or msdn. microsoft.com.

1) Match every new with a delete

2) Class design: DEFINE

   constructor,

   destructor,

3) Class design: DEFINE (or suppress)

   copy constructor,

   overloaded assignment operator

4) Use Reference Count to track aliases

   Increment with each added reference

   Decrement when alias goes out of scope

   Deallocate when count is zero

5) Explicitly transfer ownership

   Pass pointer by reference

   Assume ownership

   Reset passed (old owner's) pointer to null

FIGURE 4.5   C++ design guidelines to prevent memory leaks.

4.3.3 Garbage Collection

Memory management is difficult; common problems associated with memory management are summarized in Table 4.1. Data corruption occurs when hidden aliases permit uncoordinated updates to memory. *Errors due to data corruption are difficult to detect because they often occur far from their source.* Memory leaks occur when heap memory is not released before handles goes out of scope. Performance degradation may often be traced to poor usage of the heap. If the heap becomes too fragmented, like a hard drive, the allocator spends more time searching for available blocks. A memory request may fail when there is enough memory but it is not contiguously located. Garbage collection is an attempt to address these problems and does so with varying degrees of success.

Garbage collection involves the 'automatic' reclamation of heap memory no longer in use (garbage) and thus removes the responsibility of memory deallocation from software developers. Heap **compaction** is a separate process but may follow (or be intertwined with) garbage collection. Compaction shifts heap memory still in use to one end of the heap to maximize the amount of contiguous memory available for allocation and thus minimize fragmentation.

Garbage collection strategies date back to the development of the programming language LISP. The popularity of Java renewed interest in garbage collection algorithms and analyses. Research continues because garbage collection is not a perfect process: memory leaks still exist in Java and C#. For advanced readings and current research, please consult sun.com. In the following paragraphs, we provide only a general overview.

The standard approach to garbage collection relies on the mark-and-sweep algorithm. Example 4.9 outlines this intuitive, recursive algorithm for marking all reachable data. Developed over fifty years ago, and refined

TABLE 4.1   Common Difficulties with Program Memory

Memory Problem	Cause	Consequence	Effect
Data corruption	Hidden aliases	Ownership undermined	Data values overwritten
Performance degradation	Fragmented heap	More time to allocate memory	Software slowed Poor scalability
Memory leak	Heap memory not collected	Heap memory unusable	Lost resource
C++ memory leak	Handle to memory lost	Memory inaccessible	Memory allocated but unusable

in the intervening years, the basic algorithm has not changed. When the garbage collector is invoked, the running software is suspended. Examination of the suspended software's stack and static memory yields a **root set** of variables (data) in local or global scope. All memory blocks associated with this root set are marked. Then, each variable r (associated with a newly marked block) is examined to determine if it holds one (or more) references to any other data: this step is the call to mark(r) from the markSweep()routine. Each recursive level of mark(r) corresponds to another step in a chain of references traced from the root set. This last, recursive step is repeated until no additional blocks are marked. At this point, all reachable memory has been marked. The sweep stage then sweeps through the heap, reclaiming all unmarked blocks of memory.

Example 4.9: Classic Mark-and-Sweep Algorithm

```
// start with direct references, the root set:
//    all visible variables (active memory) at time of sweep
// trace out to all variable indirectly referenced
void markSweep()
{     for each Object r in rootSet
             mark(r);
}

// recursive depth-first marking
// terminates when all reachable objects marked
void mark(Object x)
{
      if (!x.marked)
      {       x.marked = true;
              for each Object y referenced by x
                      mark(y);
      }
}

// if heap object marked: KEEP
//    clear marked status in preparation for subsequent sweeps
// if heap object unmarked: RECLAIM (garbage)
void sweep()
{
          for each Object x on heap
              if (x.marked)           x.marked = false;
              else                    release(x);
}
```

All variables that are reachable from the root set will be marked for preservation even if such variables are not actively used in the program and should be reclaimed. *A reference that holds an address of an object that is no longer used will prevent that object from being reclaimed.* Hence, design guidelines recommend the nulling or zeroing out of pointers and references once an object is considered inactive.

For one variable to hold the address of another, it must contain a reference or pointer as a field. Whether or not a field within an allocated memory block represents a pointer requires knowledge of the type associated with that field. Some conservative garbage collection algorithms do not rely on type information and treat every collection of bytes that could represent a pointer as if it actually does. Why? To ensure that only those memory blocks that are most definitively inaccessible are reclaimed. Consequently, inactive blocks may end up being marked as 'in use' when in fact they are not. The mark-and-sweep algorithm may thus fail to reclaim all possible inactive blocks. On the other hand, it will not reclaim any blocks that are still in use. Reclaiming a block that is still in use could eventually lead to memory being allocated to two different clients simultaneously, leading potentially to unwanted aliases and data corruption.

Garbage collection thus distinguishes between live and dead data. Intuitively, when data is not longer used, it should be considered to be 'garbage' and thus reclaimed. However, only those objects (data variables) that are inaccessible are collected. An object that is no longer in use but is still accessible because its heap address 'lingers' (in some reference) cannot be reclaimed. Garbage collection may in fact miss some garbage.

Mark-and-sweep techniques require a suspension of the running program to trace out, that is, mark, all memory still in use. A pause in processing may not be a viable option for many real-time applications but may not be noticeable in others. Small applications that do not use much memory, or applications that run for only a limited time before termination (or restart), may never require garbage collection. *An advantage of garbage collection is that it requires no overhead unless the garbage collector runs.*

4.3.4 Reference Counting

Reference counting is an incremental approach: the overhead of memory management is dispersed across all allocation and deallocation requests. Each memory block has a counter associated with it that indicates how many references (or handles) refer to that memory block. Reference counting thus explicitly tracks aliases. If the reference count is zero then the memory block may be reclaimed since it is no longer in use. Reference counting tracks individual blocks while in use. This algorithm can be implemented in software when there is interest in managing large data stores internal to a program. It may be the easier technique to implement, but it cannot detect cyclic references and thus cannot collect all garbage. Figure 4.6 displays a cycle of four objects (allocated data blocks). There are no external reference to this cycle. Yet, none of the four blocks will be reclaimed because each has a positive reference count, due to a reference from another (unused) block in the cycle.

To avoid costly copying, one may implement reference counting on a class level, mimicking its implementation as a utility. This designed optimization is valuable only when data sharing is intended. Large data collections, such as registries and hash tables, are more efficiently and securely managed when data is shared rather than copied. The design trick is to centralize access, say through the class name, so that only one copy of the data is employed. Class design proceeds by suppressing all constructors (via protected or private accessibility) and providing a public, static instantiation routine. Upon the first request to instantiate, the data is allocated and the reference count set to one. Subsequent requests to instantiate involve no allocation of memory, simply an increment of the reference count: the same address of the data initially allocated is returned for all instantiation requests. Aliases abound in this scheme. Deallocation requests decrement the reference count. When the reference count reaches zero, the data may be deallocated.

Both reference counting and mark-and-sweep illustrate the effect of retaining a reference to data when that data is no longer used: the memory block cannot be reclaimed. Specious references, called lingerers or loiterers in Java, are the source of performance degradation due to heap fragmentation. The explosive growth of Java led to its quick adoption for many software projects. Often, programs were designed without adequate consideration of memory usage. Performance degradation and poor scaling results motivated more program analysis. **Profilers** followed Java on the market as developers sought to identify heap fragmentation and sources of inefficiency.

Neither reference counting nor mark-and-sweep algorithms tackle heap fragmentation, other than incidentally by returning blocks that can

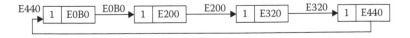

FIGURE 4.6   Reference counting defeated by cyclic references.

be coalesced with adjacent free blocks. Compaction algorithms comprise another phase of heap management. Compaction moves data, that is, reassigns allocated memory so that allocated memory resides in one section, maximizing the size of available, contiguous memory. Compaction is expensive and complicated. *To constrain fragmentation, design recommendations include minimizing allocations and use of temporaries, and allocating data in large blocks* (review Tables 3.10 and 3.11).

4.4 DESIGN: STORAGE VERSUS COMPUTATION

Memory management is complex but important. Although low-level memory management details can, and should be ignored, software design often must explicitly address memory usage. Why? Memory access can become the bottleneck of a system. Processor speeds cannot rescue a data-intensive system from a poor design. For more detail on efficient memory coding, see Loshin (1999). Here, we contrast different designs for storage versus computation.

In general, one trades space for performance. That is, increased storage requirements are justified if the additional space holds, say, (intermediate) calculations so that values can be retrieved directly with little or no computation. If requests for specific computations are frequently made and if the data values involved in such computations are infrequently modified, then storing computations for future lookup is a reasonable design option.

For example, given a stable data set that must support frequent queries that are dependent on the mean value of the set, a design that stores the mean likely yields better performance than a design that calculates the mean upon each request. Conversely, given an unstable data set (where values are frequently inserted or deleted) that must support infrequent queries, a design that calculates the mean upon request may reduce computational overhead. Example 4.10 sketches these two different designs.

Design selection may depend on estimations of the volume of queries and the stability of the data set. The more stable the data set and the more frequent the inquiries as to a computed value, the greater the benefit of storing values like the mean (minimum, maximum, etc.). The converse also holds.

Caution is recommended when a class design uses unbounded storage, such as the generic list type available in modern programming languages. Why? Generic containers are so easy to use that software designers may not explicitly evaluate how much is being stored and whether such storage is necessary. Consider Example 4.11 which encapsulates the task of monitoring access to ordered data.

Example 4.10: Storage versus Computation: C# Code

```csharp
using System;
using System.Collections.Generic;
public class storeMean
{
    private List<int>      values = new List<int>();
    private float          mean;
    ...
    public void add(int x)
    {       values.Add(x);

            int sum = 0;
            foreach (int k in values)
                    sum += k;
            mean = sum/values.Count;
            return;
    }

    public void delete(int x)
    {       values.Remove(x);

            int sum = 0;
            foreach (int k in values)
                    sum += k;
            mean = sum/values.Count;
            return;
    }

    public float mean() {return mean;}
}


public class computeMean
{
    private List<int>      values = new List<int>();
    ...
    public void add(int x)          {       values.Add(x);          }

    public void delete(int x)       {       values.Remove(x);       }

    public float mean()
    {
            int sum = 0;
            foreach (int k in values)
                    sum += k;
            return sum / values.Count;
    }
}
```

Each tracker object encapsulates a number and then process queries that test whether a proffered number is less than, equal to, or greater than the tracked number. At any given point, a tracker object may yield cumulative statistics as to the number of queries processed that were less than, equal to, or greater than the tracked number. For example, if a query passed in '5' to a tracker object that encapsulated '43' then the 'lessThan' count would be incremented. Example 4.11 illustrates a simple design.

Example 4.11: Counts Stored; Queries Discarded: C# Code

```
public class tracker
{        private int num;
         private int less = 0;
         private int equal = 0;
         private int more = 0;

         public tracker(int x) { num = x; }

     public int query(int y)
         {        if (y < num)              { less++;        return -1; }
                  if (y == num)             { equal++;       return 0;  }
                  more++;          return 1;
         }

         public int getLessCt ()          {        return less;          }
         public int getEqualCt ()         {        return equal;         }
         public int getMoreCt ()          {        return more;          }
}
```

An overdesigned response is presented in Example 4.12. The class designer uses a list to store each query and then, upon demand, must walk through the entire collection to determine the relative counts of numbers that fell below, matched, or were above the encapsulated value. A tremendous amount of storage is used, and computational overhead is increased. Any design that both maximizes storage overhead and postpones computation should be reassessed.

Example 4.12: Queries Stored: C# Code

```
using System;
using System.Collections.Generic;
public class tBigMem
{        private int          num;
         private List<int>  queries = new List<int>();

         public tracker(int x) { num = x; }
```

```
public int query(int y)
{   queries.Add(y);
    if (y < num)              return -1;
    if (y == num)             return 0;
    return 1;
}

public int getLessCt()
{   int count = 0;
    foreach (int q in queries)
            if (q < num)    count++;
    return count;
}

public int getEqualCt()
{   int count = 0;
    foreach (int q in queries)
            if (q == num)   count++;
    return count;
}

public int getMoreCt()
{   int count = 0;
    foreach (int q in queries)
            if (q > num) count++;
    return count;
}


}
```

4.5 SUMMARY

In this chapter, we examined the assignment and release of memory within a running program. Modern programming languages abstract away most memory management details. Software developers can thus design code that is more portable and maintainable because it is not directly tied to specific memory addresses.

To illustrate differences in memory management, we examined allocation and copying in C++ and C#. Examples traced the distinction between shallow and deep copying. We also summarized explicit deallocation in C++, providing common examples of memory leaks. Noting that C# and Java provide implicit deallocation, we summarized essential details of garbage collection. We also briefly commented on reference counting. Memory management is not a trivial endeavor and no approach can easily prevent all memory leaks and data corruption. Hence, the competent software developer should understand the memory models of different programming languages and their effects on software design.

At the chapter end, we contrasted different designs: storage of data for future lookup (as a means to reduce computational overhead) versus computation upon demand. Design evaluation must explicitly consider trade-offs: how much memory is required and what is the expected frequency of requests for computation? Enhanced performance can justify extra memory. Computational savings usual arise when data is stable, intermediate values can be calculated easily, and the frequency of queries is significant. Any design that requires both a significant amount of data and extensive computation should be re-evaluated.

DESIGN INSIGHTS

SOFTWARE

Memory viewed abstractly and thus treated uniformly
    Access cost dependent on location
        Cache, secondary store, etc.
Data corruption errors hard to trace
Language differences with respect to managing program memory
    Use of runtime stack and heap
    Explicit versus implicit deallocation
    Copy semantics may not be obvious
    Imprecision of memory management may not be evident
Garbage collection
    Requires suspension of executing software
    No overhead if garbage collector does not run

MODELS

Program memory: data section – heap and run-time stack
Heap more expensive than run-time stack
    Compiler lays out stack frames
        No run-time overhead
    Heap memory allocated at run-time via call to allocator
    Heap fragmentation dampens performance
Copy semantics
      Deep vs. shallow copying
      Affect data usage and class design

SOFTWARE DESIGN

Design guidelines are not enforced by the compiler
    Guidelines provide an inadequate safeguard
Judiciously allocate data in order to minimize heap fragmentation
Objects may encapsulate dynamic memory allocation

Obscure need for memory management
May suppress copying by design
C++ rests on explicit deallocation
=> programmer must manage memory
Deallocate heap memory before last handle goes out of scope
Memory leaks prevented when each 'new' matched with a 'delete'
Matching 'new' with 'delete' difficult
Parameter passing, aliasing, transfer of ownership
C# rests on implicit deallocation
Zeroing out references aids garbage collector

DOCUMENTATION

Record memory management responsibilities
Explicitly identify copy semantics
Copying suppressed, shallow copy, deep copy

CONCEPTUAL QUESTIONS

1. Describe standard views of memory.

2. What are the advantages and disadvantages of heap memory?

3. Why do Java and C# rely on implicit deallocation?

4. Why does C++ rely on explicit deallocation?

5. Why is tracking the ownership of (heap) memory difficult?

6. What is the primary difference between deep and shallow copying?

7. When is it appropriate to suppress copying?

8. What is garbage collection? How is 'garbage' defined?

9. What is compaction, and why is it necessary?

10. What are the flaws in garbage collection and reference counting?

11. List some common best practices for C++ class design and data declarations, relative to safe, and efficient use of memory.

CHAPTER 5

Design and Documentation

F ORM AFFECTS FUNCTION, in terms of ease of use and maintainability. In this chapter, we examine the design and documentation of software, using the class construct as the focal point of design. Promoting internal control of state, we cover essential functions of a class: **constructors**, **destructors**, **accessors**, **mutators**, and **private utility functions**. We note language differences when important. The intent is to scaffold software design on top of class construction, emphasizing the separation of internal elements from the external interface. We also present an effective means of documenting design, the specification of a contract between the class designer and the users of a class.

CHAPTER OBJECTIVES

- Define systematic OO class design
- Delineate standard components of class functionality
- Introduce notion of contractual design
- Define programming by contract
- Illustrate deliberate design with contractual expectations
- Identify relevant OOD principles

5.1 OBJECT-ORIENTED DESIGN

Object-Oriented Design (OOD) dominated software development in the 1990s and early 21st century. A design approach that rests on the notions of **abstraction**, **encapsulation**, and **information hiding**, OOD supported the development of many large-scale software systems and advanced the concept of **code reuse**. The popularity of **Design Patterns** publicized OOD design principles. Both OOD and Design Patterns encouraged the adoption of UML (Unified Modeling Language) as a design modeling tool.

We examine basic OOD principles for two reasons. The OO model provides a conceptual framework for cleanly delineating the different perspectives of software utility and responsibility. The organization of data, coincident with functionality, yields the **dual perspective** of designer and user. This dual perspective provides the abstraction necessary to design and maintain large software systems. Second, there are now many, many **legacy** systems written in object-oriented programming languages such as C++, Java, and C#, using OO constructs and design principles. To maintain these systems and to refactor them in preparation for continued use, one must understand the structure and effect of classic OO design. For the same reasons, we analyze design alternatives in Chapter 8.

The structural elements of OOD serve as an illustration of deliberate design, providing the foundation for comparative design and modeling. Details considered here include **lifetime** of objects, **association**, **ownership**, and **cardinality**. Are objects temporary or relatively persistent? Can object instantiation be postponed? Is the relationship (association) between two objects permanent or transient? Who owns a subordinate object? Can that ownership be transferred or shared? How many objects exist in a relationship? Is that number fixed? Other questions arise. *Deliberate design must identify all assumptions.* All these details are relevant to software design in general and are transferable to larger views of software, such as software architecture.

The reader must recognize that *compilers do not enforce design*. By following established design principles, documenting assumptions, and modeling relationships effectively, one can develop maintainable, extensible code. However, the compiler will not verify design merit for the developer; it merely follows a long, complex set of instructions for source code translation.

5.2 CLASS FUNCTIONALITY

The class construct formalized the implementation of an **abstract data type (ADT)**, and, in so doing, legitimized the idea of encapsulating data alongside functionality. Encapsulation permits a software designer to specify invariants, properties that always hold. Preservation of invariants reduces the need for testing and promotes software maintainability. Class invariants should be under the internal control of class methods, removing unneeded dependencies on the application programmer. In this manner, class design ensures that objects remain in a consistent, legal state. Two immediate benefits occur: the class may be treated as abstractly as a built-in type since the application programmer need not know any internal details, and the class is more secure because it is more difficult for an incompetent or malicious programmer to put an instance of the class in an invalid state.

We examine the systematic design of functionality within the class construct, but this categorization of functionality applies to software design in general. Functionality can be delineated by intent: initialize data; allocate, deallocate, or manage resources; change or view data values; and examine or resolve data dependencies. Fulfillment of functionality may be conditional: a request for access or change may be denied. Table 5.1 categorizes the standard functionality defined within a class design: constructors, destructor, accessors, mutators, private utility functions, and public interface functions. Functions defined within the scope of a class are often called "methods."

Regardless of category, each method in a well-designed class should support abstraction and encapsulation and, as much as possible, allow the application programmer to treat the custom type as if it were a built-in type. Responsibility for proper initialization and preservation of state

TABLE 5.1   Types of Functions Defined in Class Construct

Function	Intent	Use
Constructor	Set object in initial valid state Initialize data Allocate resources	Explicit with new operator Implicit in C++ (stack objects)
Destructor	Release resources Bookkeeping details	Language dependent
Accessor	View data values	Depends on accessibility
Mutator	Change data values Preserve validity of state	Depends on accessibility
Private utility	Preserve data dependencies Manage resources	Internal to class
Public interface	Support type definition Provide needed utility	Unrestricted Type related

should be internalized and not left for the application programmer. Hence, it is common to differentiate between private functions that may be called only from within other class methods and public functions that the application programmer can directly invoke.

To illustrate design details, we use a sample data class, Icon, that serves as a representation of a visual element in a computer game. Example 5.1 shows the C++ code for this sample class; Example 5.2 shows the C# code. Although this data type is incomplete and not immediately usable in a computer game, we use it to illustrate a type definition that is foundational but subject to variation. A computer game would be seeded with multiple Icon objects, but it is likely that there would be substantive differences between Icon objects. We define sample data fields to represent object form, and sample functions to represent movement and/or change within a game session.

Example 5.1: Sample OO Class Design in C++

```cpp
class Icon        //data members and functions, private by default
{     //data allocated for each instantiated Icon object
    double        mass, glow, energy;
    int           x, y;
    bool          active;        //dependent on energy

    //static data: ONE data member PER class
    static int    count;    //tracks #allocated Icon objects

    //private function: accessible only by Icon methods
    void adjustEnergy();
  public:
    //constructor must set state, that is, initialize fields
    //    and increment static count: one more Icon object
    Icon(...)
    {     ...
        active = (mass*glow < energy);    //invariant
        count++;
    }

    //destructor decrement count: one fewer active Icon object
    //       no resources to release
    ~Icon() {        count--;         }

    //accessor functions: control view of data member
    //      may choose NOT to return value
    double getEnergy()     const
    {       if (active)     return energy;
            return          0;
    }
```

```
bool    isActive()      const {return  active; }

int     getCount()      const {return  count; }

//mutator function: control state
//      may reject change request
bool    incEnergy(double moola)
{       if (!active || moola < mass)  return false;
        if (moola > 1)               energy + = moola;
        return true;
}
//public functions
void            oscillate()     {       ...     }
void            flair()         {       ...     }
...
};
```

Example 5.2: Icon Class in C#

```
public class Icon
{
        private double          mass;
        private double          glow;
        private double          energy;
        private int             x;
        private int             y;
        private bool            active;

        //static data: ONE data member PER class
        private static int      count = 0;

        private void adjustEnergy();

        public Icon(...) {          ...         }

        public static int       getCount() const {return    count;}
        public double           getEnergy() const   {   ...     }
        public bool             incEnergy(double)   {   ...     }
        public void             oscillate()         {   ...     }
        public void             flair()             {   ...     }

        //C# property: get (accessor) and set (mutator)
        public bool             Active
        {       get {return active;     }           }
        ...
}
```

The Icon class defines several private data members to model grid placement (x, y), size, and effect. A Boolean value (active) can be used to control whether or not an object responds to requests. Each object instantiated from this class definition will have its own copy of these data fields. One static integer tracks the number of objects instantiated from the class. If a data member is defined as static, one copy is allocated on the class level; all objects share that copy. (Static data members are initialized in the class definition for C#/Java but initialized in the .cpp file for C++.) Compare the functionality defined in this example to the types of functions summarized in Table 5.1.

5.2.1 Constructors

Constructors are special functions that are responsible for an internal and controlled initialization of objects upon instantiation. Constructors return no value and the function name is simply that of the class. The compiler patches in calls to a constructor when an object is instantiated. Thus, initialization should not be the responsibility of the application programmer; it is specified by the class designer and internally controlled. The provision of a public `initialize()` method runs counter to the design of a well-encapsulated class. As a method that can be called at any point, rather than only at the point of instantiation, a public `initialize()` method undermines class control: at any time, an object could be reset to an initial state. Constructors may be overloaded, that is, more than one may be defined, each distinguished by its parameter list.

In Java and C#, object declaration is merely a declaration of a typed reference: subsequently, the `new` operator must be called to allocate an object on the heap and place its address in the reference so declared. In C++, by default, objects are allocated on the stack, so the constructor fires implicitly upon variable declaration. Heap objects may be allocated in C++: a typed pointer variable holds the address as returned from the `new` operator. Calls to the `new` operator trigger constructor invocation.

Example 5.3 illustrates different object instantiations in C++: statements #A, #C, and #E result in calls to the no-argument (often called default) constructor; statements #B, #D, and #F result in calls in the overloaded constructor that takes an integer value as a passed parameter. In C++, when an array of objects is allocated, the compiler patches in multiple calls to the default (no-argument) constructor, one call for each array element. What if the software developer wants the objects in the array to be "constructed" (initialized) by a different constructor? Extra code is needed to overwrite array elements, as shown in statements #F and #G. Appendix B provides more detail.

Example 5.3: C++ Object Instantiation

```
//C++ variable declarion => stack allocation
myType      stackObjX;          //#A no-argument constructor
myType      stackObjY(10);      //#B overloaded constructor ...

//C++ new operator => heap allocation
myType*     heapPtrX = new myType;        //#C no-argument
myType*     heapPtrY = new myType(3);     //#D overloaded

//C++ array declaration: ONLY no-arg constructor invoked
myType      db[100];         //#E 100 calls to no-arg constructor

//overwrite default initialization
for (int j = 0; j < 100; j++)
{
    myType          replace(j);     //#F constructor takes int
    db[j] = replace;                //#G overwrite array entry
}
```

In C#, all objects are allocated on the heap, through an invocation of the new operator and thus an explicit invocation of a constructor. Moreover, an array of C# objects is really an array of references, where each reference must be assigned the heap address of an allocated object. Initializing an array of C# objects thus already requires stepping through the array via a for-loop. Example 5.4 illustrates different object instantiations in C#.

Example 5.4: C# Object Instantiation

```
//C# object variable declaration: myType reference
//      no object allocated yet
myType objA;

//C# object variable declaration and instantiation
//      object allocated on heap by new operator
myType objB = new myType();
myType objC = new myType(12);
...

//C# object variable instantiation
//      reset previously declared references objA and objC
//      to hold address of heap object allocated by new
objA = new myType();
objC = new myType(15);

//C# array declaration: array of 100 myType references
myType db = new myType[100];
```

```
//C# array initilization:
//      each reference (array element)
//            holds address of heap object allocated by new
for (int j = 0; j < 100; j++)
        db[j] = new myType(j);
}
```

Constructors are responsible for setting the initial state of an object and establishing the class invariants before any client code runs. Such initialization may include specifying default values as well as allocating resources. Not all field values must be set to a default value or to a parameter of the constructor. If a data dependency exists between two or more data members then the constructor may set the values of some data members (possibly relative to the values of other data members). For example, whether or not an Icon object is active depends on its energy level relative to its mass and glow. The constructor establishes this invariant.

5.2.2 Accessors and Mutators

Accessor methods, typically called get() functions, provide a controlled peek inside an object; such functions often return the value of a targeted private data member. For example, in containers, it is common to query the number of data items held or the size of the container. Accessor functions such as getCount() or getSize() provide this information without exposing private data members. Accessors should be const functions, that is, no accessor should modify the state of an object. Accessors may check state before returning a value, as is done in the method Icon::getEnergy(); if the object is inactive, its energy value is not returned, only the value zero.

Mutator methods, typically called set() functions, provide the means to alter state by changing the value of one or more data fields. To control the alteration of state, the implementation code of set() functions may often be conditional. A request to set a data field may be rejected if the value provided would put the object in an invalid state. Common examples of refused requests include out-of-bounds values or values that violate a dependency between two or more fields in the class definition. The mutator method Icon::incEnergy(x) in the Icon class rejects the change request if the Icon object is inactive, if the passed value x is less than the mass data field, or if x is not greater than 1. By keeping data fields private, and thus externally inaccessible, and by providing set() functions that preserve class invariants, a class designer preserves data integrity. C# provides paired set and get methods via "properties."

Design must distinguish between accessors and mutators. *Mutators alter state in a controlled, acceptable manner. Accessors do not change state.* No class method should give external access to private data, which would yield the potential to change state, unless the provision of such access is a deliberate design decision.

Example 5.5 illustrates an accessor that compromises object state by aliasing an external data variable to an internal data member. How? It is not obvious how data integrity is undermined. The accessor getControl() returns an integer value by reference (statement #A). Hence, the caller's integer variable alias is aliased, or shares the same memory space, as the private data member hiddenInt so returned (statement #C). Any subsequent changes to alias will change the private data field hiddentInt of the object insecure.

Example 5.5: Aliasing Undermines Encapsulation: C++ Code

```
class myType {
     int      hiddentInt;
   public:
     myType(int x = 101) {hiddenInt = x; }

     //mutator that rejects out of range values
     void     setValue(int    x)
     {        if       (x > 10)        hiddenInt = x;
              return;
     }

     //standard accessor: return by value
     int      myType::getValue()      { return      hiddenInt;    }

     //"get" implies accessor but a reference returned
     int&     getControl(){return hiddenInt;}          //#A
              ...
};
...
//APPLICATION CODE
myType         insecure;

insecure.setValue(200);                  //change request OK
insecure.setValue(-13);                  //change request rejected
cout << insecure.getValue() << endl;     //#B

int& alias = insecure.getControl();      //#C
cout << insecure.getValue() << endl;     //#D

alias = -13;         //#E private data member altered
cout << insecure.getValue() << endl;     //#F
```

Contrast the output values from statements #B, #D, and #F. Since the object insecure has not been legitimately changed via the defined mutator, each output statement should print "200." Yet, statement #F outputs "–13." Why? The assignment to alias statement #E results in an unseen alteration of the hiddentInt data member of object insecure. This example is in C++ but aliasing is possible in any language. See Appendix A to review return values.

5.2.3 Utility Functions

Private utility functions support functional decomposition and reuse within a class and thus reduce code complexity. In C++, a common private utility function for copying data should be used when both the copy constructor and overloaded assignment operator must be defined to correctly manage heap allocated data. Example 5.6 is the quintessential C++ class that provides support for deep copying. Appendix B contains the full class design, without a private utility function.

Example 5.6: C++ Class Memory Management

```
//good MemoryManagement:
//    constructor, copy constructor, overloaded =, destructor
class goodMM{
  private:
      int*    heapData;
      int     size;
      void    copyData(int* source);
  public:
      goodMM(unsigned s = 100)
      { size = s;    heapData = new int[size]; }

      goodMM(const goodMM&);
      void operator=(const goodMM&);
      ~goodMM() {delete[] heapData;}
      ...
};

//.cpp file: implementation details
//private utility function has access to private data (size)
void goodMM::copyData(int* source)
{    heapData = new int[size];
     for (int j = 0; j < size; j++)
          heapData[j] = source[j];
}
```

```
//copy constructor: new memory allocated, old values copied
goodMM::goodMM(const goodMM& x)
{    size = x.size;
     copyData(x.heapData);
}

//overloaded assignment operator
//           delete old lhs memory
//           copy old values from rhs into new memory for lhs
void goodMM::operator=(const goodMM& rhs)
{    if (this != &rhs)                    //skip self-assignment
     {      delete[] heapData;
            size = rhs.size;
            copyData(rhs.heapData);
     }
     return;
}
```

A private utility function may be used to internally adjust state. For example, a resize() function may expand the size of a container. Why should this method be private rather than public? The application programmer should not be responsible for maintaining the container in a usable condition. When overflow is imminent, resizing should be internally triggered to avoid capacity overflow. The application programmer uses services provided by a container, such as add and delete functions to store and retrieve data but should not manipulate internals. We present such capability in Example 5.8 when we examine priority queues.

Redefining private utility accessibility as "protected" opens access to descendants. Functions in the protected interface are those that provide utility to child classes via the inheritance construct. Protected utility functions exemplify code reuse: all derived classes can use the parent utility function so it need be defined only once.

Functions in the public interface are precisely those methods expected by the application programmer. Such functions must provide the functionality needed for the type definition. In the Icon example, key public functionality includes calls to oscillate() and flair(). In the classic stack example, key public functions would be push(), pop(), clear(), isEmpty(), and, possibly, isFull().

Design principles advocate removing any unwarranted dependencies on the application programmer as well as restricting exposure of internal details. Public interface functions then should not require knowledge of internal form. For example, an application programmer should not know or care how a queue holds its data. Arrays and linked lists are common implementations for holding data but the application programmer should program to the interface of a class not to its implementation. In the `Icon` class, for example, the calculation and control of energy consumption is internalized, as it should be. The application programmer thus cannot directly alter the rate of energy consumption or modify the relationship of mass, glow, and movement to energy consumption.

5.2.4 Destructors

The role of destructors is language-dependent. C# and Java do not have destructors but support the notion of a "finalizer." A `finalize()` routine is called implicitly by the garbage collector before an object is reclaimed. Since no one really knows when, if ever, the garbage collector runs, the `finalize()` method is of limited design utility. Destructors are essential in C++. Standard C++ design guidelines suggest that they always be defined.

Java and C# rely on implicit deallocation and thus do not need destructors. With implicit deallocation, most memory management responsibility is removed from software designers. The complexity of memory management within a program is thus drastically diminished. Heap memory may be allocated explicitly via the `new` operator but there is no `delete` operator because a garbage collector handles reclamation of dynamically allocated memory. Consequently, explicit deallocation (via destructor invocation) is not possible in C#, or Java.

If a code segment is labeled as "unsafe" in C# then pointers may be used and the programmer thus acquires indirect access to memory. The use of "unsafe" code in C# is discouraged as it compromises portability. Thus, the following short discussion applies primarily to destructors in C++.

The compiler implicitly invokes the destructor when an object goes out of scope. Like constructors, destructors return no value. The destructor's name is simply that of the class preceded by the special symbol "~." Destructors are essential when an object internally acquires resources at runtime. The destructor must then release these resources. For example, destructors could release any files opened during an object's lifetime. More commonly, if an object dynamically allocates data, a C++ destructor would deallocate this heap memory to prevent a memory leak. From Chapter 4, recall the problem of internal memory leaks in C++ classes. Refer again to Example 5.6 to review a destructor managing memory.

Destructors may also be used for bookkeeping tasks. A technique employed in resource management, as well as debugging, is to track the number of active object instances. To do so, a class can use a static count variable that is incremented upon every object construction and decremented upon object deallocation. The Icon class in Example 5.1 employs this design. Thus, a game designer who wishes to track the number of allocated Icon objects could consult the static count. Since this static data is private, as it should be, a static accessor function is needed in the class interface, as shown in Example 5.1.

5.3 PROGRAMMING BY CONTRACT

OOD reinforces a dual perspective: the application programmer (or user) manipulates types from an external view, invoking public functions to satisfy application needs; the class designer defines and implements types from an internal view, specifying relationship, defining properties, and preserving state.

Consider data storage. Ideally, containers should support functionality for data storage independent of the type of data stored. The classic stack data structure provides functions to add and remove data as well as the capability to determine if the stack is empty. Functions such as isEmpty() operate in the same manner regardless of the data type stored in the stack. This functional independence from data type is true for queues, priority queues, trees, etc. To promote consistent use (and reuse) of containers, regardless of data type stored, we must model and design generically.

Next, consider data classification systems. Whether used to delineate inventory, library materials, or courses offered at a university, for example, data types may be defined hierarchically. A basic data item definition provides a foundation for classification by collecting all common features. Specialization adds detail to the basic type definition to expand its use in a classification system. Type specialization may lead to functional variation. To promote consistent type use (and expansion), regardless of subtype specialization, we must model and design within a type framework.

These two examples, containers and classification systems, span a range of software utility. Containers are type agnostic: primary tasks of storing and retrieving data are implemented usually without regard to type. Classification systems are grounded in type: the order in which items are sorted, stored, or evaluated usually depends on (sub)type. In either case, to ensure that use is consistent with intent, software must be properly modeled, designed, and documented. There is a plethora of tools and conventions available for recording a model or design. There are also many different standards and formats for documentation. We examine here a documentation convention that effectively communicates assumptions about environment and use that must be met by application programmers.

Documentation records design intent and implementation details in support of anticipated software evolution. The notion of documentation as a contract supports the dual perspective inasmuch as the application programmer uses the provided public interface, and the class designer implements this public utility under established, published expectations. Introduced by Bertrand Meyers, the architect of the OOPL Eiffel, Design by Contract embodies a professional perspective on software development and documentation. Microsoft now advances a similar perspective, code contracts. Eiffel Software owns the registered trademark of Design by Contract.

Programming by Contract an academic rendering of Design by Contract. The central idea is that documentation serves as a contract between the application programmer and the class designer. If the application programmer adheres to the restrictions detailed in the documentation, then objects should behave as expected.

5.3.1 Defensive Programming

Programming by Contract is an alternative to **defensive programming**. It outlines a formal agreement between class designer and application programmer. The contract identifies requirements to be met on each side for safe and consistent use of the defined type. By specifying shared responsibilities for secure code between class designer and application programmer, the established contract alleviates the need for extensive testing. In contrast, defensive programming assumes nothing: software may or may not be used correctly. Hence, defensive programming incurs the overhead of extensive testing to prevent inappropriate actions.

We examine classic data structures to illustrate the differences between a contractual approach to design, as documented via Programming by Contract, and defensive programming. Consider a stack. Popping from an empty stack is illegal. What value would be returned from an empty container? How can a data value be returned from an empty container? Would an oblivious return unintentionally establish an alias to memory (data) outside the container and thus allow the modification of data owned by another object? Standard design responses to an attempt to pop() from an empty stack are either to check internally and reject the request or to assume an external check is performed before the pop() function is invoked.

A defensive approach is safe because it rejects pop() requests when the stack is empty, thus preventing unintended consequences. No precondition is thus required. Design may be tricky though. How does the pop() routine communicate a rejected request? An easy solution is to return a default value, such as zero indicating failure, when the stack is empty. However, this approach is not possible when zero, or the default value, is a legal data value that could be stored on the stack. Another option is to return the value popped through a parameter (passed by reference), allowing the pop() function to return a Boolean value: true if the pop() operation succeeds; false if it fails.

Defensive programming increases code complexity through internal checks. The overhead of unconditional testing degrades performance. In this stack example, the cost of safety is an internal check with *every* pop() call. Often, this overhead may be unwarranted and particularly onerous. Consider two scenarios: (1) an application programmer uses a stack to hold a huge data set, and extracts chunks of the data in bulk, as shown in Example 5.7; (2) a client uses a stack to reverse input for a data set of known size. In either case, a check is not needed because the client will not be accessing an empty stack. To avoid an internal check on pop(), the application programmer must know when the stack might be empty.

Example 5.7: Stack Object with Little Danger of Being Empty: C++ Code

```
myStack        dataStore;
...
for (int j = 0; j < 500; j++)
        dataStore.push(getData(j));

        ...     //no pop operations
                //      => enter for-loop with stack of 500 ints
int             transitStore[100];
//check for empty Stack unwarranted
for (int j = 0; j < 100; j++)
        transitStore[j] = dataStore.pop();
```

An alternative to defensive programming, contractual design shifts the responsibility for safety outside the class: the application programmer must meet the stated precondition (stack is not empty) before invoking pop(). Thus, the application programmer must track or check state. If a precondition is not met, the behavior of the system after the function call is undefined. Violation of the required precondition voids the contract between the class designer and the application programmer. No guarantee then remains for any resulting behavior.

Without an internal check, pop() may proceed with its attempt to remove a value from the stack data structure. Such action may result in the return of an invalid value. Consider a stack implemented as an array: the "top" of the stack is an index into the array. When the stack is empty, this index is invalid. In C++, use of an invalid index results in the extraction of an invalid data value (whatever value resident in memory so indexed). Why? C++ does not automatically provide run-time checks on array bounds. Hence, an application programmer may not know that a returned value was invalid. More problematic is the possibility of data corruption. Without internal knowledge of an invalid pop(), the routine would run as usual, decrementing the internal index controlling access to the array holding the stack data. Subsequent calls to push() would fall outside array bounds, possibly causing data corruption.

A standard precondition for pop() is that the stack object is not empty. The postcondition for pop() is that a stack object may be empty after popping an element. The application programmer should not have to count additions and removals. If necessary, the application programmer can use the query function, isEmpty(), to extract state information.

In a well-designed class, object state may change only through the execution of member functions. Member functions may specify preconditions that must be met before invocation. Unfortunately, a common result of precondition violation is data corruption, potentially leading to delayed failure—an error whose source is hard to trace.

In practice, encapsulation supports the development of reliable code because internal state is controlled: application code cannot put an object into an invalid state if the class has been designed well. Ideally, the class designer delineates the public and private functionality so that objects are always initialized correctly and that no method invocation modifies internal data without permission. With controlled and checked modification, objects thus are always in a valid state.

The tradeoffs between a defensive and a contractual design are explicit: security versus efficiency; overhead of testing versus assumptions of correct use; code clutter of extra testing (or exception clauses) versus documentation of contractual obligations. What is the difference between testing and reliance on exceptions? A conditional test is an overhead borne by all requests. Exceptions are a safeguard: code must be wrapped in a try block but there is no runtime overhead until an exception is thrown. Exceptions can be used in both defensive programming and contractual design. Note, however, that use of exceptions increases software complexity. Critics say exceptions clutter code. For more details, see Chapter 9.

Without a contract, the class designer should not depend on proper usage and so may wish to layer an internal check for empty on top of all pop() calls. In so doing, all users are penalized by the unavoidable, internal overhead. Thus, Programming by Contract presents an attractive alternative when the application programmer can track state changes and meet the stated preconditions.

Programming by Contract delineates contractual obligations across five documentation categories: function **preconditions**, function **postconditions**, **interface invariants**, **implementation invariants**, and **class invariants**. We describe each category briefly and then give an example. Table 5.2 summarizes the five categories.

5.3.2 Precondition and Postcondition

The intent of precondition and postcondition is to identify data dependencies as well as assumptions about the environment in which functions execute. To satisfy expectations as to proper use, the application programmer must meet preconditions before invoking any function. The class designer must guarantee postconditions so that the application programmer can track state, a possible prerequisite to satisfying the precondition(s) of subsequent function calls. Since encapsulation and design can guarantee data integrity, testing overhead may thus be reduced. Nonetheless, for consistent use of functions, precondition and postcondition should be used, whether or not the software is object-oriented (Table 5.3).

Function responsibilities vary. Constructors create objects in a valid state. If applicable, destructors release assigned resources and record bookkeeping details. Accessor functions return copies of data values rather than aliases to internal data. Mutator operations change state (the values

TABLE 5.2   Programming by Contract

Specification	Intent	Characteristics
Precondition	Safe entry into function	Required incoming state
Postcondition	Identify state changes	Possible altered state
Interface invariant	Promote consistent use	Services supported
Implementation invariant	Software maintenance	Design specifications
Class invariant	Communicate type and use	Designed functionality

TABLE 5.3 Common Preconditions and Postconditions

Precondition			
State satisfied	*Resource held*	*Data valid*	*Ownership*
Icon active	File handle	Within range	Callee owner
Stack non-empty	Allocated memory	Correct precision	Shared

Postcondition			
State altered	*Resource released*	*Data stored*	*Ownership*
Icon inactive	File closed	Stack full	Transferred
Stack empty	Memory released	Aged	Released

of data members) while preserving validity of state. Private utility functions provide functional decomposition within a class design. Additional methods implement the core functionality of the type defined by the class. In short, all class member functions ensure legal state transitions.

Invariants serve to document stable state conditions. Invariants also describe design decisions in the context of class structure, noting conditions and relationships that should be preserved within a class. Interface invariants are external constraints. Implementation invariants are internal constraints. Table 5.4 delineates the invariants for Programming by contract.

Preconditions enumerate all conditions that must be met before a call is made, e.g., a stack must be non-empty before pop() is invoked. The caller must fulfill all preconditions so the class operation need not verify any precondition. *The intent of preconditions is to avoid error through improper use and to reduce overhead by minimizing internal testing.* Preconditions must be published for those requesting service. Callers must recognize the potential of severe consequences if preconditions are not satisfied. Preconditions must be verifiable! How else could an application programmer invoke a function with assurance that a precondition is met? An application programmer must be able to determine if a precondition is true or not, e.g., check to determine if a stack is empty.

TABLE 5.4 Common Invariants for Programming by Contract

Interface Invariant	Implementation Invariant	Class Invariant
Constraints	Internal design	Relationships
	Data structures	Association
	Utility functions	Cardinality
Expected use	Interface (portion echoed)	Environment
Data validity	Data dependencies	Ownership
Error response	Error response	Error response

It is not always easy to verify preconditions, especially for resource management. Why? Resource use can span multiple actions. Consider long-term file use. File existence is typically a one-time check before opening a file for reading. Yet, the file could be deleted after the existence check but before reading from the file. What would be an appropriate response when attempting to read using an invalid file handle? Usually a runtime error is unacceptable. Under Programming by Contract, if the user satisfied the contract by meeting the specified precondition of "the file exists," undefined behavior would not be acceptable either. Exception handling would be an acceptable response. Although throwing an exception incurs overhead, it preserves system integrity.

In addition to specifying state, preconditions may define the validity of a passed parameter, by defining a range of acceptable values. Preconditions do not specify the type of passed parameters in a statically typed language because the compiler checks type. In a dynamically typed language like Python, for example, a precondition may specify the types for which the operation holds.

In general, postconditions specify the effect of function execution. A postcondition should identify data and state changes, such as resource acquisition or release. In the OO paradigm, postconditions identify the state of an object after a function is executed, e.g., stack is non-empty after push(), stack is empty after clear(). Postconditions are not descriptions of the function's action; they must clearly publish potential and actual state changes so that the application programmer can track state changes and verify preconditions for subsequent function calls.

Preconditions are not a new idea. Programming by Contract emphasizes the shared responsibility between the caller and the callee. Preconditions describe the required state necessary for correct behavior. If the required preconditions are not met, there is no guarantee about resulting behavior. Precondition and postcondition serve to guide the correct use of a function. Specification of precondition and postcondition thus remain relevant regardless of whether the function is declared public, private, or protected in a class or, in fact, whether the function is encapsulated in a class at all.

5.3.3 Invariants

Interface invariants provide an overview of the public use of a class and inform the application programmer of constraints. For example, if, in C++, the overloaded assignment operator and the copy constructor have been suppressed, the interface invariant would note that copying was not supported. This approach is illustrated in the definition of a priority queue in Example 5.8.

Example 5.8: C++ Overview of Priority Queue

```
class PriorityQ
{
    ...
    //private data members
    //implementation details deliberately omitted here

    //copying suppressed
    PriorityQ (PriorityQ&);
    PriorityQ& operator=(const PriorityQ&);

    //private utility functions to preserve state
    void resize();
    void age();
public:
    PriorityQ (unsigned size = DEFAULT_CAPACITY);
    ~PriorityQ ();
    ...
    int      count() const;
    bool     isStored(const Item&) const;

    void     enQ(const Item&);
    void     deQ(const Item&);
    bool     isEmpty() const;

    //possible supplemental public functions
    void     clear();
    Item&    getFirst() const;
    Item&    getLast() const;
};
```

Published prominently, interface invariants provide a higher level of abstraction than preconditions, and describe restrictions on the use of objects, often realized as preconditions that apply upon entry to all or most public functions. For example, in the Icon class, the state of an Icon (its mass, glow, and energy) affects its movement. Interface invariants may define relationships between two (or more) mutators, e.g., an inactive Icon has no energy reading (although it still may have energy reserves). Interface invariants, like preconditions, reduce the need for internal testing, as they clearly document restrictions on state and state transitions.

Implementation invariants provide detail sufficient for software maintenance. All relevant design choices should be recorded: choice and expected use of subordinate data structures, legal values of data fields, ownership responsibilities, relationships between fields (e.g., inventory value drives commission percentage), and bookkeeping details. Reasonable examples of implementation invariants include: interface of subobject echoed for utility; linked list structure used to support frequent modification of sorted data; internal (static) registry guarantees unique ID. By identifying implementation structures and design constraints, implementation invariants communicate design intent, and prioritization of requirements.

Class integrity can be more easily maintained when implementation priorities and details are clearly specified. What happens when a class design must be modified? The software developer must reexamine the class and determine the means by which additional or altered functionality can be incorporated. This task is more easily accomplished when the class design and the motives for such design are clearly documented. *Programming by Contract thus supports software maintainability by requiring an explicit record of design assumptions.* When designers must upgrade performance or expand functionality, they can refer back to the original implementation invariants to understand the initial design.

Class invariants provide a data type overview and may be less detailed than other invariants. Conceptually, class invariants represent the intersection of interface and implementation invariants, e.g., describing design decisions that affect form and function. Reasonable examples of class invariants include container stores no duplicate values; object ID is unique; ownership relative to subobjects (owned, shared, or transferable). All operations should be designed to preserve the class invariants. *The closed nature of a class gives the designer complete control over all operations that modify data fields.*

To illustrate the use of Programming by Contract, we walk through the contract specification for a **priority queue** in the next section.

5.3.4 Design Example

A standard queue typically provides enQ(), deQ(), isEmpty() functionality, and possibly the ability to clear(), and test for capacity via isFull(). A resize() function may be implemented internally to be invoked automatically if the queue exceeds capacity (in which case, the need for the query method isFull() is obviated). Items in a standard queue are added in a **FIFO** (first-in, first-out) manner so that as long as items continue to be retrieved from the queue, no item will languish in the queue indefinitely. A common analogy used is a queue of patrons waiting to buy movie tickets: no cuts in line allowed.

A priority queue is much like a queue, providing enQ(), deQ(), isEmpty() functionality as well as possibly clear() and either an automatic (internal) resizing or a test for capacity via isFull(). Externally then, a priority queue looks the same as a regular queue. However, the enqueueing process is not FIFO: items are added to the queue in order of priority. Hence, an incoming item can "cut" ahead of an item resident in the queue. A low-priority item may languish indefinitely or starve in a priority queue. To reduce the possibility of **starvation**, a priority queue may internally **age** items to increase their priority. Aging is an internal mechanism to advance items in the queue based on some combination of their priority and "age," that is, how long the item has been enqueued.

Programming by Contract should convey the restrictions and expected use of a data type. We walk through the five documentation categories of Programming by Contract for the PriorityQ type in Example 5.8. Implementation is in C++ but the concepts apply to other implementations. For each documentation category, we summarize sample specifications in a table. Some descriptions are considered "minimal" because the class design specifies these details, and hence, they should be documented. Other descriptions are denoted as "problematic" because they are inaccurate, inconsistent with the design or of questionable validity. Finally, we note descriptions that are "unnecessary" because they are directly implied by the code, enforced by the compiler, or are of questionable relevance.

The interface invariant specifies restrictions on use for the application programmer. Table 5.5 presents sample interface invariants for the PriorityQ example. What would be reasonable restrictions on the use of a PriorityQ object? Often the copying of containers is restricted to avoid the overhead of copying a large data set or to prevent data redundancy. Although it is more common to suppress copying with registries and hash tables than with queues, we illustrate this approach here with our PriorityQ type.

Details are often language specific. In this C++ example, to suppress copying, the overloaded assignment operator is declared private and not defined. Hence, the assignment "x = y;" where both x and y are PriorityQ objects will generate a compile-time error. Likewise, the copy constructor is declared private, and not defined. Call by value is thus not supported: the application programmer cannot pass PriorityQ objects into functions by value or return them by value. This suppression of copying prevents the

TABLE 5.5   PriorityQ Interface Invariants (Application Programmer)

Minimal: illegal calls (unspecified or unsupported behavior)
- Call by value not supported
- Copying via assignment not supported
- Cannot extract (`deQ()`, `getFirst()`, `getLast()`) if PriorityQ empty

Problematic: inconsistent with default behavior or internal response
- Cannot add beyond capacity (`resize()`)
- Starvation prevented (`age()` may or may not prevent all starvation)
- `deQ()` highest priority item
  - External perception of priority may differ from internal
  - `age()` may interfere with presumed priority

Unnecessary: condition enforced by compiler
- Constructor cannot pass a negative number
- Valid type (`Item&`) passed
- Constructor must provide initial size (default defined by constructor)

troubled aliasing of shallow copying, with its data corruption potential, and removes the need to provide code to support deep copying. (Recall the C++ memory management discussion from Chapter 4.)

Interface invariants do not need to document restrictions enforced by the compiler. For example, in statically typed languages, there is no need to specify the type of any parameter passed. If types do not match, the compiler will catch the error; compile-time errors are resolved well before software deployment. Any comments on use or effect must be consistent with design. Remember to consider this documentation as a contract. Hence, it is unwise to describe restrictions or error conditions that may not occur, e.g., if PriorityQ object is of fixed capacity, starvation is always avoided.

The implementation invariant documents the perspective of the class designer, providing detail on how the PriorityQ is implemented, as shown in Table 5.6. The use of a heap data structure to support efficient enqueueing and dequeueing in a PriorityQ is common. A heap data structure is essentially a short, fat binary tree, where all levels are complete except possibly the lowest level where items are stored in leftmost order. Hence, we can implement a heap data structure of n elements with an array indexed from 1 to n, where node A[i] has parent A[i/2], left child A[2*i], and right child A[2*i + 1]. For further detail, see a good data structures text.

The internal effects of using a heap data structure should be documented. Why was the heap data structure chosen to implement a priority queue? Immediate answers include (1) efficient access via an array, (2) reduced memory overhead, (3) support for ordering (the relative priority

TABLE 5.6   PriorityQ Implementation Invariants (Class Designer)

Minimal: implied by interface, internal data structures, private utility functions
- Dynamically allocated array used to implement PriorityQ
  - Underlying heap data structure (with heapify() etc). Why?
    - Efficient access and resizing
    - Ordered collection, with efficient reordering
- Copying via assignment not supported
- Call by value not supported
- No default behavior for accessors
- Nop if clear () called on empty PriorityQ
- age () strives to avoid starvation
  - Age factor associated with data value for internal priority
  - Outline aging algorithm: linear or proportional scaling?
- resize () will double internal array when capacity reached

Problematic: of questionable validity or relevance
- Ordered Array (NO!: min or maxheap supports item extraction via root index)
- No starvation (may be difficult to guarantee)

Unnecessary: implied by function prototype
- isEmpty () non-destructive (implied by const)
- enQ () and deQ () trigger reordering (implicit in heap functionality)

of queue items), even with additions and deletions, and (4) ease of resizing. Aging priority queue items is also relatively straightforward to implement: one need only to traverse the underlying array structure. If this PriorityQ class must be modified in the future, say to change the notion of priority, these implementation details should be known so that modification may be as easy as possible.

For software maintenance, it is advisable to identify internal data structure(s) and comment on effect of such choice. Implementation invariants do just that. Implementation invariants also outline any internal functions or algorithms that impact structure. In the priority queue example, the heap order property of the underlying array is not undermined if our aging mechanism simply increments an age factor that is then added to the data value to derive a composite priority value. In contrast, if aging proportionately weights items so there is a nonlinear adjustment, the heap may become disordered, requiring an internal reordering, an additional overhead.

Preconditions remind the application programmer of the prerequisites of a legal call. To avoid the overhead of defensive programming, preconditions must specify any required state(s) before function entry. For example, containers must be non-empty before any data is extracted and much have sufficient capacity for data insertion (or provide internal resizing capabilities). See Table 5.7 for descriptions of preconditions for our PriorityQ example. One need not specify the data types of permissible values that are enqueued: function prototypes provide these details.

Postconditions must document state changes so that state may be tracked externally if needed. The connection between postconditions and function invocation may not be obvious. The explanation is one of cause and effect. To ensure that the application programmer satisfies any preconditions that involve object state, the application programmer must be able to query state. For the application programmer to know when it is necessary to query state, the application programmer must know when an object has the potential to change state.

The application programmer can discern information about external data and resources. If a file must be opened before a call, the application programmer can do so, or determine that it cannot be done. State information about an object, however, is internal. State changes are also internal and are not immediately discernible.

Table 5.8 describes postconditions for our PriorityQ example. Whenever an item is added to the queue, the queue can no longer be empty.

TABLE 5.7   PriorityQ Preconditions

Minimal: implied by above invariants
- Extract (deQ(), getFirst(), getLast()) only from non-empty PriorityQ

Problematic: of questionable validity
- isStored() cannot be called with empty PriorityQ

Unnecessary: implied by function prototype
- enQ() has valid item

TABLE 5.8   PriorityQ Postconditions

Minimal: describes state or potential for state change
- PriorityQ may be empty after deQ()
- PriorityQ empty after clear()
- PriorityQ non-empty after enQ()

Problematic: of questionable validity or relevance
- DEAFULT_CAPACITY is public

Unnecessary: describes what functions does
- PriorityQ object exists after constructor fires
- PriorityQ unchanged by getFirst(), getLast() (const functions)
- One fewer item in PriorityQ after deQ()

Whenever an item is removed from the queue, the queue may be empty. It is unnecessary to describe what functions do. Programmers should be aware of the effect of class methods. After a constructor fires, an object has been instantiated and placed in an initial state. After a mutator executes, an object has likely been updated and so forth.

Class invariants provide an overview of the type defined, its use, and expectations. Table 5.9 describes the characteristics of our priority queue, along with design details that affect use, such as the avoidance of starvation and overflow. Class invariants often appear as a common subset of interface and implementation invariants. It is not surprising then that, for the PriorityQ, the class invariant notes the suppression of copying via both assignment and call by value. Again, this documentation technique is akin to specifying a contract. Do not suggest excessive or application-specific restrictions, such as no duplicate values contained in the queue, when such restrictions are not enforced.

To emphasize the demarcation between form and use, an effective design must document its structure and intended use, both for the application programmer and for the class designer. Documentation standards attempt to provide the means to do so. More than an arbitrary convention,

TABLE 5.9   PriorityQ Class Invariant

Minimal: implied by above invariants
- Container stores data
  - Highest priority item dequeued first
  - Priority is combination of age and value
  - Items aged (internally) to avoid starvation
- Container capacity
  - Default capacity
  - Size may be specified upon instantiation
  - Internal resizing averts capacity overflow
- Call by value not supported
- Copying via assignment not supported
- Extract (deQ(), getFirst(), getLast()) only from non-empty PriorityQ

Problematic: of questionable validity
- No starvation
- PriorityQ objects do not contain duplicate values
  - Perspective: aging changes composite value
  - Application dependent

Unnecessary: implied by type definition
- Starvation possible

Programming by Contract, with its emphasis on shared responsibility, effectively reflects software design. It capitalizes on the encapsulated design of objects, with separation of public and private interfaces, and thus clearly details the dual perspectives of application programmer and class designer.

5.3.5   Contractual Expectations

A contract emphasizes responsibilities from both internal and external perspectives. Internal responsibilities lie with the class designer. At minimum, control of an object's state should be internalized. The standard alternative to a contractual relationship is defensive programming. No assumptions are made about correct input or fulfillment of preconditions in defensive programming. Hence, this approach requires extensive error checking. Class methods must check arguments and object state. This overhead is acceptable for infrequently invoked functions but becomes expensive for repetitive calls.

To determine the bounds of the contract, the class designer must estimate consequences of contract violation. Although testing may be reduced with a contract, and its assumption of correct use, the impact of error must still be assessed. What would be the impact of data corruption and memory leakage? Is failure acceptable? What failures are acceptable? How often is error expected? The cost of failure cannot be too large.

In evaluating the costs and impact of software design, consider current and future applications. Is high performance desired? Confirm that preconditions are reasonable and verifiable. Move beyond the standard tradeoff of safety versus efficiency; consider amortized overhead, both for software development and for use. Anticipate expectations. How is the class to be used?

Contractual obligations, as enumerated by Programming by Contract, are important when making design decisions. In Chapters 6 and 8, we will examine design options. *When design alternatives exists, utility, and preference are more easily identified if assumptions as to use and maintenance are clearly documented.*

5.4 OO DESIGN PRINCIPLES

Our discussion on class form, functionality, and documentation covered basic design principles. Additional comments may be made with respect to OOD. Yet, such comments can be distilled down to the software engineering emphasis on low coupling and high cohesion. Several OO principles relative to class design embody these two principles. The two principles noted below summarize concepts covered in this chapter.

Single Responsibility Principle (SRP)
Every object should have a single, encapsulated responsibility.
Thus, there can be only one reason to modify a class.

Responsibility Driven Design (RDD)
Identify all object responsibilities (functionality) and required information.

Single responsibility emphasizes the notion of cohesion and promotes software maintenance. By focusing class functionality on a primary goal, the class designer precisely targets use, and potential reuse. Class integrity is easier to preserve. Our example of the priority queue exemplifies this principle: the queue stores items in order of importance; the queue does not do anything else. When conditions for preservation of state (implementation invariant) are consistent with expectations of use (interface invariant), the single responsibility principle holds.

Responsibility-driven design works in tandem with Programming by Contract to specify design and all contractual expectations as to use. The implementation invariant specifies the design of the object, with a focus on functionality and internal responsibility for state. The interface invariant specifies the public functionality and any client responsibility for consistent use. Clear and cohesive interfaces reinforce class design. Thus, a priority queue provides the public functionality to store, retrieve, and check for data. Internally, the priority queue implements the functions to resize the container when needed and to periodically age the stored data items so as to prevent starvation.

5.5 SUMMARY

In this chapter, we used the class construct to illustrate a systematic design of software. Following principles of OOD, we emphasized design that controlled internal elements as separated from the form of an external interface. Standard class methods were differentiated along the lines of functionality (constructor, destructor, accessor, mutator, private utility, and core public utility). When relevant, we discussed language differences between C++ and C#/Java.

Programming by Contract was concisely but thoroughly summarized as an effective means of documenting design. The clear specification of code expectations across five categories (preconditions, postconditions, interface invariant, implementation, invariant, class invariant) streamlines the process of uncovering and documenting design assumptions. Documentation then yields a contract between the class designer and those who use the class. We closed the chapter by noting two design principles that are sustained by the class construct and Programming by Contract. Concepts covered here promote the development of usable and reusable software.

DESIGN INSIGHTS

SOFTWARE

Compilers do NOT enforce design

MODELS

Dual Perspective
External utility: client
Internal implementation: class designer
Advanced by ADT and class construct
Supported by notion of contract
Programming by Contract
Alternative to defensive programming
Contractual design
Specifies correct usage and guaranteed response
Reduces need for extensive testing

SOFTWARE DESIGN

Class design encapsulates and protects state
Minimizes exposure of internal details
Removes dependencies on application programmer
Client cannot place object in an invalid state
Class functionality
Constructors: initialize objects
Public initialize() method undermines encapsulation
Accessors provide controlled view
Should not change state
Mutators control state change(s)
Change request may be rejected

      Private utility functions
          Provide internal functional decomposition
          Promote code reuse
          Reduce code complexity

DOCUMENTATION

Deliberate design must identify all assumptions
Invariants
      Reduce need for testing
      Promote software maintainability

CONCEPTUAL QUESTIONS

1. What is the notion of internal control?

2. Describe the major components of a standard class design.

3. What are the differences in C++ class design versus C# class design?

4. Why is a constructor needed?

5. What are the benefits of private utility functions?

6. Why should a class designer minimize the provision of set and get routines?

7. When are destructors needed?

8. What are the major differences between defensive programming and contractual design? What are the benefits and drawbacks of each approach?

9. Describe the major components of Programming by Contract.

10. How does Programming by Contract support the dual perspective?

III

Software Design

CHAPTER 6

Structural Design

Building on the previous chapter, we examine how class designs may be used together. We cover the basic relationships modeled in **Object-Oriented Design** (OOD): **has-a**, **holds-a**, and **is-a**. These relationships are also known as **composition**, **containment**, and **inheritance**, respectively. Each type of relationship is examined in detail, with examples and descriptions of intended use. The relevance, costs, and benefits of each design are evaluated. A comparative evaluation of these relationships reinforces the underlying impetus for each design.

Understanding OOD is important for constructing reliable, large-scale systems. Moreover, it is now essential for understanding legacy systems and **design patterns**. Analysis of structural relationships and evaluation of their characteristics yields insights applicable to software design in general. Relationships define the connection between structure and effect. Their characteristics support the processes of evaluating form, intent, and maintenance.

The software engineering goals of **low coupling** and **high cohesion** supersede any preference for a particular type of design. Likewise, the conscious tracking of **association**, **ownership**, and **cardinality** transcend design perspectives. Hence, this chapter closes by placing well-known and accepted OOD principles into context.

CHAPTER OBJECTIVES
- Define basic relationships in OOD
- Motivate appropriate use of relationships
- Illustrate composition, containment, and inheritance

- Examine the relevance of association, ownership, and cardinality in design
- Evaluate the imperative of code reuse
- Identify relevant OOD principles

6.1 RELATIONSHIPS

We begin by examining the structure of interdependent types. Using relationships found in object-oriented programming, we describe criteria relevant to software design and maintenance, characteristics such as association, cardinality, and ownership. An association between two objects may be temporary, stable, or for the lifetime of the primary object. Cardinality may vary, sustaining a one-to-one or a one-to-many relationship. Ownership implies that the primary object has a responsibility for the secondary object, requiring allocation, deallocation, replacement, or transfer of responsibility.

We consider basic structural relationships: has-a (composition), holds-a (containment), and is-a (inheritance). Traditionally, OOP texts have discussed **aggregation**, which defines a structure wherein the aggregate object contains many subobjects of the same type. We find it more useful to distinguish between relationships where there is a type dependency, as in has-a, and where there is not, as in holds-a. *Aggregation merely addresses form and less so intent and effect.* For example, both a container and a building toy (such as a Lego set) may be described as aggregates. As we shall see, however, a container illustrates a holds-a relationship. In contrast, a building toy is strongly dependent on its components and thus illuminates a has-a relationship. In the context of has-a and holds-a, we can readily evaluate essential characteristics such as ownership and association.

The simplest relationship is none: two types do not interact. Next in simplicity is the uses-a relationship, that is one type uses, typically by call by value or call by reference, another type in a transient fashion. This perspective, with its focus on interface, is that of the application programmer. The remaining relationships represent associations that are more enduring and that may represent some type dependency. We examine these relationships in detail.

6.1.1 Composition

To model composition, we use an intuitive example: a plane has-a engine. Type dependency clearly exists in the has-a relationship: a plane is not well defined without an engine, and in fact is inoperable. In the has-a relation, the subObject affects the state of the composing object because it provides functionality: the state of the engine affects the state of the plane. If an engine is in a failed state then the functionality of the plane is compromised.

In composition, the association between the composing object and the subobject is stable. Lifetimes are often directly correlated; that is, the subobject exists for the lifetime of the object. The cardinality of a sub-object is usually fixed within the lifetime of the object. For example, if a plane model is designed with two engines then it must have two engines. Likewise, if the plane design dictates four engines, as in Figure 6.1, then the plane must have four engines.

As a data member of the class, the subobject would typically be instan-tiated upon object construction. However, it is possible to postpone the construction of a subobject until use, employing the same logic as just-in-time manufacturing. In this case, the object becomes responsible for subobject allocation (and possibly, deallocation) and must determine the legality of copying and assignment. Review Example 6.1, keeping in mind that internally allocated heap memory requires careful design in C++ (as shown in detail in Chapters 4 and 5).

Example 6.1: Postponed Instantiation of SubObject: C++ Code

```cpp
class justInTime
{       // need appropriate memory management details
        // Suppress or define: copy constructor and operator=
        bigData*     generator;
        ...

    public:
        justInTime() {   generator = 0;   }
        ...

        void process()
        {
            if (!generator)         generator = new bigData;
            generator.process();
        }
    ...
};
```

FIGURE 6.1   UML diagram for plane has-a (4) engines.

In a typical has-a relation, the subobject, like a plane engine, is owned by the object and is not usually shareable or transferable. Although it may be replaceable, replacement should be considered carefully and, if supported, controlled via qualifying conditions and testing.

6.1.2 Containment

Standard containers model the holds-a relationship quite easily as there is no type dependency on the subobjects. A stack provides the same utility no matter what type of data it holds or how much data it holds. A stack is well defined when empty, full, or in-between. The operations of push(), pop(), clear(), etc. function in the same manner regardless of the type of data processed. The data held provide no direct (public interface) functionality for the container.

To model containment, we use another intuitive example, sketched in Example 6.2: a student holds-a calculator. Initially, this relationship may not appear to be that of a standard container like a stack, queue, dictionary, or hash table. However, if a student is well defined without a calculator then a student may have zero calculators and still function as a student. A student is not dependent on a calculator if calculators do not drive student functionality, or if another tool, such as a cell phone, can replace a calculator. *When an internal data structure provides some functionality but could easily be replaced without compromising functionality, a holds-a relation may suffice.*

Example 6.2: Student Holds-a Calculator: C++ Code

```
class Student            // simple, fixed calculator
{        Calculator   c;    // automatically instantiated
      ...
     public:
      ...
       Student() {}
       void replace(Calculator     value)
       {    c = value;      // bitwise copy: value transfer     }
};

// ownership of subobject(s) implies memory management
```

```cpp
// => must provide destructor
// => support or suppress overloaded assignment operator
class StudentOwner          // replaceable calculator
{       Calculator* c;      // handle only, no object yet
        ...
    public:
        ...
        // assumption constructor: ownership of transfer assumed
        StudentOwner(Calculator*&  transfer)
        {   c = transfer;
            transfer = 0;
        }
        // again ownership transferred in
        bool replace(Calculator*&  bkup)
        {   Calculator* temp = c;
            c = bkup;
            delete temp;
            bkup = 0;
        }
};

class PrecisionStudent       // zero, one or more calculators
{       Calculator* c;
        int         numCalc;
    public:
        ...
        PrecisionStudent(unsigned   quantity)
        {   numCalc = quantity;
            c = new Calculator[numCalc];
            ...
            // initialization
        }
};
```

In contrast to the has-a relation, the holds-a relation does not imply ownership. The student may or may not own a calculator, may share, borrow, or lend a calculator. The student is not typically responsible for the creation or destruction of calculator(s) because the perspective is that any ownership responsibility is only temporary. If the student must dispose of a calculator, the response differs according to ownership details. If the calculator is shared, the reference count would be decremented. If the student is the sole owner and the calculator is dynamically allocated, say upon demand, then the calculator should be "destroyed" (reference zeroed out or destructor invoked). Ownership could also be transferred out to another student or a reclamation site.

A container may hold subobjects, copies of subobjects, or references to subobjects. The number of subobjects may vary across the lifetime of a container. Likewise, a student may hold varying numbers of calculators. In fact, considering the different types of calculators available (simple, graphing, pocket), the actual subtype of calculators held may vary over the lifetime of the student. Only a temporary association exists between the object and the subobject. The student need not hold the same calculator for a lifetime. The subobjects may be passed in and out, may be shareable, or may be absent.

Independent of the implementation language, *a containment relationship provides much flexibility because of its variability in cardinality, ownership, and association.* However, design differences do exist because of language differences. Recall the memory management discussions in Chapters 4 and 5. In C++, memory management must be addressed for any object with internally allocated heap memory. The class must track ownership so that all heap-allocated memory is deallocated before objects owning the heap-allocated memory go out of scope. In all languages, aliases should be tracked so that dead objects may be reclaimed and also so that data is not corrupted.

Copying in containers is an essential design decision. What does the container hold? References? Copies of data? Original data? Is the container responsible for copying? What are the effects of supporting or suppressing copying? Copying becomes interesting whenever data is referenced indirectly, that is, via a reference or a pointer. What does one copy? The address holder (reference or pointer) or the actual data values? Recall the difference between shallow and deep copying. Appendix B and Chapter 4 cover memory management concepts in detail.

In both C# and C++, *a decision must be made about copying.* If no decision is made in C++ (the means to copy is neither defined nor suppressed), the compiler generates, by default, a copy constructor and an overloaded assignment operator that will yield shallow copies, unintended aliasing, and possibly data corruption. If no decision is made in C#, no copy constructor will be provided.

6.1.3 Class Design: Has-a or Holds-a?

When modeling type interaction, how does one decide whether to design for composition (has-a) or containment (holds-a)? First, consider type dependency. If the state of the subobject affects the object then type dependency is clear. If the object must use some functionality provided by the subobject then the object is dependent on the subobject. In both cases, one should model composition (has-a). Dependency suggests that the composing object is of little value without the subobject.

To evaluate design differences, we return to our plane/engine and student/calculator examples. Since an engine provides core functionality, the relationship modeled must be has-a. However, a calculator may or may not be perceived as providing essential functionality. If a liberal arts student is not dependent on a calculator for core functionality and can exist without a calculator, a holds-a relationship is appropriate. In contrast, if an engineering student must use a calculator, a has-a relationship is implied.

In addition to type dependency and functionality, consider cardinality. How many subobjects exist? Can the number be zero? Is the number of subobjects determined upon construction? Is the number of subobjects fixed across the object's lifetime? Can the number of subobjects vary directly through public add or delete methods or indirectly via state changes for the object? The more stable the structure, the more likely that a has-a relationship should be modeled. If a subobject goes in and out of use, then evaluate association. A subobject may be considered less essential if it can be missing. If the association between object and subobject(s) is transitory, it is likely that a holds-a relationship should be modeled.

Whether an object contains one or more subobjects, consider ownership. Who owns the subobject(s)? Is ownership permanent? Ownership implies responsibility, even with implicit deallocation, and suggests a has-a (composition) relationship. Yet, the ability to transfer ownership of a subobject, either assuming or releasing ownership, does not solely imply either has-a or holds-a. One must carefully examine conditions under which such transfers occur. Frequent and unconditional transfers suggest a weak dependency on the subobject and hence a stronger affinity to a holds-a relationship. If transfers occur to update state or for replacement value, then a has-a relationship may be warranted.

6.2 INHERITANCE

Inheritance (is-a) is a key OO principle, providing immediate **code reuse** and establishing a type relationship between the **parent** (or **base**) class and the **child** (or **derived**) class. Note the inconsistent terminology. When C++ came to the forefront of the software community in the late 1980s, inheritance design guidelines used the term "base" to indicate the base or foundation of an inheritance hierarchy. The word "derived" referred to any class that inherited from another class, whether the derived class was an immediate descendant or transitive progeny (grandchild, etc.). Ten years later, when Java emerged as a popular alternative to C++, inheritance design guidelines used the term "parent" to indicate the immediate ancestor in an inheritance relation and the term "child" for the class that inherited directly from a parent class.

Many designers, especially those well versed in C++, prefer the terms base and derived, possibly because of familiarity but also because the term "derived" is inclusive of all descendants, whether the inheritance relation is immediate or transitive. We use both sets of terms but prefer to use parent and child when considering only a pair of classes and base and derived when examining a deep class hierarchy.

Syntactically, a child class declares itself to be an extension of the parent class. Clearly, the parent class must have already been defined. Child class(es) inherit ALL data members and member functions from a parent class but cannot access any parent data or functionality that is declared private. Examples 6.3 and 6.4 provide sample C++ and C# code, respectively, that manipulates objects declared from a parent class and two different child classes. Inheritance defines a relationship between parent and child (and, transitively, between parent and grandchild). Sibling relationships are not defined or supported.

Example 6.3: Inheritance in C++=> Child Stands in for Parent

```
Parent        pObj;
Child1        c1Obj;
Child2        c2Obj;

pObj.parentFn();                // cannot invoke pObj.childFn()

// child objects can invoke inherited public functionality
c1Obj.parentFn();               c2Obj.parentFn();
c1Obj.childFn();                c2Obj.childFn();

// function invocation restricted to parent interface
pObj = c1Obj;         // sliced: child additions not accessible
pObj.parentFn();      // access only parent functionality

// Substitutability: an instance of a derived class
//            can stand in for an instance of a base class
// Not a symmetric relation: parent cannot stand in for child
Parent*       pPtr;
...
// pPtr: handle of type Parent =>
//   Parent functionality accessible; child functionality not
pPtr = new Parent;   pPtr->parentFn();      delete pPtr;
pPtr = new Child1;   pPtr->parentFn();      delete pPtr;
pPtr = new Child2;   pPtr->parentFn();      delete pPtr;

// COMPILATION ERRORS: NO SIBLING RELATIONSHIP
c2Obj = c1Obj;                 c1Obj = c2Obj;
```

Example 6.4: Inheritance in C#=> Child Stands in for Parent

```
Parent          pObj;
// Substitutability:
//    parent object (reference) can hold address of child object
// Not symmetric: child reference cannot hold parent address
// pObj: handle of type Parent =>
//    Parent functionality accessible; child functionality not
pObj = new Parent();            pObj.parentFn();
pObj = new Child1();            pObj.parentFn();
pObj = new Child2();            pObj.parentFn();
```

As shown in Examples 6.3 and 6.4, the application programmer can invoke public parent functionality through an instance of the child class. A child class variable may be assigned to a parent class variable, but not vice versa. Why? Since a child inherits from a parent, the child can provide what the parent provides. Thus, a child object can be used in place of a parent object. Since a child class may define additional functionality (and/ or data) that is not present in the parent class, the parent cannot stand in for a child because the parent would not be able to provide this additional capability. When an application programmer manipulates a variable of a specific type, any function defined in that type's public interface should be callable. Thus, child class functions (that expand the inherited parent interface) cannot be invoked through a parent class variable.

Inheritance introduces an additional level of accessibility: **protected** interfaces. Protected data and functionality are essentially closed (private) to external entities but open (public) to descendants in a class hierarchy. There are no sibling relationships in class hierarchies. An object may access only its own or its ancestors' data and functionality. It cannot access any data or functionality from a sibling class unless those data and functionality are public.

A child class has access to all public data and functionality of the parent (base) class as well as all protected data and functionality of the parent. When manipulating a parent class object, the application programmer has access to all public data and functionality of the parent class. When manipulating a child class object, the application programmer has access to all public data and functionality of the parent as well as all public data and functionality of the child.

Purity of the inheritance relation is not guaranteed. A child class can close off access to inherited functionality for both its descendants and/ or the application programmer. C++ supports direct suppression: derived classes may **override** an inherited public or protected method with a private method thus preventing invocation of the parent function through a child object. C# and Java do not permit a child class to reduce an inherited interface: a compiler error stops a child class from restricting access to an inherited method by redefining an inherited public method as protected or private (or an inherited protected method as private). *But this restriction has only syntactical impact.* Whether or not access can be restricted, a child may redefine, override, or NOP inherited functionality. Thus, in C# or Java, if a child class does not wish to support an inherited function, it can simply redefine it and provide a null or meaningless implementation. This design option is also possible in C++ (see Examples 6.5 and 6.6).

Example 6.5: C++ Direct Suppression of Inherited Functionality

```
class Child: public Parent
{ …  // fields private by default
        void parentFn() { // now private => suppressed }
    public:
            …
};
…
Parent          pObj;
Child           cObj;
pObj.parentFn();
cObj.parentFn();       // compilation error: not accessible
```

Example 6.6: C# Designed NOP of Inherited Functionality

```
public class Child: Parent
{ …
    public void parentFn() {// NOP}
            …
}
// application code
Parent          pObj = new Parent();
Child           cObj = new Child();
pObj.parentFn();       // parent functionality
cObj.parentFn();       // compiles & runs & does nothing
```

6.2.1 Automate Subtype Checking

When is an inheritance design valuable? When is it not? Unfortunately, these questions are often not asked. Yet, *software designers should know when to use inheritance, and when not, especially since inheritance can be simulated with composition.* To illustrate an effective inheritance design, we revisit the `Icon` example from the previous chapter, where the design goal was to represent `Icons` and their movement in a computer game. We expand the `Icon` type definition to include the data and functionality needed to support movement. `Icons` can spin, slide, or hop, with the restriction that any particular icon is capable of only one type of movement. A spinner cannot hop, a hopper cannot slide, etc. Furthermore, the type of movement associated with an `Icon` does not change. Thus, a slider cannot spin, not now, not ever. We incorporate into our design the ability to track what "type" of movement an `Icon` object exhibits. Example 6.7 shows the monolithic class design accommodating these features.

Example 6.7: C++ Monolithic Class for Icon Movement

```cpp
class Icon
{     float     speed, glow, energy;
      int       x, y;
      int       subtype;        // spinner, slider or hopper

      bool      clockwise;      // need for spinner
      bool      expand;         // need for spinner

      bool      vertical;       // need for slider
      int       distance;       // need for slider

      bool      visible;        // need for hopper
      int       xcoord, ycoord;       // need for hopper

      void spin();
      void slide();
      void hop();
public:
      // constructor must set subtype: client must pass value
      Icon(unsigned value)
      {      ...
          subtype = value;      // use enum for readability
          // and then use conditional to set associated fields
      }
      // tedious subtype checking: subtype drives movement
      void move()
      {       if (subtype == 1)               spin();
              else if (subtype == 2)          slide();
              else                            hop();
      }
      // tedious subtype checking: subtype drives flair details
      void flair()
```

```
{           if (subtype == 1)                ...        // spinner
            else if (subtype == 2)           ...        // slider
            else                             ...        // hopper
}
    ...
};
```

What are the limitations of this monolithic design? One huge class carries all data and (private) functionality needed for the specialized movements. Each `Icon` object should behave consistently, according to its "type" of movement. That is, spinners do not hop, hoppers do not slide, sliders do not spin, etc. Consequently, the class designer must track movement "subtype." Movement determines power consumption and the value of energy reserves and thus the state of an `Icon` object. The constructor must set the "subtype" and then in every method impacted by movement, there must be a "subtype" check. This tedious, error prone approach is shown in the `Icon::move()` method.

This `Icon` design is neither cohesive nor extensible. If a fourth type of movement were to be later incorporated, say a zigZagger, the `Icon` class must be modified to add the data and functionality needed to support zigzagging. All methods that require special movement, such as `move()` and `flair()`, must be modified to include an extra test for the `zigZagger` subtype. Example 6.8 shows this tedious, error-prone means of expanding a type system without inheritance.

Example 6.8: Tedious Type Expansion without Inheritance

```
// ALL methods in Icon that check subtype must be altered
// ERROR PRONE software maintenance
void Icon::move()      // subtype drives movement
{           if (subtype == 1)              spin();
            else if (subtype == 2)         slide();
            else if (subtype == 3)         hop();
            else                           zigzag();
}
//tedious manner of checking subtype
//    subtype drives details of function flair
void Icon::flair()
{           if (subtype == 1)              ...        // spinner
            else if (subtype == 2)         ...        // slider
            else if (subtype == 3)         ...        // hopper
            else                           ...        // zigZagger
}
    ...
```

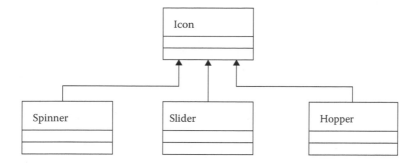

FIGURE 6.2 UML diagram for inheritance.

Since each specialized type of movement demands its own data and functionality, this "subtype" must be tracked. It is onerous and error-prone to do so "manually," that is, via a switch statement. An inheritance design provides an attractive alternative, as illustrated in Figure 6.2. Example 6.9 provides the corresponding code. Cohesion and readability are improved by the isolation of specialized movement in child classes.

Example 6.9: C++ Icon Class Hierarchy

```cpp
class Icon
{ protected:
     float          speed, glow, energy;
     int            x, y;
   public:
     // constructor sets base values
     Icon(…)        {…}
     void move()    {…}
     void flair()   {…}
     …
};

class Spinner: public Icon
{ protected:
     bool           clockwise, expand;
     void spin();
   public:
     // constructor may invoke parent constructor
     Spinner(…):Icon(…)     {…}
     void move()            {spin();…}
     void flair()           {…}
     …
};

class Slider: public Icon
{ protected:
```

```
     bool             vertical;
     int              distance;
     void slide();
  public:
     // constructor may invoke parent constructor
     Slider(…):Icon(…)        {…}
     void move()              {slide();…}
     void flair()             {…}
     …
};

class Hopper: public Icon
{ protected:
     bool             visible;
     int              xcoord, ycoord;
     void hop();
  public:
     Hopper(…):Icon(…)        {…}
     void move()              {hop();…}
     void flair()             {…}
     …
};
```

The base Icon class models the commonality of movement: location, speed, power consumption, and energy reserves. Derived classes specialize movement: clockwise or counterclockwise spinning; vertical or horizontal sliding; and, hopping. What happens if a zigZagger subtype is needed? Add another child class. In Figure 6.2, a fourth child class could derive from the parent class without affecting any of the other, defined classes. The Icon class is not affected. **Type extension** should not impact the parent class.

Icon data members are declared protected so that derived classes may access such data. Parent classes may also provide protected utility methods. Designing an inheritance relation, and determining accessibility (protected or private), may be tricky. Private accessibility restricts access to the immediate class and thus ensures design consistency. Protected accessibility opens access only to descendants, but the number (and time of development) of descendants is not constrained.

In the Icon inheritance hierarchy, specialized data and functionality associated with each type of Icon movement is incorporated into the child classes. What happened to the subtype field that was defined in the monolithic Icon class of Example 6.7? It is no longer needed because subtype is no longer "manually" tracked. The derived class name denotes the subtype. When a game designer wants a Hopper, a Hopper object is instantiated. When a game designer wants a Spinner, a Spinner object is instantiated, etc. We may now easily add a zigZagger subtype simply by defining another derived class. Inheritance often is preferred because it supports this extensibility. zigZagger is added without impacting the base Icon class, as defined in Example 6.9, or any of the derived (sibling) classes.

Inheritance is not always the best design approach. Design extensions may undermine previous design decisions. We revisit this example in Chapter 8 to evaluate the long-term viability of design decisions.

6.2.2 Inheritance Design

From a design perspective, an inheritance relation may be seen as **inheritance of interface** or **inheritance of implementation**. We consider each approach independently. Design complexity increases when the two motives are mixed. There is no software mechanism to enforce separation of these two design perspectives. Some languages attempt to steer design toward inheritance of interface. Modeled in part on Smalltalk, both Java and C# provide an "object" class that serves as an implicit base class for all defined classes. That is, even if a standalone class is defined, it will inherit automatically from the Object class. Thus, all types have an is-a relationship with the Object class. Although this language construct does not yield any better OO designs in general, it does force conformance to an implicit, common interface.

Inheritance of interface is considered type extension and thus the "pure" form of inheritance. The central concept is that the child operates as the same type as the parent. The child can stand in for the parent, that is, a child object can serve as a substitute for a parent object (**substitutability**) because it supports the same interface as the parent. An implicit design assumption of type extension is that the child may extend but should not constrain the functionality provided by the parent. The child class retains all properties of parent class but may add attributes and/or methods only if such **extension** does not interfere with the notion of the parent type. Hence, the child class may provide a larger set of functionality. In short, the parent type is not compromised by the definition of the child class.

An intuitive example of type extension is a categorization of athletes. A biAthlete is-a runner (a runner who also bikes). A triAthlete is-a biAthlete (a bi-athlete who also swims). This pure form of inheritance is said to unambiguously support the is-a relationship because the child type is a pure extension of the parent type: the child type retains, supports, and possibly extends parent interface. Figure 6.3 displays this example of expanded functionality in child classes.

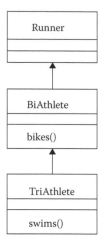

FIGURE 6.3 Type extension.

Inheritance of interface rests on an external perspective: how are types used and what functionality do they provide? In contrast, inheritance of implementation rests upon an internal perspective: develop a type by incorporating existing code. Inheritance of implementation is also known as code reuse and is considered an expedient, practical approach to software design even though it can compromise type consistency.

Inheritance of implementation is often described as an impure form of inheritance since it may not completely support the is-a relationship. The child class inherits all data and functionality from the parent class but suppresses all or part of the parent interface. Thus, the child cannot stand in as a substitute for the parent. Inheritance of implementation is often called **contraction** because the child class represents a more restricted form of the parent class. The child class may redefine or limit properties of parent class. To provide functional variety in a class hierarchy, a child class overrides or redefines behavior inherited from a parent.

Opinion may be divided as to the form of inheritance used in a particular design. Compare the standard queue to the priority queue. Both queue types typically provide enQ(), deQ(), isEmpty() functionality and, possibly, the ability to clear(), and either an automatic (internal) resizing or a test for capacity via isFull(). Externally, a priority queue looks the same as a regular queue. Internal perspective differs. Items in a standard queue are added in a FIFO (first-in, first-out) manner while items in a priority queue are enqueued by a measure of value (priority). Moreover, internal aging mechanisms can modify an item's relative priority placement in a priority queue.

Since the queue and the priority queue types provide the same interface, making substitutability possible, many argue that a priority queue is-a queue. Specifically, a priority queue is a specialized version of a queue. One can use a priority queue in place of a standard queue, especially if ordering is not important and starvation is unlikely. A counterargument is that the two different containers may yield different effects. In an active, fluid environment of adding and removing items from a container, a queue can guarantee no starvation but a priority queue cannot. In handling a stream of requests, a queue can guarantee service in order of request but a priority queue cannot. One may need to guarantee no starvation. One may desire FIFO ordering. Thus, the effects of using the two different types may drive the choice of data structure. Hence, one cannot unequivocally state that the two types are interchangeable.

Software design and maintenance responsibilities are most confusing when a class uses a mix of inheritance of interface (type extension) and inheritance of implementation (code reuse). With mixed motives, it becomes critical that goals, priorities, and assumptions be documented in the implementation and class invariants.

Inheritance gives software no more computational power than any other structural relation. However, the inheritance construct, as supported by object-oriented programming languages, enables the software designer to easily specify type relationships. One can reuse code without having to handle many tedious and laborious syntactical details. Frequently, software development time is reduced and software maintenance is improved when using inheritance. Yet, many professionals prefer composition over inheritance. Why? We contrast the cost and benefits of inheritance versus those of composition in the next section.

6.3 CODE REUSE

How is class design affected when one must reuse code? Assume we have been given a simple class minMax that has already defined, as shown in Example 6.10. This class accepts incoming streams of numeric data, tracking the minimum and maximum values. Many resource management and inventory problems need to track minimum and maximum values: a resource allocator may track the upper and lower bounds of memory requests; inventory control may wish to note the values of the most and least expensive items; a meter may record the maximum and minimum readings; etc. The minMax type encapsulates this functionality.

Example 6.10: Simple Data Class: C++ Code

```
class minMax
{ ...
          unsigned min, max;
     public:
          minMax() {max= 0;        min = MAX_INT;}

          void rec(unsigned x)
          {        if (x > max)    max = x;
                   if (x < min)    min = x;
          }
          unsigned getMin()        {return min;}
          unsigned getMax()        {return max;}
};
```

After the successful design, implementation, testing, and deployment of the minMax class, the need for a minMaxMean class arises. One could design this second class from scratch or reuse the minMax class. When functionality is already in place, with a known interface, enthusiasm for clean-slate design evaporates. The existing class can be incorporated into a new design using either an inheritance or a composition relationship. *Selection of the most appropriate relationship must identify implicit trade-offs*, as well as design effects.

Inheritance offers immediate reuse, support of the is-a relationship, and access to protected data and functionality. Composition also offers immediate reuse, but without access to protected data and functionality, and does not support the is-a relationship. Since the minMax class does not have a protected interface, or any protected data, will employing inheritance or composition to reuse minMax make much difference? Not structurally. Both the minMaxMeanInherit class and the minMax MeanCompose class contain exactly one minMax component. The min MaxMeanInherit class holds one minMax parent component and the minMaxMeanCompose class contain exactly one minMax data member. The two classes thus have the same memory overhead. Compare the two classes, and their interfaces, as defined in Example 6.11.

Example 6.11: Reuse via Inheritance versus Composition (C++)

```
class minMaxMeanInherit: public minMax
{ ...
        unsigned sum, count;
    public:
        minMaxMeanInherit() {sum = count = 0;}

        void rec(unsigned x)  // not recursive
        {   minMax::rec(x); // resolve scope
            count++;             sum += x;
        }
        float getMean()  {return sum/count;}
};


class minMaxMeanCompose
{ ...
        minMax        m;
        unsigned      sum, count;
    public:
        minMaxMeanCompose() {sum = count = 0;}
        void rec(unsigned x)
        {   m.rec(x);
            count++;             sum += x;
        }
        float getMean()  {return sum/count;}

        // echo subobject interface
        unsigned getMin()        {return m.getMin();}
        unsigned getMax()        {return m.getMax();}
};
```

With inheritance, the application programmer automatically receives access to the parent component functionality via a derived object so the class designer need not echo the interface. In contrast, when a minMax component is held as a subobject, the application programmer cannot access this encapsulated data member of minMaxMeanCompose. Hence, any required public functionality of minMax must be echoed. Small, echoed functions, such as accessors, would most likely be inlined.

Consider another newly requested type: maxRange, which is a class that must track the interval, that is, the magnitude difference between the minimum and maximum values. The minMax class can be reused again. Which approach, inheritance or composition, is most appropriate? Again, there is no difference with respect to space requirements: both forms of reuse require exactly one minMax component. Contrast the two classes defined in Example 6.12: they seem almost identical. Why bother with the distinction between code reuse via inheritance or composition?

Example 6.12: Reuse via Inheritance versus Composition (C++)

```
class maxRangeInherit: public minMax
{ …
     public:
           unsigned getRange()    {return getMax() - getMin();}
};

class maxRangeCompose
{ …        minMax    m;
     public:
           unsigned getRange()    {return getMax() - getMin();}

           // subobject interface echoed
           unsigned getMin()      {      return m.getMin();}
           unsigned getMax()      {      return m.getMax();}
};
```

Without a designed echo or deliberate suppression, the interfaces of the maxRange classes would be different. Under the inheritance relationship, the application programmer can extract the min and the max values via the public parent methods getMin and getMax because maxRangeInherit is-a minMax object. In contrast, under the composition design, the application programmer has no access to minMax methods because minMax is a private subobject. To achieve equivalent, broad interfaces, the public interface of minMax may be echoed in the composition design, as it was in Example 6.11. Alternatively, to achieve equivalent, narrow interfaces, the inherited public functions may be suppressed (via declaration as private functions). In Example 6.13, neither class supports the public interface of the reused minMax type. Downgrading an interface is called "closing down a class" because of the loss of access to functionality; it is permissible in C++ but not in Java or C#.

Example 6.13: Suppressed Interface (C++)

```
class maxRangeInherit2: public minMax
{ …         // inherited interface suppressed
           unsigned getMin()          {}
           unsigned getMax()          {}
     public:
```

```
            unsigned getRange()       {return getMax()
                                       - getMin();}
};
class maxRangeCompose2
{ …
            minMax    m;
    public:
            unsigned getRange(){return m.getMax() - m.getMin();}
};
```

Choosing inheritance rather than composition, or vice versa, yields little difference in this example. Code is reused either way. There is no variability in the relationship between the `minMax` component and the `minMaxMean` type (or the `maxRange` type). Each design defines an object with exactly one embedded `minMax` component. The relationship between parent and child (or object and subobject) is fixed, in terms of lifetime association, unit cardinality, and ownership. Moreover, substitutability is not imperative. That is, there appears to be no client need for an object that could be of type `minMax` at one point and then of type `minMaxMean` at another point.

Contrast this `minMax` example to the `Icon` class hierarchy and to the `TriAthlete` example. `Icons` provided varying behavior, according to subtype, while `BiAthlete` and `TriAthlete` augmented behavior. Both class hierarchies suggest a strong type dependency on the parent class and also a need for substitutability. Both class hierarchies define a set of related subtypes that would likely be used in a heterogeneous collection. Inheritance design is thus more strongly warranted.

6.3.1 Class Design: Has-a or Is-a?

In choosing an appropriate design, one must evaluate implicit tradeoffs, as well as the effects of the relationship in question. What are the costs and benefits of deriving a child class from a defined class? Alternatively, what are the costs and benefits of using an instance of a defined class as a data member? The consequences of using inheritance instead of composition may not be obvious. Structurally, the layouts of the two designs are similar, whether an instance of the reused class serves as a parent component or as a private data member. However, design involves more than form. What is the impact on ease of use? Conceptual understanding? Interface flexibility? Software maintainability?

Table 6.1 summarizes the key characteristics of composition, containment, and inheritance. With inheritance, the child class may access the

TABLE 6.1   Relationship Details: Class to Subordinate (or Parent)

Standard Characteristics of OO Relationships					
Relationship	Association	Cardinality	Ownership	Dependency	Replacement
Composition	Stable	Variable	Transferable	Yes	Yes
Containment	Temporary	Variable	No	No	Not relevant
Inheritance	Permanent	Fixed: 1-1	Implied	Yes	No

public and protected interfaces of the parent class. Externally, the application may access the public interface of the parent object through a child object. In contrast, composition shuts off all external access to the subobject. Internally, the composing object may access the public but not the protected interface of the subobject. The composing object may shoulder the responsibility of managing the subobject. To avoid overhead, instantiation of the subobject might be postponed until use. With delayed instantiation, construction, and cleanup responsibilities must be assumed by the class.

Inheritance supports type extension; composition does not. With type extension comes **substitutability** and **polymorphism** (covered in detail in Chapters 7 and 8). In addition to the flexibility of runtime selection of functions, software maintainability is enhanced. New subtypes may be added without breaking application code, as seen in the Icon example. Additionally, an application programmer familiar with a parent interface may more easily adjust to an extended child interface. One could argue that composition permits the definition of a polymorphic subobject, thus magnifying the flexibility of this relationship. See Chapter 8 for an expanded discussion on polymorphic subobjects.

In comparison to inheritance then, composition reduces accessibility, increases internal responsibility, and cannot provide the benefits of substitutability and extensibility. Yet, practitioners prefer composition over inheritance. Why? A popular answer is control: *the composing object has more design options with respect to manipulating a subobject than a child object has for its parent component.* A composing object may replace or discard its subobject. Using a null reference or pointer, the overhead of a subobject may be avoided by postponing instantiation. The class designer may choose what portions, if any, of the subobject's interface to echo.

Table 6.2 summarizes the design effects of has-a, holds-a, and is-a. Composition may also be preferred over inheritance because of reduced overhead. With inheritance, a child object always has an implicit parent class component. This unavoidable overhead should be warranted. The

TABLE 6.2   Design Effects of OO Relationships

| | Object Use of Subordinate (or Parent) Subobject | | | | |
Relationship	Internal Access	External Access	Overhead	(Subobject) Interface	Control
Holds-a	Public	None	Minimal	Not relevant	None
Has-a	Public	None	Variable Avoidable	Suppressed May echo	Replacement Deferred instantiation
Is-a	Public Protected	Public	Unavoidable	Support Extend Suppress	None

parent component of the child object's memory is automatically initialized: the compiler generates code to invoke the parent no-argument constructor before the child constructor fires. The child class designer can specify the invocation of a different parent constructor but cannot circumvent the allocation or initialization of this parent component.

Inheritance is a precisely defined, implicit structural relationship that offers less flexibility than composition. Each child object has exactly one parent component, no more, no fewer. This parent component is not replaceable; it may be considered owned by the child object but cannot be deallocated before the child object goes out of scope. Essentially, a lifetime association exists between parent and child.

Inheritance increases coupling, as the child type is tightly coupled to the parent type, and decreases cohesion because the type definition is spread across the inheritance hierarchy. However, a has-a relationship also increases coupling and decreases cohesion for the same reasons. Yet, inheritance is a valuable design option. If a child class must support another interface, then inheritance provides access automatically; composition requires the interface to be echoed. If the application requires polymorphism or substitutability then inheritance is the best approach. If type extension is anticipated, then, for software maintainability, inheritance is preferred.

A standard motive for inheritance is code reuse in order to reduce development time and thus cost. The class targeted for use as the parent in an inheritance relationship is already designed, implemented, debugged, and tested. However, this class could also be used as a subobject in a composition relationship. If an extended type should reuse functionality, either inheritance or composition provides that capability. Thus, when considering whether to use inheritance or composition, code reuse as an argument is moot: *the class will be reused either way; it is the impact of design that must be evaluated.*

The argument for inheritance that rests on access to protected data and functionality is also somewhat moot. While inheritance provides access to protected and public data and functionality, composition provides access only to public. However, one can easily define a wrapper class for the sole intent of opening up a protected interface. This derived class could then be used in a composition relationship to mimic inheritance.

Say, as in Example 6.14, a class defines a protected function, such as getKey(). If access to this function is desired, an inheritance design seems the obvious choice. However, a derived class, that serves only to expand the accessibility of getKey(), may be defined. This intermediary class can then be used, in place of the original parent, as a subobject. This extra step seems silly. After all, the publicEyes class incurs the overhead of inheritance that a composition relationship seeks to avoid. However, the flexibility of composition, including delayed instantiation, may now be achieved by the deCode class.

Example 6.14: Opening Up Protected Interface: C++ Code

```cpp
class familyEyes
{ ...
   protected:
      int              getKey();
      ...
};

class publicEyes: public familyEyes
{ ...
   public:
      // open access
      int           getKey()    { return   familyEyes::getKey();}
      ...
};
class deCode
{ ...
      publicEyes*    p;
   public:
      int           getKey()
      {        if (!p)    p = new publicEyes(...);
               return     p->getKey();
      }
      ...
};
```

The external benefit of reuse via inheritance may be limited. Although every object of a derived class may be substituted for an object of the base class, public utility is still restricted to that published in the parent class interface. If a child class extends its inherited interface by defining additional methods, one cannot call those additional methods through a parent handle. In Example 6.15, the child function LOL() cannot be invoked through a parent handle.

Example 6.15: Parental Interface Limits Use: C++ Code

```
class narrowParent {..};

class widerChild: public narrowParent
{    ...
  public:
     // method added to interface, not in parent interface
     void LOL();
     ...
};

// application code
narrowParent*        db[100];
for (int j = 0; j < 100; j++)
     db[j] = GetObj();
for (int j = 0; j < 100; j++)
{
     db[j]->process();        // ok, in parent interface
     db[j]->LOL();            // COMPILATION ERROR}
}
```

A preference for has-a over is-a, or vice versa, with respect to software maintenance, cannot be unilaterally supported without consideration of future application needs. If a class hierarchy may be extended or if heterogeneous collections must be supported, then inheritance should be preferred. If a class interface is unstable or the overhead of a parent component should be avoided, then composition may be preferred.

When evaluating design options, software maintenance arguments must be posited carefully. *Predicting the cost of future software maintenance is not equivalent to comparing existing differences in overhead.* To reduce software maintenance costs, software developers should adhere to good software design principles, such as the **open closed principle** (OCP, see chapter end), high cohesion, low coupling, and thorough documentation.

When determining the most appropriate relationship to model, assess intended use. What is the expected impact? Evaluate current priorities and predict future demands. Standard review includes breadth of the public interface, anticipated reuse, stability, memory usage, and cost (size).

Documentation details about an object's relationship to a subobject include:

Accessibility
Private
Full or partial access
   Echoed functionality
Association
Temporary or permanent
Delayed instantiation
Stable but replaceable
Cardinality
Fixed by class design
   Same for all objects
Fixed at instantiation
   Stable for object lifetime
Variable within object lifetime
Ownership
Owned (internal responsibility)
External resource
   Shared, transferable

We evaluate the merit of inheritance in more detail in the next chapter by examining substitutability and heterogeneous collections.

6.3.2 Contractual Expectations

Contractual obligations, as enumerated by Programming by Contract, may drive design decisions when choosing between inheritance and composition. Either design can be perceived as beneficial. What does the application currently demand? What of future demand?

Inheritance preserves an interface, offering familiarity to an application programmer. As shown in more detail in the next two chapters, inheritance supports the use of heterogeneous collections, and, in this manner, promotes extensibility. However, it is a rigid design, with unavoidable overhead.

Composition wraps the subobject, hiding its interface, and removing responsibility from the application programmer. Composition yields a class design with more control over, and thus more responsibility for, subobjects. A chief benefit of composition is flexibility with respect to cardinality and instantiation. It also isolates application code from unstable interfaces.

6.4 OO DESIGN PRINCIPLES

Several OO design principles summarize observations made in this chapter. The composite principles states practitioners' preference for composition over inheritance. Why? Composition is a more flexible relationship, and offers more control over internal design than inheritance. For low coupling, class designers may adhere to the principle of least knowledge. Ideally, when classes interact, in any relationship, class design should not be dependent on private implementation details of any other class. In concert with clear documentation, deliberate design identifies relationships and their consequential effects.

Composite Principle
Use composition in preference to inheritance.

Open Closed Principle (OCP)
A class should be open for extension and closed for modification.

Principle of Least Knowledge
Every object should assume the minimum possible about the
structure and properties of other objects.

Nonetheless, inheritance is an attractive design option, especially if one desires substitutability and the support of heterogeneous collections. A good inheritance design adheres to the open closed principle (OCP): individual classes are preserved but type extensions are seamless. OCP promotes software maintainability. When a class hierarchy, like the Icon class hierarchy, relies on implicit subtype selection to distinguish appropriate functionality (movement), it illustrates an effective use of inheritance. Type extension is thus seamlessly supported.

6.5 SUMMARY

Building on the foundation of maintainable class design, and clear documentation of assumptions, we examined the basic relationships modeled in Object-Oriented Design (OOD). Composition, containment, and inheritance were each examined in detail, with examples, descriptions, and comparative evaluations. By modeling different relationships, contrasting designs, extending analysis to software maintainability, we thus motivate intentional design.

Since composition and inheritance both readily promote code reuse, *software developers must understand the effects of different designs to choose appropriately.* Inheritance is warranted when substitutability and type checking is needed. Inheritance typically suggests better maintenance due to the ease of type extension. Cut-and-paste programming, a technique known to be error-prone and a maintenance headache, is avoided with inheritance.

We close this chapter with a comment on professional goals of software design. Software developers should understand the costs and benefits of different design approaches to appropriately choose among alternatives. Comparative analyses may be difficult when short-term and long-term priorities conflict. Nonetheless, one should anticipate design impact on performance as well as software maintainability. Whether working inside the OO realm or outside, a professional developer must be able to recognize basic design concepts. A competent software designer can simulate missing features and determine when and how to avoid expensive approaches. In essence, design effectively.

DESIGN INSIGHTS

SOFTWARE

Assessing current overhead differs from predicting future cost

MODELS

Type dependency should be evident
    Inheritance: Common Interface
        Substitutability
        Polymorphism
    Composition: Internalized functionality
        Varying cardinality
        Postponed instantiation
Aggregation defines form
    Not type dependency

SOFTWARE DESIGN

Strength of type dependency driven by
    Association
    Ownership
    Cardinality
Inheritance supports maintainability
    Built-in type checking
    Extensibility
Composition may wrap unstable interface

Code reuse achievable via either inheritance or composition
    Different effects
    Different impact on maintainability
Containment models collections with weak type dependency
Composition suggest type dependency
    Stable association, lifetimes correlated
    Flexible ownership, cardinality, association

DOCUMENTATION

Explicitly record design decisions
    Why inheritance chosen?
    Why composition chosen?

CONCEPTUAL QUESTIONS

1. What is the relevance of design details such as lifetime, association, cardinality, and ownership of memory?

2. Describe the major differences between has-a and holds-a.

3. When is type dependency important in design?

4. Describe the major differences between has-a and is-a.

5. What type of design yields the most effective code reuse?

6. What are the language differences with respect to inherited interfaces?

7. When is the composite principle not applicable?

8. When is the open closed principle in conflict with the composite principle?

CHAPTER 7

Behavioral Design

PROGRAMMING LANGUAGE SUPPORT for automatic type checking greatly advanced the pace and breadth of software development. Chapter 6 explored this capacity for reuse as supported via the inheritance construct. This chapter continues the examination of inheritance with a focus on its support for dynamic function selection, also known as **polymorphism**. We begin by defining three forms of polymorphism used in software and then examine subtype polymorphism in depth.

To highlight an effective design using subtype polymorphism, we examine **abstract classes** and the resulting support of **heterogeneous collections** and ease of **software maintenance**. In addition to small, intuitive examples, we dissect code from a real-world software tool, a **disassembler**, to illustrate appropriate use of abstract classes. To understand process and cost, and to expose readers to a truly elegant software solution, we carefully explain and illustrate **virtual function tables**. Such an examination is unusual in a text; more often, background processes are dismissed as tedious. However, in the author's experience, this knowledge successfully reinforces an understanding of polymorphism. To assess unavoidable, but common, design difficulties, the chapter closes by looking at **type introspection** and specific language requirements.

CHAPTER OBJECTIVES
- Define common forms of polymorphism
  - Overloading, generics, and subtyping
- Contrast static and dynamic binding

- Illustrate effective use of dynamic binding
- Examine the structure and utility of virtual function tables
- Define and demonstrate the utility of abstract classes
  - Analyze production code for disassembler
- Demonstrate the use and benefits of heterogeneous collections
- Assess the cost of type identification
- Identify relevant OOD principles

7.1 INHERITANCE FOR FUNCTIONALITY

In the previous chapter, we examined structural design with an emphasis on inheritance, the hallmark construct of object-oriented design. As noted there, the mere structural design of inheritance can be mimicked with composition. A composing class can gain access to all the public data and functionality of the "parent" component. If access to protected data and functionality is desired, then a wrapper class can be defined with the sole purpose of opening up the protected data and functionality. What then is so important about inheritance, the major design construct of OOD?

The true power of inheritance is not structural reuse but behavioral modification. By defining an interface in the base class and providing variant behavior in descendant classes, a class designer can provide quite a range of functionality, all maintainable under a uniform interface. Heterogeneous collections and **substitutability**, two design touchstones of extensible code, are feasible only under a common interface.

We examine the design of class hierarchies and how functionality (behavior) can vary within class hierarchies. OOPLs support polymorphism, that is, dynamic binding of function calls so that a single object handle can provide access to varying behavior at runtime. What are the costs and benefits of polymorphism? How does one design effectively using polymorphism? We address these questions and also consider abstract classes as the means to standardize form within a class hierarchy.

7.2 POLYMORPHISM

Looking at the Greek roots of the word "polymorphism," we discern its meaning: many (*poly*) and form (*morph*). Polymorphism in software then refers to a function, method, class, or type name that is associated with more than one form or implementation. Software employs different types of polymorphism in design.

7.2.1 Overloading

Ad hoc polymorphism refers to function overloading. A single function (or method) name can have more than one definition. The **function signature** (the function name and the number, type, and order of passed parameters) distinguishes each different implementation. Constructors are commonly **overloaded**. Object instantiation often invokes the default, or no-argument, constructor. When inheritance is used, the compiler invokes the parent default, or no-argument, constructor unless the class designer specifies an alternative constructor.

Many functions that provide routine processing are commonly overloaded. Take care to distinguish between two different design motives for overloaded functions: (1) each implementation executes modified instructions so the function bodies look different; and, (2) each implementation executes essentially the same actions on different data so the function bodies look the same.

Overloaded constructors exemplified the first case. Example 7.1 illustrates another, intuitive example—variants of an initialization routine. An array could be reset or initialized in different ways: all elements initialized with a common value such as zero, all elements initialized with a specified integer value, all elements scaled up or down by an additive or multiplicative factor.

Example 7.1: Overloaded Functions: Altered Functionality

```
void reset()
{       for (int k=0; k < size; k++)
            A[k] = 0.0;
}

void reset(double value)
{    for (int k=0; k < size; k++)
            A[k] = value;
}

void reset(bool op, int factor)
{    if (op)
            for (int k=0; k < size; k++)
                A[k]*= factor;
```

```
        else
            for (int k=0; k < size; k++)
                A[k] += factor;
}
```

The second case is illustrated by functions that have the same function body but operate on different types of data. Example 7.2 illustrates the swapping of a pair of values. Many versions of the same function must be defined in a statically typed language because the type of the values swapped differs. Such functions are candidates for **templates** or generics.

Example 7.2: C++ Overloaded Functions:
Consistent Behavior => Generic functions

```
void swap(int& x, int& y)            void swap(float& x, float& y)
{       int hold = x;                {       float hold = x;
        x = y;                               x = y;
        y = hold;                            y = hold;
}                                    }


template <typename someType>
void swap(someType& x, someType& y)
{       someType        hold = x;
        x = y;
        y = hold;
}
```

7.2.2 Generics

The swap routine is a classic example of an overloaded function that provides the same functionality regardless of data supplied. Swapping two values entails the same actions, whether for integers, reals, Icon objects, etc. Likewise, regardless of data type, the same actions unfold for sorting, searching, and often finding the minimum or maximum. Consider an iterative version of binary search. The code for the algorithm always looks the same. In fact, even the comparison operators are used in the same manner. When the type of the underlying data does not matter, why not use a placeholder for the data type? The placeholder could then be replaced with an actual type when needed. That is exactly what **generic**, or templated, code does. Overloaded functions that differ only by type of data used (such as swap, sort, etc.) are good candidates for templated or generic code.

Parametric polymorphism refers to generic or templated code. Generics are functions, methods, or classes that are defined without a specific type provision. The multiple overloaded swaps in Example 7.2 are easily written in one generic version, with a placeholder for the type of data swapped. The compiler can then generate multiple versions, each instantiated with a specific type as supplied by the application programmer.

A data structure that serves primarily to store and retrieve data, that is, any container, is a good candidate for template code: the functionality of storing and retrieving is not affected by type. A stack pushes, pops, tests for empty, and clears no matter the type of data it contains. Likewise, functionality is independent of the data type in a queue, a set, etc. A priority queue stores data in order; so as long as the data type stored supports comparison, a priority queue also functions independent of type. C++ advanced the use of generics by developing and disseminating the **Standard Template Library (STL)**.

7.2.3 Subtype Polymorphism

Table 7.1 summarizes three different types of polymorphism. Relative to OOD, however, we are most interested here in **subtype polymorphism**: the use of one name to signify any one of a number of (sub)types in a class hierarchy. The key utility of subtype polymorphism is increased flexibility for runtime functionality. That is, the static resolution of a function call (the compiler's translation into a direct JUMP statement) is replaced by dynamic resolution. To do so, the compiler must generate code that supports an indirect jump.

Dynamically bound functions or **virtual** methods usually have multiple implementations in a class hierarchy. Calling a virtual method through a polymorphic handle can thus yield different results on different runs of the same software. How? Function call resolution is postponed until

TABLE 7.1   Types of Polymorphism

	Overloading	**Generic**	**SubType**
Functions	Different versions	Type-less	Overridden
Identified	Function signature parameter list	Type placeholder	Class scope same function signature
How used	Constructors Function variants	Compiler generates code with type	Heterogeneous collections base class interface
Impact	Common name	Design reuse	Dynamic binding

runtime—the compiler does not resolve virtual function calls. By waiting until runtime to bind a function call to actual function code, function selection is postponed and thus can vary at runtime. When a function call is not permanently associated with a specific function address, software is more flexible. Subtype polymorphism thus enables the design of flexible and extensible software because of dynamic binding. In the next section, we trace a sample class design, comparing static and dynamic binding.

7.3 STATIC BINDING VERSUS DYNAMIC BINDING

Conceptually, a function call is a JUMP statement where, at the point of call, statement execution is transferred to the first instruction of the named function. For efficiency, function calls are statically bound, that is, resolved at compile-time. The compiler translates the function invocation into a JUMP statement, generates the code necessary to store and transfer data, and to record the program counter (which holds the address of the current instruction) so that control can be transferred back to the point of call once function execution terminates. When a function call is resolved at compile-time, by translation to a direct JUMP statement, the same function is always called.

In C++ and in C#, function calls are statically bound by default. Example 7.3 shows the design of a simple C++ class hierarchy, where all defined functions are statically bound by default. The C# class design is similar, as will be shown in Example 7.6. The base (FirstGen) class defines two public functions (whoami) and (simple), in addition to an overloaded constructor. Its immediate descendant, (SecondGen), redefines one of these two inherited functions, (simple), and defines a new function (expand) as well. At the third level of the class hierarchy, the ThirdGen class redefines the inherited functions (simple) and (expand) and defines another public function (grand).

Example 7.3: C++ Class Design: Default Static Binding

```
// C++ class design - by default, function calls statically bound
//           efficient but rigid
class FirstGen
{    protected:
        int    x, y;
        int    level;
     public:
        FirstGen(int a = 1, int b = 10)
```

```
        {     x = a;  y = b;  level = 1;        }
        int whoami(){    return level;    }
        int simple(){    return x + y;    }
};

class SecondGen: public FirstGen
{    public:
        SecondGen(int a = 10, int b = 100): FirstGen(a,b)
        {     level = 2;        }
        int simple(){    return x * y;    }
        int expand(){    return x * y * level;        }
};

class ThirdGen: public SecondGen
{ public:
        ThirdGen(int a = 100, int b = 1000):SecondGen(a,b)
        {        level = 3;        }
        int simple(){    return x * y + x + y;    }
        int expand(){    return x * y * level + x + y + level;    }
        int grand() {    return (x+y)*(x+y) * level;    }
};
```

To explore the differences between static and dynamic binding, especially with respect to (sub)type identification, we analyze the class hierarchy of Example 7.3 in detail. All three classes define a default (no-argument) constructor with specified default values. The FirstGen class defines a whoami function that returns the value of the protected data member level. Since the value of level is set in each class constructor, whoami effectively identifies the subtype of an object instantiated from the FirstGen class hierarchy: 1 for a FirstGen object; 2 for a SecondGen object; 3 for a ThirdGen object. The whoami function thus does not have to be redefined in each descendant class: the value of level as set in each constructor will be picked up by the whoami function defined in the FirstGen class.

whoami is a classic design technique used to build in type identification. As long as the application programmer tracks the correspondence between an integer value and its associated type, this design is extensible: any subsequently derived class need only initialize the protected data member level to the unique value that is to be associated with the new class definition. The phrase "as long as" implies a significant dependency, one that may be beyond an individual's control. Modern language constructs provide an alternative to functions such as whoami, as shown in this chapter, thus removing dependencies on software maintenance and client code.

The FirstGen class hierarchy expands the inherited interface at each
level, yielding three different definitions for the simple function and two
different definitions for the expand function. Here, we consider only the
simple function and evaluate how design impacts utility at the application level. Example 7.4 provides sample code that declares and manipulates objects from the class hierarchy defined in Example 7.3. Recall that
a pointer (reference) typed to hold the address of a base class object can
hold the address of a base class object or the address of any derived class
object. Thus, the firstPtr pointer array may hold the address of any type
in the FirstGen class hierarchy, whereas the secondPtr pointer array
may hold addresses of SecondGen and ThirdGen objects. Statements
#A, #B, and #C show the varied initialization of the two pointer arrays.
Figure 7.1 shows sample memory layout of the typed pointer arrays and
objects defined in Example 7.4.

Example 7.4: C++ Binding: Dependent on Class Design

```
int main()
{       FirstGen        f1;     // default internals, x=1, y=10
        SecondGen       f2;     // default internals, x=10, y=100
        ThirdGen        f3;     // default internals, x=100, y=1000

        FirstGen*       firstGPtr[3];
        SecondGen*      secondGPtr[2];

        firstGPtr[0] = &f1;                             // #A
        firstGPtr[1] = secondGPtr[0] = &f2;             // #B
        firstGPtr[2] = secondGPtr[1] = &f3;             // #C

        // invocation thru C++ stack objects ALWAYS statically bound
        // same as cout << FirstGen::simple(&f1) << endl;
        cout << f1.simple() << endl;  // #D: output 11 = 1 + 10

        // same as cout << SecondGen::simple(&f2) << endl;
        cout << f2.simple() << endl;  // #E: output 1000 = 10*100

        // same as cout << ThirdGen::simple(&f3) << endl;
        cout << f3.simple() << endl;  // #F: output 101100

                                //      = 100*1000+100+1000
        // invocation thru C++ pointer can be dynamically bound
        //      BUT NOT HERE!
        for (int i=0; i< 3; i++)
                cout << firstGPtr[i] -> simple();       // #G
        for (int i=0; i< 2; i++)
                cout << secondGPtr[i] -> simple();      // #H
        return 0;
}
```

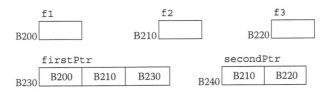

FIGURE 7.1   Sample memory layout for Example 7.4.

The values printed at tagged lines #D, #E, and #F in Example 7.4 are as expected: the output is consistent with the type of object through which the call to simple is invoked. The values printed at statement #G are according to the type (FirstGen) of the typed pointer: simple thus computes "x + y," yielding 11, 110, and 1100, although the definition of the function simple is overridden in each descendant class! Since each pointer in the firstGPtr array holds the address of a different subtype, one might expect the simple function to compute "x * y" and "x * y + x + y" for a SecondGen object and a ThirdGen object, respectively.

Why does the output statement at point #G yield 11, 110, and 1100 and not the same output as statements #D to #F, namely, 11, 1000, and 101100? After all, the first element of the pointer array contains the address of f1, the second element contains the address of f2, and so forth. Since C++ employs static binding by default, each simple function call through a firstGPtr array pointer is resolved at compile-time. Most likely, the simple function call is inlined so that code to compute "x + y" is generated in place. The compiler processes statements individually so it does not track the type of the object whose address is placed in a firstGPtr array pointer.

A trace of the messages printed at output point #H yields a similar uniformity: simple always computes "x * y," yielding 1000 and 100,000, despite the fact that the two pointers in the secondGPtr array hold addresses of objects of different subtype. Each simple call is statically bound, and most likely inlined, computing "x * y" upon each call. In essence, with static binding, the subtype of the object whose address is held in the pointer does not matter.

To achieve dynamic binding in C++ (and C#), one must specify that a function is "virtual" in the base class. Simply adding the keyword virtual to a function name is the only change needed in Example 7.3 to make dynamic binding possible. Example 7.5 shows this modification. Once a function has been tagged virtual in a class, all descendant classes inherit that function as a virtual function, with the potential for dynamic binding. We explain subsequently why a function is "once virtual, always virtual." Using the class FirstGen, as modified by the virtual keyword in Example 7.5, the application code in Example 7.4 would now produce dynamic function resolution at statement #G, yielding output: 11, 1000, 101100.

Example 7.5: C++: Virtual for Dynamic Binding

```
// C++ - dynamic function identified by keyword virtual
// ONLY change to Example 7.3 to achieve dynamic binding
class FirstGen
{     protected:
          int   x, y;
          int   level;
      public:
          FirstGen(int a = 1, int b = 10)
          {   x = a; y = b;  level = 1;  }

          int whoami(){    return level;   }
          virtual int simple(){   return x + y;   }
};

class SecondGen: public FirstGen
{     public:
          SecondGen(int a = 10, int b = 100):FirstGen(a,b)
          {     level = 2;      }

          virtual int simple(){   return x * y;   }
          virtual int expand(){   return x * y * level;   }
};

class ThirdGen: public SecondGen
{     public:
          ThirdGen(int a = 100, int b = 1000):SecondGen(a,b)
          {     level = 3;      }

      virtual int simple(){   return x * y + x + y;   }
      virtual int expand(){   return x * y * level + x + y + level;   }
      virtual int grand()  {   return (x+y)*(x+y) * level;   }
};
```

With respect to dynamic binding, C# operates much like C++: static binding is employed by default; methods must be declared "virtual" to postpone function resolution until runtime. In C#, to override an inherited, virtual function, a method must be labeled "override." Attempts to redefine, and thus provide alternative behavior, without using the key word "override" will trigger compilation errors. This forced pairing of "virtual" with "override" clarifies the intent of class design, and is illustrated in Example 7.6. The class hierarchy in Example 7.6 is the same as that in Example 7.5 except that it is written in C#.

Example 7.6: C# Virtual Functions Tagged and then Overridden

```
// C# class design - tagged function calls dynamically bound
//    redefined functions must be labeled 'override'
class FirstGen
{    protected int  level;
     public Gen(int a = 100, int b = 1000)
     {      level = 1;      }

     public virtual int simple(int x, int y)
     {      return x + y;      }
}

class SecondGeb: FirstGen
{    public SecondGen(int a = 100, int b = 1000): base(a,b)
     {      level = 2;      }

     public override int simple(int x, int y)
     {      return x * y;      }

     public virtual int expand(int x, int y)
     {      return x * y * level;      }
}

class ThirdGen: SecondGen
{    public ThirdGen(int a = 100, int b = 1000): base(a,b)
     {      level = 3;      }

     public override int simple(int x, int y)
     {      return x * y + x + y;      }

     public override int expand(int x, int y)
     {      return x * y * level + x + y + level;      }

     public virtual int grand(int x, int y)
     {return (x+y)*(x+y) * level;}
}
```

The application code in Example 7.7 is analogous to that of Example 7.4 except that it is written in C#. At output point #G, the values printed are "11," "1000," and then "101100." Why? The function call to simple() is not resolved until runtime. That is, the compiler does not translate the method invocation into a direct JUMP statement. Instead, the compiler generates the code necessary to determine, at runtime, which function to call.

Example 7.7: C# Application Code for Example 7.6

```
// application code
FirstGen              a = new FirstGen();
SecondGen             b = new SecondGen();
ThirdGen              c = new ThirdGen();

FirstGen[]            firstGPtr = new FirstGen[3];
SecondGen[]           secondGPtr = new SecondGen[2];

firstGPtr[0] = a;
firstGPtr[1] = secondGPtr[0] = b;
firstGPtr[2] = secondGPtr[1] = c;

for (int i=0; i< 3; i++);
    Console.WriteLine(firstGPtr[i].simple(2,3));        #G

for (int i=0; i< 2; i++)
    Console.WriteLine(secondGPtr[i].simple(2,3));       #H
```

In Example 7.7, each reference in the firstGPtr array is examined at runtime in order to determine the type of the object whose address is held therein. Since firstGPtr[0] holds the address of a type FirstGen object, the simple function from class FirstGen is invoked. Since firstGPtr[1] holds the address of a type SecondGen object, the simple function from class SecondGen is invoked, etc. Similar reasoning verifies that the output at point #H will be "1000" and then "101100."

If the keywords "virtual" and "override" were missing in the class hierarchy of Example 7.6, then the C# application code in Example 7.7 would have yielded the same static binding effects as that acquired from the C++ class hierarchy in Example 7.3. What about Java? Java uses dynamic binding so all methods are implicitly virtual. Java does not then have (or need) a keyword "virtual." Java application code is thus more consistent than either C++ or C#: there is no guesswork with respect to binding, and no need to consult the class hierarchy; function call resolution is consistently postponed until runtime. We explain the technical details for dynamic resolution of function calls in a later section.

Figure 7.2 shows sample memory diagrams for the C# application code in Example 7.7, illustrating C# object layout. C# programmers need not deviate from their usual manipulation of objects, since objects are references; C++ programmers must use base class pointers to acquire dynamic binding. Why? The (sub)type of an accessed object may easily change when that object is accessed via a reference (or pointer). How? Change an address, change the object (and thus possibly the subtype) referenced. The type of a stack object cannot change.

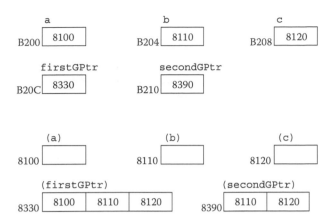

FIGURE 7.2   Sample memory layout for C# application code in Example 7.7.

In both Examples 7.4 and 7.7, the sample arrays firstGPtr and secondGPtr represent **heterogeneous collections**: aggregates of different types of data that can be treated uniformly. Heterogeneous collections are a powerful data structure that supports a standard (common) interface for all types within the collection. Varying functionality (behavior) results when each different subtype satisfies the standard interface but implements different responses to the same call. In the FirstGen example, the simple function comprises the standard interface; the message output, as it differs per class, signifies the variable response or implementation.

The whoami function in Examples 7.3 and 7.6 need not be virtual. The whoami function is defined in the base class and not redefined in any descendant classes. Since this function returns the protected data member level, as set by each class constructor, it accurately reflects the identity of the subtype of the object. The accuracy of the whoami design depends on the vigilance of both the class designer and the application programmer. If the class designer omits the correct initialization of the protected data member level in any subsequently designed descendant classes, the design falters. If the application programmer misinterprets the value returned from the whoami function, the design falters. We re-evaluate the utility of the whoami function when we examine design options in Chapter 8.

7.3.1 Heterogeneous Collections

Polymorphism promotes **extensibility**—the ability to extend a given class hierarchy without breaking any pre-existing application code. Additional classes, say FourthGen, FifthGen, and SixthGen, could easily be added to the class hierarchy in Examples 7.5 and 7.6. Such a type extension would not break the application code: neither for-loop exercising the polymorphic functionality would need to change. The only needed change would be the initialization (and, possibly, size) of the heterogeneous collection.

To design for software maintainability, isolate code that deals directly with type. Example 7.8 illustrates an effective wrapping of C++ initialization code in a routine, GetObjAddr(). Similarly, Example 7.9 illustrates an effective wrapping of C# (Java) initialization code in a routine, GetObj(); the C# code is the same as C++ code except a base class reference is returned (instead of a pointer). The more important difference is that C++ programmers must manage heap memory. If the class hierarchy used in Examples 7.5 and 7.6 is extended by the definition of additional derived classes, such as a FourthGen or FifthGen, the only code that needs to change is that in GetObjAddr() or GetObj().

Example 7.8: C++ Polymorphic Object Creation

```
// function that evaluates environment, possibly file input
//    generates an object of some type from class hierarchy
//    => can return address of any object from class hierarchy
//    => subtype of object allocate determined at run-time
//    BASE pointer can hold address of ANY class hierarchy object
// at compile-time:
//         return pointer holding address generated at run-time
//         cannot 'guess' what (sub)type of object allocated
FirstGen* GetObjAddr()
{
    if (condA)        return new FirstGen;     // base class
    else if (condB)   return new SecondGen;    // derived type
    else if (condC)   return new ThirdGen;     // derived type II
       ...
}    // ownership of object passed back
```

Example 7.9: C# Polymorphic Object Creation

```
// function that evaluates environment, possibly file input
//    generates an object of some type from class hierarchy
//    => can return address of any object from class hierarchy
//    => subtype of object allocate determined at run-time
// BASE reference can hold address of ANY class hierarchy object
// at compile-time:
//    return reference (address of object generated at run-time)
//          cannot 'guess' what (sub)type of object allocated
```

```
FirstGen GetObj()
{
    if (condA)      return new FirstGen();    // base class
    else if (condB) return new SecondGen();   // derived type
    else if (condC) return new ThirdGen(); // derived type II
    else throw new IndexOutOfRangeException("Bad condition");
}       // ownership of object passed back
```

As shown in Examples 7.10 and 7.11, code that traverses a heterogeneous collection is stable. Nowhere in either sample application code is the subtype of a particular object known. This design technique of isolating initialization code to promote software maintainability may be used across programming languages.

Example 7.10: C++ Heterogeneous Collection

```
// initialization of heterogeneous collection:subtype hidden
// at compile-time, do NOT know type of object generated
FirstGen*           bigPtrArray[100];
for (int k = 0; k < 100; k++)
    bigPtrArray[k] = GetObjAddr();

// dynamic behavior
for (int k = 0; k < 100; k++)
    bigPtrArray[k]-> simple();

...
// MEMORY MANAGEMENT: release heap memory before leaving scope
// deallocate dynamically allocated objects
for (int k = 0; k < 100; k++)
    delete    bigPtrArray[k];
```

Example 7.11: C# Heterogeneous Collection

```
// initialization of heterogeneous collection:subtype hidden
// at compile-time, do NOT know type of object generated
FirstGen[]  bigArray = new FirstGen[100];
for (int k = 0; k < bigArray.Length; k++)
    bigArray[k] = GetObj();

// dynamic behavior
for (int k = 0; k < bigArray.Length; k++)
    bigArray[k]-> simple(3,9);
```

Using a function to isolate initialization code is an effective design technique. Constructors embody this idea. However, initializing a heterogeneous collection of polymorphic objects of, say, base type Z, is a *responsibility external* to the class Z. The code shown in Examples 7.10 and 7.11 initialize heterogeneous collections external to the FirstGen class.

In a statically typed language like C++, C#, or Java, the only method that may not be virtual is the constructor. Why? To allocate an object on the stack in C++, the compiler must know the size, and therefore, the type of the object. C# and Java follow the same programming language design as C++. However, several design patterns mimic virtual construction (Gamma, 1995).

7.4 VIRTUAL FUNCTION TABLE

What code is generated by the compiler so that function resolution is postponed until runtime? The solution is both elegant and efficient: a jump table. When the compiler processes a dynamically bound function call, it generates code for an indirect jump using a collection of jump tables. Essentially, each class has its own table, called its **virtual function table** or **vtab**. By storing the addresses of each dynamically bound (virtual) function, the vtab provides the means to resolve a function call at runtime. For more details, see Ellis (1990).

Each virtual function in a class definition is associated with an offset within the virtual function table (vtab). We sketch out an example vtab for conceptual reinforcement. Function addresses may not be laid out exactly as displayed here: language standards need not specify layout. However, for any one particular function, the offset in every vtab for that class hierarchy will be the same.

Assuming that a pointer (address) is allocated (defined by) 4 bytes, the first virtual function address will be stored at offset 0; the second

TABLE 7.2   Vtabs for Example 7.5

	FirstGen **virtual function table (vtab)**	
Table Entry	Virtual function	Address (class definition)
Offset 0	`simple()`	`FirstGen::simple()`

	SecondGen **virtual function table (vtab)**	
Table Entry	Virtual function	Address (class definition)
Offset 0	`simple()`	`SecondGen::simple()`
Offset 4	`expand()`	`SecondGen::expand()`

	ThirdGen **virtual function table (vtab)**	
Table Entry	Virtual function	Address (class definition)
Offset 0	`simple()`	`ThirdGen::simple()`
Offset 4	`expand()`	`ThirdGen::expand()`
Offset 8	`grand()`	`ThirdGen::grand()`

virtual function address will be stored at offset 4, the third virtual function address will be stored at offset 8, etc. As shown in Table 7.2 (the virtual function tables corresponding to Example 7.5), the offset for function simple is always 0; the offset for function expand is always 4, etc. Only the addresses of those functions tagged as virtual are placed in the class vtab. Recall that the functions simple, expand, and grand were all denoted virtual in Example 7.5. whoami was not labeled virtual.

Rather than translating a function call directly into a JUMP statement, as done with statically bound calls, the compiler generates additional instructions:

1. Dereference the pointer through which the function is invoked

2. Get the type tag of the object whose address is stored in pointer

3. Go to the class vtab of the object whose type was just resolved

4. Add the offset associated with the function name for the vtab entry

5. Extract the address of the target function from the vtab entry

6. Jump to the extracted address

These instructions extract the desired function address out of the appropriate vtab at runtime. The compiler lays out the **indirection** needed for dynamically bound function calls. The programmer need not become enmeshed in function pointers, as illustrated in Appendix C, in order to support dynamic binding.

In Java, all calls are dynamically bound: a flexible but costly model. In C++ and C#, to acquire dynamic binding, the class designer must label functions that are to be dynamically bound with the keyword virtual. This virtual tag is a flag to the compiler to store the function address in the class virtual function table (or vtab). In C#, the class designer must use the keyword override in a descendant class to redefine the function. Note that every redefined function must be labeled "override." C# thus makes it clear when an inherited function is redefined, suggesting polymorphic behavior. The vtabs for Example 7.6 (C# code) would be essentially the same as those displayed in Table 7.2.

By default, C++ object variables are allocated on the stack, that is, assigned a (relative) address within a stack frame by the compiler. When an object is assigned a (relative) memory address, a space for all its data members is also allocated and mapped. A stack object's type cannot then change because of the potential change in size. Function invocation through a C++ object thus cannot be postponed because the type of a stack object cannot vary. Hence, one cannot achieve dynamic binding *directly* through C++ objects. In contrast, Java and C# define objects as references. Since base class references are address holders that can contain the address of any type defined in the class hierarchy, dynamic binding is immediately achievable through such variables.

In C++, dynamic function invocation is a two-step process: (1) declare a function virtual in the base class and (2) call the virtual function through a base class pointer. Why use a pointer? So that type may vary at runtime! C++ stack objects cannot "change type" but a base class pointer can hold the address of a base class object, or the address of any derived class object. Pointer values (addresses of objects) can change at runtime. Really, the C++ approach of using pointers is the same as the C# and Java object model since a reference is a just pointer that the compiler dereferences.

Appendix C provides a detailed analysis of software design with respect to the use of virtual functions. Appendix C evaluates different designs, starting with a non-extensible, non-OO approach, and tracing through iterative modifications, ending with the simplest and most extensible design—one that employs virtual functions.

7.5 SOFTWARE DESIGN

Polymorphism promotes extensibility: it is trivial to add a new class FourthGen to the previous examples. The only code that would have to change would be the object selection functions shown in Examples 7.8 and 7.9. The array of base class pointers need not change: it can store the addresses of FourthGen objects as easily as it stored the addresses of SecondGen objects. Polymorphism thus supports extensibility and heterogeneous collections, as also demonstrated in Examples 7.5 to 7.11. One can traverse a heterogeneous collection and trigger varying behavior via polymorphic calls. The only constraint is that the polymorphic call must conform to the interface as defined by the base class.

Polymorphism also promotes the OO tenet of substitutability: the address of any object from the class hierarchy can be held in a base pointer (or reference). Hence, any object can stand in for a parent object and support the parent's interface whether through inherited or overridden functionality.

Dynamically bound function calls provide a great degree of flexibility. Yet the impact on performance is significant. The software must absorb the runtime overhead of resolving function addresses. Moreover, the key optimization technique of inlining function calls cannot be applied. Recall from Chapter 3 that a function is inlined when the function call is replaced by the actual function code. The intent is to avoid the loss of instruction-level parallelism that occurs whenever nonsequential code, such as a JUMP statement, is executed. Inlining is most feasible when the function is small. However, if one cannot determine which function to invoke at compile-time, the compiler cannot substitute actual function code for a function call, no matter how small the function. Thus, it can be especially costly to implement virtual set and get methods.

7.5.1 Abstract Classes

Heterogeneous collections support polymorphic objects: an element of the collection can be any subtype in a given class hierarchy. With polymorphic objects, dynamic binding may yield differing behavior (if one or more derived classes override an inherited virtual function). Heterogeneous collections thus rely on the interface as defined in the base class. Any function invoked from a heterogeneous collection must be declared publicly in the base class interface. Through the base (common) interface, the invocation of the same named function is resolved at runtime. What if the base class cannot completely define or provide all functionality? Use **abstract classes**.

An abstract class is an incomplete type definition, providing form but not all the implementation details needed for a complete definition. That is, not all the methods specified in the abstract class interface are implemented, as shown in Example 7.12. An application programmer cannot instantiate objects from an abstract class, as shown in Example 7.13. Inheritance must be used so that derived classes may complete the class definition. In essence, abstract classes provide a common interface for a class hierarchy and serve as a placeholder for extension, thus clearly supporting the is-a relationship.

Example 7.12: C++ Abstract Class Shape: Pure Virtual Function

```
// C++ class design: abstract class due to pure virtual methods
class Shape
{       public:
```

```
                virtual void rotate(int) = 0;
                virtual void draw() = 0;
                ...
};

// inherited methods defined => descendant class not abstract
class Circle: public Shape
{               point    center;
                int      radius;
        public:
                Circle(point p, int r):center(p), radius(r) {}

                // once virtual, always virtual, need not tag as
                // virtual void rotate(int){}

                // for readability tag as virtual
                virtual void draw();
                ...
};
```

Example 7.13: C++ Code: Cannot Instantiate Abstract Class

```
// application code
Shape       s;      // cannot instantiate object from abstract class
Shape*      sptr;       // Utility: hold address of derived objects

// given abstract class Shape and derived subtypes
//          Circle, Square, Triangle, Star, ...
// initialize array of Shape pointers
// each pointer can contain address of different subtype
// given input function GetObject() that constructs
//          some Shape subtype (on heap) and returns its address
//    contents of array could be dependent on input file
int main()
{
    Shape* composite[100];
    for (int i=0; i<100; i++)
            composite[i] = GetObjectAddr();
            ...
    // what is drawn?
    for (int i=0; i<100; i++)
            composite[i]->draw();
}
```

Abstract classes may provide default or NOP (no operation) behavior but remain incomplete to force descendant classes to satisfy the inherited interface. How does one define an incomplete class? Java and C# provide a keyword `abstract` that indicates that a class or function is abstract, that is, its definition is incomplete, as shown in Example 7.14. C++ does not provide a keyword. Instead, the idea of "initializing a function to zero" is emphasized. By setting the function header of a virtual function "=0;", a class designer specifies a virtual function without a definition, that is, a **pure virtual** function. Any function that has no implementation is abstract and depends on derived classes to provide implementation details. Since it has no implementation, a pure virtual function has an entry in the class vtab initialized with the value "0."

Example 7.14: C# Abstract Class

```
abstract class Shape          // abstract easily noted with keyword
{     public virtual void rotate(int);
      public virtual void draw();
          ...
}
```

In the classic Example 7.12, the Shape class is an abstract class and the descendant Circle class must provide a definition for each inherited pure virtual function. Hence, the application programmer can instantiate Circle objects but cannot instantiate any Shape objects. The same design effect could be met by making the Shape constructor protected without providing any additional (overloaded) public constructors. The Shape class would then be abstract because the application programmer would have no public constructor to invoke. The descendant Circle class would have to provide a public constructor in order not to remain abstract.

Without using the keyword abstract, which is unavailable in C++, one can design an abstract class in two primary ways. If a class definition has at least one declared but undefined function then the class is abstract. In Example 7.12, both rotate() and draw() are pure virtual functions, forcing Shape to be abstract. The compiler cannot support instantiation of Shape objects because it cannot resolve function calls to rotate() and draw(). An abstract class forces the design and implementation of descendant classes. The derived class(es) must define each pure virtual (also known as **deferred** or abstract) method inherited from the base class. If the derived class does not define an inherited but undefined function, the derived class remains abstract, like its parent class. If the descendant Circle class did not define either rotate() or draw(), it would remain an abstract class.

A second means of designing an abstract class without the keyword abstract is a careful manipulation of constructors. Failure to provide public constructors makes a class abstract. Why? If a class definition provides no public constructors then the application code cannot directly instantiate any objects from this class. However, if the base class defines at least one protected constructor then inheritance may be used. When a derived class defines at least one public constructor, derived class objects may be instantiated. If the base class defines only protected constructors, the design and implementation of descendant classes are forced. Why? *A derived class can invoke a protected constructor but an application programmer cannot.* The application programmer must have a public constructor to invoke. If the base class provides only a protected constructor and the derived class provides a public constructor, then the application programmer can invoke only the derived constructor. At which point, the compiler patches in a call to the parent of the derived class. The subtle detail is that the application programmer is not invoking the base constructor; the derived class is doing so.

Abstract classes enforce a common interface for a class hierarchy, thereby promoting extensibility. A uniform interface supports the manipulation of polymorphic objects, typically in heterogeneous collections. Applications that handle data with common core functionality, but varying details, are served well by abstract classes. For example, inventory systems support common functionality (toy selection in stores, car models in a dealership) but hold data with varying characteristics. Classification systems also benefit from abstract classes. Table 7.3 summarizes the intent and effects of abstract classes. As explained in Chapter 8, abstract classes

TABLE 7.3 Abstract Classes

Design Intent	Implementation Details	Effects
Incomplete type definition	Not all functions defined	Cannot instantiate objects
Deferred methods	Function prototypes serve as placeholders	Inheritance required
Base class defines uniform interface for class hierarchy	Derived class(es) override or augment behavior	Inheritance anticipated
Polymorphism: calls through base-typed pointer (reference) resolved wrt base interface	Typed pointer or reference holds address of derived object	Heterogeneous collections Varying behavior Extensibility
Generalization of overriding	Derived class(es) define behavior	Derived class remains abstract unless it redefines inherited deferred methods

are a noted design type. In the next section, we examine a real-world design and implementation that rests on the use of abstract classes.

7.6 REAL-WORLD EXAMPLE: DISASSEMBLER

To illustrate the utility of abstract classes, we analyze a real-world example: part of the code design for a disassembler. C++ code provided here is similar to production code but is simplified for presentation (T. Hildebrandt, private communication, 1999). A disassembler is a reverse engineering tool and is often used by embedded systems engineers to quantify code coverage.

Conceptually, a disassembler is the inverse operation of an assembler: it translates machine code into assembly language code. Machine code lacks symbolic constants and comments. More problematic, it contains variable-width instructions and manipulates different types of storage where the size of memory used may be unknown. Hence, the task of regenerating all the assembly code corresponding to an execution of a program is a difficult one.

In a disassembler, the process of identifying type, and thus inferring size, is one of trial and error. Consequently, the disassembler must be written in a manner that supports multiple passes at resolving the type of a value. Consider resolution of an arbitrary value as a guessing game. What details help resolve type? Is the value read only? Does the value have an address? Does the value derive from a known class? Can the value be cloned? Think of a value as being held in some location. Characteristics of this location yield more clues about the possible type of the value. Is the location a register or an addressed memory location? Is the location sized to hold an integer or a real?

To guess, and then guess again, the disassembler needs a malleable representation for storage in a computer until it can resolve the location type, and then the type of the value held in that location: As shown in Example 7.15, the design of the disassembler rests on an abstract base class called `AbsoluteLocation`. The disassembler must determine whether a value is constant (cannot be written) or variable (value may be updated at runtime). Constants may be stored in a symbol table by the compiler and then retained by a debugger but do not require physical storage when the program runs. Since variables may change value at runtime, some memory must be assigned to contain that value. Physical storage options include registers and memory locations. Design details are summarized in Table 7.4.

Example 7.15: Abstract Base Class for Disassembler (C++)

```
class AbsoluteLocation
{
  protected:
      enum Class{unknown, constant, variable, constantInt,
          constantFloat, memory, aRegister};
  public:
      virtual ~AbsoluteLocation() {}

      virtual AbsoluteLocation* Clone() const = 0;

      virtual bool IsKnown()        const {return false;}
      virtual bool IsReadOnly()     const {return true; }
      virtual bool HasAddress()     const {return false;}

      virtual Class GetClass()      const {return unknown;}

      virtual bool IsA(Class C)     const {return (C == unknown);}
      virtual bool DerivesFromA(Class C) const {return IsA(C);}

      // various Set()      - NOP as default
      // various GetAs()    - zero (cast) returned as default
};
```

The disassembler must track the fundamental types supported by the program language whose trace is being disassembled. Typical candidates include float, double, int, long, bool, but for simplicity, we consider only float and int here. For readability, the enumerated type "Class" in the AbsoluteLocation class definition lists the many types that must be tracked. The enum value is used for readability when testing and tracking type. A simplified class hierarchy encapsulating this example is presented in Figure 7.3.

TABLE 7.4   AMC Disassembler Design

Design for Memory Location Discernment		
Disassembler	**AbsoluteLocation Class**	**AbsoluteLocation Interface**
Gathers information about locations	Defines abstraction handling of location	Supplies self-identification functions
View trace	Supports collection of different locations	IsA(), derivesFromA(), IsReadOnly(),...
Note access to address	Defines interface for manipulating locations	Supports reinterpretation of data
Postpone resolution of contents(type) of address	Support evaluation of multiple perspectives on one location	Simulates different views of processor

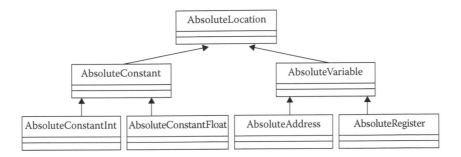

FIGURE 7.3   Disassembler type hierarchy.

The iterative evaluation conducted by the disassembler is supported by the use of subtypes (within a class hierarchy) to represent a location, whose identity is to be determined through the process of elimination. Essential functions of the `AbsoluteLocation` interface are summarized in Table 7.5 and include: `Clone()`, which makes a copy of the object; `IsKnown()`, which returns a Boolean, affirming (or denying) the classification of location; `IsA()`, which returns a Boolean, affirming (or denying) ancestry; `HasAddress()` and `IsReadOnly()`, which return Boolean values, affirming the need for (or the lack of a need for) physical storage, respectively; and `GetClass()`, which returns an enumerated value, identifying type. Multiple `GetAs()` and `Set()` functions support evaluation of multiple perspectives on one location.

The middle tier of descendant classes defines the need for storage: none for constants; physical storage for variables. These derived classes provide additional information on the value but remain abstract because `Clone()` cannot be not defined without more precise knowledge of type.

TABLE 7.5   *AbsoluteLocation* Interface: Key Virtual Functions

Function Name	Purpose	Details
Clone	Makes copy	Uses this pointer
IsKnown	True only if type known	Default false
IsReadOnly	True only if no storage	Default true
HasAddress	True only if needs storage	Default false
GetClass	Returns class enum value	Default unknown
IsA	Verify type test	Default: compare to unknown
DerivesFromA	Verifies ancestry	Default: invoke IsA
Set	Supply value for address	Default NOP
GetAs	Translation between various address types	Default return 0

Additionally, as shown in Example 7.16, the AbsoluteVariable class redefines the inherited NOP set functions as pure virtual, forcing descendant classes to define their own set functions. Why? Descendant classes gain enough type information to implement set methods. For utility, child classes of the AbsoluteVariable class must provide a set function to identify the result of type interpretation.

As shown in Example 7.17, those descendant classes that define Clone() are no longer abstract. Not until the type of variable or constant is known can the derived class provide an implementation for Clone(). Why? Data cannot be copied without size information! The disassembler code can instantiate objects from this tier of classes and hold the addresses of these objects in base (AbsoluteLocation) pointers.

Example 7.16: Derived Classes Still Abstract: C++ Code

```cpp
// abstract base class for constants
//    remains abstract because Clone() not defined
class AbsoluteConstant: public AbsoluteLocation
{
 public:
     virtual ~AbsoluteConstant() {}

     virtual bool IsKnown()        const {return true;}
     virtual Class GetClass()      const {return constant;}
     virtual bool IsA(Class C)     const {return (C == constant);
}
     virtual bool DerivesFromA(Class C) const
     {return IsA(C) || AbsoluteLocation::DerivesFromA(C);}
};

// abstract base class for variables
//    remains abstract because Clone() not defined
//    pure virtual set() functions
//          => force each derived class to define set()
class AbsoluteVariable: public AbsoluteLocation
{
   public:
     virtual ~AbsoluteVariable() {}

     // variables require memory so IsReadOnly overridden
     virtual bool IsReadOnly()  const {return false;}
     virtual Class GetClass()   const {return variable;}
     virtual bool IsA(Class C)  const {return (C == variable);}

     virtual bool DerivesFromA(Class C) const
     {return IsA(C) || AbsoluteLocation::DerivesFromA(C);}

     // plus various set(), each "=0;"
};
```

Example 7.17: Derived Classes: Clone() Defined: C++ Code

```cpp
// class NO LONGER abstract: Clone() defined
class AbsoluteConstantInt: public AbsoluteConstant
{    unsigned long  value;
  public:
    AbsoluteConstantInt(unsigned long val): value(val) {}
    virtual ~AbsoluteConstantInt() {}

    virtual AbsoluteLocation* Clone() const
            {    return new AbsoluteConstantInt(*this);    }
    virtual Class GetClass() const        {return constantInt;}
    virtual bool IsA(Class C) const
            {    return (C == constantInt);    }

    virtual bool DerivesFromA(Class C) const
    {return IsA(C) || AbsoluteConstant::DerivesFromA(C);}

    // + various GetAs() - retrieve object of correct size
};

// class NO LONGER abstract: Clone() defined
class AbsoluteConstantFloat: public AbsoluteConstant
{    float   value;
  public:
    AbsoluteConstantFloat(float val): value(val) {}
    virtual ~AbsoluteConstantFloat() {}
    virtual AbsoluteLocation* Clone() const
            {    return new AbsoluteConstantFloat(*this);}
    virtual Class GetClass() const       {return constantFloat;}
    virtual bool IsA(Class C) const
            {    return (C == constantFloat);}

    virtual bool DerivesFromA(Class C) const
    {return IsA(C) || AbsoluteConstant::DerivesFromA(C);}

    // + various GetAs() - retrieve object of correct size
};

// class NO LONGER abstract, represents processor register
//          Clone() and set() functions defined
class AbsoluteRegister: public AbsoluteVariable
{    RegHandle       handle;
  public:
    AbsoluteRegister(RegHandle r): handle(r) {}
    virtual ~AbsoluteRegister() {}
    virtual AbsoluteLocation* Clone() const
            {    return new AbsoluteRegister(*this);    }
    virtual Class GetClass() const    {return variable;}
    virtual bool IsA(Class C) const    {return (C == a Register);}

    virtual bool DerivesFromA(Class C) const
```

```
        {return IsA(C) || AbsoluteVariable::DerivesFromA(C);}

        // plus various GetAs() & set(), each defined
};

// class NO LONGER abstract: Clone() and set() defined
// represents an absolute memory address
class AbsoluteAddress: public AbsoluteVariable
{      unsigned long   address;
  public:
      AbsoluteAddress(unsigned long a): address(a) {}
      virtual ~AbsoluteAddress() {}
      virtual AbsoluteLocation* Clone() const
              {          return new AbsoluteAddress(*this);      }
      virtual Class GetClass()        const {return memory;}
      virtual bool HasAddress()       const {return true;}
      virtual bool IsA(Class C)       const {return (C == memory);}
      virtual bool DerivesFromA(Class C) const
      {return IsA(C) || AbsoluteVariable::DerivesFromA(C);}

      // plus various set(), each defined
};
```

7.6.1 Virtual Function Table

Table 7.2 represented the virtual function table, also known as vtab, generated by the compiler for each class in Example 7.3, as revised with functions tagged as virtual in Example 7.5. In the FirstGen/SecondGen/ ThirdGen example, there was one additional virtual function in each descendant class so there was one additional entry in each descendant class vtab. In the Disassembler example, not counting SetAs and GetAs functions, there are eight virtual functions in the base class AbsoluteLocation. Thus, there are at least eight corresponding entries in each subtype vtab. Function entries are ordered within the table so that all classes in the class hierarchy can use the same offset for a specific function name. For example, assuming that function addresses are laid out in an order corresponding to function declaration, the Boolean function IsKnown() is always the third entry in the class vtab, for all classes in the AbsoluteLocation class hierarchy. Hence, when the compiler encounters a function invocation for IsKnown(), the compiler may equate this function invocation with an offset of 8 bytes (offset of 0 for first function; offset of 4 for second function; etc.) into the class vtab.

When a class designer defines a child class, the compiler copies the parent vtab over as a default vtab for the child class. For each inherited virtual function that the child redefines, the compiler updates the corresponding entry in the child class vtab so that it contains the address of the child class method. Overridden functions should be evident in Tables 7.6 through 7.9, the vtabs for the dissembler example.

The dictum, relevant to C++ and C#, *once virtual ALWAYS virtual* makes sense. When a function is defined as virtual, it will be virtual in all descendant classes. Why? Polymorphic calls are made through a base class pointer (or reference). The *compiler checks the base class for function accessibility and form and will then determine if the call is virtual or not.* If it is, the compiler generates the extra instructions needed to extract an appropriate function address from the vtab at runtime. It does not matter if the derived class then fails to declare the function virtual: the derived class already has an entry in its vtab, initialized with the base class function address if it is not overridden. Although it is not necessary in C++ to label an inherited virtual function as `virtual`, design guidelines recommend using the keyword virtual so that class designs are as self-documenting as possible. C# code is clearer than C++ because designers must use the keyword `override` when redefining an inherited virtual function.

TABLE 7.6 *AbsoluteLocation* Virtual Function Table (vtab)

Table Entry	Virtual Function	Address (Class Definition)
Offset 0	`~AbsoluteLocation()`	`AbsoluteLocation::`
Offset 4	**`AbsoluteLocation* Clone()`**	**`Undefined: no address`**
Offset 8	`bool IsKnown() const`	`AbsoluteLocation::`
Offset C	`bool IsReadOnly()`	`AbsoluteLocation::`
Offset 10	`bool HasAddress()`	`AbsoluteLocation::`
Offset 14	`Class GetClass()`	`AbsoluteLocation::`
Offset 18	`bool IsA(Class C)`	`AbsoluteLocation::`
Offset 1C	`bool DerivesFromA(Class C)`	`AbsoluteLocation::`

TABLE 7.7 *AbsoluteConstant* Virtual Function Table (vtab)

Table Entry	Virtual Function	Address (Class Definition)
Offset 0	`~AbsoluteConstant()`	`AbsoluteConstant::`
Offset 4	**`AbsoluteLocation* Clone()`**	**`Undefined: no address`**
Offset 8	`bool IsKnown() const`	`AbsoluteConstant::`
Offset C	`bool IsReadOnly()`	`AbsoluteLocation::`
Offset 10	`bool HasAddress()`	`AbsoluteLocation::`
Offset 14	`Class GetClass()`	`AbsoluteConstant::`
Offset 18	`bool IsA(Class C)`	`AbsoluteConstant::`
Offset 1C	`bool DerivesFromA(Class C)`	`AbsoluteConstant::`

TABLE 7.8   *AbsoluteConstantInt* Virtual Function Table (vtab)

Table Entry	Virtual Function	Address (Class Definition)
Offset 0	~AbsoluteConstantInt()	AbsoluteConstantInt::
Offset 4	**AbsoluteLocation* Clone()**	AbsoluteConstantInt::
Offset 8	bool IsKnown() const	AbsoluteConstant::
Offset C	bool IsReadOnly()	AbsoluteLocation::
Offset 10	bool HasAddress()	AbsoluteLocation::
Offset 14	Class GetClass()	AbsoluteConstantInt::
Offset 18	bool IsA(Class C)	AbsoluteConstantInt::
Offset 1C	bool DerivesFromA(Class C)	AbsoluteConstantInt::

TABLE 7.9   *AbsoluteConstantFloat* Virtual Function Table (vtab)

Table Entry	Virtual Function	Address (Class Definition)
Offset 0	~AbsoluteConstantFloat()	AbsoluteConstantFloat::
Offset 4	AbsoluteLocation* Clone()	AbsoluteConstantFloat::
Offset 8	bool IsKnown() const	AbsoluteConstant::
Offset C	bool IsReadOnly()	AbsoluteLocation::
Offset 10	bool HasAddress()	AbsoluteLocation::
Offset 14	Class GetClass()	AbsoluteConstantFloat::
Offset 18	bool IsA(Class C)	AbsoluteConstantFloat::
Offset 1C	bool DerivesFromA(Class C)	AbsoluteConstantFloat::

Design decisions may be difficult. Design variants often imply different effects. To clarify impact, Table 7.10 summarizes the key similarities and differences of function name reuse. *The choice between inheritance and composition often rests on the importance of type extensibility versus the need to avoid fixed overhead and to filter interface changes.*

Polymorphic functionality, via a common interface, supports type extension and usually justifies the overhead of inheritance. If applications are likely to require heterogeneous collections then inheritance is an obvious choice. However, if the base class cannot provide a stable interface, then a robust design employing polymorphism is unlikely. In contrast, a wrapped interface, via composition, buffers the client from interface modifications. As repeatedly recommended, document whatever design choice(s) are made.

Polymorphism is a key object-oriented construct. Polymorphic objects yield different behavior by postponing function resolution until runtime. Essential to such design is the use of virtual functions. Compilers use hidden virtual function tables (vtabs) to retrieve appropriate function addresses at runtime. Polymorphic designs are flexible, promote

TABLE 7.10   Function Name Reuse

Overloaded	Number, type and order of parameters varies
	Selection based on function signature
	Parameters drive selection
	Constructors often overloaded
	Overloaded for type => Generics
Overridden	Same name, same signature, same class hierarchy
	Return type NOT part of function signature
	May or may not be dynamically bound (C#, C++)
	Redefines inherited functionality
	Masks parent functionality
	May NOP inherited method
Virtual	Same name, same signature, same class hierarchy
	Return type NOT part of function signature
	Dynamically bound
	Requires vtab == overhead of indirect call
	Type of this pointer not known until run-time
	Prevents function inlining
	May be overridden in derived classes
	Extensible

substitutability, and support heterogeneous collections but incur the overhead of runtime binding. Software maintainability is improved by its use of a common interface, support of type extension, and "automatic" type resolution. However, *polymorphism is not free*. Extra instructions must be executed at runtime to support the indirect jump needed for runtime resolution. Most importantly, dynamic function calls cannot be inlined.

7.7 LANGUAGE DIFFERENCES

Software development should start at a high level, moving from requirements to modeling, to architecture, to design, and then to implementation. By retaining an abstract perspective as long as possible, software may be developed with minimal dependencies on language features. Unfortunately, especially when dealing with legacy systems, software design may not always proceed independent of the implementation language. In this section, we examine some language details that may impact design.

7.7.1 Type Introspection

Polymorphism removes need for "manual type checking" as a means to select functions at runtimes. Appendix C traces the design iterations of an inventory system dependent on type checking. Please consult this appendix to understand fully the overhead of type checking, from a design perspective. After following this comprehensive example, readers should appreciate the built-in support for polymorphism as provided by OOPLs.

What if legacy code did not anticipated the need for subtype extension and did not incorporate virtual functions into a widely used class hierarchy? In Java, there is no problem because all functions are dynamically bound so there is no need to label functions as virtual. But such an omission impacts C++ and C# code since both languages use static binding as the default. Nonetheless, in C++ and C#, type extension is still possible. A common solution is the simulation of dynamic binding. Essentially, the application programmer must check for (sub)type and then select the appropriate function.

Type introspection is the examination of object type at runtime via a language construct. C++ provides the `dynamic_cast` operator, Java provides `isa`, and C# provides `as`. Considered a tool for application programmers, type introspection often exposes poor design or failure to model system requirements for extensibility.

The tedious and error-prone nature of forced type checking is illustrated in Examples 7.18 and 7.19: a lengthy switch (or a multi-arm if-else) statement is needed to check for all possible subtypes. Type extraction is not implicit, as it is for virtual functions. Wherever the application programmer must select functionality based on subtype, this process of elimination must be repeated—not an extensible approach. If a new subtype is created, every place that performs type checking must add another arm to the if-else or switch statement. Some improvement may be realized when type checking code is isolated in a function but such improved functional decomposition does not mitigate the difficulty of ensuring all updates in a large software system.

Type checking code in an application implies inadequate design. The principles of OOD have been compromised. Why? Forced to verify type before action, an application programmer thus assumes the burden of state control that should have been internalized. Software that must include type checking is not maintainable. Application programmers must remember to check for subtype in all appropriate places: a vulnerable proposition in the modern era of large-scale, long-lived software systems. Say subtype extraction is performed in 15 different places of a software system. What happens if a new descendant is added to the type hierarchy? This type extension forces an update in those 15 different places. What happens if one update is missed? Software becomes inconsistent and possibly unreliable.

Testing type, incrementally, as shown in the multi-arm if statement of Examples 7.18 and 7.19, is inefficient. If one must exclude 8 subtypes before a match is found on the 9th subtype, then 9 dynamic casting operations (language independent) are required. Excessive type verification can be ameliorated somewhat by building whoami functionality into the base class. This approach was illustrated previously in Example 7.3, where the whoami function, as defined in the base FirstGen class, returned the value of the data member level, as set in each descendant constructor. The key idea is that one call to a whoami function returns the identity of the subtype, typically a number (or an enumerated value for readability). The application programmer can then use that number and a static cast to reclaim type, as shown in Example 7.20, thereby reducing the number of casts to one. The whoami design fix effectively reduces the cost of determining type but responsibility for correct usage still resides externally. Type-checking methods cannot compensate for poor maintainability due to a lack of virtual functions.

Example 7.18: Type Extraction in C++

```
class Base
{   public:
      virtual void surprise();

      // NOT virtual => statically bound call
      // => even if overridden, always yields Base functionality
      void process();
};


// APPLICATION CODE: heterogeneous collections
//    virtual function surprise() == automatic type checking
//    non-virtual function process() == no type checking
//    => manual type-checking if Derived behavior desired
//    when function is not virtual in the Base class

//    process() non-virtual => forced type checking
// dynamic_cast -
// run-time type check of object whose address held in pointer
//    pointer value returned if type matches
//    zero if cast fails

for (int i=0; i<100; i++)
{
  // elegant: compiler sets up dynamic invocation
  HeteroDB[i]->surprise();

  // clunky, tedious, not extensible
```

```
   if (Child1* ptr = dynamic_cast<Child1*> (HeteroDB[i]))
      ptr->process();
   else if (Child2* ptr = dynamic_cast<Child2*> (HeteroDB[i]))
      ptr->process();
   else if (Child3* ptr = dynamic_cast<Child3*> (HeteroDB[i]))
      ptr->process();
   …          // for all relevant subtype variants, test cast
   else …     // catchall: process unmatched subtype
}
```

Example 7.19: Type Extraction in C#

```
// same setup: Base class with virtual surprise()
//                  and non-virtual process()
// APPLICATION CODE
for (int i=0; i<100; i++)
{   // elegant: compiler sets up dynamic invocation
    HeteroDB[i].surprise();

    // clunky, tedious, not extensible
    if (HeteroDB[i] is Child1)
    {     Child1 x = HeteroDB[i] as Child1);
          x.process();
    }
    else if (HeteroDB[i] is Child2)
    {     Child2 x = HeteroDB[i] as Child2);
          x.process();
    }
    else if (HeteroDB[i] is Child3)
    {     Child3 x = HeteroDB[i] as Child3);
          x.process();
    }
    …              // for all relevant subtype variants, test cast
    else …     // catchall: process unmatched subtype
}
```

Example 7.20: Type Reclamation with Static Cast in C++

```
// virtual whoami() in class hierarchy yields identifying int
//   myObj is base class pointer, just like HeteroDB[i]
int typeId        myObj->whoami();

switch             typeId:
{   case 0: SubType0     ptr = static_cast<SubType0*> (myObj);
            ptr->process();
            break;
    case 1: SubType1     ptr = static_cast<SubType1*> (myObj);
            ptr->process();
            break;
    …
    case 8: SubType8     ptr = static_cast<SubType8*> (myObj);
            ptr->process();
}
```

For completeness, we next examine two anomalies particular to C++: destructor invocation and accessibility. Actually, once the compiler's actions are understood, neither aberration turns out to be an anomaly: the compiler generates code consistently.

7.7.2 C++ Virtual Destructors

Without language support for implicit deallocation, C++ relies on programmer expertise and convention to properly handle heap memory. Common C++ guidelines for class design, with respect to memory management, were discussed in Appendix B as well as Chapters 4 and 5. We complete this examination by a brief look at destructors in a class hierarchy when derived classes allocate heap memory.

Destructors fire in reverse order of constructors, from derived to base. Since the compiler patches in destructor calls, invocation is not the responsibility of the application programmer. Yet, as noted earlier, a C++ class designer must carefully specify cleanup details when memory is internally allocated in a class. To avoid memory leaks and data corruption, *the class designer must make an explicit decision about copy semantics: suppress copying or support deep copying.* That is not all, however! Correct memory management becomes more complex when heterogeneous collections are used and derived classes allocate heap memory.

When an object goes out of scope and the object is of type Base, *only* the Base destructor is invoked. When an object goes out of scope and the object is of type Derived, first the Derived destructor is invoked and *then* the Base destructor is invoked. The Base destructor is implicitly invoked from the Derived destructor. When the delete operator is invoked through a handle, if the handle is of Base type, *only* the Base destructor invoked. If the handle is of Derived type, *both* Derived and Base destructors are invoked.

When a Base class handle goes out of scope, with a statically bound destructor call, the Base class destructor is invoked. When a Base class pointer contains the address of a Base object, there is no problem. What if the Base class handle holds the address of a Derived object? The compiler does not track the effect of the assignment; the compiler resolves calls based on the type of the pointer. Hence, with static resolution the Base class destructor is invoked and the Derived class destructor is not. Failure to invoke the Derived class destructor is not a problem unless the Derived class allocates dynamic memory. In which case, there is a memory leak.

Why? The Derived class destructor was not invoked so the deallocation code in the Derived destructor did not run.

Consider Example 7.21. Test this code yourself. When delete is called on the base class pointer b, the call to the destructor is statically bound so only the Base class destructor fires: the 500 integers allocated on the heap for the Derived class object thus leak, through no fault of the application programmer. Memory leaks arise because the Derived class allocates heap memory but the Derived destructor was not invoked.

Example 7.21: C++ Memory Leak: Only Base Destructor Called

```
// class hierarchy: Base ok; Derived class allocates heap memory
class Base
{    …
  public:
    Base() { … }    // #A
    ~Base() { … }
    …
};

class Derived: public Base
{    int*          ptr;
     int           size;
     …
     // copying suppressed
  public:
    Derived(int    aSize = 900)
    {      size = aSize;
           ptr = new int[size];    // heap memory allocated
           cout << "allocated" << size << "ints";
    }

    ~Derived()
    {      delete[] ptr;           // deallocate heap memory
           cout << "deallocated" << size << "ints";
    }
    …
};

void hiddenProblem() // Application code correct BUT MEMORY LEAK
{    Base*          b = new Derived(500);
     …
     // Destructor call statically resolved:
     //     Base destructor non-virtual
     //     compiler resolves call based on type of pointer b
     // Base destructor invoked: 500 ints leak
     //     => Derived destructor not invoked!!
           => MEMORY LEAK
```

```
delete  b;       // #B   destructor invoked

Base*           db[10];

for (int k = 0; k < 10; k++)
        db[] = new Derived;

for (int k = 0; k < 10; k++)
        delete db[k];  // #C   destructor invoked
return;
}
```

Base class pointers often hold addresses of Derived class objects. In statements #B and #C of Example 7.21, the application programmer correctly calls delete for each heap object. Since the destructors are statically resolved, only the Base class destructor is invoked: the Derived destructor is not invoked through a Base handle. Big problem! The application programmer has followed all the rules (match every new with a delete; deallocate when ownership is surrendered but not transferred) and yet there is an invisible memory leak!

How does the class designer ensure the invocation of the derived destructor when delete is invoked with a base class pointer? Through dynamic resolution of destructor invocation. The setup is the same as with other virtual functions. A Base class pointer may hold the address of Derived object. Thus, the (sub)type of the object whose address is held in the base class pointer must be examined at runtime to trigger the execution of the proper destructor. The firing of a Derived destructor yields the subsequent execution of the Base destructor.

The fix is easy: make the Base destructor virtual. That is all! We do not take the space needed to replicate Example 7.21. All code is the same except the keyword virtual is placed in front of the Base class destructor in statement #A. Hence, when "delete b" (in statement #B) or "delete db[k]" (in statement #C) is compiled, the compiler patches in an indirect call to the destructor via the virtual function table. As with other dynamically invoked calls, the choice of destructor will be postponed until runtime. If the Base class pointer holds the address of a Derived class object, the Derived class vtab will yield the address of the Derived class destructor, triggering a call to the Derived destructor first, followed by a call to the Base class destructor. Rerun the application code in Example 7.21, once the Base class has been defined with a virtual destructor. No memory leaks!

7.7.3 Accessibility of C++ Virtual Functions

In Chapter 6, we discussed the possibility of suppressing an inherited inter-face. C++ allows direct suppression: a class designer may redefine a public inherited method as private or protected (as well as redefining a protected inherited method as private). Java and C# do not allow such "closing down" of a class. On the one hand, the approach taken by Java and C# might appear to be a simple syntactic constraint since a public inherited method could be redefined, still as public but with no meaningful func-tionality. In this manner, an inherited interface could be effectively nar-rowed, regardless of language.

On the other hand, consistent accessibility reduces code complexity and makes it easier to reason about control flow and so forth. Consider the inter-play of accessibility and virtual functions in C++. Example 7.22 defines a class hierarchy with both virtual functions and reductions in inherited accessibility.

Example 7.22: C++ Derived Class: Partial Suppression

```
// virtual functions in base
// derived class suppresses part of inherited interface
class Diva
{    ...
  public:
      virtual void sing()    {...}
      virtual void hum()     {...}
      ...
};

class Shy: public Diva
{    ...
      // public inherited virtual function SUPPRESSED
      virtual void sing()    {...}
  public:
      // public inherited virtual function overridden
      virtual void hum()     {...}
      ...
};
```

The class definitions in Example 7.22 suggest that an application pro-grammer may call two functions, `sing()` and `hum()`, through a base class object but only one, `hum()`, through a derived class object. Yes, that is true. Example 7.23 provides sample application code. All code except statement #D compiles. Since `sing()` is a private method in the Shy class interface, the call to `sing()` through a Shy object triggers a compilation error.

Example 7.23: C++ Dynamic Invocation of a Private Function

```
Diva          b;
Shy           d;
b.sing();     // #A
b.hum();      // #B
d.hum();      // #C
d.sing();     // #D compiler error, Shy::sing() private


Diva*         bPtr = &b;
bPtr->sing();          // #E
bPtr->hum();           // #F


bPtr = &d;   // d Derived object; Derived::printMsg() private
bPtr->sing();          // #G
bPtr->hum();           // #H
```

What happens when calls to virtual functions are made through base class pointers? Remember that, to support dynamic binding, the compiler generates the extra instructions needed to extract a function address, at runtime, from the appropriate class vtab. The compiler looks only at the type of the pointer through which a function call is made. Thus, the compiler examines the base class, class Diva in Example 7.23, to match the invoked function with a declared function in the base class interface and to verify that it has public accessibility.

Virtual function sing() does have public accessibility in class Diva. Thus, all the function calls in statements #E through #H compile and execute. To the compiler, statement #G is no different than statement #E. What is the outcome? The private function Shy::sing() is executed at runtime. An application programmer has thus defeated a restricted interface!

The interplay of accessibility and dynamic binding, when an inherited, virtual function is suppressed, may seem counterintuitive. Once the compiler's actions are analyzed, however, the software response is logical. The compiler resolves the legality of a call relative to the type of the handle through which the call is made. Then the compiler generates the code needed for dynamic function resolution (an indirect jump). The (sub)type of the object whose address is held in a base class pointer (reference) at runtime is immaterial at compile-time. This (sub)type is used at runtime to identify the appropriate vtab: accessibility is not rechecked at runtime. Put a simple output message in the class methods of Example 7.22 and test this code yourself!

7.8 OO DESIGN PRINCIPLES

Once again, the open close principle (OCP) applies to our emphasis on software maintainability. Polymorphism is used when a base type defines key functionality but defers complete implementation to descendant classes, or when variant behavior among subtypes is to be supported within a heterogeneous collection. As software evolves, the base class should be stable (closed to modification). Furthermore, the design of additional descendant classes is expected (open for extension).

The Liskov Substitution principle (LSP) implies the power of heterogeneous collections. Any subtype can stand in for a base class object. Great variability can thus be achieved in stable software systems.

Open Close Principle (OCP)
A class should be open for extension and closed for modification.

Liskov Substitution Principle (LSP)
Given a type T with a subtype S defined via inheritance, any object of subtype S can serve in place of an object of type T.

7.9 SUMMARY

This chapter examined and illustrated the functional impact of employing inheritance in software design, noting the major benefits of substitutability and heterogeneous collections. Polymorphism provides tremendous support for the design of elegant and extensible software and thus, if properly used, improves software maintainability. Abstract classes were also illustrated. Using a real-world example, we demonstrated that careful and deliberate design uses abstract classes and polymorphism in a meaningful manner.

In this chapter, we took the unusual tact of explaining virtual function tables, and clarifying use via examples. Knowledge of this background process will surely aid the reader. We closed the chapter by looking at type introspection, a couple of subtle language differences and relevant design principles.

DESIGN INSIGHTS

SOFTWARE
Software maintenance enhanced by well-designed polymorphism
Heterogeneous collections, abstract classes, extensibility

Dynamic binding provides flexibility at a cost:
    Incurs the run-time overhead of an indirect jump
    Prevents function inlining, an effective optimization
Static binding is efficient but rigid
Compilers process statements individually and do not track assignment
Type checking in client code implies inadequate design

MODELS

True power of inheritance is not structural reuse
    Behavioral modification!
Inheritance versus composition
    Type extension versus possibly reduced overhead
    Polymorphism versus buffer for unstable interface
    Substitutability versus flexibility

SOFTWARE DESIGN

Isolate code that is highly dependent on explicit type
whoami is a designed type extraction method
    Reduces overhead of reclaiming type
    Rests on external dependencies
Common interface required for heterogeneous collections
    Abstract classes
    Interface construct
Polymorphism
    Promotes type extension
    Suggests software maintainability
    Removes need for external type validation
Polymorphism is NOT free
    run-time binding overhead
    unable to inline functions

DOCUMENTATION

Explicitly record design decisions
Evaluate expectations for
    Substitutability, polymorphism, type extension

CONCEPTUAL QUESTIONS

1. What are the three common forms of polymorphism?

2. How is the notion of type relevant in each form of polymorphism?

3. How does each type of polymorphism impact software maintainability?

4. What is the essential difference between static and dynamic binding?

5. Describe the different effects of static and dynamic binding.

6. Why would static binding be a reasonable choice for default behavior?

7. When would a heterogeneous collection be useful?

8. What does the phrase "once virtual, always virtual" mean?

9. What is an abstract class, and how is it used?

10. Why is tracking (sub)type not desirable?

11. Define type extensibility.

CHAPTER 8

Design Alternatives and Perspectives

D ESIGN RECORDS CHOICE. Frequently, multiple solutions exist for a given problem. How does one recognize an optimal, or even a preferable, design? How does a class designer balance short-term and long-term costs and benefits?

To highlight and explain design evaluation, we contrast different design solutions in this chapter. We begin by examining the class construct from design and use perspectives. Bjarne Stroustrup, the architect of C++, enumerated several different design types of classes, and we illustrate some of them here to identify motives for selection and clarify terminology. We then examine different inheritance designs, as compiled by Timothy Budd, a noted author in OOD, again identifying motives for selection and use of each different type of design.

The latter half of the chapter returns to the question of design choice: when is inheritance preferred over composition? The discussion here, however, is rooted in the necessity of modeling **multiple inheritance** when a language does not support such a design. Various approaches to simulating multiple inheritance are examined and then contrasted to the provision of multiple inheritance in C++. The chapter concludes by summarizing characteristics relevant when analyzing design options.

CHAPTER OBJECTIVES

- Define and illustrate common class design types
  - Concrete, abstract, node, wrapper, delegate, handle
- Examine common inheritance design intents
  - Specialization, specification, extension, limitation, generalization
- Contrast composition and inheritance
  - Polymorphic subobjects
- Discuss multiple inheritance
- Illustrate and analyze design alternatives to multiple inheritance
- Identify relevant OOD principles

8.1 COMPARATIVE DESIGN

Bits are bits and loops are loops. Why care about variability in structure if the resulting behavior is the same? Reasons abound but one of the strongest design incentives is software maintainability. Software evolves, that is, changes over time. Some changes may be obvious, such as user interface modifications. Other changes may not be readily apparent, such as performance under heavy load, porting software to a new platform, augmenting error processing, or incorporating a data mining algorithm. No matter the modification, software that conforms to the modeled and documented requirements is easier to modify than code that is not.

Isolation and comparison of design options is part of deliberate design, an approach that evaluates immediate use and anticipates change. By clarifying intent and effect, one can more easily evaluate trade-offs, such as short-term versus long-term use, efficiency versus generality, etc. We examine multiple design approaches and variants, including the application of and simulation of inheritance.

8.2 CLASS DESIGN TYPES

Design intent affects modeling, use, and reuse. Stroustrup identified different class designs and their utility in OOD (Stroustrup, 2000). Using these designs and clarifying commonly used terms, we examine the following class design types: **concrete**, **abstract**, **node**, **delegate**, **interface** (**wrapper**), and **handle**. Each class design type implies a distinct use and/or form.

8.2.1 Concrete Class

A **concrete class** is the representation of a relatively simple concept with all operations defined to support that type. In early object-oriented programming (OOP), common examples of concrete classes included vector, date, and complex number classes. Currently, these types are often built-in (or provided via libraries). Recall the concrete `minMaxRec` class from Chapter 6: its utility is confined; its design simple. Concrete classes have a clear, targeted use and, typically, constrained functionality.

A concrete class is immediately usable because its class designer provides a fully functional, complete interface. Design is streamlined because there is a one-to-one correspondence between interface and implementation. Member function calls are statically bound; consequently, function calls may be inlined. Concrete classes are thus considered efficient.

Concrete classes may be considered standalone type definitions. Design and effect should be understood in isolation, without reference to other classes. Inheritance is not anticipated. Some OOPLs provide the syntactical means to suppress inheritance. To prevent a class from being used as a base for inheritance in Java, one labels a class 'final'; in C#, one labels a class 'sealed'. C++98 provides no keyword for directly suppressing inheritance, but could support a workaround via design—a tedious and less maintainable solution, as detailed below.

By defining all constructors private, a class designer prevents instantiation at both the public (application programmer) level and the protected (descendant) level. Inheritance is suppressed because a child class is unable to invoke any parent constructor. Application use is also suppressed: no object can be directly instantiated. The class designer must then define a public, static method that can be called through the class name. The method must be static because, without a public constructor, the client is not able to instantiate an object (through which to invoke public class methods). As a class method, this static function can access private data and functionality and thus instantiate an object and return its address to the caller. This approach is essentially the Singleton pattern, a collapsed version of the Factory pattern that is used to control instantiation (Gamma et al., 1995). C++11 provides a special identifier 'final' that, when used, forces the compiler to suppress redefinition.

Contrast the clarity of using a language construct to suppress inheritance, as shown in Example 8.1, with the use of a more complex design to control instantiation, as shown in Example 8.2. Note that the C++ solution does more than prevent inheritance; it forces instantiation through a public static method—an unnatural process best reserved for the Singleton pattern. Thus, in legacy code, C++ programmers often did not attempt to suppress inheritance.

Example 8.1: Suppressing Inheritance in C# and Java

```
// C#                              // Java
sealed class Childless            final class Childless
{     ...     }                   {     ...     }
```

Example 8.2: Suppressing Inheritance via Design in C++

```
// failure to provide public and protected constructors
//    => class unusable except through its own public interface
//    => first call must be through static method getInstance
class Childless
{     // private constructor, copy constructor, overloaded =
      Childless();
      Childless(const Childless&);
      void operator=(const Childless&);
   public:
          // call through class name to get handle to object
          static Childless*     getInstance();
          ...
          // public functions
};
```

A concrete class has no relationships with other classes (other than, possibly, simple composition). Programming by Contract details are thus fairly constrained. The interface invariant clearly specifies the intended use of the class, as defined by the public functions. The implementation invariant records assumptions, preferences for internal data structures, and design priorities such as efficiency or maintainability.

8.2.2 Abstract Class

In contrast to a concrete class, whose design yields immediate utility, an **abstract** class is a placeholder for extensibility and is not immediately usable. Inheritance is anticipated; in fact, it is required for any functionality to be exercised. The base class defines a common interface for the class hierarchy. The base class need not implement any functionality for its declared member functions, although it is possible for the base class to define default or minimal behavior. Abstract classes are designed for generality, for heterogeneous collections. Common examples of abstract classes are *Shape, Vehicle, Toy, Ad*. In the previous chapter, we saw the AbsoluteLocation class as an abstract class that established and enforced a uniform interface. Contrast Figure 8.1 with Figure 8.2. The two UML class constructs look the same, except the name of an abstract class is italicized.

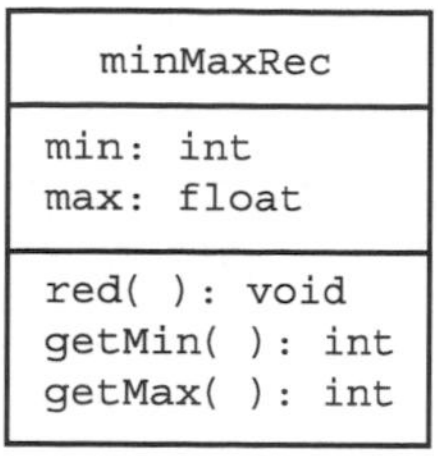

```
┌──────────────────────────┐
│       minMaxRec          │
├──────────────────────────┤
│ min: int                 │
│ max: float               │
├──────────────────────────┤
│ red( ): void             │
│ getMin( ): int           │
│ getMax( ): int           │
└──────────────────────────┘
```

FIGURE 8.1   Concrete class in UML.

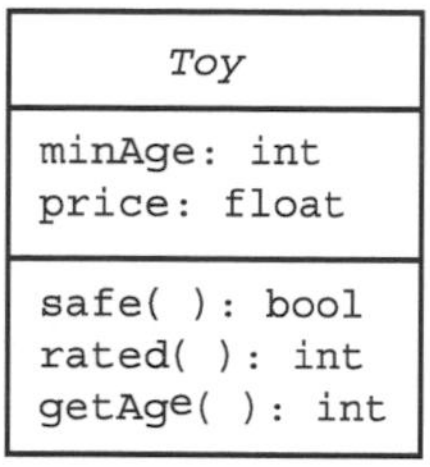

```
┌──────────────────────────┐
│          Toy             │
├──────────────────────────┤
│ minAge: int              │
│ price: float             │
├──────────────────────────┤
│ safe( ): bool            │
│ rated( ): int            │
│ getAge( ): int           │
└──────────────────────────┘
```

FIGURE 8.2   Abstract class in UML.

We covered abstract classes in Chapter 7 but expand our discussion here. Abstract classes define a common interface that supports the use of heterogeneous collections. Implementation of functionality is typically deferred to derived classes. A **deferred method** is a function that has been declared but not defined in a class. How could an invocation of a deferred method be resolved? It cannot: there is no possible translation to a JUMP statement. Without a function implementation, there is no function code to lay out in memory and thus no address associated with the function. A compiler cannot then resolve a function invocation. To forestall such errors, the compiler prevents object instantiation from an abstract class.

Later edition OOPLs provide the keyword `abstract` so that software designers can clearly label abstract classes, thus increasing readability and software maintainability. As shown in Chapter 7, with or without a key-word, design techniques can prevent the instantiation of objects from a class meant to be abstract. In a class design, if no constructor is public but at least one constructor is protected, then only a derived child can invoke a constructor from that class. Hence, inheritance is required. If a class contains at least one function that is declared but not defined, then the class is abstract. In other words, if a class contains a method that has no corresponding implementation code, then the method is abstract (or pure virtual). Since there is no means to execute an abstract function then one cannot instantiate an object from a class with an abstract method. Again, contrast the clarity of using a self-documenting language keyword to define an abstract class, as shown in Example 8.3, with a design solution to define abstract classes, as shown in Example 8.4.

Example 8.3: Abstract Classes in C# and Java

```
abstract class Vehicle
{    ...    }
```

Example 8.4: Abstract Classes in C++

```
// no keyword abstract => at least one method must be pure virtual
class Toy
{    public:
          virtual bool safe() = 0;
    ...
};
// no keyword abstract
//    => protected constructor, no public constructor
class Vehicle
{
    protected:
          Vehicle();
    public:
    ...
};
```

An abstract class defines the interface for its descendants and establishes a dependency on descendants. Thus, the interface invariant for an abstract class must note the expected use (and any restrictions) of the public interface. The implementation invariant must describe the responsibilities to be met by descendant classes, the intended utility of polymorphic methods, and any default behavior that the abstract class may provide.

8.2.3 Node Class

In between the concrete and abstract class design types lies an intermediate class design type. A **node** class sits in the middle of a class hierarchy: it is neither the root (base) class defining the interface for the class hierarchy nor is it a terminal leaf node that is not intended for further derivation. As a middling node, a node class relies on the services provided by the base class or the interface defined by the base class. However, a node class implements some services itself, for the application programmer or descendant classes. Thus, inheritance is anticipated but not immediately required. Tied to both parent and child, a node class increases coupling and also decreases cohesion because it expands a type definition across multiple classes.

A node class may itself be abstract but further refines the abstract notion of type as defined by its parent. Commonly, node classes provide some (possibly default) services. This type of "mix" design increases software complexity so the design contributions of a node class should be warranted. An intuitive example is an *Aircraft* class that extends a *Vehicle* class (*Aircraft is-a Vehicle*) and serves as parent for *Jet, Fighter, PropPlane* classes. Similarly, a *Watercraft* class could extend the *Vehicle* class (*Watercraft is-a Vehicle*) and serve as parent for *Sailboat, Freighter, Yacht* classes. In the disassembler example from Chapter 7, the node classes AbsoluteConstant and AbsoluteVariable were descendants of AbsoluteLocation and parents of AbsoluteConstantInt and AbsoluteAddress, respectively, as previously noted in Figure 7.1.

A node class must clearly document inherited and extended data and functionality. The implementation invariant must distinguish between utility code and public, possibly deferred, methods. Assumptions, design limitations, and prioritization of qualities (efficiency, extensibility, etc.) should be recorded.

8.2.4 Wrappers

The meanings of concrete, abstract, and node classes are clear and their applicability is straightforward. In contrast, the class design types called wrapper, delegate, and handle are not clearly distinguished from each other. These terms are often used interchangeably when their meaning and intent differ. The critical design differences are succinctly noted here. A wrapper defines and *controls* a consistent interface that may be layered over one of multiple implementations. A delegate serves to provide functionality; it may be replaceable or polymorphic and thus provides flexibility in subordinate behavior. A handle promotes access to target data without being tied to a specific object or data set.

Wrappers are what the name implies: an extra layer or coating. *A wrapper class layers an interface over an existing class (or set of classes) to isolate users* from an unstable class or interface. As an added interface layer, wrappers are commonly used to buffer application code from change. Although they may provide extra functionality, wrappers primarily serve to maintain a stable interface. Wrappers streamline the reuse of legacy code by defining a more modern or palatable interface.

A **wrapper** class provides a shell to encompass an existing class, and thus promotes software maintainability. By wrapping the interface of proprietary software, a wrapper class isolates application code from change. If a new version of the wrapped code is released with a modified interface, the internals of the wrapper class may need to be modified but its interface can usually stay the same. Thus, application code need not be modified immediately. For any code, a wrapper class can provide a more uniform, general, or simpler interface. This extra layer removes dependencies on wrapped code and decreases coupling, which is especially desirable when the wrapped code is unstable. Hence, if used well, this type of class design reduces software complexity.

Wrapper classes are also known as interface classes and are a common solution in Design Patterns, e.g., *Façade* (Gamma et al., 1995). Wrappers promote the reuse of existing classes for new or modified applications. Wrappers may redefine interfaces and modify class functionality or accessibility to meet client needs. An effective reuse of code, wrappers may set up a uniform means to customize code for different clients.

Although counterintuitive, wrappers may also be used to expose an interface. Say that a class designer wishes to reuse a class with a protected interface but does not wish to support an inheritance relationship. How can one gain access to the protected interface if composition is used in place of inheritance? Use a wrapper class to open up the protected interface. This approach is especially useful when simulating multiple inheritance with single inheritance and composition, as will be seen in Example 8.17.

Typically, wrappers are designed using composition: the wrapper has-a subobject and wraps up the interface for the subobject class. The interface invariant details of a wrapper class are similar to those of any class: describe core utility provided and restrictions on use. The implementation invariant should explain what is being wrapped and why. Is the wrapped code unstable, proprietary, or dated? What dependencies are hidden? How does the wrapper streamline use for the client? Record expectations with respect to maintenance and/or performance.

Consider an application that must support multiple queries across a stable collection of numeric values. It is expedient to reuse an existing container type. Figure 8.3 illustrates a modQuery wrapper class that wraps a priority queue alongside an integer that tracks the number of queries. The wrapper provides a public interface that retrieves (but does not delete) min, max, and random values. By wrapping a priority queue, the modQuery class suppresses unwanted public functions, such as clear() and

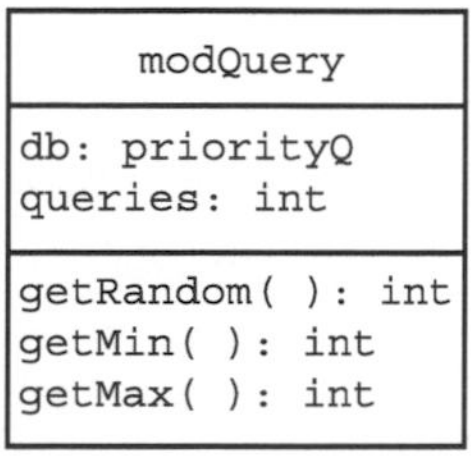

```
┌─────────────────────────┐
│        modQuery         │
├─────────────────────────┤
│ db: priorityQ           │
│ queries: int            │
├─────────────────────────┤
│ getRandom( ): int       │
│ getMin( ): int          │
│ getMax( ): int          │
└─────────────────────────┘
```

FIGURE 8.3   Wrapper class in UML.

isEmpty(), while supporting the retrieval of data. The type of internal container manipulated by the modQuery class is irrelevant to the application programmer. If the modQuery class were to replace the priority queue with a stack or a simple array, the client would not know or care.

8.2.5 Delegate

A **delegate** class provides functionality and promotes flexibility. Delegates are often held as subobjects inside another class, and may be instantiated internal or external to the containing class. A delegate can be replaced or varied without impacting the external interface. Figure 8.4 illustrates an idVerifier delegate class. The delegate supports a public interface that provides validation of proper ID initialization as well as age and ID verification. Consider a class that desires an ID parameter but does not want to reimplement verification, validation, or age requests. An idVerifier instance may be used as a delegate: forward all requests through the delegate to avoid the unneeded cost of reimplementing known functionality (see Example 8.5).

Delegates provide functionality to an enclosing class, thus isolating the application code from change: the enclosing class can easily modify or replace its delegate. Furthermore, if a delegate is a polymorphic subobject, as shown in Example 8.6, a variety of functionality may be provided. Consider

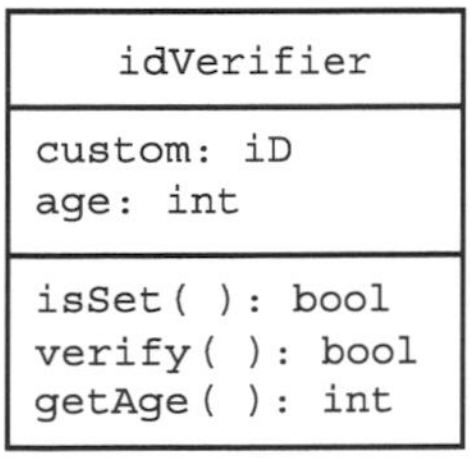

```
┌─────────────────────────┐
│       idVerifier        │
├─────────────────────────┤
│ custom: iD              │
│ age: int                │
├─────────────────────────┤
│ isSet ( ): bool         │
│ verify( ): bool         │
│ getAge ( ): int         │
└─────────────────────────┘
```

FIGURE 8.4   Delegate class in UML.

the class hierarchy in Figure 8.5. If each delegate subtype provides a different implementation of process(), then a call to dynamicProcess() will yield variant behavior. When a delegate is typed to hold the address of a base class object, any object in the class hierarchy can be used. C# offers a specific delegate construct.

Example 8.5: Delegate Use in C++

```
class seminarAttendee
{       // delegate could be object or pointer
        //      indirection supports postponed instantiation
        idVerifier              delegate;
        ...
        void replaceDelegate(...)
        {       idVerifier              newImproved(...);
                delegate = newImproved;
        }
    public:
        // class functionality, including constructor
        ...
        // pass requests to delegate
        bool registerD()        {       return delegate.isSet(); }
        bool isValid()          {       return delegate.verify(); }
        bool renew()
        {       if (!registerD() || ! isValid())        return false;
                return (delegate.getAge() > 18)
        }
};
```

Example 8.6: Polymorphic Delegate in C++

```
// contrast simple echo with indirect (layered) echo
class HasADelegate
{       idVerifier              delegate;
        BaseType*               polyD;

        void replaceDelegate()
        {       delete      polyD;
                if (...)                polyD = new MinType(...);
                else if (...)           polyD = new MaxType(...);
                else if (...)           polyD = new MeanType(...);
        }
    public:
        // simple echo
        int getAge()    [       return      delegate.getAge();      }
        // additional layer of indirection supports polymorphism
        void dynamicProcess()
        {       return      polyD->process();}
        ...
};
```

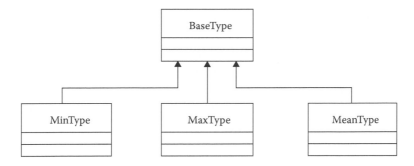

FIGURE 8.5   Delegate polymorphism.

What is the difference between a delegate and a wrapper? A delegate is an internal data member that provides functionality. A wrapper is an external class that isolates the client from change or streamlines an interface. The two overlap. A wrapper could wrap up a delegate. Differences may be slight and focus on intent. *A delegate serves to provide utility. A wrapper serves to redefine an interface.* The interface invariant details of a delegate class should describe core utility provided and restrictions on use. Documentation should indicate if the application programmer has any responsibility for seeding or replacing a delegate. The implementation invariant should explain the motivation for using delegates and enumerate cardinality, ownership, and stability (replacement) details.

8.2.6 Handle: Smart Pointers

Colloquially, a **handle** refers to the means of accessing data or an object. Every variable is an abstraction of an assigned memory location but provides direct access to data through its name. Pointers and references hold data that is interpreted as addresses and thus provide an indirect means to access data (but the layer of indirection is not obvious when using a reference). Regardless of type then, variables are all considered handles. One piece of data may have multiple handles, as is evident when a pointer variable holds the address of another variable.

What then is a handle class design type? Conceptually, a handle supports the dual perspective of internal functionality versus external use. A type definition can be viewed in two parts: the handle is the user interface and the representation is the object state. Internal details for managing state are independent of external use of the handle. Thus, the class designer may vary implementation without changing the interface. The Bridge design pattern is essentially a handle: a consistent means of access that supports varying functionality and/or varying data representation (Gamma et al., 1995).

How does a handle class differ from a delegate? Significant differences are not obvious. A handle class controls access to data but does not augment or alter functionality. See Table 8.1.

Smart pointers, such as the `unique _ ptr` and `shared _ ptr` template classes in C++11 STL, embody handles. A smart pointer is just a wrapped pointer that serves the essential need in C++ to manage internal class memory. By wrapping a raw pointer inside a class, with a defined destructor, the memory leaks illustrated in Chapters 4, 5, and 7 may be avoided.

Example 8.7 illustrates two wrapped pointers: a simple wrapped pointer as well as a wrapped pointer that assumes ownership of the pointer so wrapped. A `wrappedPtr` object is instantiated with a pointer, passed in by the client. When this `wrappedPtr` object goes out of scope, its destructor is automatically invoked so the deallocation of wrapped heap memory is guaranteed. The second class design differs only in that the `grabMemoryPtr` constructor assumes ownership of the memory whose address is held in the passed pointer. The passed pointer is zeroed out, preventing the caller from using the raw pointer after it has been wrapped. Thus, the `grabMemoryPtr` class design may be viewed as more secure. Nonetheless, both designs depend on the application programmer constructing the smart pointer with a valid address.

TABLE 8.1   Stroustrup Class Design Types

Design Type	Characteristics	Interface	Base for Inheritance
Concrete	Simple, efficient	Tight, cohesive	Not desired
Abstract	Defines interface of class hierarchy	Common general	Required
Node	Intermediate in class hierarchy	Inherited	Anticipated
Delegate	Wrapped subobject	Layered	Unlikely
Handle	Object management	Transparent	Possible

Example 8.7: Wrapped Pointers in C++

```
// automatic invocation of destructor prevents memory leaks
//    dependent on convention:
//         Application programmer MUST use wrapped pointer
//              should not (but can) use raw pointer
class wrappedPtr
{       SomeType*        ptr;
    public:
         // address copied from pointer passed by value
         wrappedPtr(SomeType* p): ptr(p) {}

         ~wrappedPtr()    {delete ptr;}

         // forward call transparently
         SomeType* operator->()   {return ptr;}
};


// automatic invocation of destructor prevents memory leaks
// Constructor
//    assumes ownership of memory addressed by pointer parameter
//    =>  Application programmer cannot use raw pointer
//    does NOT support sharing via aliases
class grabMemoryPtr
{       SomeType*        ptr;
    public:
         // pointer passed by reference: value zeroed out
         grabMemoryPtr(SomeType*& p): ptr(p)    {p = 0;}

         ~grabMemoryPtr()                {delete ptr;}

         // forward call transparently
         SomeType* operator->()   {return ptr;}
};
```

Use of a smart pointer forces the invocation of a destructor when a pointer goes out of scope, and in so doing, prevents memory leaks. Why is a smart pointer considered a handle rather than a delegate? *The smart pointer provides no functionality other than heap protection: it does not delegate a subset of behavior*; it does not have any other critical type-dependent functionality.

Our frequent use of the term "wrapper" in the discussion of handles indicates why the term "wrapper" has colloquially subsumed the "term" handle. Formally, however, it is interesting to evaluate why a smart pointer is considered a handle rather than a wrapper. A smart pointer does not wrap up an interface. In fact, with judicious operator overloading in C++, calls to the functionality provided via the wrapped pointers may be forwarded transparently. The overloaded `operator->()` does just that. For more details, see Appendix D.

8.3 DESIGN SPECIFICATIONS FOR INHERITANCE

An interface usually publishes class functionality. However, the full design utility and usability of a class often cannot be fully comprehended in isolation. How are classes to be used together? The distinction between different types of class design helps determine the appropriate use of a type in context. Design may be problematic when it is difficult to identify the appropriate variety of class design to employ. Our brief discussion of the subtle differences between handle, delegate, and wrapper classes illustrates such confusion. Whatever type of class design is selected, a software designer still must evaluate tradeoffs and document carefully.

As outlined above, class design takes different forms with different intent. Similarly, the structure and use of inheritance is also variously motivated and implemented. We examine here five of Budd's different categories of inheritance designs, distinguishing between original (clean-slate) design and modified (reused) design (Budd, 2002). Clean-slate designs support the is-a relationship associated with inheritance. Code-reuse designs typically do not.

The first three inheritance design examples listed in Table 8.2 all support the is-a relationship. Not surprisingly, these design setups are best pursued with clean slate development. **Specialization** describes subtyping, that is the child class inherits core functionality from the parent class but redefines or overrides some inherited behavior. Our `Icon` class hierarchy from Chapter 6 illustrated the specialization of movement by the different child classes of the parent `Icon` class. Many class designs, where the parent provides default behavior and the child augment or redefines that behavior, under the same interface, illustrate specialization.

TABLE 8.2   Budd's Inheritance Design Classes

Inheritance Design	Characteristics	Inherited Interface	Relationship
Specialization	Redefines behavior	Retained	Is-a
Specification	Completes abstract base	Implemented	Is-a
Extension	Type expansion	Extended	Is-a
Limitation	Restrict use of parent	Suppressed	Code reuse
Generalization	Inverted class hierarchy	Compromised	Code reuse

As noted earlier, a priority queue may be viewed as just another queue because the external interfaces of the two queue types are the same. However, the internal ordering of items in the priority queue may undermine the is-a relationship. Why? The possibility of starvation may preclude the use of a priority queue in place of a regular queue. Nonetheless, this example underscores the subtle interpretation of specialization: it may not unambiguously support the is-a relationship.

Specification refers to node classes that inherit a common but not fully functional interface from an abstract parent class. The child class must define (specify) the behavior outlined by the parent class because the parent class definition is incomplete. Since the parent class is thus an abstract class, no object can be instantiated from the parent class. The key difference between specification and specialization is that, under specification, the parent type definition is incomplete and thus unusable until a child class is defined. In our Icon example, if the move() method was an abstract method then the client could not instantiate any Icon objects. The Icon class would then provide no utility until a child class "specified" the move() function by providing implementation details (that is, the function body of the move() method).

The power of specification comes from the common interface defined by the base class. All derived classes must conform to this interface, must define the functions whose forms were declared but not defined, and thus must implement a core set of required behaviors to be usable. Specification classes are thus candidates for polymorphism, and may likely be used in heterogeneous collections. *Specification differs from specialization in that the child class is not a refinement of existing usable type but a realization of incomplete abstract specification.*

A car is-a vehicle is a clear example of specification. Vehicle's definition ensures that all derivations (car, plane, boat) move but implementation details have been deferred to child classes. The same postponement of utility was seen in Figure 8.2: a Toy object is not usable because it is abstract; derived Toy objects may be instantiated, however, assuming the derived classes provide implementation of inherited abstract methods. The disassembler example from Chapter 7 is a real-world example of specification.

Extension is the pure form of inheritance. The inherited parent interface is extended but not compromised or redefined. Each child class introduces new abilities by adding new methods but does not override parent class methods. In this manner, the is-a relation is supported. In contrast, subtyping (specialization) retains the is-a relationship but its modification of inherited behavior may compromise the notion of substitutability.

As noted in Chapter 6, a simple example of extension is a TriAthlete class. A TriAthlete is-a BiAthlete, that is a TriAthlete runs and bikes like a BiAthlete but also swims. A BiAthlete is-a Runner, that is a BiAthlete runs like a Runner but also bikes. Extension differs from specification in that the base class is not abstract but an existing usable type. Extension differs from specialization in that the derived classes extend, and do not compromise, the inherited interface.

The last two types of inheritance design delineated in Table 8.2 describe class designs that reuse existing classes. Both these designs exhibit obvious flaws. Forced reuse of software often is not effective or a good return on investment. When software designers do not have the luxury of designing from scratch, optimal design may not be easily achieved. Frequently, insufficient resources (time, labor) are available to refactor and thus improve existing software. Software designers thus must reuse classes that have already been designed, developed, tested, and deployed. When reusing classes, a key design question is: should composition be preferred over inheritance for reuse?

Limitation is a special case of subclassing for specialization where the behavior of the subclass is smaller than that of the parent. Often a portion of the inherited interface is suppressed or redefined in a more restricted manner. For example, a double-ended queue (deque) supports insertion and deletion from both ends of the queue. One can derive a stack from a deque by simply suppressing access to one end of the queue. Although utility is then easily realized, the derived stack class cannot function as a deque. Therefore, substitutability is not supported, unlike the specification design of the priorityQ.

Generalization is a contorted application of inheritance whose primary motive is the expedient reuse of code to create a more general class design. Say a class design has already been deployed but demand arises for more flexiblity or broader utility. What options should a class designer pursue? Redesigning an existing class is not attractive when software development must proceed with severe time constraints. A Player is-a Warrior is an intuitive example of an inverted relationship: a Player is a generalized notion of an actor in an online game; a Warrior is a specific realization of such. Ideally, the Player class should rest at the top of the class hierarchy and the Warrior class should be a descendant class. When a class hierarchy is inverted and no true is-a relationship exists, the parent

(Warrior) interface most likely will be compromised as the Player subclass must modify and generalize the properties of parent class.

8.4 INHERITANCE VERSUS COMPOSITION

Inheritance is one of the most touted constructs of OOP. We examined this construct in detail, and contrasted it to composition, in both Chapters 6 and 7. We revisit it here with an emphasis on polymorphic subobjects.

A common observation leading to an endorsement of inheritance is that the parent class has already been designed, implemented, debugged, and tested. Perceived as an easy means to reuse code and shorten the development life cycle, inheritance is thus often overused. Yet, for any class X that is already designed, implemented, debugged, and tested, code reuse is possible whether X serves as the base for inheritance or is the type of a subobject defined in a composition relationship. Although both design variants profit from code reuse, inheritance yields different effects from composition. We compared these design approaches in Chapter 6, noting the classic composite principle: prefer composition over inheritance.

Many professionals adhere to the composite principle. Their underlying assumption is that the need for the is-a relationship often is not significant enough to justify its costs. When using composition, the class designer maintains more control over the class, and thus can more easily acquire efficiency and/or flexibility. The authors of the seminal Design Patterns book (Gamma et al., 1995) state a preference for composition over inheritance. Yet, many patterns detailed in this classic book rely on inheritance.

What does inheritance provide that composition does not? Type extension, substitutability, and support for heterogeneous collections. When the precise type of object needed is not known until runtime and, in fact, could easily change, as in the disassembler example in Chapter 7, polymorphism is required and thus inheritance is warranted. When extensibility is needed because anticipated code modifications may add new subtypes, as in the Icon example, inheritance is again justified. When the contents of a collection may vary and the heterogeneous subtypes contained therein offer polymorphic behavior, inheritance is required. Reasonable designs that use inheritance must take advantages of some of the key benefits of inheritance: support of is-a relationship, type extension (extensibility), immediate access to protected data and functionality, code reuse, substitutability, and polymorphism.

The practical motive for inheritance is code reuse. Hence, inheritance is valued for expedient software development. The designer of the child class can automatically reuse the functionality of the parent class. The child class has access to all public data and functionality of parent and all protected data and functionality of parent. If parent functionality can be reused, software development time can be reduced significantly. However, if the parent interface is not essential, the child class could just as easily gain use of the parent's public functionality via composition.

With inheritance, the child class has an implicit parent class component, which implies unavoidable overhead because the parent component is always part of a child class object's memory. The parent component is initialized by a parent class constructor. Thereafter, for state or data changes, the child class is restricted to the parent's public and protected data and functionality.

Inheritance is often perceived as a rigid design. A child class object has exactly one parent component. The relationship is fixed: the child absorbs the overhead of the parent component even if the parent is not used. The parent component is not shareable, other than through the risky venture of an aliased pointer. The parent component is thus considered owned by the child object. This lifetime association prevents replacement of the parent component. If more than one parent component is desired, the child class may resort to composition to obtain additional parent component copies.

In contrast to inheritance, *composition affords design variety in terms of cardinality, association, ownership, and subobject instantiation.* Thus, composition offers control in design and thereby explains the professional preference embodied in the composite principle.

Through composition, a class design may:

Wrap up existing code
   Providing isolation from change
Alter cardinality
postpone instantiation
Support replacement
Transfer or share ownership

An immediate benefit of composition is the ability to avoid overhead when desired.

What benefits are lost when inheritance is replaced by composition? Is the primary drawback the loss of access to the protected data and functionality of the parent class? No! One need only define a wrapper class to open up this protected interface to circumvent this restriction, as was shown in Chapter 6. No, the primary drawbacks of using composition as a design alternative to inheritance is the application's loss of polymorphism and the resulting absence of substitutability and support for heterogeneous collections.

In determining design motives, perspectives, and alternatives, one must evaluate costs and benefits with respect to immediate and future use. If inheritance is a viable option, consider the client code's need for extensibility, heterogeneous collections, and substitutability. Consider the stability of the parent class and the desirability of sustaining its interface through child classes. Examples 8.8 and 8.9 contrast the use of inheritance versus a composition design with polymorphic subobjects. The code is in C++ but, without the interface construct, the effect is the same in C#.

Example 8.8: Inheritance versus Composition (C++)

```cpp
class B
{       protected:
                virtual void filter();
        public:
                ...
                virtual void store();
};

class QueenInheritB: public B
{       public:
                // keyword used for documentation
                // once virtual always virtual!!
                virtual void store()
                {       B::store();
                        filter();
                        ...
                }
                ...
};

class QueenComposeB
{
                B       subObject;
        public:
                // cannot access protected B::filter()
                // virtual character of B::store() not relevant
                void store()
                {       subObject.store();
                        ...
                }
                ...
};
```

Example 8.9: Composition with Exposed Interface (C++)

```
class Be: public B
{      public:
           ...      // make inherited protected method public
                void filter()              {       B::filter();    }
};

class QueenComposeB2
{                Be         subObject;
         public:
                // can filter by using intermediary class
                void store()
                {        subObject.store();
                         subObject.filter();
                }
};
```

In Example 8.8, `queenInheritB` illustrates classic inheritance while `queenComposeB` displays an alternative using composition. Does this design choice greatly impact utility? Both `queenInheritB` and `queenComposeB` contain a `B` object: under inheritance, the `B` object is the parent component; under composition, the `B` object is a data field. The public `B::store()` method is accessible to both `QueenB` classes. The protected `B::filter()` method is not. Yet, this restriction is avoided with the introduction of the `Be` class that promotes the `filter()` method to public visibility. As shown in Example 8.9, the `QueenComposeB2` class regains access to the protected `filter()` method using a wrapper subobject of type `Be`, where `Be` inherits from `B` and opens up its protected interface. Thus, the `QueenComposeB2` class, in Example 8.9, provides utility comparable to that of the `QueenInheritB` class in Example 8.8. In both classes, the `store()` method makes two statically resolved calls: one to `B::store()` the second to `B::filter()`.

The differences between inheritance and composition as design for code reuse largely rest on the perceived need for extensibility and support of the parent interface. If neither substitutability nor use of heterogeneous collections is a priority then the flexibility offered by composition seems attractive. The variability afforded by composition with respect to cardinality and instantiation of subobjects becomes even more attractive when one considers polymorphic subobjects, as in Example 8.10. Rather than settling for a permanent 1-1 relationship with a parent, a composing class can interact with a variety of polymorphic subobjects.

Example 8.10: Polymorphic Subobjects: C++

```
class flexQueen
{
          B*        subObjP;
     public:
          flexQueen()
          {       //      subObjP = 0;
                  subObjP = new B;
                  //      subObjP = new Be;
                  //      subObjP = new Bee;
                  //      subObjP = new B[size];
              ...   // other choices
          }

          virtual void store()
          {       subObjP->store();        // dynamic behavior
              ...
          }

          void replaceB(B*&      worker)
          {       delete subObjP;
                  subObjP = worker;
                  worker = 0;
          }
          ...
};
```

Despite its silly name, the QueenB example illustrates simple design variants that impact control and flexibility as well as manipulation via interfaces. Consider a hierarchy of B types (B, Be, Bee, BeNot,...), where each subtype can override the inherited virtual store() method. With an internal base class pointer (or reference), we can define a polymorphic B subobject. In this manner, we define different QueenB types. Would this design be preferred to inheritance? Once cannot answer this question without knowing the design imperatives of the client code that will use QueenB objects.

flexQueen holds a pointer to a B object and thus displays the most flexibility. Since this pointer may hold the address of any type of object in the B hierarchy, it serves as a polymorphic handle: flexQueen may hold a subobject of any type from the B hierarchy, yielding a variety of functionality via the virtual store() method. In contrast, in Example 8.8, both queenInheritB and queenComposeB are constrained to the functionality of store() and filter() as provided by the base B class. Why? The parent component of queenInheritB is stable, and of fixed type, B. The subObject data field of queenComposeB2 is stable and of fixed type, B.

Additional flexibility is afforded by (1) retaining a handle to a type B object, rather than storing a B object directly, (2) postponing instantiation of the polymorphic B object, (3) assuming ownership of an external polymorphic B object, (4) replacing a polymorphic B object, and (5) sharing polymorphic B object. Technically, the pointer could also hold the address of the first element in an array so flexQueen could alternately be designed to hold an array of a variable number of B objects. One could also design a subobject to be an array of pointers to yield a heterogeneous collection.

8.5 MULTIPLE INHERITANCE

Multiple inheritance specifies the derivation of a class from two or more base classes. The derived class thus has two (or more) is-a relationships, affording the usual benefits of reuse via the parent classes, support for heterogeneity, and polymorphism. The child class then, of course, assumes the overhead of two (or more) parent components. Ideally, it should be clear what data and functionality is inherited from which parent. Such clarity is possible when the parent classes do not overlap in form or function; in which case, the parent classes are described as **orthogonal** (see Figure 8.6).

Even with orthogonal parent classes, multiple inheritance increases software complexity. Minimally, cohesion decreases because the child class definition is spread across three or more different classes. Coupling increases because the child class is tied to two or more parent classes. Multiple inheritance also may yield two specific design difficulties: **ambiguity** and **redundancy**. We examine these constraints subsequently.

C++ supports multiple inheritance. C# and Java do not. We conjecture that multiple inheritance is not supported in C# and Java because these languages, developed after C++, were better positioned to weigh the costs and benefits of supporting such a complex design technique. To compensate for the restricted use of inheritance, C# and Java provide an interface construct. Why? An interface forces the definition of a function. Thus, if

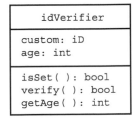

FIGURE 8.6 UML orthogonal parent classes.

a class implements an interface then it must define all functions declared in the interface. Example 8.11 illustrates a simple interface: media() is the only function prototype declared. Every class that implements this interface must define this function. Using interfaces, the class designer ensures that many different classes can support the same interface while providing differing functionality.

Example 8.11: C# Interface

```
public interface ISocial
{       string          media();        }

// classes must implement methods defined in interface
public class chat: ISocial
{       ...
        public string media()           { return "lol";         }
}

public class twit: ISocial
{       ...
        public string media()           { return "memememe"; }
}

public class tweet: ISocial
{       ...
        public string media()           { return "and then they...";}
}
```

With some attention to detail, classes may be designed to mimic multiple inheritance while retaining the ability to support heterogeneous collections. The key idea is to replace all but one parent class with an interface. Clearly, the functionality of the mimicked parent must be replicated, as must any data. However, consistency of use, via a common interface, is supported.

We examine multiple inheritance as directly supported in C++ and as simulated in C++, C#, and Java. We walk through design alternatives for the same example so that the reader understands the impact of different design choices. It is difficult to provide a real-world example of multiple inheritance that cannot be designed as well, or better, by simulating multiple inheritance.

Our first example models members of a university community: students and employees. Both types contain data associated with location and identity: name, address, identification number, email address, etc. The student type must have functionality and data associated with taking and completing courses: registration, tuition payment, term schedule, transcript,

Student
DOB: date GPA: float…
active( ): bool classR( ): int getAge( ): int

Employee
SS: int DOH: date…
fullT( ): bool rank( ): string getAge( ): int

FIGURE 8.7   Student and employee types.

date of graduation, GPA, etc. The employee type must have functionality and data associated with work: position, pay, vacation hours, supervisor, date of hire, etc. (see Figure 8.7).

Multiple inheritance becomes a design option when we consider StudentEmployees. StudentEmployees should retain all the data and functionality associated with the Student type and most of the data and functionality associated with the Employee type. How then to model a StudentEmployee in a manner that reuses the Student and Employee types? Four options come readily to mind: (1) multiple inheritance; (2) inheritance from Employee alongside composition with a Student subobject; (3) inheritance from Student alongside composition with a Employee subobject; and (4) composition with both Student and Employee subobjects. We examine each option in turn.

8.5.1 Multiple Inheritance Imperfections

Multiple inheritance is supported in C++, that is a child class can directly derive from two parents, e.g., a StudentEmployee can inherit directly from both Student and Employee. The StudentEmployee class reuses the code and data from the Student class, just as if it were single inheritance. Likewise, the StudentEmployee class reuses the code and data from the Employee class, just as if it were single inheritance. Hence, the StudentEmployee class can specify the invocation of specific parent constructors and can override virtual functions. A StudentEmployee object may access public and protected data and functionality from either of its parent classes. As shown in Figure 8.8, inherited functionality includes queries for active state, full-time status, class rank, and employee rank. One nagging detail is that the getAge() method has the same signature in both parents. Which method is invoked?

Ambiguity is an implicit design problem with multiple inheritance. If two parent classes yield an interface subset that contains identical

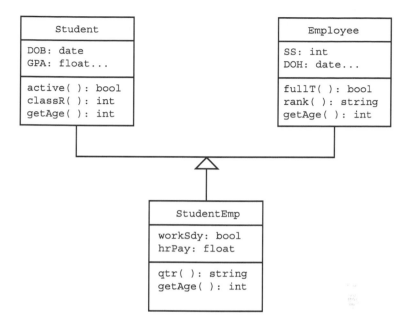

FIGURE 8.8 StudentEmployee via multiple inheritance.

functions, then which one of the same-named functions should be called through a child object? In this example, both parents provide a public getAge() query and the design of the child class did not produce such a function for the child component. Which inherited query should be called? Who knows? There is no obvious choice. The C++ language standard does not identify any assumptions about the order in which parent classes are declared in multiple inheritance. In other words, one cannot design or program in a manner dependent on the order of parent declaration. Thus, compilers cannot use this order as a means to select functions from overlapping interfaces. Since there is no rule for the compiler to follow, when faced with overlapping interfaces, the compiler generates an error.

Ambiguity is managed by forced override. The child class, by design, must override the getAge() function to resolve the inherited ambiguity. The overridden function in the child class may call zero, one or both parent functions in crafting an appropriate response. The overlapping function getAge() highlights a design flaw that is primarily syntactic: there would be no ambiguity if the Employee class had named its function something like getSeniority(), as aptly named in Example 8.12. Note that the StudentEmployee class can internally invoke public or protected parent class functionality from either parent by resolving scope.

Example 8.12: Resolving Ambiguity: C++ Multiple Inheritance

```
class StudentEmployee: public Employee, public Student
{     ...
      public:
              int getAge()          {return Student::getAge();}
              int getSeniority()    {return Employee::getAge();}
};
```

Compilers do not deal well with ambiguity. In translating HLL source code to executable code, compilers systematically follow long, complex sets of rules. When faced with a choice, a compiler must be able to look up the resolution of that choice. Compilers cannot capriciously determine the selection of alternatives. Hence, the intent of all code statements must be clear. When resolving a function call, it must be obvious to the compiler which function to invoke. Hence, the class designer of the multiple inherited child class must override overlapping function(s), determining internally what, if any, of the inherited parent functionality to use.

With multiple inheritance, the possibility of overlap arises when parent types do not serve distinct purposes. In our example, both Student and Employee types model members of a university community. Some commonality then is to be expected. Consider schedules. Students have a schedule of classes and Employees have a work schedule; each type of schedule may have different characteristics. Class schedules cannot be modified after the drop date, and work schedules may be subject to approval. If the Student class had the functionality to test the ability to change a schedule and the Employee class also had the functionality to test the ability to change a schedule, then there is an overlap. The StudentEmployee class designer must resolve the ambiguity before the code compiles.

Redundancy is an implementation complexity in multiple inheritance. The compiler does not force its resolution. Let us refine the Student, Employee, and StudentEmployee classes as illustrated in Figure 8.9: Student inherits from a Person class and Employee does also. This design yields **diamond inheritance**.

Conceptually, there is no problem: a Student is-a Person and an Employee is-a Person. Implementation protocol, however, yields space inefficiency and may interfere with data consistency. Why? Recall the fixed overhead of inheritance: a derived class object is laid out with an implicit parent class component, whether or not that component is used. Thus, a Student object has a Person component and an Employee object has a

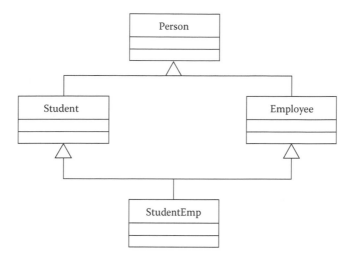

FIGURE 8.9   Diamond inheritance.

Person component. Since a StudentEmployee object has both a Student component and an Employee component, it then has two Person components: one Person component via its Student component and another Person component via its Employee component (see Figure 8.10).

Data duplication is clear. Why would redundancy be more problematic than simply wasting a few bytes? Data consistency may be undermined. Say that Person class has a chgAddr() function. This function is overridden by the Student class, possibly to distinguish between school and home addresses but is not overridden by the Employee class. An instantiation of the StudentEmployee class can be accessed via a StudentEmployee handle, a Student handle, or an Employee handle. Invoking chgAddr() on this particular object but through handles of different types will modify different (grand)parent address components. Thus, it is possible to have incompatible, conflicting addresses (without awareness of such). Data inconsistency is a problem when data is retrieved from different sources but assumed to be the same. Thus, an altered address

personObj   studentObject   employeeObject

studentEmployeeObject

FIGURE 8.10   Redundancy of diamond inheritance.

may be problematic if the address value is subsequently accessed via an Employee handle and then assumed to be the same as that accessed via a Student handle.

C++ offers a syntactical solution to the data redundancy of diamond inheritance: **virtual inheritance**. The class designer must anticipate the possibility of diamond inheritance and derive each parent class "virtually" as demonstrated in Example 8.13. If any parent is not derived virtually from the common ancestor, then the compiler will not suppress redundant copies of that ancestral component.

Example 8.13: Virtual Multiple Inheritance (C++)

```
// diamond inheritance anticipated => use virtual inheritance
class Student: public virtual Person {      ...        };
class Employee: public virtual Person {      ...        };

// regular (non-virtual) inheritance
class Consultant: public Person {   ...         };

// NO REDUNDANCY: both parents derived virtually from Person
//      => compiler suppresses redundant Person component
class StudentEmp: public Student, public Employee {...};

// REDUNDANCY: one parents did NOT derive virtually from Person
//      => compiler does NOT suppresses redundant Person component
class StudentConsultant: public Student, public Consultant{...};
```

Aside from the confusing and overloaded meaning of the key word virtual, virtual inheritance is not widely applicable. Correct foresight as to the future use of classes is required. This provision is akin to suggesting that a class designer have a crystal ball to see into the future. Tagging every inherited relationship as "virtual" is overkill, especially since multiple inheritance is a relatively uncommon design choice.

If multiple inheritance is used, the child class should override every function that accesses common, but redundant, ancestral data to confine use to a specific ancestral component. More importantly, great care must be taken to use handles appropriately so that data integrity is preserved. In other words, the client must now track usage according to type, despite the promise of OOD to remove type checking as an external responsibility. Simulating inheritance via composition does not remove the redundancy but does provide more explicit control.

Despite its drawbacks, multiple inheritance offers strong support for heterogeneous collections. Since Student is-a Person and Employee is-a Person, a heterogeneous collection based on the Person type could reference objects of type Person, Student, Employee, and StudentEmployee.

8.5.2 Single Inheritance with Composition

Without language support, multiple inheritance must be simulated. The interface construct facilitates support of heterogeneous collections but the class designer must reclaim the functionality lost through a restricted use of inheritance. A common solution is to use single inheritance with composition. Ideally, the derived class inherits from the class with which it has a stronger type association (or dependency) and contains a subobject of the second type. We examine both alternatives for single inheritance with composition for the StudentEmployee design.

If StudentEmployee2 derives from the Employee class and contains a Student subobject, as shown in Examples 8.14 and 8.15, then every StudentEmployee2 is-a Employee. Since the interface of the Employee type is accessible via the StudentEmployee2 type, all Employee public functions may be called through a StudentEmployee2 object. The Student class, however, is hidden as a data member in StudentEmployee2. Thus, the StudentEmployee2 class must wrap up all Student function calls; that is, echo a portion of the delegate interface. Use of the interface construct in C# and Java forces the interface (of the subobject) to be echoed, presumably yielding fewer design omissions. Moreover, a C# StudentEmployee2 object can substitute for an Employee or Student object while, without multiple inheritance, a C++ StudentEmployee2 object cannot. Why? C++ does not have the interface construct. Thus, in C++, the class designer is not forced to echo the `Student::active()` method, and a StudentEmployee2 object cannot be viewed as a Student object.

Example 8.14: C++ StudentEmployee: Employee Parent

```
class StudentEmployee2: public Employee
{               // contain data member for Student component
                Student        s;
        public:
                // echo desired Student functionality
                bool  active() {      return s.active();      }
        ...
};
```

Example 8.15: C# StudentEmployee: Employee Parent

```
interface IStudent
{      bool    active();
       …
}

public class StudentEmployee2: Employee, IStudent
{      // contain data member for Student component
       private       Student       s;

       // interface forces echo of Student functionality
       public bool   active() {    return s.active();     }
       …
}
```

When simulating inheritance via composition, one type must be deemed subordinate. The subordinate type loses the is-a relationship and no longer offers substitutability and extensibility as afforded by inheritance. The strength of type dependency may drive this design decision. The stronger the association between a parent type and a child type, the more utility the child may derive from the parent interface. Whenever a type is subordinated, a portion of its interface may be echoed.

This second design, StudentEmployee2 is-a Employee, is workable but likely inferior to situating the Student class as the parent of StudentEmployee. Why? StudentEmployee should derive more of its functionality from the Student class because its type dependency is stronger. The resulting implication is that the design should maximize the direct reuse of inherited functionality without having to wrap it.

When StudentEmployee3 derives from the Student class and has an Employee subobject, as shown in Examples 8.16 and 8.17, then every StudentEmployee3 is-a Student. This design makes more intuitive sense than the previous one because a Student becomes an Employee to finance education: education remains, or should remain, the paramount focus. Hence, it is likely that a larger portion of the interface inherited from the Student class will be used than that from the Employee class.

Example 8.16: C++ StudentEmployee: Student Parent

```
class StudentEmployee3: public Student
{             // contain zero or more Employee components
              Employee*     e;
       public:
              // echo desired Employee functionality
       …
};
```

Example 8.17: C# StudentEmployee: Student Parent

```
interface EmployeeI
{...}

public class StudentEmployee3: Student, EmployeeI
{
        private      Employee      e;

        // interface forces echo of Employee functionality
        ...

}
```

This third design, StudentEmployee3 is-a Student and contains an Employee object, offers the additional benefit of flexibility relative to the cardinality, association, and lifetime of the Employee subobject. A StudentEmployee3 could have two jobs, zero jobs, or be in-between jobs and still remain a student. The enduring type value of Student to a StudentEmployee3 indicates why it is less desirable to subordinate Student to Employee.

A drawback to modeling inheritance with composition is loss of access to the protected interface. Say the Employee class has protected functionality for computing reimbursement. The StudentEmployee3 has no access to that functionality if the Employee is a subordinate object rather than a parent. Brunt force design suggest that the functionality merely be copied or reimplemented. However, such a cut-and-paste approach to programming is known to be deficient, in regards to both testing and maintenance. Another approach is to introduce an intermediary class, whose sole intent is to open up the protected interface of the Employee class, as was shown in Chapter 6 and Example 8.9.

With the protected interface of Employee opened via an intermediary class, the StudentEmployee3 class now has indirect access to the protected `reimburse()` functionality via its subobject. The wrapper class could be used by software, other than the StudentEmployee3 class, possibly undermining design intent. Nonetheless, the wrapper is an effective fix for the loss of access to protected data and functionality when simulating inheritance.

8.5.3 Simulated Design without Inheritance

The fourth design alternative avoids inheritance completely, as shown in Example 8.18. StudentEmployee4 is composed of both an Employee subobject and a Student subobject. Any portion of either interface that should be supported must be echoed. In C++, heterogeneous collections cannot be easily supported because the StudentEmployee is not an Employee, is not a Student and thus, due to the complete lack of inheritance, is not a Person. The use of interfaces in C# and Java, however, do support streamlined use of heterogeneous collections.

Example 8.18: C# StudentEmployee4: No Parents

```
interface IEmployee                  interface IStudent
{    ...}                            {        ...}

public class Employee: IEmployee {...}
public class Student: IStudent {...}

public class StudentEmployee4: IStudent, IEmployee
{
        private      Employee      e;
        private      Student       s;

        // interface forces Employee & Student functionality
        ...
}
```

Evaluation of the different design options begins with an assessment of the costs and benefits as enumerated in Table 8.3. In general, composition offers greater flexibility in both design and implementation. Cardinality can vary: a composing object can hold more than one subobject; the number of subobjects may be fixed by design or may vary. The association between composing object and subobject is malleable: the composing object may replace, null out, or transfer ownership of subobject. The lifetime of a subobject, as suggested by its varying association, is neither fixed nor permanent: a composing object may postpone instantiation of a subobject until needed and may delete a subobject well before its own lifetime is terminated.

TABLE 8.3   Multiple Inheritance Design Options

Student	Employee	Benefits	Costs
Parent	Parent	Maximal heterogeneity Substitutability, etc.	Software complexity
Subobject	Parent	???	Counterintuitive
Parent	Subobject	Reflects logical type dependency May hold 0 or more jobs	Loss of is-a
Subobject	Subobject	Type neutrality	Not extensible Design overhead

8.6 MULTIPLE INHERITANCE DESIGN

Selecting a design from alternatives may be difficult. The StudentEmployee3 type is a straightforward example because the Employee subtype is clearly subordinate to the Student subtype. What happens when it is not so obvious which subtype to subordinate? We return to the Icon examples from Chapters 5 and 6, repeating our initial monolithic class design in Example 8.19.

Example 8.19: C++ Monolithic Class for Icon Movement

```
class Icon
{
    float       speed, glow, energy;
    int         x, y;
    int         subtype;            // spinner, slider or hopper

    bool        clockwise;          // need for spinner
    bool        expand;             // need for spinner

    bool        vertical;           // need for slider
    int         distance;           // need for slider

    bool        visible;            // need for hopper
    int         xcoord, ycoord;     // need for hopper

    void        spin();
    void        slide();
    void        hop();
public:
    // constructor must set subtype, possibly input externally
    Icon(...)
    {       ...
            subtype = value;        // use enum for readability
            // and then use conditional to set associated fields
    }

    void move()
    {       if (subtype == 1)       spin();
            else if (subtype == 2)  slide();
            else                    hop();
    }
    ...
};
```

Under the design imperative to write extensible code, in Chapter 6, a base class and three descendant classes replaced this monolithic Icon class. As was evident in Figure 6.2, the Icon class hierarchy easily absorbed additional subtypes, such as zigZagger, whereas the original monolithic class could not. What if an Icon object with multiple movement capabilities is now needed? When asked to design a SpinHopper or a SlideSpinner sub-type, multiple inheritance might be an immediate choice for C++ program-mers. However, this design yields diamond inheritance and its associated drawbacks. If implementation is in a different language, multiple inheri-tance is not an option, and a subordinate parent must be chosen. Unlike the StudentEmployee example, it is not clear which type to subordinate. Whether inheritance is used or is simulated via composition, it is difficult to avoid redundancy of data members declared in the base Icon class.

Is a return to the monolithic class, a poor design, as shown in Example 8.20, warranted? Probably not! Poor design cripples the possibilities of extension. Moreover, the logic needed to track subtypes, now that multiple-movement subtypes are incorporated, is labyrinth and thus not maintainable.

Example 8.20: C++ Monolithic Class for Icon Multi-Movement

```cpp
class Icon
{       float       speed, glow, energy;
        int         x, y;
        int         subtype;        // spinner, slider or hopper

        bool        clockwise;      // need for spinner
        bool        expand;         // need for spinner

        bool        vertical;       // need for slider
        int         distance;       // need for slider

        bool        visible;        // need for hopper
        int         xcoord, ycoord; // need for hopper

        void        spin();
        void        slide();
        void        hop();
    public:
        // constructor must set subtype, possibly input externally
        Icon(…)
        {       …
                subtype = value;        // use enum for readability
                // and then use conditional to set associated fields
        }

        void move()
        {       if (subtype == 1)       spin();
```

```
           else if (subtype == 2)   slide();
           else if (subtype == 3)   hop();
           else if (subtype == 4)   // spinSlider
           {     prepHalf();
                 spin();
                 prepHalf();
                 slide();
           }
           else if (subtype == 5)   // spinHopper
                 ...
           else                     // slideHopper
                 ...

        }
        ...
};
```

How design proceeds depends on whether we have the luxury of clean-slate design or are working with existing code (the monolithic `Icon` class or the `Icon` class hierarchy). With clean-slate design, we can anticipate the difficulties of multiple inheritance and also note the lack of clear subordination in subtypes.

What is essential in our design? If game designers need heterogeneous collections of `Icon` objects then a common interface is required. C++ enforces commonality via an abstract class; C#/Java do so via an abstract class or interface.

Examples 8.21 and 8.22 illustrate an abstract `Iconclast` class, providing the essential interface for heterogeneous collections: move (and other) capabilities. Any class that inherits from `Iconclast` must define the move() function; otherwise, the derived class will also be abstract.

Example 8.21: C++ Abstract Class and Descendants: Data Missing

```
class Iconoclast // abstract
{   public:
      virtual void move() = 0;
      ...
};

class Spinner: public Iconoclast
{      bool            clockwise;    // need for spinner
       bool            expand;       // need for spinner
     public:
       Spinner();
       ...
       virtual void move()    {        ...        }
};
```

```
class Slider: public Iconoclast
{    bool          vertical;       // need for slider
     int           distance;       // need for slider
    public:
      Slider();
      …
      virtual void move()    {        …        }
};

class SpinSlider: public Iconoclast
{    Slider          firstMovement;
     Spinner         secondMovement;
    public:
      SpinSlider();
      …
      // use subobjects for movement
      virtual void move()    {        …        }
};
```

Example 8.22: C# Abstract Class and Descendants: Data Missing

```
abstract class Iconoclast
{    public virtual void move();
     …
}

class Spinner: Iconoclast
{    private     bool        clockwise;      // need for spinner
     private     bool        expand;         // need for spinner
     public Spinner();
     …
     public override void move()    {        …        }
}

class Slider: Iconoclast
{    private     bool        vertical;       // need for slider
     private     int         distance;       // need for slider
     public Slider();
     …
     public override void move()    {        …        }
     …
}

class SpinSlider: Iconoclast
{    private     Slider      firstMovement;
     private     Spinner     secondMovement;
     public SpinSlider();
     …
     // use subobjects for movement
     public override void move()    {        …        }
     …
}
```

The common interface ties together all Iconoclast types. Thus, any number and order of Iconoclast objects may be held in the same heterogeneous collection, as demonstrated by both C++ and C# application code in Example 8.23. The SpinSlider design uses composition to mimic inheritance but gains familiarity via the Iconoclast interface.

Example 8.23: Heterogeneous Collection of Iconoclast Objects

```
// C++ array of base class (Iconoclast) pointers
Iconoclast*          icon[100];
...
// GetIcon() returns base class pointer, address held therein
//    may point to any (sub)type in class hierarchy
for (int j = 0; j < 100; j++)
     icon[j] = GetIcon();
...
for (int j = 0; j < 100; j++)
     icon[j]->move();

// C# array of references typed to abstract class Iconoclast
Iconoclast[]         icon = new Iconoclast[100];
...
// GetIcon() returns base class reference, address held therein
//    may point to any (sub)type in class hierarchy
for (int j = 0; j < 100; j++)
     icon[j] = GetIcon();
...
for (int j = 0; j < 100; j++)
     icon[j].move();
```

Yet, these examples are incomplete. Where are all the common data members: energy, glow, speed, and the coordinates x and y? If defined directly in the base Iconoclast class then SpinSlider will have three copies: one inherited from Iconoclast, one indirectly through Spinner, one indirectly through Slider. If defined by derived classes, then SpinSlider will have two copies: one indirectly through Spinner; one indirectly through Slider. Clearly, it is easier for a multiple-movement Icon class to resolve redundancy across two copies than three copies. Data members defined in any base class can be provided default values. Data members can also be held indirectly, via a pointer or reference, and stubbed out when not needed. Hence, the base class could provide overloaded constructors so that at least one constructor would opt out of instantiating redundant data members when multiple copies are not needed. This solution, however, increases software complexity.

When using established classes, design can be difficult. If we must add a SpinSlider using the definition of the monolithic class, as illustrated in Example 8.19, the most expedient route is demonstrated in Example 8.20. However, this modification violates the tenets of OOD. Every function that relies on subtype identification must use a multiarm if-else, or a case statement, to determine object subtype. Whenever a new subtype is defined, the class must be opened up again, requiring the recompilation of the Icon class, and possibly many other recompilations. Recompilation is not a trivial endeavor for a large software system.

Given an Icon class hierarchy, and the need to add a multi-movement Icon such as SpinSlider, we have the same choices as faced with the StudentEmployee example. If simulating multiple inheritance with composition, the choice of subordinate subtype would be arbitrary, however.

8.6.1 Evaluating Design Options

What are the general costs of using composition in place of inheritance? As shown earlier, loss of access to the protected interface may be a limitation but it can be overcome using a wrapper class. Most significant is the loss of the is-a relationship. Interfaces somewhat mitigate this loss by preserving the ability to place objects in heterogeneous collections. Interfaces, however, do not readily address design with respect to redundant data members. Compensation for loss of inheritance may unavoidably increase design complexity. Table 8.4 enumerates the effects of inheritance design.

TABLE 8.4   Inheritance Effects

Motivation	Benefits	Costs
	Inheritance of Interface	
Design type system	Type familiarity	Fixed overhead
Is-a relationship	Substitutability	Fixed cardinality
Type extension	Extensibility	Lifetime association
Polymorphism	Heterogeneity	Dependency on parent
	Inheritance of Implementation	
Code reuse	Access to protected data	Code complexity
Reduced dev time	Access to protected methods	Increased coupling
Reduced test time	Stability of parent component	Decreased cohesion
Less code replication	Not responsible for parent	Fixed relationship

Cost of change may be correlated to the strength of the type dependency in a relationship, as well as the stability of an interface. If a parent class is modified—an undesirable but possible outcome—a child class receives such updates "automatically" through recompilation. Yet, a child class may need to make its own modifications, in response to parental changes, especially if the inherited interface changes. Any change to a common interface in a class hierarchy may significantly impact the client. If a subobject class is modified, the composing class may be forced to recompile if either the size or the interface of the subobject changes. A composing object, however, can isolate its application code because it wraps its subobject: if the subobject's interface changes, the composing object is not forced to modify its external interface.

8.6.2 Relevance of Type

To choose an appropriate relationship, the relevance of type is a dominant factor. Recall that the modeling of StudentEmployee as a Student that wraps an Employee was preferred to modeling StudentEmployee as an Employee and wrapping a Student. The preeminence of Student functionality drove that distinction, as it should.

What if we added a StudentAthlete type? Must we thoroughly examine all possible options, as explored previously for StudentEmployee? Unlikely. In our previous design evaluations, it became evident that the Employee type should be subjugated to the Student type because, ideally anyway, the essence of being a student is more important to a StudentEmployee than being an Employee. Nonetheless, both Student and Employee types are central definitions in a university system: one can be a Student without being an Employee and vice versa. The same type relevance is not evident for Athlete. One can be a Student without being an Athlete. One cannot be an Athlete on campus without being a Student. There is no expectation of managing, say, a database of Athletes who are not Students, as there was for manipulating Employees who were not Students. Hence, the notion of an Athlete can easily be subjugated to that of a Student.

As noted in Chapter 6, the design impact of inheritance may be difficult to ascertain. Pure inheritance, or type extension, focuses on interface retention. This support of the is-a relationship suggests a continuity of type. Practical inheritance, or code reuse, strives to expeditiously develop code by reusing functionality and structure that has already been designed, implemented, and tested. Expectations for maintenance should factor prominently in design. Maintenance costs are dependent on design but

TABLE 8.5   Use of Composition to Simulate Multiple Inheritance

Motivation	Design Benefits	Costs
Missing language support	Control	No protected access
Clear subordinate type	Variable cardinality	No substitutability
Efficiency	Replaceable subobject	No extensibility
Polymorphic subobject	Postponed instantiation	No heterogeneous containers
Conflicting types	Insulating layer	No direct polymorphism

it is often difficult to predict how classes may be used as software evolves. Classes more likely to be modified may be preferentially wrapped, especially if interfaces are unstable.

Multiple inheritance makes it more difficult to evaluate design impact because of the possibility of mixing the two motives of type extension and code reuse. One parent could provide code reuse while another provides type extension. Table 8.5 summarizes the costs and benefits of simulating multiple inheritance.

Examine design rationales carefully. While it is true that inheritance increases coupling because the child class is tightly coupled to the parent, the composing class will be similarly tightly coupled to its subobject in composition. Cohesion is decreased whenever a single type definition spans multiple classes. Inheritance decreases cohesion because the child class type definition is spread across the inheritance hierarchy. Composition also dilutes cohesion: the functionality of a composing class may be understood best by examining the subobject. *Coupling and cohesion then are not necessarily convincing arguments for choosing either inheritance or composition.*

Critical differences between inheritance and composition include flexibility and type support. In composition, the subobject may easily change because there is no external dependency on its hidden interface. If the type of the subobject class is changed, application code should not be impacted. With inheritance, type variability, via substitutability, and type extension are promoted via built-in language constructs. Tracking subtype then is not the responsibility of the application programmer.

8.7 OO DESIGN PRINCIPLES

Two design principles exalt interfaces as a key component in design. The interface segregation principle (ISP) promotes high cohesion and low coupling by confining the breadth of an interface. Narrow interfaces focus the intent of a class design and imply specific and thus clear utility. Wide interfaces undermine cohesion and maintainability. The Program to Interface Not Implementation (PINI) principle underscores the OOD tenets of abstraction and encapsulation by serving to isolate the application programmer from volatile or arbitrary implementation details. These two principles drive class design, especially when classes are designed together, whether for inheritance or composition.

The Dependency Inversion principle (DIP) reinforces the importance of an extensible, possibly abstract, interface at the base of a class hierarchy. The unappealing Generalization inheritance design (Player is-a Warrior) illustrates the deficits of dependency inversion: the parent class depends on the child class to promote broad utility and type extensibility. When designing composition relationships, DIP suggests choice when determining which class type to subordinate: the application programmer should be isolated from the least abstract type. Then, if any lower-level implementation details must change, the client code is shielded.

Interface Segregation Principle (ISP)
Interfaces should be small and contain only a few, related methods.

Program to Interface, Not to Implementation (PINI)
Use abstract classes and interfaces to model functionality independent of implementation.
Implementation can then vary independently.

Dependency Inversion Principle (DIP)
High-level abstractions are more stable and less prone to change.
It is preferable that low-level abstractions depend on high-level abstractions.

8.8 SUMMARY

Software design's immediate goal is to achieve required functionality in a manner that meets user expectations. Longer-term goals may add performance criteria, software maintainability, extension of a software product line, etc. Software design thereby becomes a complicated endeavor, with implicit tradeoffs. *The inability to optimize all criteria simultaneously requires that the software designer remain aware of tradeoffs in design.* Thus, this chapter focused on design alternatives and perspectives.

The reader should now be able to assess different design motives and structures for class design and inheritance relationships. Designs alternatives for simulating multiple inheritance should be well understood. Additionally, the costs and benefits of directly modeling multiple inheritance, if supported by the implementation language, should be evident.

Solution selection, model structure, and *design should depend on goals and priorities rather than comfort due to experience.* Inheritance supports the is-a relationship, yields code reuse, type familiarity, interface recognition, direct polymorphism, and substitutability. Composition supports the has-a relationship, yields code reuse, buffers an unstable interface, and provides flexibility with respect to cardinality, ownership, and overhead. As a model for software development, OOD clearly illustrates tradeoffs and supports an evaluation of both long-term and short-term cost and benefits.

DESIGN INSIGHTS

SOFTWARE

Compilers do NOT handle ambiguity
Interfaces promote consistency and use of heterogeneous collections

MODELS

Inheritance for specialization models refinement
Inheritance for specification models abstraction
Inheritance for extension models type extension

SOFTWARE DESIGN

Multiple inheritance may be simulated
    Type dependency drives selection of subordinate type
Composition offers more flexibility than inheritance
Wrappers support an external perspective
    Isolate unstable code
    Redefine interfaces
        Possibly supplementing or modifying functionality
Delegates support an internal perspective
    Provide utility and flexibility
        Replaceable
    May be polymorphic
Handles control access to data and manage resources
    Do not provide or alter functionality

DOCUMENTATION

Design options require choice
    Tradeoffs must be evaluated
    Immediate use versus anticipated change
Design records choice
    Document intent and effect

CONCEPTUAL QUESTIONS

1. Why is the choice between is-a and has-a important?

2. How can inheritance be suppressed?

3. Explain the value of protected constructors.

4. When would suppression of inheritance be appropriate?

5. What are the costs and benefits of multiple inheritance?

6. How can multiple inheritance be simulated?

7. Describe the notion of type subordination and how it affects design choices.

8. What are the key differences among wrappers, delegates, and handles?

9. Are the language differences, with respect to abstract classes, important?

10. When should composition be chosen in lieu of inheritance, and vice versa?

IV

Software Durability

CHAPTER 9

Software Correctness

H OW CORRECT IS SOFTWARE? Many questions arise with respect to the notion of software correctness. Does software run without error? How does it handle error conditions? Does it meet specified requirements? Does it satisfy user expectations?

In this chapter, we provide short summaries of both exception handling and software testing. As a part of software design, exception handling catches runtime errors so that software execution is not interrupted. Software testing is an essential part of the software development life cycle, charged with verifying (and thus preserving) functional and nonfunctional properties as software ages.

CHAPTER OBJECTIVES
- Summarize intent and design impact of exception handling
- Provide a high-level view of testing
- Examine testing with respect to: scale, perspective, and coverage
- Discuss the relevance of software qualities to software correctness

9.1 EXCEPTIONS

Error processing is essential for modern software. It is preferable to catch and possibly correct a small error (such as a data value or format error) than to terminate running software. Normal control flow is interrupted when a hardware error or an encoded software error (such as division by zero) is detected: current scope is exited and control transfers to error-handling code. Exception objects represent error events and are either built into the language implementation or defined by the software developer. Exception handlers are code segments designed to handle (process) specific errors (exceptions). Thus, handlers are matched to exception objects. Some handlers can be designed to catch (or handle) a wide range of errors.

Exceptions automate some error processing. Upon an error condition (exception), the normal flow of execution branches to an exception handler, where error-handling code is executed, and then control flow returns to normal processing. The compiler generates code that sets up the required context changes when standard, expected control flow jumps to exception handlers.

As a built-in error-processing language construct, exceptions provide a software design alternative to excessive conditional evaluations. Moreover, *exceptions can detect and respond to errors that cannot be uncovered via conditional evaluation.* For example, when a library routine receives erroneous input or enters a state that prevents continued processing, an exception could alert the caller that the request could not be completed normally.

Most hardware exceptions are handled "automatically." Low-level kernel code or device drivers translate most interrupts and some processor exceptions into events. Other processor exceptions are translated into software exceptions. For example, code that attempts to access off-limits memory (such as memory allocated to the operating system), generates an exception. Other memory exceptions include stack overflow and failure to satisfy a heap allocation request. If these exceptions are "caught," the error condition can be "handled" and, ideally, normal control flow resumed.

Three statements typically support exception handling in modern programming languages: try, throw, and catch. In many languages, these three specific words are, in fact, reserved words. A try block is the specification of a code block that is to be guarded or enclosed by exception handling. Essentially then, the try block is a signal to the compiler that, when the software runs, if exceptions are thrown in the guarded code then execution should jump to the appropriate error-handling code. A catch block is an **exception handler,** the specification of code to execute when an exception arises. A named catch block is associated with one or more exceptions that are identified. An unnamed catch block processes all (remaining) exceptions. Throw is an intentional, direct raising of an exception.

Exception handling is an oft neglected component of software design. Code should be analyzed to determine its vulnerability to error. The expected frequency and severity of error should be estimated alongside the cost of error response. What type of errors merit the overhead of exception handling? This question cannot be answered independent of an application, and its prioritization of design goals.

When disruptive errors are anticipated and exception handling is to be used, code is placed in a try block. The try block is followed by one or more "catch" blocks and an optional "finally" block. Example 9.1 illustrates some common exceptions, using pseudo-code that is similar to exception handling code in modern languages. Figure 9.1 shows the corresponding possible execution paths through this code.

Example 9.1: Pseudo-Code for Exception Handling

```
try                     // exact syntax is LANGUAGE DEPENDENT
{
    x = y/z;                // A1: division by zero possible
    ptr->data = 100;        // A2: null pointer possible
    if (myExceptionCond)    // A3: throw specified exception
            throw new MyException("Error", and_other_data);
    ...
}
catch (ZeroDivide& e)       // code block B
{
    // Re-throw if we cannot handle this exception.
    if (! this.CanHandle(e))       throw;
    ...
}
catch (nullAccess& e)       // code block C
{       ...     }
catch (myException& e)      // code block D
{       ...     }
catch (...)                 // "catch-all": all exceptions not
                            yet caught
{       ...     }           // code block E
finally                     // code block F
{    // code executed upon normal exit and after any catch
}
```

What is the cost of exception handling? First, we examine how exceptions are processed to gauge runtime effect. Subsequently, we consider cost from the software design perspective.

Each exception arises or is thrown at a particular point in a running program: that code location is recorded in the program counter. Each

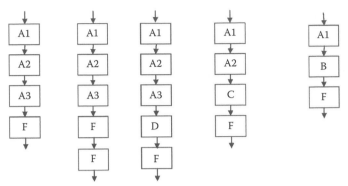

No error   Other Exception   Exception A3   Exception A2   Exception A1

FIGURE 9.1   Possible control paths for Example 9.1.

exception handler is also associated with a code location, the address of the first instruction tied to the corresponding named catch block. Processing exceptions consist of matching a thrown exception to its handler. The runtime system must attempt to find an exception handler that matches the thrown exception. The search proceeds from the point of the exception being raised or thrown. The current scope (the scope in which the exception is thrown) is searched first. If no match is found, and there is no catch-all block, scope is exited, the stack unwinds (pops off a stack frame), and the search continues. From the current scope upward, if there is a valid cast from the exception object type to a catch clause type, then that catch clause is selected, and its code executed.

Code within a finally block is executed regardless of the exit path from scope. If the code runs correctly, the finally block is executed. If an exception is thrown and caught, the finally block is executed. If an exception is thrown and not caught in scope, the finally block is executed. If an exception is thrown and caught and another exception arises (or is thrown) in the catch block, the finally block is executed. This possibility of multiple execution paths is shown in Figure 9.1.

If a catch clause is executed, then the exception is considered handled. Normal execution then resumes after the execution of the corresponding finally clause. The try block is not re-entered, unless it is in a loop. A catch clause may re-throw the caught exception or throw a new exception: both actions cause the exception so thrown to propagate up, after executing the finally clause. An exception may also be thrown within a finally clause, again causing scope to be exited and the exception to propagate.

In the search for a matching exception handler, successive stack frames are released, one after another, until a matching catch clause is found. Control repeatedly pops out of current scope until the exception is matched to an appropriate catch clause. If no matching catch clause is found, the application will exit. Such drastic termination is usually unexpected and has the undesirable side-effect of releasing all resources allocated to the application, including any of the user's unsaved data. Hence, the application architect should consider a catch-all or finally clause at a point where the user's data is still available. Some applications automatically save all pertinent data and attempt to restart the application when an unexpected exception bubbles up to the application level.

When a hardware exception—for example, an integer overflow—occurs, the runtime environment creates an object of the appropriate type and then jumps to the exception handler in the context of the currently executing routine. In this way, hardware-generated exceptions are handled uniformly, using the same mechanism as software-generated ("thrown") exceptions.

When an exception is thrown, the exception object (along with its execution context) is constructed and control is transferred to an exception handler. Execution of a throw statement interrupts normal control flow: control is transferred to the named exception handler. The contents of the stack and any global data structures remain accessible. All the information in the nested frames (popped off the runtime stack) is lost, unless it is explicitly retained.

Resources management should anticipate premature exit from scope due to error and error handling. A return statement should be allowed after resource allocation only if those same resources are released in the finally clause. C# provides a using statement that ensures the release of resources allocated within its control clause regardless of how the controlled statement is exited (normally, or due to an exception or return statement).

In a debugging environment, the exception handler tracks the stack frames unwound in response to an exception. If the exception is unhandled (or caught by the debugger), the analyst can then extract a crude stack trace, which is potentially helpful in determining the cause of the exception. In execution environments using garbage collection for memory management, it is feasible to maintain the entire execution context between the point when an exception is thrown to the point when it is handled. The "exception analyzer" feature introduced in Microsoft Visual Studio 2010 does so.

9.1.1 Exceptions and Software Design

Exceptions reflect a structured approach to processing errors. All executions change the state of a program; *the intent of exception handling is to recover from the state of an error condition so that normal processing may resume.* An exception handler may generate a summary or detailed trace of the execution state when an exception occurs, but is not required to do so. Normal execution, and its associated output, is suspended while the exception handler unwinds the stack and looks for a matching catch clause.

From the software design perspective, what does exception handling cost? To some, the wrapping of code in try blocks, with associated catch blocks, clutters code. *Specification of error conditions obscures the fundamental intent of code segments.* The presence of multiple exception handlers shifts the focus away from normal control flow toward error processing. Software design should accommodate exception handling as needed. The distinction between normal and exceptional control paths should be preserved. It is easier to follow normal control flow. Using exceptions places additional design and documentation responsibilities upon the developer. One must document:

1. When exceptions may arise

2. Reasons for throwing an exception

3. How exceptions are handled (or not) and why

4. How exceptions (and handling) affect the calling routine

Design and documentation must be explicit when using exception handling.

Although arguments for sustained readability and constrained software complexity have merit, especially if exception handlers are poorly specified or layered inappropriately, *readability must be balanced with the need to handle error.* Exceptions may be underused. When considering the use of exceptions, evaluate language support and cost as well as application priorities (such as performance versus safety). The stigma of additional memory and execution overhead associated with exceptions remains. Commonly, developers consider exceptions to be optional—it being implied that supporting exceptions is more expensive than not.

Assess expected use and cost. In a trial execution, how many times is an exception of a given type thrown? How effective is recovery? And so forth. As objects, exceptions can be instantiated from a type hierarchy. Development tools aimed toward normal software development can be used in the design and visualization of exception class hierarchies. Profiling tools that track the lifetimes of objects of a given type can provide insight into the runtime behavior of exception objects.

Exceptions do not directly advance the targeted functionality of a piece of software and thus may be underused or not incorporated thoughtfully into a design. In prototyping, exception conditions are commonly ignored or handled only as they arise. Hence, when prototype code is converted into production code, it is not uncommon to skip a thorough review of exception conditions and corresponding handlers. In addition, documentation of exceptions is usually inadequate.

In a modern development environment, one can analyze a code base and list any and all exceptions that could be thrown. However, documentation is still necessary to indicate the conditions under which each exception may arise and how best to handle the exceptions. The complexity of such analysis may be significant, as would be the resources (manpower) necessary to conduct it. Yet, failure to make a decision about error response is the same as the decision to let runtime errors interfere with normal processing.

9.2 TESTING DESIGN

Software testing is a large subject area, both commercially and academically. In this section, we provide an overview of models and techniques used. Our motivation is to provide fundamental information and define common terms used in testing vocabulary. Our quick examination is not at all comprehensive. Readers are encouraged to consult a good software testing text for more information (Ammann and Offult, 2008; Perry, 2006). Several sites provide information on software testing information including http://softwaretestingfundamentals.com/software-testing-methods/.

9.2.1 Scale

Software must be verified that it works as intended. Both functionality and nonfunctional properties (such as performance or security) are relevant. Since it is infeasible to test exhaustively, test case design is critical. At what level is software tested? What is the granularity of the tests? Table 9.1 summarizes standard delineation of tests.

TABLE 9.1   Levels of Testing

Type	Motive	Details
Unit	Small scale Functional	Embedded, repetitive Can be automatic
Integration	Correct use of interface Resolve incompatibilities	Difficult Legacy software
System	Meets specifications	Nonfunctional may be difficult to verify
Acceptance	Meets expectations Contractual fulfillment	Formal Can be extensive

Unit testing rests on individual software units. The preponderance of the class construct in Java and C#, with the ability to embed a main routine in any class design, facilitates unit testing. When unit tests are so embedded, preservation of functionality is more easily verified after code changes. Unit tests may be stubbed out until the function or class is fully defined.

A unit should be the smallest testable portion of software. In a procedural language, it would be a function. In an object-oriented language, it would be a method or set of methods associated with a class. Modules are not considered units because they usually contain many functions and data fields. Unit testing offers the clear advantage of uncovering defects or deficits early in the development cycle, a much cheaper prospect than discovering errors during system or acceptance testing. Unit testing also facilitates debugging because errors may be confined in scope. The use of a version control system in concert with unit testing streamlines the task of tracking changes.

Integration testing aims to uncover defects or deficiencies in interfaces and interactions between components. Integration testing may be difficult, especially if there is little control over use of previously developed packages. A good software architectural model provides the foundation for component level and integration testing. Testing typically simplifies the execution environment. A common assumption is that components can be tested independently. Caution should be exercised, however, because this assumption is not always valid: the software architecture or model should identify dependencies between components.

System testing follows integration testing and seeks to verify that the integrated system meets the specified requirements. Terminology may be inconsistent here: some refer to system integration testing. Acceptance testing formally determines whether the software satisfies the acceptance criteria: it may be internal (as an alpha release) or external. Conducted within an organization, internal acceptance testing must be conducted by professionals who are not directly responsible for software development. External acceptance testing is performed outside an organization. Often a distinction is made between customer and end-users. Customers are the clients who requested the software development or modification and hence approved the requirements specifications. End-users evaluate software use directly or in an embedded product.

Testing aims to confirm that software meets expectations. We distinguish **verification** from **validation**. Software verification confirms that the software meets specified requirements. Verification may be staged throughout the development process by reviewing requirement specifications, models of software architecture, design specifications, and even code. Test cases are designed to mirror requirements. Validation evaluates software more broadly by determining if the software meets user needs. Validation measures whether the correct system was built, in addition to verifying that the system was built according to specification. If the requirements specification is inaccurate or incomplete, a software system could be verified but not validated.

9.2.2 Perspective

Structurally, there are two perspectives on testing: white box testing and black box testing. In black box testing, the internal characteristics of the software are not known. No assumptions may be made about structure, design, or implementation. Hence, most black box testing is functional. In white box testing, software internals are known. Hence, tests may be targeted directly toward the software structure, design, and implementation. Although opaque and transparent may have been more accurate terms, the terminology for black and white box testing meant to imply the ability to look inside the "box" of software and see the internals.

As an example, consider, again, our math tutor software. What might black box testing entail for such a system? To answer this question, we review the specified functionality. Minimally, the operations (addition, subtraction, etc.), the types of input (integers, reals, etc.), and the range of values (negative, positive, two digits, etc.) must be known. Additional analysis is needed to evaluate probable input for user queries, repetition, tutorials, etc. Once specified, functionality must be translated into

TABLE 9.2 Functional Verification for Math Tutor

Validate	Input	Expected Response	Assumptions
Legal input	Non-numeric data	Error message	Number of errors may be bounded
	Numeric data, improper format	Error message Possible default correction	Automatic corrections should be simple
Valid input	Numeric data, improper value	Error message Review of properties possible	Division by zero, integer exponent, etc.
	Numeric data Incorrect value	Correct math fact	Possible hint or example
	Numeric data Correct value	Verification Congratulations	May correlate with automatic level of difficulty increase

a pairing of input and output values. The pairing of legal input with correct response forms the foundation for testing. To verify appropriate error processing, illegal or invalid input must also be vetted. See Table 9.2 for a sample summary of test input. In contrast, white box testing would entail testing targeted at the software structure.

9.2.3 Coverage

Testing begins with the design and review of a test plan, that is, specification of what is to be tested, desired outcomes, and frequency of analysis. Test plans focus on requirement specifications, and should include a schedule with an estimate of required resources. Test cases or scripts are designed and reviewed relative to the plan. Test data must be carefully scoped. The test environment must be set up to mimic the end-users environment. Test execution results in verification or a defect report. A test report yields composite results.

Testing is essential but expensive. Some may argue that testing is developmental overhead because it does not directly advance the completion of functional software. Nonetheless, core functionality and user interface touchstones must be tested. How much more must be tested? The answer is application specific. Test coverage measures how much of a software system is exercised during testing.

Table 9.3 summarizes common quantifications of test coverage. Code coverage is perhaps the most familiar; it measures how much of the code has been exercised. Specific inquiries as to what has been covered (such

TABLE 9.3   Test Coverage

Type	Intent	Details
Code	Proportion of code exercised	Tracks frequency
Branch	All alternatives exercised at decision points?	If-else structures Switch statements and so forth
Condition	Both true and false outcomes?	Optimization may consider results
Function	How often function called	Identify most frequently called functions and functions not invoked
Feature	How often feature requested	May result in multiple function calls
Path	All possible control paths executed?	Exhaustive Expensive
Model	Verify functionality	Broad category Many models

as, has a particular path been executed?) fall under particular types of test coverage (such as branch coverage). Some types of coverage are easier to automate than others.

A system model or architecture may serve as a scaffold for automated testing. Typically, it is infeasible to comprehensively test a large software system. Test developers must then devise appropriate test cases to exercise core functionality, verify UI responsiveness, confirm the relevance and value of error processing, detail recovery options, etc. One must be able to interpret outputs, especially those in response to error conditions. Testing becomes more intricate when valid input ranges are not static or are state-dependent. Determining valid input ranges and interpreting error responses experimentally can be expensive.

9.2.4 Data Values

What is in a test? Data and requests for service that will exercise the software. Specific inputs are correlated with expected outputs. Unexpected output thus indicates a problem. How are appropriate data values determined? There are a variety of techniques. Table 9.4 lists common means of determining data values. Equivalence partitioning separates or partitions all possible data values into different sets, where the values in each set cover a particular condition (or trigger a particular response) in the software. That is, the data values in any one partition are equivalent. If testing uses one data value from each partition then all conditions of the software should be covered. In this manner, equivalence partitioning reduces the number of tests required to cover functional responses in the software.

TABLE 9.4   Testing Techniques

Technique	Type	Details
Equivalence partitioning	Black	Reduce testing by noting equivalent values
Boundary value analysis	Black	Boundary values as error conditions
Control flow testing	White	Could be exhaustive
Branch testing	White	Force execution of seldom exercised branches
Scenario testing	White	Nonfunctional properties

Equivalence partitioning is used in conjunction with boundary value analysis, a software testing technique that focuses on values that straddle the boundary of partitions. Partitions are in essence ordered since the set of all partitions represent all possible data values, both valid and invalid. Invalid data is not illegal; it is just not relevant to the structure or function under test. Unless requirements prohibit error processing (possibly due to overhead), *test data should include invalid data in order to verify an appropriate response to erroneous input.*

For example, 27 is a legal value for a day in the month of February; 30 is not; 29 rarely but sometimes is. Hence, the partitions for data values for days in the month of February would include <=0; 1...28; 29; >=30. Boundary values would then be 0, 1, 28, 29, and 30. The minimum and maximum values that straddle a partition are boundary values. Both sides of a boundary should be tested. Thus, there are two boundary values to test for each boundary.

Control flow testing strives to exercise the different execution paths that might be followed during software execution. Appropriate data values must be selected to exercise each path. Branch testing is similar to control flow testing but strives to execute all possible branches, even those rarely taken. For software that must be reliable, or is high-risk and must be secure, it may be essential to verify response for all possible actions.

A collection of test cases designed to test specific portions or functionality of software is called a **test suite**. Each group of test cases may be associated with environmental requirements or state prerequisites before the test cases can be run. A test script is a list of instructions to be executed when a test case is run.

A **test harness** is a collection of code (execution engine), accompanied by data (test suites), used to exercise software. A harness is an automated framework: test cases are run under specific, varying conditions, and the behavior and output of the software tested is recorded. In essence, targeted functions are called, often multiple times, with different parameter values, and the resulting execution(s) are observed. Test harnesses provide consistency to the testing process as the same test suites may be used over and over again. The construction and content of the test harness depends on the type of testing executed.

Thus far, we have outlined testing with an emphasis on software functionality. What of software qualities, the **nonfunctional properties** of software? Software qualities may shift the emphasis in testing. We next examine several qualities, mostly nonfunctional properties, starting with security.

9.3 SOFTWARE QUALITIES

Security testing is a huge field that continues to grow as distributed and concurrent computing applications increase. Such applications demand privacy and safeguards for data. Hence, software designers must provide minimum guarantees of protection from malicious (or haphazard) attack. Security testing falls across half a dozen categories: confidentiality, integrity, authentication, availability, authorization, and non-repudiation. Security testing mandates an assessment of vulnerabilities and response. Once vulnerabilities are potentially identified, attacks may be simulated.

Security measures tested are listed in Table 9.5. Security testing is but one type of testing that is associated with a nonfunctional property (NFP). Table 9.6 enumerates general nonfunctional properties, including security, that are frequently tested.

TABLE 9.5   Security Measures

Measure	Response	Intended Guarantee
Confidentiality	Confirm information disclosed ONLY to intended recipient	Privacy Data integrity
Integrity	Verify correctness of data	Reliable transmission
Authentication	Confirm identity Verify access rights	Trusted communication
Availability	Ensure software available	No denial of service attacks
Authorization	Verify validity of request	Access control
Non-repudiation	Verification of send and receive	Sender cannot deny transmission Receiver cannot deny receipt

TABLE 9.6   Nonfunctional Testing

Type	Motive	Details
Compatibility	Comparable behavior across platforms	Product consistency
Conformance	Meets standard	Content and interface
Load	Comparable behavior under different loads	May identify stress points
Performance	Efficiency Reliability and so forth	Broad category
Recovery	Assess recovery cost	Consistent resumption
Security	Function without interference	Broad category
Scalability	Sufficient resources for load	Cost of scaling
Stress	Test load for failure	Simulate excessive demand
Usability	Assess ease of use Consistent interaction?	Selective test subjects Need domain knowledge?

Compatibility testing verifies that a software package operates comparably across differing platforms. For example, web applications must be tested on different web browsers to verify that presentation and response are similar. Compatibility with databases, peripherals, and operating systems may be tested. Mobile phone applications require testing on different hardware.

Conformance (or compliance) testing determines whether software conforms to applicable standards. For example, compilers must meet the specifics of a language standard. Compliance testing may need to be external to provide impartial verification of standards compliance, especially if independent certification is desired.

Load testing evaluates system response and performance under normal load conditions as well as expected peak load conditions. The intent is to model actual use of the application at periods of normal demand as well as high demand and then to identify any failure states or bottlenecks. Load testing is frequently used to evaluate the performance of software designed for multiple users, such as e-commerce applications.

Closely related to load testing, stress testing assesses system response in overloaded conditions, such as excessive concurrency or denial of service attacks. Scalability testing is similar to load and stress testing. The software system is tested for its ability to scale up or out when user load increases, number of transactions increases, data volume or communication load increases, etc.

To verify a timely and acceptable resumption of normal execution, recovery testing forces software failure. Data integrity, data transmission, network connectivity all may need to be evaluated after recovery. Multiple modes of failure (hardware, network, database, excessive load, etc.) may trigger extensive recovery testing.

Our curtailed review of nonfunctional testing is not exhaustive. For more information, please consult a modern software engineering text and/or testing text. We close by briefly summarizing regression testing, an essential process when software is refactored to sustain software quality characteristics such as modularity, low coupling, etc.

Regression testing determines whether changes to legacy software have or have not compromised the functionality and/or performance of the system. Test case reuse is common with regression testing, as is the use of tools for automated regression testing. To verify that system functionality and/or performance have not been compromised, tests are run and evaluated against a fixed set of expected results. If the results deviate from expectations, then the regression analysis indicates that the new version of software has altered the system in an unexpected or undesirable manner.

9.4 SUMMARY

Exception handling is often overlooked despite providing an automated and effective means of handling runtime errors. Software design impacts the ease of implementing and layering exception handling. Inappropriate coupling increases the difficulty of isolating potential error conditions and constructing an appropriate and efficient error response. Well-designed software minimizes coupling, implying an effective delineation of structure and isolated functionality. With low coupling, updating software in one component is less likely to trigger a fault elsewhere in the software; **cascading changes** are thus less likely to occur. Clear and cohesive design remains essential as software ages.

Software testing is essential for verifying and preserving functional and nonfunctional properties as software ages. Software design impacts the ability to systematically test software.

DESIGN INSIGHTS

SOFTWARE

Run-time errors usually unacceptable
Error recovery suggests an unrestricted return to normal processing
Software must be verified to work as intended

Functional and non-functional properties
Testing of invalid data verifies error response

MODELS

Exception handling built into software design
Exception handling layered
    Exceptions propogate up
Resource management must consider premature exit

SOFTWARE DESIGN

Exceptions
    Can catch errors not identified by conditional evaluation
    Control error response
    Prevent run-time disruption
Exceptions
    Increase code complexity
        Readability must be balanced with error control
Assess
    Expected frequency and severity of error
    Cost of error response

DOCUMENTATION

Requirements aid black box testing
Models and software architecture aid white box testing

CONCEPTUAL QUESTIONS

1. When is conditional evaluation insufficient for error processing?

2. Why is functional decomposition valued when designing exception handling?

3. What are the tradeoffs associated with exception handling?

4. How do Java and C# support unit testing?

5. Why are nonfunctional properties relevant to software design and testing?

6. When is security considered a functional requirement?

7. How does an accurate system model assist the testing process?

8. How does system design impact testing?

CHAPTER 10

Software Longevity

I F PUBLISHED YEARS AGO, this book would end before this chapter. Why? Software development has changed: emphasis has shifted away from clean-slate software construction and toward maintaining legacy systems. **Software evolution** and **software integration** are now essential. Software developers must work with existing software and applications. In addition to providing functionality, software developers should address the central question, relative to software longevity: What makes software viable?

In this chapter, we review the traditional perspective of **software maintenance** alongside a more recent emphasis on software evolution. We describe several nonfunctional properties and note their increased relevance to software. From a high level, we examine refactoring, the process of changing the internal structure of code without modifying external functionality. In extreme cases of software degradation, software must be reengineered. Hence, we close the chapter by describing reverse engineering.

CHAPTER OBJECTIVES

- Close the book with an orientation toward future study
- Define and establish relevance of software maintenance
- Distinguish software evolution from software maintenance
- Summarize key nonfunctional properties
- Define and provide an overview of refactoring
- Identify the relevance of reverse engineering

10.1 SOFTWARE MAINTENANCE

Software maintenance dominates the software life cycle, consuming well over half the resources devoted to software development. Software maintenance encompasses more than just bug fixes: platform upgrades; UI modifications; functional, interface, and/or hardware extensions; integration with new components (databases, browsers, etc.); performance enhancements; porting; and other maintainability enhancements.

As the final stage of the waterfall model, *software maintenance was defined as reactive: correcting software errors.* Viewed as a postdelivery activity, software maintenance was not perceived as accommodating new functionality or hardware advances. To limit software maintenance costs, professional and academic research efforts focused on making software development more precise, more streamlined, and thus safer and cheaper. If software development could just be "done right" the first time, then the software maintenance phase could be minimized. To accommodate hardware changes and extended user expectations, software updates now suggest that software evolution is an essential part of the software life cycle. Successful software product development must include plans for efficient maintenance.

In addition to correcting deficits in existing systems, software maintenance must accommodate requirements changes that drive new or modified functionality as well as expanded UIs. To more accurately represent the responsibilities of the software maintenance stage, and to counter the negative connotations of this term, we use a newer term, "software evolution." In the next section, we examine the causes, responses, techniques, and effects of software evolution.

10.2 SOFTWARE EVOLUTION

Why discuss software evolution? Over the past several decades, huge amounts of money and time have been invested in developing and maintaining software. Such systems are integral to most business operations, including medicine, transportation, government, education, etc., and must be maintained. Trepidation about software development costs underlies an accepted reluctance to replace systems in their entirety, that is redesign (and implement and test and deploy) a system from scratch. Yet, change is inevitable. Hardware advances, expansion (or contraction) of customer bases, algorithmic or data mining improvements, and product line changes all drive software change. Additional functionality, or demand for improvement in nonfunctional properties, such as reliability, performance, or usability, also drives software change. *Whether to expand or preserve market presence, or to support the infrastructure of business, software must maintain its utility in the face of technological advances.*

Business needs and technology advances continue to spur software upgrades and extensions. How can the impetus for software change be categorized? Lehman and Belady enumerated laws of software change, some of which are listed in Table 10.1.

Software must evolve as systems age. Exposed to advancing technology, users expect more responsive, more reliable, safer software. Additional functionality, performance upgrades, expanded GUI, security, etc. all impact system structure. An accumulation of small changes erodes the original design, especially if not documented thoroughly.

Software systems that are maintained, usually for commercial reasons, are called **legacy systems**. Large systems are typically difficult to modify. When updating software, developers must work around restrictions: working software cannot be taken offline (without replacement), user expectations must be met (for continuity of use), and performance criteria cannot degrade even if more functionality must be integrated and so forth. Targeted change must be incorporated into the existing model and design. The cost and difficulty of such modifications increase tremendously when expectations of evolution are not anticipated.

TABLE 10.1   Lehman and Belady Laws of Software Change

Property	Motive	Details
Continuing change	Modifications required to satisfy increased user expectations	System value degrades if not updated
Increasing complexity	Add-ons and modifications increase software complexity	Internal restructuring needed (refactoring)
Self-regulation	Assess and retain measures of effectiveness	Support functional and performance evaluation
Conservation of familiarity	Steady incremental expansion (increased complexity)	Users remain competent wrt UI and software utility
Continuing growth	Increase functionality to retain users	Maintain user satisfaction as technology advances
Declining quality	Inevitable decline unless adapted to technological advances	Environment changes regardless

Insufficient modeling, design, and documentation impede software evolution. System functionality may not be readily understood when requirements or design specifications are missing, poorly documented, or incomplete. Moreover, when successive, small software updates are not reflected in documentation, a system's model may not match its implementation. Hence, a valid system perspective may be compromised. Nonetheless, software developers must understand the underlying intent and organization of a legacy system to properly integrate new components and/or sustain continued maintenance efforts. Reverse engineering is thus often employed to extract an accurate model.

Software evolution often is a form of reengineering, where the goal is to understand a system to then transform it. Systems are restructured to remove deficiencies or to meet performance or cost expectations. Software must absorb additional functionality to retain appeal. Reengineering is required when a portion of a system bears excessive maintenance costs or when a customer base demands modernization. Refactoring is a form of reengineering specific to an internal restructuring of software.

Software evolution is not clean-slate modeling or design (Table 10.2). The mandate to update, port, or extend existing software begins by assessing the current state of the software, juxtaposed with new expectations: *one cannot merely guess.* Identifying obsolete features and scheduling their removal may be part of evolution. Verification of functionality must be confirmed via **regression testing**: unmodified portions of the system must preserve their essential functionality and nonfunctional properties; modified portions of the system must reflect desired changes.

TABLE 10.2   Software Evolution Stages

Stage	Typical Motive	Goal
Requirements	Update expectations	Validate change
Architecture	Migration to new environment	Reengineering Maintenance
Design	Preserve functionality Maintainable code	Restructure software to better absorb modification
Test case	Modification and addition of test cases	Verification of functionality and nonfunctional properties
Data	Migration to new database schema	Verification of information preservation
Runtime	Modify system without disruption	Reconfiguration, adaptation, and upgrade
Language	Integration needs	Handle incompatibilities

10.3 NONFUNCTIONAL PROPERTIES

Traditionally, software development focused on implementing required functionality within desired performance constraints. Little attention was paid to nonfunctional requirements such as usability, readability, and extensibility. Less attention was paid to software maintenance; design was often idiosyncratic. *Modern software development places more emphasis on modeling, design, and testing, with retention of legacy systems as an explicit goal.*

Software requirements enumerate required functionality. Thus, even when tied to specific hardware configurations and data sets, requirements emphasize software utility. With expanded software use, however, requirements have increasingly emphasized user experience. How are the user needs and expectations met? Ease of use, security, performance, etc. are not strictly functional properties because achievement of such characteristics does not advance or support required functionality. Qualities that reflect the operation of the software rather than its functionality can make one product more attractive than another. Called constraints or the "ilities," nonfunctional properties (NFPs), or requirements, are usually difficult to design and measure.

We categorize NFPs, as shown in Tables 10.3 through 10.5, according to whether the nonfunctional property primarily pertains to error-handling response, performance, or structure. Starting with security, we provide a brief overview of several NFPs in these categories but note that this examination is not exhaustive.

Security is a rather broad term, covering data integrity, service protection, privacy, and performance. Security implies a systematic defense against intrusion that would interfere with normal processing. Adherence

TABLE 10.3   Error-Sensitive NFP

NFP	Meaning	Relevance
Security	Only authorized changes Only authorized views	Protection of service Data integrity Privacy
Robustness	Respond reasonably to erroneous or uncommon input	Stable software execution
Recoverability	No data lost due to failure	Data persistence
Availability	Operate with limited resources	Stable software execution
Reliability	Provide predictable results	Preserve functionality
Safety-critical	Fail safe for high risk ventures such as aviation software	Reduce catastrophe and liability

to protocols and verification are usually required in any secure system. Security may be perceived as a functional requirement, particularly for applications such as for banking and e-commerce. Nonetheless, for many systems, security remains pure overhead.

Robustness characterizes the ability to withstand error and continue processing. Robust software does not crash in adverse conditions such as erroneous data errors, invalid requests, peak capacity loads, and malicious attacks. A system is said to be robust if very few errors cause software to abort or malfunction. Clearly, critical software such as monitoring software, aviation software, etc. must be robust. Less obvious, however, is that robust software is costly: design must include significant error processing, state testing, and recovery paths in addition to the required functionality.

Recoverability is a term traditionally associated with databases: the ability to roll back to a state prior to aborted transactions to preserve data integrity. The notion of recoverability with respect to a general software is the same: the ability for a system to recover from spurious input or erroneous states and resume normal processing.

Availability is an engineering term that is related to reliability: the more reliable the system, the more it is available for use. Once a system is functional, its availability can be measured directly: the proportion of time a system is functional. Measures associated with availability include mean time to failure (MTTF) and mean time to repair (MTTR). If the MTTF is 990 hours and the MTTR is 10 hours then the availability is MTTF/(MTTF + MTTR) = 990/1000 = 99.00%. The unavailability is (1 − availability): 1.00%. One can only predict, not assess, the availability of a system model or design.

Reliability has long been studied in engineering and is a measure of the mean time between failure (MTBF). The many definitions of reliability include the ability of a system to remain functional for a specified period of time; the probability that a system will remain functional; the ability of a system to fail well. Reliability is especially important in embedded and real-time systems. Like availability, reliability is hard to measure precisely until a system has been built. However, if one can quantify expected input and correlate it to error processing responses, one can estimate the probability that a system remains functional.

Safety-critical software must not be allowed to fail and, thus, demands, intense scrutiny. Safety is functionally built into the system through the design, implementation, and test phases. Requirements analyses include the identification of hazards, faults, as well as sources of error and inconsistency. Failure modes can then be built into the software system. Response to failure and error must ensure continued operation and control hazards. Often, design strives to minimize the number and complexity of safety-critical components, interfaces, and functions.

Summarized in Table 10.4, performance NFPs assess the operation of the software: how does the system run from a qualitative perspective? Users expect stability and consistent response. Acceptable performance then is often perceived as fulfillment of expected functionality without much variation in response time, regardless of load.

Accessibility is a common term used to describe the extent to which a product, service, or system is available, generally without restriction, to any user. Accessibility is often used in context of assistive technology, that is, technology aimed for users with special needs or disabilities. Accessibility measures the ability to directly access software functionality, despite possible vision, or hearing impairment. With respect to software systems, accessibility has also been used to measure Internet access, a quality that may have legal and/or political concerns in addition to technical.

Usability differs from accessibility with respect to target audiences, level of satisfaction, and directed outcomes. How easy is software to use? When a user must make a selection, valid options should be presented so as to facilitate choice. Information regarding correct usage should be readily available (via help screens, tutorials, etc.). User-friendly is an older term subsumed by usability. Usability includes the notion of effective functionally where user-friendly did not.

TABLE 10.4   Performance NFP

NFP	Meaning	Relevance
Accessibility	Usable by wide audience	Reduce dependency on standard vision, hearing, etc.
Usability	Intuitive access Small response time	Shallow learning curve Access consistent with use
Performance	Rapid response	Timely
Efficiency	Resource use reasonable to load	Contain cost Maximize use
Operability	Provide required functionality in timely manner	Usable
Stability	Insensitive to external factors such as load	Indiscernible variation in performance

Usability is gauged by satisfaction with respect to expectations of efficiency and/or outcome. Is the software responsive? Is the user interface appealing? Are user selections obvious, or heavily dependent on domain knowledge? When an interface presents an intuitive organization of material, and supports online learning, the software is considered usable. When an interface is overly cluttered, requires extensive domain knowledge or prior consultation with a manual, it is not considered usable. Usability must be evaluated with respect to the expertise and experience of actual or targeted users.

Performance as a specific NFP is assessed as the running time of a piece of software. Classically, analysis focused on algorithmic complexity that is a measure of how processing time increases when the size of input data increases. Succinctly put, algorithms with smaller growth rates scale better. Why use a linearly bounded search on sorted data when a logarithmic algorithm can search in less time? Tricky details, such as data representation and linkage, affect the use and efficiency of specific algorithms. Standard tradeoffs between time and space impact many algorithms. For more details, see any standard algorithms text. Since efficient algorithms often are harder to understand, and thus maintain, a general guideline is to use simple solutions for small problems.

Efficiency is defined as effective processing using resources commensurate with workload. Performance and efficiency may be impacted by the need to support nonfunctional properties, such as security. Additionally, software design for generality (extensibility) often impedes efficiency. For example, to be more flexible, dynamic evaluation may be preferred (over static type checking and/or static function calls) despite the performance overhead incurred.

Operability is another engineering term. It refers to the ability to keep a system running in a safe and reliable condition. With respect to software systems, operability is a measure of the system's ability to meet functional expectations, that is, provide all needed functionality. With the growth in distributed systems, operability becomes more complex as many, distributed components must work together, use a variety of communication protocols, and meet expectations relative to response time.

Until a system is built, performance NFPs may be no easier to directly measure than other NFPs. However, the complexity of response time and resource usage can be theoretically bounded. Such analysis, however, depends on formal specification of the algorithms and data structures used in support of software qualities.

Structural NFPs may be measured against the form of the software. Are hardware details isolated, and thus amenable to change? If so, then portability is supported. Are the software components decoupled and easily identified? If so, then maintainability is anticipated. Are inventory and classification systems designed to incorporate new types of items? If so, then extensibility is expected. Table 10.5 enumerates common structural NFPs.

Maintainable software should be easy to update. Typical modifications include correct a fault, extend functionality, port to different platform, accommodate new requirements, adjust user interfaces, modify data storage, enhance security, etc. The cost of software maintenance depends on system structure, design, and readability.

Extensibility is an NFP meant to assess the ability to *extend* the software system as different needs develop or the spectrum of users expands. Whether extension incorporates new functionality, modifies existing functionality, or alters the user interface, system updates should minimally impact the current system. Maintaining legacy software by extending its capabilities should be as cheap and as easy as possible. Extensibility is hard to measure, as it requires predictive power. Nonetheless, a stable system architecture should absorb change and curtail the impact of modification.

Interoperability measures how easily a system can interface with other systems or components without restriction. Interfaces must be known, data must be used in a common format and communication must rest on a standard protocol. Interoperability thus implies adherence to standards and minimizes the design of standalone, incompatible (proprietary) software.

Portable software may be easily moved to different hardware platforms and still operate. Closely related to portability is compatibility: the use of software in different environments. To maximize commercial gain,

TABLE 10.5   Structural NFP

NFP	Meaning	Relevance
Maintainability	Easy to modify	Retention of legacy systems
Extensibility	Easy to add features	Software evolution
Interoperability	Works with other software	Software integration
Portability	Works on many platforms	Broad software usage
Compatibility	Used in different environments	Broad software usage
Scalability	Can work on larger problems	Handle variable workload
	Can accommodate more users	Functions under peak demand
Testability	Easy to place in accessible state	Verification

software is often developed for several, different computing platforms. To streamline installation, configuration files are placed in specified locations and are used to store hardware- and software-specific information. Specific programming languages, such as Java and Javascript, are used within common browsers to support portability and compatibility for web applications.

Scalability is an engineering term denoting the ability of a system or network to be enlarged, or "scaled" up, in response to increased workload. Scalability is not achieved simply by adding more hardware. Search engines and algorithms for communication, computation, and data storage must efficiently handle an increased load. Latency and throughput must remain at acceptable levels. A scalable system demonstrates improved performance with additional capacity, with such improvement proportional to added capacity. A system that fails when load increases does not scale.

Horizontal scaling (scaling out) implies the extension of system structure, such as adding more nodes to a network or more servers to the client–server model. An example of horizontal scaling is cluster computing, that is, the configuration of hundreds of desktop computers. In place of a high-performance computer, a cluster distributes a problem and solves it incrementally. Increased demand for data storage often accompanies horizontal scaling. Vertical scaling (scaling up) implies an internal increase in resources, such as the addition of more CPUs or memory.

Testability, how thoroughly a system can be systematically tested, cannot be directly measured until the software system is relatively complete. Can testing be *automated*? Is component functionality clearly documented and *understandable*? Can component state be *controlled*? How easy is it to *observe* state change and test results? *Software structure supports or impedes testing.* Component coupling interfers with testing if **emergent behavior** is not confined to clearly defined interfaces. Clear **separation of concerns**, where each component has a single, well-defined responsibility, eases testing. Unit testing and test-driven development have increased the awareness of the necessity of testing.

Whew! So many nonfunctional properties! And we did not even cover all known NFPs. It is unlikely that any one system will prioritize so many nonfunctional properties. NFPs are difficult to model. Yet, requirements should explicitly identify essential nonfunctional properties. Design should deliberately incorporate prioritized nonfunctional properties.

10.4 REFACTORING

Refactoring is the internal restructuring of software that does NOT modify the software functionality. In other words, code is altered, but externally, the system runs in the same manner: a client should be unaware of any refactorings. Typically, refactoring is undertaken in preparation for planned or anticipated changes. Since well-designed software permits easier, and thus cheaper, integration of new features, refactorings strive to improve a system's internal structure.

Software longevity often implies degradation of structure, especially if successive modifications have been incrementally incorporated. Yet, for viability, software must be updated to absorb technological advances and meet rising user and performance expectations. Refactoring thus is an essential software development activity. Martin Fowler's (1999) book, *Refactoring: Improving the Design of Existing Code*, brought refactoring to the forefront of software maintenance endeavors. Fowler's book has a distinct Java (and thus OO) orientation but provides a systematic delineation of refactoring, with intent and effect clearly noted.

Refactoring is applicable to OOD, especially when relationships are neither adequately modeled nor appropriately designed. A common deficit is the overuse or misuse of inheritance. As discussed in earlier chapters, "manual" type checking is not extensible and can be costly: case statements are rigid and error-prone and should not be used to select functionality. The likelihood of cut-and-paste programming (a maintenance problem) increases when inheritance is missing. However, if inheritance is overused, performance may be impacted. As noted in Chapter 8, composition is often preferred over inheritance.

Fowler categorized different motives for refactorings. When data storage or retrieval is too costly, employ a refactoring to organize data. When methods (functions) are too large or too small or require too many parameters, apply a refactoring to resolve granularity. When cohesion is too low or coupling too high, choose a refactoring that restructures classes. Additional types of refactorings include simplifying conditional expressions or method calls. Some refactorings in this classic text are due to language limitations. Java has no structs, no pointers (and thus no function pointers) and constrained parameter passing. Just as some patterns are not needed in a particular language, some refactorings are not relevant either. For more information, see the text or Fowler's web site: http://www.refactoring.com.

Across all stages of software development (modeling, design, implementation, testing), documentation is usually insufficient, inconsistent, and/or incorrect. Personnel turnover, distributed development, deadline pressures, and a singular emphasis on code production over design all contribute to poor documentation. Many refactorings are simply renamings that make code more self-documenting.

Renaming may seem as a mechanical, uninspiring type of refactoring but it can expose duplicate code, identify poor encapsulation, indicate an interface that is too wide or too narrow, etc., leading to additional refactoring (see Example 10.1). Renaming must adhere to a standard convention, use the same name for the same meaning, and avoid arbitrary dependencies (such as type or size) in name selection. Renaming should give meaning to code and clearly delineate functionality, use, and/or effect. Software tools now automate many renaming refactorings, thus streamlining the tedious processes of updating all references to a name.

Example 10.1: Renaming to Expose Duplicate Code: C#

```
// 3 differently named functions: each produces same effect
//                 double all array elements equal to passed value
void       doubleValue(int[] intArray, int value)
{
           foreach (i in intArray)
                  if (value == intArray[i])
                         intArray[i] *= 2;
           return;
}


// renaming refactoring should expose redundancy
void       magnifyElem(int x, int[] myDB)
{
           foreach (i in myDB)
                  if (x == myDB[i])
                         myDB[i] = myDB[i] * 2;
           return;
}

// renaming refactoring should expose redundancy
//                 even with variant structure
void magnifyElem(int p, int[] iArr)
{
           for (int i = 0; i < iArr.Length; i++)
                  if (p == iArr[i])
                         iArr[i] = 2* iArr[i];
           return;
}
```

Refactoring targets key pieces of software, often the most critical or most frequently executed pieces of code. Dependencies must be identified to suppress ripple effects of change. After each refactoring, the software must be tested to ensure that system functionality is unaltered. Test cases verify functionality in an automatic or embedded fashion. Prior to a refactoring, code is copied before modification so that it may be restored, if needed. The refactoring is then applied, the code compiled, and tested.

Fowler and Beck summarized many software characteristics that make maintenance and evolution difficult and described these characteristics as "code smells." Tables 10.6 and 10.7 delineate some of these smells according to whether they occur due to insufficient design (or maintenance) or overdesign.

Refactoring must not undermine an effective design. Explicit and documented design helps prevent excessive refactoring. For example, delegation is used to isolate callers from proprietary code, unstable classes, or unstable interfaces. Layering via delegation decouples client code from legacy system constraints. Delegation that appears excessive must be placed in the context of the larger system. Perhaps, delegation is needed to protect client code. The cost of replacing delegation with inheritance can be significant.

TABLE 10.6   Fowler's Code Smells and Refactorings: Insufficient Design

Code Smell	Details	Refactoring(s)
Duplicated code	Same expression	ExtractMethod
	Same code	ExtractClass
	Similar code	FormTemplateMethod
	Same problem	SubstituteAlgorithm
Long methods	Insufficient decomposition	ExtractMethod
	Loss of delegation	DecomposeConditional
	Poor maintainability	ReplaceMethod
Large class	Expensive, not extensible	ExtractClass
	Poor cohesion	ExtractInterface
	Duplicate functionality	ExtractMethod
Long parameter list	Tedious design	ReplaceParameterWithMethod
	Not maintainable	IntroduceParameterObject
	Dependency on caller for acquiring data	PreserveWholeObject
Divergent change	Poor cohesion	ExtractClass
	Change in different directions	
Switch statements	Not extensible, rigid	ReplaceTypeCodeWithSubClass
	Is selection criteria dependent on type or method?	ExtractMethod
		MoveMethod

TABLE 10.7   Fowler's Code Smells and Refactorings: Over Design

Code Smell	Details	Refactoring(s)
Speculative generality	Overdesigned Excessive delegation Excessive abstraction Not maintainable	CollapseHierarchy InlineClass RemoveParameter
Message chains	Excessive delegation Long call sequences Excessive accessor calls	HideDelegate ExtractMethod MoveMethod
Middleman	Excessive external delegation Extra intermediary classes	InlineMethod ReplaceMiddleman ReplaceDelegateWithInheritance
Incomplete library	Cannot modify library Use wrapper	IntroduceForeignMethod IntroduceLocalExtension
Comments	Code not self-documenting Poorly designed code needs explanation	Renamings… ExtractMethod IntroduceAssertion
Refused bequest	Child does not use inherited methods	PushDownMethod PushDownField ReplaceInheritanceWithDelegation

Caution must be taken when considering replacing inheritance with delegation. Although composition is often preferred over inheritance, consider software evolution. Extensibility is compromised if inheritance is replaced with delegation. Consider the smell, Refused Bequest in Table 10.7. Refactoring to replace inheritance with delegation because a particular class does not use inherited functionality is risky. Why? Immediate use is not necessarily a good predictor of future need. Software designers must evaluate the need for extension and not compromise future design.

Some smells may be language dependent. For example, Fowler identifies Primitive Obsession as a smell in his foundational book and provides refactorings that replace primitive data with objects. Relevant examples given, in Java, do indicate a proliferation of primitives that may be better organized via the class construct in Java. However, C++ and C# provide the struct construct, and thus are more amenable to mixing procedural and object-oriented design. Appropriate refactoring may differ according to the implementation language.

Refactoring risks include the introduction of error, inappropriate refactorings that compromise design intent, excessive refactoring that degrades the system structure, and a low-level focus on relatively unimportant code segments. Low-level refactorings must be applied judiciously: system-level goals should not be neglected or obscured.

Refactoring is prominent in software evolution. *Refactoring to Patterns* by Joshua Kerievsky (2005) summarized techniques used to refactor code so that the revised internal structure reflects proper use of design patterns. Code is restructured to be more extensible and better able to absorb modifications. Processes employed in refactoring to patterns include extracting (refactoring code so as to implement pattern), removing (inappropriately used), and transforming a pattern.

Refactoring in Large Software Projects, by Roock and Lippert (2003), examines and details large refactorings (e.g., API, DB). Large-scale refactoring resembles reengineering. Explicit requirements and acceptance tests must verify the preservation of functionality. Architectural structure and interconnection among subsystems, packages, and layers must be explicitly outlined. The authors stress granularity: subsystem integration may be more important than discerning internal structure. Architectural drift or erosion, incompatible refactorings, and cyclic dependencies all contribute to costly refactoring.

Clean-slate software design is the modeling, design, and implementation of a system without the impediment of retaining or reusing existing software. *Clean-slate design is an ideal;* most systems, even if designed from scratch, reuse libraries, or other utilities and thus must conform to established interfaces. Legacy systems support established interfaces. Users may be familiar with these interfaces, even if they are designed suboptimally. Migration to a refined system then poses more than technical challenges.

Legacy software is often poorly understood. Documentation may be inadequate or so voluminous as to be incomprehensible. Documentation can be incomplete, poorly organized, misleading, dated, and/or impenetrable.

Software is difficult to modify when it is large, hard to read, insufficiently layered, or inadequately modularized. Overdesigned software is problematic. Constructs established for generality (such as abstract classes) may not be essential but still increase software complexity: consider removal if performance is compromised by the overhead of flexibility. Underdesigned code is also problematic. Insufficient class and relationship design results in insufficient encapsulation (or internalization) of functionality, leading to excessive external analysis, and duplicate code, such as manual type checking. Code is easily replicated via "cut and paste," and pundits refer to "cut-and-paste programming" to describe poorly designed duplicate code. Cut-and-paste programming leads to error propagation, code bloat, and degraded software design.

TABLE 10.8   Poor Software Causes

Sin	Results	Details
HASTE	Compromised quality Incomplete functionality Incomplete error processing Incomplete user interface	Schedule constraints => Insufficient Documentation Inadequate Testing
LAZINESS	Expedient solution Longevity not considered	Poor configuration control
PRIDE	External software not used	"not invented here"
APATHY	Failure to anticipate change Lack of reusable design	No long-term vision Insufficient decomposition
BIAS	Idiosyncratic designs	No alternatives evaluated
GREED	Insufficient modeling Inadequate design Poor or no documentation	Insufficient abstraction Excessive complexity Inadequate testing
IGNORANCE	Depend only on experience Poor choices	Dependency on language, platform, tools, etc.

Source: Adapted from Bates, M. E., *The Online Deskbook*, Pemberton Press, 1996.

In a large system, incompatible or redundant details may degrade performance but do complicate maintainability. Design defects compromise longevity. Refactoring addresses internal deficiencies and transforms code into software that more easily absorbs modifications as the system evolves. As a form of reengineering that orchestrates internal change to meet new standards or performance expectations, refactoring aims to reduce software complexity. Refactoring is an iterative process, involving multiple internal modifications to alter the software structure so that it may absorb future changes or upgrades. Incremental adjustments include renaming for readability, restructuring for consistency, and reducing code duplication for maintainability.

Table 10.8 summarizes the "root causes" of inadequate software development (Bates, 1996; Brown et al., 1998). The presentation plays on the notion of the "seven deadly sins." Whether or not the humor resonates with the reader, it should be clear that rushed development, without sufficient resources for modeling, design, and testing, more likely leads to compromised software. We reiterate then the need for refactoring.

10.5 REVERSE ENGINEERING

Software systems designed and developed from a model support a comprehensive, global perspective. Without a model or sufficient documentation, a developer lacks the high-level view necessary to determine minimal testing requirements and to integrate modifications. With diligence, developers can **reverse engineer** a software system, that is construct a model of the software from the software itself.

Reverse engineering is an established engineering methodology used to extract product knowledge by exposing the underlying design, structure, functionality, and operation of a device (or software). Motivations for reverse engineering include building a replica and extracting a model. This last motivation is the intent of analyzing legacy software: circumvent inadequate documentation to maintain, and possibly integrate, a legacy system with more modern software.

Reverse engineering dissects a system to understand it. Reverse engineering must (1) identify system components and (2) evaluate connectors and relationships between components. Also recommended is the construction of a system model to advance the high level of abstraction associated with an extensible and malleable system. As reverse engineering recovers the software architecture, requirements, design models, and implementation details, documentation must be updated.

Program comprehension is tedious and time-consuming since modern systems can be constructed from millions of lines of code. System core functionality must be distinguished from user interface behavior. Inputs, outputs, memory, and transformations must be classified and correctly mapped. Often, in poorly organized software, UI functions are interspersed with functional code. Such code is brittle because one cannot modify either the UI code or core functionality independently. Selective refactoring may expose features obscured by excessive coupling.

Profiling tools help determine core functionality, resource management, and use. Profilers, test cases, and traces help establish the base functionality of a system and evaluate the UI. Profilers identify persistent and temporal data as well as the most frequently exercised control paths. Debuggers allow the setting of breakpoints, precise locations in the software, so that the state of the software can be examined at critical junctures. By manually changing state during a debugging session, alternative execution paths can be evaluated. Reverse Engineering techniques include tracing execution, analyzing functional provisions as well as version comparison.

Assessing dynamic behavior is difficult. Exhaustive coverage is infeasible and incomplete coverage may be misleading. Correlation of outcomes to specific scenarios should be explicit. Analyses of real-time systems, embedded systems, and concurrent or distributed systems may be highly variable.

Specifying functional obligations is a form of contract analysis. At an architectural level, contractual analysis identifies essential components and connectors. A timeline of past modifications to the software system can be retrieved through version analysis. Is the system design stable? Architectural drift or erosion may be uncovered. At the code and integration level, contractual (functional) analysis must identify how classes (components) collaborate or how data is used. Difficulties arise when an interface is not used as intended. A misconstrued UI indicates poor structure or delineation of functionality. Internal misuse of a class interface indicates poor design and decomposition. Design or model inconsistencies may warrant examination of the source code for type casting, aliasing, and improper accessibility (all problematic techniques discussed in Chapters 4–8).

Reverse engineering is often conducted bottom-up. Construction of a system model proceeds in stages, identifying deficiencies and inconsistencies as they arise. Legacy software is tested to establish functionality, code is analyzed to establish structure, structure is evaluated to determine architectural form, and then, at the highest level of abstraction, the requirements of the system are enumerated.

Some reverse engineering efforts focus on extracting an accurate system model from legacy software that is not documented well or whose documentation is dated and not reflective of the system in use. When legacy software is owned or licensed, the source code is often available. Reverse engineer efforts may seek to replicate software or modify proprietary software so that (illegal) copies may be made. In these cases, the source code is not typically available.

Software **cracking** is the modification of software with the intent to remove or circumvent restrictions on use. The software may not be owned or may have been purchased or licensed with restriction. Cracking software seeks to disable features such as copy protection; adware; verification via serial number, hardware key, data check, or CD check. Software patents and licensing agreements exist so cracked copies are illegal. We mention software cracking because its first steps are reverse engineering: the software's executable image (binary) is analyzed to avoid the branch that requires verification, triggers adware, or prevents copying. The operation code for branching is replaced with an NOP (no operation). Another cracking technique is to replace the expiration date on trial software. Debuggers, disassemblers, decompilers, and UML tools can be used in software cracking.

10.6 SUMMARY

Modern software development must support legacy software, whether integrating new features or upgrading platforms or enhancing user interfaces. Software maintenance is a critical, and oft revisited, stage of software development. In this chapter, we review the traditional perspective of software maintenance alongside the more recent emphasis on software evolution.

From a high level, we examined refactoring, the process of changing the internal structure of code without modifying functionality. A legacy software system may need to be refactored. Typically, the intent is to improve the design of the software by removing inefficient code or tightly coupled code. Refactoring may be necessary for desired performance improvements or to prepare a legacy system for anticipated modifications. Simplification of the software may also be warranted for the sake of prototyping, feasibility studies, or performance analysis. In extreme cases, software must be reengineered, or at least understood on a structural level, so we close the chapter by describing reverse engineering with respect to software.

DESIGN INSIGHTS

SOFTWARE

External pressures drive software evolution
    Technological advances
    User expectations
Software maintenance involves more than bug fixes
Software maintenance (evolution) keeps legacy systems viable
Nonfunctional properties address user experience
Key software qualities
    Security, performance and structural NFPs

MODELS

Models provide a global perspective for software evolution
Reverse engineering can extract models from legacy systems
Requirements traditionally have a functional emphasis
Modern software requirements must model non-functional properties

SOFTWARE DESIGN

Refactoring alters the internal structure of code
=> future modifications better absorbed

Refactoring should not impact the functionality of existing software
   Regression testing used to verify consistent functionality
Refactoring can improve performance and reduce software complexity
   Renaming may expose duplicate code, etc.
Retention of legacy systems is modern software design goal

DOCUMENTATION

Documentation not consistently updated as software evolves
Documentation needed for refactoring but often dated or incomplete

CONCEPTUAL QUESTIONS

1. What is a legacy system?

2. Why not design software from scratch?

3. What are the primary objectives of software maintenance?

4. How does software evolve?

5. Why is the term software evolution preferred?

6. Why did nonfunctional properties become important design criteria?

7. Which are the most important nonfunctional properties?

8. What are the main differences between security, performance, and structural NFPs?

9. When is reverse engineering relevant to software development?

10. What is refactoring and why is it more relevant now than 30 years ago?

11. Why is regression testing used in refactoring?

Glossary: Definitions and Conceptual Details

absolute address: is the actual address to which a variable is mapped, which is the memory location that holds the variable's value.

abstract class: is a class definition that is not fully implemented; one or more class methods remain undefined with the result that no objects can be instantiated from the class.

abstract data type (ADT): is a conceptual model of form and function; a data definition is separated into an interface and an implementation where the implementation details are hidden so that an ADT is characterized by its utility, which is the functionality provided via its interface. For example, a stack is an ADT that provides a LIFO (last-in, first-out) ordering of data; implementation details of the stack container are not relevant to its use.

abstraction: in software design is the separation of conceptual information from implementation details. For example, a variable name is an abstraction of a memory location, a class interface is an abstraction of its functionality, a flowchart is an abstraction of control flow.

accessor: is a class method that accesses encapsulated (hidden) data internal to the class. Such functions typically return data by value.

ad hoc polymorphism: refers to function overloading: two or more functions use the same name but can be distinguish by their function signatures (the number, order, and type of passed parameters).

age: refers to an internal accounting of how long an item has been resident in a collection; typically used to advance low priority items in a priority queue to avoid starvation.

aggregation: is a form of object composition where the composing object usually contains multiple subobjects but may not necessarily own these subobjects. The subobjects do not typically provide functionality to the composing object.

agile software development: is an incremental (iterative) software development methodology based on adaptive planning: requirements and design evolve; interactions with stakeholders drive rapid responsive; code is valued over documentation.

aliasing: occurs when two or more handles (variables) reference the same memory location. Call by reference, for example, sets up an alias between the formal and the actual parameters. Aliasing may be used for efficiency since it allows data to be shared, and thus avoids copying. However, aliases must be tracked carefully for data integrity.

ambiguity: describes a lack of precision that confounds analysis. Compilers cannot handle ambiguity. For example, in a multiple inheritance relationship, when two parent classes define the same named function, it is unclear which method is invoked through a child class object. The compiler cannot resolve such an ambiguous call. Hence, the class designer must resolve the ambiguity by redefining the method (which can simply redirect the call).

assembly language: is a computer language tied to the processor on which it runs and is one step up from machine level code. An assembler translates assembly language code into an executable form (machine code).

association: is the manner in which two or more variables are related. Typically used to refer to ties between objects in OOD, association may be flexible or fixed. For example, a derived class object has a permanent, fixed association with its parent component.

base class: is the topmost (or original ancestor) in a class hierarchy. In a single inheritance relationship, the parent class could also be referred to as the base class. This term is more often associated with C++ than C# or Java.

binary: is the numerical basis of computing: a number system based on two values 0 or 1. Numerically, 10 is 2, 11 is 3, 100 is 4, 101 is 5, etc. Yet, binary string values can be interpreted in multiple, different ways (as characters, as real numbers, etc.).

bit: is the smallest storage unit in memory. A bit holds a zero or one.

Boolean logic: governs the representation of true and false values as well as the rules that determine the truth value of a given equation. For example, the truth value of a conjunction (AND) of two Boolean values is true if and only if both values are true; the truth value of a disjunction (OR) of two Boolean values is false if and only if both values are false.

branch prediction: is the process of predicting which way a branch (if-else) will go to preserve, if possible, the low-level parallelism of the instruction pipeline.

business logic: is also known as domain logic and is the portion of software that handles the required functionality (data processing) of the (business) application.

byte: is 8 bits and is the standard size of a collection of bits.

caching: is the storage of frequently accessed data so that it can be retrieved quickly. Modern processor chips have on-chip caches. Programmers may design their own caches to avoid the overhead of memory access, but should do so with care due to the difficulty of ensuring data integrity with two or more copies of the same piece of data.

call by reference: is a parameter passing mode that is considered efficient but insecure. No local memory is allocated for values passed in and/or out. Instead, aliases are established, thereby avoiding the overhead of data allocation and initialization. However, local modification of data does affect external values.

call by value: is a parameter passing mode that is considered secure but inefficient. Local memory is allocated and initialized for values passed in and/or out. Thus, local modification of data should not affect external data values. References and pointers undermine the security of call by value.

cardinality: is a measure of the number of items in a set, and, in OOD, reflects the number of subobjects defined in a relationship. For example, containers have a varying cardinality of subobjects, ranging from zero for an empty container to unbounded for a resizable container.

cascading changes: imply that modification to one piece of software will necessitate modification to a second piece of software, which will then necessitate modification to a third piece of software, and so on. Tightly coupled code is more prone to cascading changes.

child class: is the immediately derived or descendant class in an inheritance relationship and, as such, inherits all the parent data and functionality but may access only that data and functionality that is public or protected.

class construct: is a language construct supported in modern OOPL. A class construct is used to define a type by specifying data fields (members) and member functions (methods). Essentially an ADT with encapsulation, the class construct distinguishes between public (external) and private (internal) accessibility to defined member data and functions.

class invariant: is a documented summary of the properties and characteristics of a class that should always hold. A class invariant specifies constancy in state (such as range of values, dependencies between fields, data characteristics), with the implied guarantee that manipulating objects instantiated from the class via the class methods should not violate any part of the class invariant. Under Programming by Contract, the class invariant specifies design details and documents intent for software evolution.

clean slate: is a colloquial term that refers to software design that starts from scratch. That is, the software designer need not reuse, support, or integrate any existing code.

code bloat: is the generation of excessively large amounts of code, often unnecessarily. Causes of code bloat include inappropriate optimizations (such as function inlining and loop unrolling), poor software design, and redundant instantiation of templates.

code complexity: is a term used to describe how easy or difficult software is to read, understand, and maintain. Like software complexity, code complexity is not a performance measure.

code obfuscation: refers to the deliberate design of code so that it is hard to read and understand. Code obfuscation (hiding) attempts to safeguard proprietary code from reverse engineering.

code reuse: is the use of existing software to build new software. Software libraries are well-known examples of code reuse: the utilities provided by libraries, such as I/O and pseudo-random number generators, are used over and over again by many different software systems. Code reuse may be more formally known as software reuse.

cohesion: is a software engineering measure of functional or type integrity within a design. Cohesion describes how well a software entity (function, class, component) hangs or sticks together. The more cohesive an entity is, the less dependent it is on external entities and thus the more maintainable.

compaction: is the shifting of allocated memory to one portion of the heap to reduce fragmentation and thus improve software performance. Like the reclamation phase of garbage collection, compaction is pure overhead.

compiler: is the software program that translates the high-level language (HLL) source code written by a software developer into assembly or machine code. Work done by the compiler is typically called static (static typing, static binding) because it does not change at runtime.

composite principle: refers to the preference in software design of composition over inheritance. This design principle is popular with practitioners and has been advanced by the Gang of Four in their seminal Design Patterns book.

composition: is the structure of a complex data type as defined by the composite of several data fields (members), where each data member is an essential element and provides some functionality to the more complex data type. Composition models the has-a relation.

concrete class: is a class definition that is fully implemented; all class methods are defined so that objects can be instantiated from the class.

configuration management: is the process of tracking and controlling changes in large software systems. Software configuration management (SCM) tools assist with version control etc.

connector: is a software architectural term referring to what connects two components: function call, communication protocol, interface component, etc.

constant: is an identifier that does not need memory allocated because its value does not change. The compiler can thus substitute in the constant value wherever this identifier occurs.

constructor: is a special class method that is called by the compiler when an object is instantiated, thus removing the need for an application programmer to call an initialize() routine. It should be designed to set the object in a valid, initial state. Constructors return no value and have the same name as the class.

container: is a data structure whose primary responsibility is to hold or contain data. Common containers include stacks, queues, and sets.

containment: is a conceptual model of the holds-a relation. An object contains or holds one or more subobjects. The subobjects do not provide functionality and are not typically owned by the container.

contraction: refers to an inheritance design that reduces (contracts) the inherited parent interface by suppressing (or NOPing) one or more inherited public functions.

control flow: is the trace of the statements executed in sequence as software runs, which is the software's executable path.

copy constructor: is the constructor that initializes a newly allocated object by copying the state (value of all data members) of a passed object. If not defined by the class designer, the C++ compiler generates a copy constructor that performs a bitwise copy on all fields—a design landmine if a C++ class allocates heap memory internally. C# does not provide a copy constructor.

coupling: is a software engineering measure of the degree of dependency between two software entities. Low coupling implies little dependency on external entities.

CPU: is the abbreviation for central processing unit, the computational core of a computer.

cracking: software cracking is the deliberate reverse engineering of proprietary software to make copies and/or avoid verification checks (such as valid date, specific hardware). Cracked copies are illegal.

cut and paste programming: is a programming technique whereby functionality or structure is replicated by copying the code statements defining the functionality or structure from one portion of the software system to another. Highly susceptible to error, cut and paste programming should be avoided as it undermines software maintainability.

data corruption: occurs when two or more handles (variables) unknowingly reference the same memory location. One handle can thus change the value of the memory location unbeknownst to the other handle.

data mining: is a colloquial term often used in place of data analytics. Most often interpreted as the process of scouring large databases in search of patterns or correlations between data items, data mining has commercial and artificial intelligence applications.

deep copy: refers to the allocation and initialization of a complete copy of a piece of data. Safe but expensive, deep copies are often avoided by using aliasing.

default constructor: is older, C++ terminology for the constructor that is provided, by default, by the compiler when the class designer does not provide one. The default constructor takes no arguments. Hence, the term is often confused with no-argument constructor.

defensive programming: is a style of programming in which no assumptions are made about correct usage of the software. Hence, the software must build in many tests for error conditions, such as illegal input, or use exception handling to prevent improper usage from interrupting program execution.

deferred methods: also known as abstract methods, deferred methods are functions declared in a class interface but not defined. Definition (implementation) is deferred to derived classes.

delegate: is an object that serves to provide functionality or services. Typically, a delegate is a data member composed within another object. If so encapsulated, delegates may be easily replaced or modified. Delegation is an established software design technique: consider the Proxy pattern. Delegates may be polymorphic.

dependency inversion principle: prioritizes designs that move from the abstract to the concrete. High-level abstractions are stable; low-level abstractions are not. Therefore, high-level abstractions should not depend on low-level abstractions.

derived class: is a descendant or child class in an inheritance relationship. This term is more often used with C++ than with C# or Java. Technically, it is more inclusive because a derived class may be a grandchild class and so forth.

design patterns: are a collection of established solutions to reoccurring problems. A design pattern is a general and reusable code solution with expected costs and benefits. For example, several creational patterns address the need for virtual construction in a statically typed language.

destructor: is a special class method in C++ that is called by the compiler when an object goes out of scope. It should be designed to release any resources (such as heap memory) held by the object but may also be used to update bookkeeping details. Destructors return no value and have the same name as the class, preceded by the special "~" symbol.

diamond inheritance: occurs in multiple inheritance when a child inherits from two parents that share a common grandparent. Diamond inheritance suggests data redundancy in multiple inheritance because the grandchild class inherits two copies of the grandparent component (one through each parent).

disassembler: is a software tool that examines the executable (object code) of another program and extracts a representation similar to the original assembly language code.

distributed system: refers to a software system with components distributed in different locations where the underlying network coordinates actions via message passing.

dual perspective: describes two different views of software development. Externally, the application programmer uses a defined class via its published interface, and thus is interested in utility but not implementation details. The class designer has an internal perspective and must structure the class to meet design expectations. The class designer must: choose implementation structures; decide what functions to overload, override, suppress, or NOP; define invariants and implement so as to maintain internal control of state.

dynamic binding: refers to the runtime resolution of a function call. An alternative to static binding (when the compiler translates a function invocation to a JUMP statement), dynamic binding postpones function resolution until runtime using a virtual function table. Dynamic binding supports polymorphism and heterogeneous collections.

e-commerce: is electronic commerce: the purchase, sale, and/or exchanges of goods and services over the Internet.

embedded system: is a special-purpose software system, responsible for a few dedicated functions, which is embedded in another device. Examples abound, including digital watches, traffic lights, vacuum machines, etc.

emergent behavior: may be difficult to quantify because it is the behavior of the system as a whole and thus cannot be easily determined by isolated analysis of the system's constituent parts.

encapsulation: is a key characteristic of OOP and OOD: the data members and associated functionality of a type are bundled together (encapsulated) in a class definition, thus promoting high cohesion.

exception: is a hardware or software error that disrupts the execution of software. Exceptions can be named and processed within software so that runtime errors are avoided.

exception handling: is a systematic response to exceptions. Errors so raised are processed and normal execution resumes. Exception handlers are (small) pieces of code that execute when associated exceptions are raised.

explicit allocation: is the direct allocation (acquisition) of heap-allocated memory via a runtime call, e.g., use of the new operator in C++/C#/Java.

explicit deallocation: is the direct deallocation (release) of heap-allocated memory via a runtime call, e.g., use of the delete operator in C++.

extension: is a pure form of inheritance where the child class preserves inherited functionality but also extends the functionality provided by the parent.

extreme programming (XP): is an incremental software development methodology that emphasizes short development cycles (incorporated with stakeholder feedback) so that requirements and code are built incrementally.

FIFO: is a popular abbreviation for first-in, first-out. FIFO ordering describes containers, like queues, that release data in the order in which it was stored.

fragmentation: of the heap occurs when the pattern of memory allocations (and, possibly, deallocations) yields lots of holes in the heap, that is, many small chunks of free memory dispersed among many allocated blocks. Heap fragmentation causes the allocator to slow down, as it must spend more time searching for free blocks and may cause memory requests to fail if there is not enough contiguous memory available.

framework: is a reusable software platform used to develop applications. The user can selectively override specific functionality for customization. Examples include APIs, compilers, code libraries, and tools sets.

friend: is a C++ construct that permits a class designer to selectively open up the class to external functions and classes. Any function or class declared a friend in classX has access to all the data and functionality of classX, even that declared private or protected. The friend construct is not symmetric, transitive, or inherited.

function signature: is defined by the function name and the number, type, and order of parameters passed into the function.

functional decomposition: is a style of programming also known as structured decomposition or top-down programming. A program or function is designed first at the high level, breaking major tasks into lower level functions.

garbage collection: is the reclamation of heap memory no longer in use (garbage). Garbage collection removes responsibility for memory deallocation from the programmer but is an imperfect process. Executing software must pause for the garbage collector to run. Garbage collection is not controlled by the programmer and may in fact not ever be invoked for small or short-lived applications that use little heap memory.

generalization: is a less desirable form of inheritance where the derived class strives to makes the inherited functionality and interface more general, typically in preparation for further, future derivations.

generic: functions and types are definitions wherein the structure and primary functionality are defined but the primitive data types are not defined internally, rather a type placeholder is used. For example, one can define a generic swap routine, capable of swapping values of any type. Likewise, it is common to define generic containers, such as stacks and queues, and then, when needed, define the type of data held in the container.

handle: is a the means of accessing data stored in memory. A variable is a handle. A handle class controls access to data but does not provide or alter functionality.

hard coding: is a discouraged practice whereby a programmer uses literals (such as "3.14") rather than constant variables (such as `const float pi = 3.14`). Hard coding is not maintainable: if a value changes, all occurrences of those literals must be updated. In contrast, use of constant variables promotes maintainability: if a value changes (say, `const float pi = 3.14159`), the programmer need only update one statement—the constant variable.

has-a: is also known as composition. A class has-a data member that provides essential functionality to the composing object. This relation is often preferred to inheritance because it affords more flexibility relative to cardinality, association, and ownership.

heap: has multiple meanings: (1) data structure and (2) portion of memory in a program. The <u>heap data structure</u> is a tree structure that can be easily (and efficiently) represented by an array, where A[1] represents the root node, A[2] represents the left child of the root, A[3] represents the right child of the root,…. For a given array element A[i], the left child is A[2*i], the right child is A[2*i + 1], and the parent (for i > 0) is A[i/2]. Priority queues are often implemented via the heap data structure because of this efficient representation and the ease of traversing the tree by directly accessing array elements. The <u>(runtime) heap</u> is a portion of program memory that is used for the dynamic allocation of memory. Heap memory provides much flexibility but incurs runtime overhead and can result in performance degradation if poorly managed.

heterogeneous collection: is a container of many objects where each object can be of any type in a specific class hierarchy, which is a collection of polymorphic objects. Support for heterogeneous collections is a key benefit of dynamic binding.

hexadecimal: is a base-16 numbering system: 0, 1, 2, 3, 4, 5, 6, 7, 8, 9, A, B, C, D, E, F. Commonly used to denoted memory locations.

high-level language (HLL): is a programming language that provides built-in control structures, and the means to define composite data structures. HLLs provide a significant degree of abstraction, isolating the programmer from hardware details.

holds-a: is also known as containment; a class holds one or more data members but does not derive any utility from these subobjects, thus implying a lack of type dependency.

identifier: is a (user-defined) name that refers to an entity in source code, such as a constant, variable, function, etc.

implementation: of a class is the code that provides functionality and embodies the design decisions made with respect to internal structure and support for a defined type. Algorithms and data structures are key design decisions.

implementation invariant: is a set of design decisions, software characteristics, or properties that must hold for any implementation of the defined class. As a documentation artifact under Programming by Contract, the implementation invariant provides a design record for class maintenance.

implicit allocation: is the indirect allocation (acquisition) of memory, without explicit calls to the allocator. Either the compiler allocates memory, via stack frames, or memory is automatically allocated at runtime (as in dynamically typed languages like Python).

implicit deallocation: relies on garbage collection to reclaim heap-allocated memory because no action is taken in the software to deallocate memory when handles go out of scope.

indirection: refers to the ability to access memory indirectly, via a pointer variable, or to invoke a function indirectly, via a delegate or function pointer.

information hiding: is an ideal in software design that specifies the hiding of implementation details so that the application programmer not design software that is dependent on arbitrary implementation characteristics. Information hiding is difficult to realize because compilers need type information (size) to lay out objects correctly.

inheritance: is a key OO relationship where a child class is defined in terms of its parent class. The child class "inherits" all data and functionality defined in the parent class. Inheritance supports the is-a relationship. The child class can directly use all public and protected data and functionality so inherited. Structurally, inheritance can be mimicked with composition but inheritance designs are more maintainable, especially when polymorphism is used. OOPLs provide the inheritance construct to automatically pull in the data members and functionality of the parent class.

inheritance of implementation: describes the impure form of inheritance: code reuse. The child class reuses code from the parent class but does not necessarily support the inherited interface.

inheritance of interface: describes the pure form of inheritance where the derived class maintains the interface and functionality of the base class so the derived object is-a base object.

inlining: is a compiler optimization technique that replaces a function call with the body of the function, thereby avoiding the overhead of function call and return. Inlining can thus improve performance. However, inappropriate inlining can lead to code bloat and, ironically, decreased performance.

instantiation: refers to the allocation and initialization of an object. This term implies the invocation of a constructor to place the object in a known, initial state.

interface: is the set of functions defined for a class (or component, or module). A class interface may be delineated by accessibility: public for the client; protected for descendants; private for internal utility.

interface invariant: is a set of properties, state conditions, or means of use that must be observed for the public interface of a class to support the application programmer's expectations. As a documentation artifact under Programming by Contract, the interface invariant is a contractual specification for the client.

interface segregation principle: is the ideal of a maintainable interface: small and cohesive. Different functionality should be isolated in different interfaces.

invariant: a portion of code that should remain the same. Loop invariants describe a condition that should hold true with every execution of a loop. Class invariants describe a condition that should hold true for all objects instantiated from the class.

is-a: is an inheritance relationship where the derived class maintains the interface and functionality of the base class so the derived object is-a base object. Substitutability is possible when the is-a relationship is supported.

legacy code: is existing software that continues to be used, despite the availability of newer technology or improved methodologies. Often such systems function for convenience of established users' needs. Typically, replacement cost is considered prohibitive.

lifetime: is the length of time that a variable (piece of data) remains allocated. Note allocation does not imply utility or access.

limitation: is an undesirable form of inheritance where the derived class limits substitutability by restricting some of the inherited parent behavior (either through suppression or NOP).

liskov substitution principle: is the OOD principle that verifies the interoperability of (sub)types defined in a class hierarchy. The key idea is that inheritance designs support the substitution of a derived class object in place of a base object.

literal: is not associated with memory, and thus cannot be modified. A literal is a value that is just as it appears, e.g., "7," "Hello." For maintainability, if a literal value is subject to change as software evolves, it is recommended to use constants instead.

model view controller (MVC): is an architectural pattern commonly used in software to separate out three entities: the data (model), the view (of data), and the controller (update and manipulate data). MVC supports code and reuse and maintainability because modifications to the view do not impact data representation and so forth.

modular programming: is a software design that strives to separate a program's key functionalities (behaviors or concerns) into separate components. Modular programming reduces coupling, increases cohesion, and promotes code reuse.

mutator: is a class method that alters the value of one or more data members of an object. A mutator need not induce a state change. For example, popping an item off a stack object does not necessarily change the state of the stack, unless the stack transitions from a non-empty stack to an empty state.

no-argument constructor: refers to a constructor that takes no arguments. Ideally, this term should be distinguished from the default constructor, which is the (no-argument) constructor provided by the compiler when the class designer fails to define any constructors.

node class: is an intermediate class in a class hierarchy that inherits form (and possibly some functionality) from a parent class and anticipates extension. A node class itself may be partially abstract.

nonfunctional property (requirement): defines expectations or limitations on the design or implementation of a software system that are not directly related to functional requirements. These software qualities include performance criteria as well as quality measures such as maintainability or scalability.

NOP: stands for No Operation and is an operation code (opcode) that indicates that no operation should be undertaken.

object-oriented design (OOD): refers to software design that rests on the definition and use of objects, as well as the specification of appropriate relationships between objects.

object-oriented programming language (OOPL): support OOD by providing the class construct and built-in constructs for inheritance and polymorphism. A software developer can thus easily define an inheritance relationship with dynamic binding, without using arcane constructs such as function pointers.

open closed principle: specifies that a class should be open for extension but closed for modification, and is a key design principle of OOD.

operating system: is the software, typically preloaded onto desktop computers, that handles the basic tasks of the computer such as IO (input from keyboard, output to screen or file), scheduling processes, organizing files and directories, and executing applications.

operator overloading: is the definition of class methods that can be invoked in application code through a symbol, such as the symbol "+." C++ fully supports operator overloading but, in some cases, must rely on the somewhat controversial friend construct to do so. Java does not support any operator overloading. C# selectively supports operator overloading.

orthogonal: refers to different entities that do not overlap so they can be treated separately. In a multiple inheritance relationship, if two parent classes are orthogonal, their interfaces have no common functions and thus do not confound design with ambiguity.

overloaded: functions are functions that share a name but are distinguished by different parameter lists. Constructors are commonly overloaded in class definitions.

overridden: functions occur in class hierarchies when a derived class redefines the implementation of an inherited function. Overridden functions must have the exact same function signature as the method inherited from the parent (or base) class.

ownership: refers to the handle (variable/object) responsible for a piece of data (another object). Ownership should be tracked to avoid memory leaks and data corruption due to unwarranted aliasing.

parametric polymorphism: is another name for templated or generic code. A templated class or function is written with a type placeholder. When explicitly instantiated, a type (or, the type parameter) is supplied and the compiler generates a copy of that class or function with the parameter type filled in.

parent class: is the foundation of derivation in an inheritance relationship, and establishes the interface to be used in the is-a relationship. Conceptually, there is no limit on the number of child classes that can derive from a parent class.

peripherals: are devices ancillary to a computer, such as printers, secondary storage, modems, etc.

pointer: is a variable that holds the address of data in memory. The pointer construct provides the programmer with the power of indirection and explicit aliasing but is not available in all languages.

polymorphism: is the dynamic binding of function calls within the scope of a class hierarchy. All calls are dynamically bound in Java. In C++ and C#, a base class must specify a method as "virtual" for the function to be dynamically bound. A derived class may override an inherited function, and thus provide variant behavior for a virtual function. When a virtual function is called through a base class pointer or reference, the base class function is called if the reference holds an address of a base class object; the derived function is called if the reference holds an address of a derived class object. In this manner, a single (polymorphic) call may yield many (different) results.

portability: is a measure of whether a software program can run on multiple hardware platforms or not. That is, how easy it is to move (port) a software program from one platform to another.

postconditions: are conditions that hold after a function finishes execution. By evaluating postconditions, an application programmer can track state and thus ensure the legitimacy of subsequent calls.

preconditions: are conditions that should be met before a function executes. By satisfying stated preconditions, an application programmer ensures correct execution of a function.

principle of least knowledge: is a design guideline that promotes low coupling by stating that one object should know as little as possible of another.

priority queue: is a queue that provides the same interface as a standard queue. Internally, although, a priority queue orders items by priority, not in FIFO order. If data is low priority, then when queued in a priority queue, it may be stored indefinitely, that is, starve.

private: confirms the encapsulated nature of class data members and methods. Any method or data member declared to have private accessibility cannot be externally accessed by either the application programmer or descendant classes.

process: is a computer program, or instance of a computer program, running concurrently with other programs (processes).

profiler: is a software tool that runs other software programs and tracks details of usage. Profiles may provide execution traces, track memory usage, and collect coverage data. Profilers can be used to evaluate heap fragmentation (to identify memory leaks or excessive use of temporaries). Profilers can assess the frequency of function calls so that optimization efforts may be targeted.

program counter: holds the address of the currently executing instruction. In modern hardware architectures, the program counter is stored in a special register. The value held in the program counter is pushed onto the runtime stack when a function is invoked so that, when the function terminates, control can be returned to the caller.

protected: accessibility restricts access to class data members and methods to descendants. Any method or data member declared to be protected cannot be externally accessed by the application programmer but can be accessed by descendant classes.

pseudo-code: refers to a English-like coding form that is used to represent the encoding of a software solution when it is not desirable to follow the precise syntax of a particular programming language (such as C or Java).

public: denotes opens access to class data members and methods. Any application programmer or class may access public data and methods. Public data members violate encapsulation and are thus discouraged.

pure virtual: is a C++ term that refers to a function declared but not defined in a class interface. Also known as deferred or abstract methods, pure virtual functions make a class abstract. Inheritance is anticipated because descendant classes must provide implementation details.

queue: is a standard data structure that serves as a container. Items are stored in a FIFO (first-in, first-out) order. Thus, enqueueing adds to the back of the queue; dequeueing removes from the front of the queue.

readability: refers to how easy it is to read and understand a piece of software. Readability directs impact software maintainability. Software construction guidelines suggest coding techniques such as functional decomposition, encapsulation, and self-documenting code to promote readability.

redundancy: is an inheritance problem that occurs when a child inherits from two parents that share a common grandparent. The child class object thus receives two copies of the grandparent components. Data integrity may be a problem. C# and Java do not support multiple inheritance and thus do not encounter this problem. C++ designs may avoid such redundancy through virtual inheritance.

refactoring: is the iterative and systematic alteration of the internal structure of existing software. External behavior is preserved! Refactoring is performed in anticipation of software upgrades so that the code is better structured to absorb change.

reference: is a variable that holds the address of data in memory. Multiple references can address the same memory, thereby establishing aliases and supporting sharing. However, poorly tracked aliases (references) can lead to data corruption. One can view a reference as a pointer that the compiler automatically dereferences.

reference counting: is a garbage collection technique that associates a reference count with each allocated memory block. Every reference to this block increases the reference count. Each time a reference is reassigned or goes out of scope, the reference count is decremented. A reference count of zero indicates that there is no access to this memory block, and thus, there is no use of this memory block and it may be reclaimed.

reflection: is the ability of a computer program to examine type (and modify) code at runtime without knowing precisely the names of the interfaces, fields, and methods.

regression testing: evaluates software after an upgrade to ensure that system functionality and/or performance has not been altered from one version to the next. Tests are run and evaluated against a set of fixed results. Conformance to expectations indicates that the tests pass.

relocatable: code is not assigned an absolute address. Rather, the relocatable address is the combination of a base address and an offset. Typically, the number of bytes in an offset represents the distance of the code (function or data) from the starting address of the component's layout. Since the component can be loaded into any open memory address, the base address can vary but the offset remains constant. The code is relocatable because whenever it is loaded into memory, addresses are recalculated using the new base and the constant offset.

requirements: are specifications that define the essential functionality of a software system, i.e., what a software system should do. Behavioral requirements can be modeled with state charts, sequence diagrams, etc. Requirements that include nonfunctional characteristics (such as performance) are often distinguished as NFR (nonfunctional requirements).

responsibility driven design: is the design principle that stresses the clear identification of class functionality (actions) and dependencies.

reverse engineering: is the analysis of a hardware or software system to determine its structure and functionality. Historically, reverse engineering was undertaken to reproduce an existing product when the design blueprints were unavailable (as in replicating a competitor's product) or whose original design has degraded due to successive modifications. In software, reverse engineering is often undertaken to understand an existing system that is inadequately documented.

root set: is the set of variables in scope when program execution is paused so that the garbage collector may run. A trace emanating from the root set identifies all active variables so that the garbage collector will not reclaim active variables.

scalability: is a measure of how well a software system performs under increased load conditions (when additional resources are added).

self-documenting code: is the deliberate selection of identifier names that describe use and intent. Variable names such as min and max clearly imply intent as do function calls like Fibonnaci(n).

separation of concerns: is a design approach that separates the major, different features or functionalities of the program into different modules and yields more maintainable code that is easier to reuse.

shallow copy: refers to establishing an alias (a secondary reference) to a piece of data to avoid the overhead of allocation and initialization of a true copy. Efficient but vulnerable, shallow copies may lead to data corruption.

side-effect: is an unintended or secondary effect of a direct action. Side effects are commonly associated with function calls, where an indirect result of the call will be a change in value for some memory (the direct result of the function call being the functionality associated with the function called).

single responsibility principle: is the design principle that prioritizes the encapsulation of the primary functionality in a class design, and no more.

smart pointer: is a wrapped pointer that serves to guard against memory leaks in C++. When a smart pointer goes out of scope, its destructor is invoked so that any heap memory referenced by the smart pointer is appropriately deallocated. The auto_ptr construct in the STL is essentially a smart pointer.

software architecture: has many different definitions. A structural definition considers software architecture to be the layout of the different components of a software system and the relationships between those components.

software complexity: is an assessment of software's structure, readability, and maintainability. How intricate, layered, complex is the software? Common measures of software complexity include control flow, coupling, branching, data, data access, and cyclomatic complexity (the number of independent paths through the software).

software development life cycle (also known as software development process): is the set of processes undertaken to develop a software system. Typical stages include requirements gathering, design, implementation, testing (verification), and maintenance. Different methodologies exist for undertaking software development.

software engineering (SE): is the application of engineering principles to developing and managing software systems. SE covers the requirements analysis, design, implementation, testing, maintenance, and reengineering of software.

software evolution: is a more modern term referring to adaptive software maintenance, which is the upgrading of an existing software system to provide more functionality, improved performance, etc.

software integration: is the combination of several software subsystems into a working software product. Using predefined subsystems, such as databases, UIs, etc., developers can shorten the implementation and testing phases of software development.

software maintenance: is the modification or upgrade of a software system. Traditionally, software maintenance was assumed to be corrective: fixing software defects or improving performance. Much of software maintenance, however, involves the support of an expanding software system and thus includes functional enhancements, refinements of UIs, platform extensions, etc.

source code: is a set of executable instructions, usually written in a high-level language, that comprise a program.

spaghetti code: is unstructured code that is not readable or maintainable. Spaghetti code is a style of programming usually associated with the emergence of computer programming in the 1960s and extensive use of the GOTO statement.

spatial locality: refers to the use of data elements that are stored in proximity to each other.

specialization: is a form of inheritance where the derived class modifies or extends the parent functionality in a manner that specializes the behavior according to subtype.

specification: is a form of inheritance where the derived class fills in details or provides implementation that is missing in the abstract parent class.

stack: has multiple meanings: (1) data structure and (2) portion of memory in a program. The <u>stack data structure</u> is a common container that stores data in a LIFO (last-in, first-out) order. Its classic interface supports pushing (storing) and popping (retrieving) items. The <u>runtime stack</u> is a portion of program memory that holds functions and data currently in scope. Upon function entry, an activation record (or stack frame) is pushed onto the runtime stack. Upon function exit, its activation record (or stack frame) is popped off the runtime stack.

stack frame: also known as an activation record, a stack frame is a layout of the composite data necessary to correctly process a function call and thus includes the program counter as well as space for local variables.

standard template library (STL): for C++, provides generic versions of standard data structures, such as stacks and vectors, as well as standard algorithms for operating on these containers.

starvation: is a possible side-effect of using a priority queue: a low-priority item may be continually bumped in line as higher-priority items are enqueued ahead of it. Use of an internal aging mechanism may be used to avoid starvation.

static binding: refers to the resolution of function calls by the compiler. Static binding is not flexible but is efficient. Once resolved, a function call cannot be modified, but no overhead is incurred at runtime to process the call.

static function (method): refers to functions that are declared and defined within class scope but are not accessible via an instantiated object. Rather such functions are invoked through the (scope of the) class name.

static variable: refers to data members that are declared and defined within class scope but are not accessible via an instantiated object. Rather data members are invoked through the (scope of) the class name. When a class definition is loaded, one instance of the static variable is allocated. Every object instantiated from the class definition thus shares this one copy.

structured programming: is often heralded as the emergence of software design, as well as a response to overuse of the GOTO. Structured programming promotes functional decomposition and appropriate use of control constructs. The deliberate organization of data and functionality should make the underlying structure or design of the software evident.

substitutability: is an effect of the is-a relationship: a derived object can stand in for, or act as a substitute for, a base class object.

subtype polymorphism: rests on inheritance and dynamic binding. A derived class can override (redefine) an inherited function. If this function is dynamically bound then, at runtime, either the base or a derived class method is invoked, dependent on the (sub)type of object through which the method is invoked.

syntactic sugar: is a derogatory term that implies that a language construct does not provide significant additional design support but merely sweetens the code.

templates: are the generic type and generic function support in C++.

temporal locality: refers to the use of data elements within a relatively small time window.

test coverage: evaluates how much of a software program has been "covered" or tested.

test driven development (TDD): is an incremental software development methodology that emphasizes tests. Tests are written first and then code is developed to pass the test. This code is then refactored to adhere to good design principles.

test harness: is a set of test code and data used to test targeted software, often by varying test conditions from one test run to another.

test suite: is a collection of test cases used to test software; often, the test suite targets specific functionality or behavior.

`this` **pointer:** is a construct in OOPLs that facilitates data access while maintaining data integrity. The `this` pointer is the address of the object through which a class method is invoked. The compiler automatically patches it in as an implicit parameter whenever a class method is invoked through an object. Static class methods are called through the class name and thus do not have a `this` pointer as an implicit parameter.

thread: is a lightweight process, the smallest unit of a running program that can be scheduled by the operating system. A process may contain multiple threads that share resources, such as memory.

type extension: is typically viewed as a pure form of inheritance: the derived class extends, by adding functionality and/or data, the capabilities of the parent class.

type introspection: refers to the ability to examine the (sub)type of a variable at runtime.

unified modeling language (UML): is a standardized, graphical, modeling language freely available to model both structure and behavior in OO software systems. See uml.org.

unit testing: promotes the testing of software components on a unit level (function, class, module). Tests are written after the code is designed and implemented.

user interface (UI): is the layer of software responsible for supporting human (the user's) interaction with the software system. Traditionally, operating systems provided rudimentary UIs. Modern UIs are typically GUI (graphical user interface).

validation: assesses whether the system satisfies the specified requirements as well as client expectations; that is, does the system function correctly and behave as needed?

variable: is a data identifier that is associated with memory. Thus, the value held in a variable may change (vary).

verification: determines whether or not software performs as expected. Unlike validation, software verification seeks to assess functionality relevant only to the specified requirements.

version control: is the formal management of changes to software. Different versions are numbered and identified with a timestamp.

virtual function: is a function tagged in its class definition so that it can or will be dynamically bound.

virtual function table (VTAB): is a table of function pointers associated with a class. Each entry contains the address of the corresponding function declared in the class interface. When a function is defined, its address is placed in the table. If it is undefined (abstract), then the vtab entry contains a zero.

virtual inheritance: is a tagged definition of inheritance in C++ that attempts to resolve the redundancy problem.

weak reference: a reference (address holder) that provides the same capability to address memory as a (strong) reference but will not prevent the garbage collector from reclaiming an object.

wrapper: is a class that serves to wrap up, or encapsulate, an existing class. Wrappers typically facilitate code reuse by adjusting interfaces while retaining existing functionality.

References

Ammann, P., and Offutt, J., *Introduction to Software Testing*, Cambridge University Press, 2008.

Bates, M. E., *The Online Deskbook*, Pemberton Press, 1996.

Blaha, M., and Rumbaugh, J., *Object-Oriented Modeling and Design with UML*, 2nd edition, Prentice-Hall, 2005.

Brown, W. et al., *AntiPatterns: Refactoring Software, Architectures and Projects in Crisis*, Wiley, 1998.

Budd, T., *An Introduction to OOP*, 3rd edition, Addison-Wesley, 2002.

Bulka, D., and Mayhem, D., *Efficient C++: Performance Programming Techniques*, Addison-Wesley, 1999.

Dingle, A., 2002, Tracking the Design of Objects: Encapsulation through Polymorphism, *OOPSLA '02*, pp. 48–52.

Dingle, A., and Hildebrandt, H., *C++ Memory First*, Franklin, Beedle & Associates, 2006.

Ellis, M., and Stroustrup, B., *The Annotated C++ Reference Manual*, Addison-Wesley, 1990.

Fowler, M., *Refactoring: Improving the Design of Existing Code*, Addison-Wesley, 1999.

Gamma, E., Helm, R., Johnson, R., and Vlissides, J., *Design Patterns*, Addison-Wesley, 1995.

Gomaa, H., *Software Modeling and Design*, Cambridge University Press, 2011.

Hammer, K., and Timmerman, T., *Fundamentals of Software Integration*, Jones & Bartlett, 2008.

Jorgenson, P., *Modeling Software Behavior*, CRC Press, 2009.

Josuttis, N., *The C++ Standard Library*, 2nd edition, Addison-Wesley, 2012.

Kerievsky, J., *Refactoring to Patterns*, Addison-Wesley, 2005.

Lakos, J., *Large-Scale Software Design*, Addison-Wesley, 1996.

Larman, C., *Applying UML and Patterns*, Prentice-Hall, 2005.

Loshin, D., *Efficient Memory Programming*, McGraw-Hill, 1999.

Martin, R., *Clean Code: Handbook of Agile Software Craftsmanship*, Prentice-Hall, 2009.

Meyers, S., *Effective C++*, 2nd edition, Addison-Wesley, 1998.

Perry, D., and Wolf, A., Foundations for the study of software architecture, *Software Engineering Notes*, vol. 17, no. 4, Oct 1992, pp. 40–52.

Perry, W., *Effective Methods for Software Testing*, John Wiley & Sons, 2006.

Roock, S., and Lippert, M., *Refactoring in Large Software Projects*, John Wiley & Sons, 2003.

Schacter, D., *Seven Sins of Memory: How the Mind Forgets and Remembers,* Houghton Mifflin, 2003.

Seacord, R., *Secure Coding in C and C++*, 2nd edition, Addison-Wesley, 2013.

Shaw, M., and D. Garlan, 1996, *Software Architecture: Perspectives on an Emerging Discipline*, Upper Saddle River, NJ: Prentice-Hall.

Stroustrup, B., *The C++ Programming Language*, special edition, Addison-Wesley, 2000.

Stroustrup, B., *The C++ Programming Language*, 4th edition, Addison-Wesley, 2014.

Torkel, K., *The Overflowing Brain*, Oxford University Press, 2009.

Appendix A: Memory and the Pointer Construct

THIS APPENDIX REVIEWS PROGRAMMING LANGUAGE constructs that enable programmers to address program memory within software. We cover the C++ pointer construct and examine references, as supported in C++ and used in C# and Java. We review parameter passing as a means to reinforce an understanding of references. This appendix supplements discussions in Chapters 2, 4, 5, and 7. Readers are not expected to have experience with either C or C++.

A.1 POINTERS

Chapter 2 outlined the evolution of programming languages and software development. The benefits of increased abstraction were noted, as was the move away from programming based directly on system hardware. Freedom from tedious details, such as mapping out memory assignments and tracking specific locations of data, made software development easier, faster, and more appealing. Code without hard-coded memory locations better supported software maintenance and portability.

Nonetheless, as programming languages became higher level, and programmers farther removed from the hardware, the desire to directly access memory remained. Hence, in C, and then C++, the pointer construct was provided to hold addresses. Using pointers, programmers can indirectly access data stored in memory. What is the difference between direct and indirect access? Direct access is when data is accessed directly (one step) through its variable name, as in: "index++;." Indirect access reflects an additional layering. Since a pointer holds an address of a variable, two steps are needed to access or store data in that address: (1) the address of the desired variable is extracted from the pointer and (2) the desired variable so addressed is accessed. Step 1 is called "deferencing a pointer" and is accomplished using the "*" in front of the pointer variable. The statement "(*indexPtr)++;" illustrates these two steps.

Syntactically, it does not matter whether a pointer holds the address of memory on the runtime stack or the heap, but any memory accessed must be within range of the addresses allocated to the running program. If a pointer variable contains an invalid address, that is, a value outside the range of program memory, a runtime error results if that pointer variable is deferenced. *At the abstract level of software design, there is no easy means to distinguish invalid addresses from valid addresses.* Hence, care must be taken to initialize and maintain appropriate values in pointer variables. A pointer variable should be initialized to the address of a variable, or to zero (or null) to indicate that it currently does not contain a valid address.

Example A1 illustrates the declaration of a simple integer variable and a pointer variable. The symbol "*" following the type name in a variable declaration defines the variable to be a pointer, see line #A. The symbol "*" could also immediately precede the variable name, as in line #B. Note that "*" does not distribute: line #C declares two variables: an int pointer and an int. Placement of "*" is somewhat arbitrary. *Software developers should be consistent: pick a convention and stick with it.*

Example A1: C++ Pointer Declaration, Initialization and Simple Use

```
// C++ code: two variable declarations
int  x;              //stack allocation of integer variable
int* iPtr;           //stack allocation of pointer variable    #A
int  *iPtr2;         //stack allocation of pointer variable    #B
int* iPtr3,x2;       //stack allocation of pointer and then int #C


x = 100;             //x initialized to hold value 100          #D
iPtr = &x;           //iPtr initialized to hold address of x   #E

cout << x << &x << endl; //output x's value and then address   #F
cout << *iPtr << iPtr << endl;   //same as above               #G

cout << ++x << x++ << endl;      //outputs 101 101             #H
cout << x++ << ++x << endl;      //outputs 102 104             #I
```

```
*iPtr = 200;                      //indirect access              #J
cout << x << endl;                //is 104 or 200 output? Why?    #K

cout << ++(*iPtr) << (*iPtr)++ << endl;    //outputs 201 201    #L
cout << (*iPtr)++ << ++(*iPtr) << endl;    //outputs 202 204    #M

cout << x << endl;                //is 104 or 204 output? Why?
cout << *iPtr << endl;            //is 104 or 204 output? Why?
```

The symbol "&" in front of a variable name tells the compiler to extract the memory address of that variable, as in statement #E of Example A1. The symbol "*" in front of a pointer variable name tells the compiler to extract the value located in memory whose address is held in the pointer. Compare the output of statements #F and #G.

Figure A1 displays a sketch of sample memory assignments for the variables x and iPtr in Example A1. Initially, both variables are declared but not defined. That is, no value is assigned to either variable. The memory diagrams in Figure A1 reflect this lack of assigned value with question marks. Actually, there would be values in memory: whatever residual bit string lingers in a variable's memory location would be interpreted as its value. Convention suggests that one always initialize variables. The danger of using uninitialized pointers is particularly negative.

Consistent with the notion of an int type, the variable x holds the value of a whole number, the value 100 as assigned in statement #D. Consistent

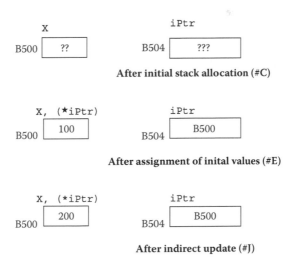

FIGURE A1   Memory sketch for Example A1.

with the notion of a pointer type, the variable iPtr holds the value of the memory address of variable x, as assigned in statement #E. Any variable on the left-hand side of an assignment statement is subject to an altered value. Unless declared as const, pointer values can change, just like any other type of variable.

Example A1 displays a classic contrast between pre- and post-increment of an integer value. The first set of cout statements (#F and #G) uses the integer variable x. As a pre-increment operation, ++x increases the value of x from 100 to 101 before the value of x is displayed. As a post-increment operation, x++ increases the value of x from 101 to 102 *after* it is displayed. Hence, 101 is displayed twice (#H). The cout statement #I reverses the use of pre- and post-increment, so the output is 102 and 104.

Statement #J illustrates an indirect assignment via a pointer variable. *iPtr indicates to the compiler that the assignment targets the data value whose memory address is stored in the pointer variable iPtr. Hence, the value of 200 is written into memory location B500, which is the memory address associated with the integer variable x in Figure A1. The value of the pointer variable is not altered; the value held in the memory that it addresses is altered.

In Example A1, the #L and #M cout statements mimic #H and #I. Instead of referring directly to our stored integer, via the variable x, we use the dereferenced pointer *iPtr. Note that *iPtr and x are aliased: they refer to the same memory. Hence, a change to one is equivalent to a change to the other. Thus, when *iPtr assumes the value 200, the data altered is the data resident in memory location B500. That is, x is now 200. In statements #L and #M, increments to *iPtr are really increments to the integer variable x.

Due to precedence constraints, we must enclose *iPtr in parentheses before applying the post-increment operator. Failure to do so will not result in a compilation error. What would happen of statements #L and #M used *iPtr++ instead of (*iPtr)++? Let us reason through the syntax. *iPtr++ represents two operations: dereferencing a pointer and post-increment. The post-increment operator is invoked first because ++ has higher precedence than *. What would be incremented?: iPtr, the value of the pointer variable. Hence, B500 would be incremented to B504, assuming pointers are allocated 4 bytes. Then the value of the "integer" stored in B504 would be output, which is not the value expected. Yet, after the cout statements execute, iPtr would still be perceived as a pointer variable holding an appropriate address. Any changes to memory made through this pointer will result in data corruption.

Why? iPtr would no longer hold the address of x. It holds the address of memory 4 bytes beyond x. Who knows what values would be altered?

Pointers are typed in C++. Why? To more strongly regulate the use of pointer variables, pointers may be assigned only the address of a variable whose type matches its own. Thus, int pointers may hold only addresses of int variables; float pointers may hold only addresses of float variables and so forth. Type incompatibilities trigger compilation errors. Any statement assigning the address of an int variable to a float pointer variable will not compile and so forth. This restriction is relaxed somewhat with respect to inheritance: a base class pointer may hold the address of a derived class object, as seen in Chapters 7 and 8.

Pointers are not so constrained in C. An untyped pointer, the void pointer, is broadly used in C code. The address of any type of variable may be held in a void pointer. Use of void pointers in C++ is discouraged.

Example A2 shows the declaration, initialization, and use of differently typed pointer variables. Figure A2 show the corresponding sample memory allocation. What does the output statement #B yield? 9.9 for the float value. What int value is output? Who knows? Although clearly iPtr holds the address of y, y was not initialized. Whatever bit string was left in the memory associated with y is output.

Example A2: C++ Typed Pointers

```
float        a = 7.5;      //stack allocation of float variable
float        a2;           //stack allocation of float variable
float        b = 107;      //stack allocation of float variable
int          y;            //stack allocation of int variable

float*       fPtr;         //stack allocation: pointer variable
float*       fPtr2 = &a;   //stack allocation & initialization
int*         iPtr;         //stack allocation: pointer variable

fPtr = &y;    //error: float pointer cannot hold address of int
iPtr = &a;    //error: int pointer cannot hold address of float
// #A Initial stack allocation complete here

fPtr = &a2;    //pointer holds address of uninitialized float
fPtr2 = fptr;  //pointer value can be overwritten
               //two different pointers can hold same address
*fPtr = 9.9;   //float 'pointed to' by fPtr is assigned new value

iPtr = &y;    //pointer holds address of uninitialized int

cout << *fPtr << *iPtr << endl;
// #B pointer values updated by this point
```

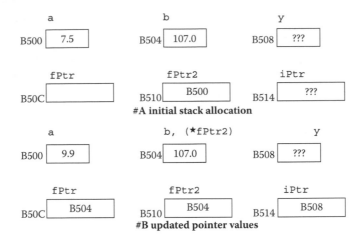

FIGURE A2   Memory sketch for Example A2.

A.2 INAPPROPRIATE USE OF POINTERS

Example A3 illustrates illegal and unwise manipulations of pointers. Figure A3 sketches the corresponding memory allocation. A pointer may not hold the address of a constant value. Nor may a pointer point to a literal value. Why? There is no program memory associated with constants or literals. The cross-through statements in Example A3 indicate compilation errors. *More problematic are statements that compile but have unknown effect because the pointer variable may or may not contain a valid address.*

Example A3: Danger of the Uninitialized: C++

```
// C++ code: missing and illegal initialization
float*        fPtr3;          //uninitialized pointer variable
int*          iPtr3 = 0;      //pointer initialized to zero
const float   pi = 3.14159;

fPtr3 = &pi;                  //pointer cannot hold address of constant
iPtr3 = &1000;               //pointer cannot hold address of literal

if (iPtr3)    *iPtr3 = 100;       //Safety check. Effect?    #A

*fPtr3 = 99.99;                   //will compile. Effect?    #B
```

Consistent with convention, iPtr3 was initialized to zero (points to nothing). What happens if iPtr3 were dereferenced?: a runtime exception. Why? The memory location 0 is in the operating system domain and is inaccessible to user programs. Modern software uses exceptions to preserve software

Pointers that do not contain valid addresses should not be dereferenced

FIGURE A3   Pointer variables with invalid addresses.

integrity. It is preferable to generate a runtime exception from a null pointer than to permit data corruption. To avoid runtime errors, a simple safety check, verifying that the pointer is not null or zero, can be performed, as in statement #A of Example A3. What happens when statement #A executes? iPtr3 was initialized to zero (false), indicating that it does not contain a valid memory address. Thus, 100 is not assigned to the memory "pointed to" by iPtr3.

What is troubling about statement #A in Example A3? fPtr3 was not initialized! *Lack of initialization does NOT mean that variables have no value.* It means that no one knows what value they have: whatever bit string resides in the memory associated with the variable will be interpreted as its value. Thus, whatever bit string resides in the memory associated with the pointer fPtr3 will be interpreted as an address of a float. If the residual bit string yields an address outside the range of valid program addresses, a runtime error occurs. Otherwise, the memory location is overwritten by the value 99.99. Data corruption! *Although unintentional data alterations often do not affect running software, data corruption can lead to failure.* Such errors can be hard to trace since they may occur far from the source. Design guidelines explicitly recommend that programmers initialize pointer variables either to the address of an appropriate variable or to zero (or null), indicating that pointers point to nothing.

Multiple handles (pointers) can hold the same address, giving programmers multiple ways to access a specific memory location. Thus, pointers support the sharing of data. Pointers may lead to data corruption if the value in memory is changed through an alias without the knowledge (or permission) of other aliases.

A.3 REFERENCES

C++ has pointers. Java does not. C# supports pointers in a restricted manner and only in unsafe mode. Is there indirect addressing in C# or Java? Yes! All three languages have references. Like a pointer, a reference is an address holder. Unlike a pointer, a reference is an established alias. Thus, the programmer cannot change the association between a reference variable and its aliased memory location.

Example A4: C++ References

```
// C++ code: aliases (two or more handles point to same memory)
int        z;
int&       alias = z;   // reference to int variable declared
int&       illegal,     // compile-time error: no alias specified
int*       iPtr = &z;   // int pointer declared and defined
// #A Initial stack allocation complete here

z++;
alias++;
cout << z << alias << *iPtr << endl;
// #B post increment of (uninitialized) variables complete here

z = 100;
cout << z << alias << *iPtr << endl;
// #C assignment to int z

alias = 1;
cout << z << alias << *iPtr << endl;
// #D assignment to alias complete here
```

Example A4 illustrates the declaration, initialization, and use of C++ references. Figure A4 sketches the corresponding memory allocations. A reference is manipulated in the same syntactical manner as the variable

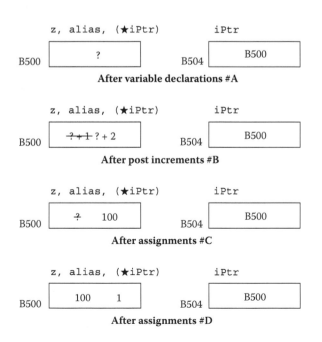

After variable declarations #A

After post increments #B

After assignments #C

After assignments #D

FIGURE A4   Aliased int.

with which it is aliased. Contrast that to a pointer variable. One must use "*" to dereference a pointer variable and "&" to extract the address of a variable. A common saying is that a reference is a pointer that the compiler dereferences for you. The reference is conceptually the same in C# and Java.

A.4 THE this POINTER

Pointers provide the means to address memory, and thus potentially undermine portability. Yet, pointers are used extensively in object-oriented programming (OOP). How then can OOP be more abstract than structured programming? *OOP hides many pointers*, specifically, a special type of pointer called the this pointer.

The this pointer/reference is defined for each object instantiated in an OO program, whether the code is written in C++, C#, or Java. The this pointer/reference holds the address of the object with which it is associated. The this pointer/reference is needed to resolve access to data members and member functions defined in a class but referenced in individual objects. We walk through Example A5 to explain this concept.

Example A5: Sample C++ Class Definition

```
// class definition in.h file
class hitCount
{       int     count;
        int     min;
        ...
    public:
        hitCount()              { count = 0; min = 0;}
        void    query()         { count++;}
        bool    threshold(int);     // function defined in .cpp
        ...
};


...
hitCount        a, b, c;
a.query();              // #A equivalent to hitCount::query(B100)

for (int k = 0; k < 10; k++)
        b.query();      // #B equivalent to hitCount::query(B108)

for (int k = 0; k < 100; k++)
        c.query();      // #C equivalent to hitCount::query(B110)
```

Example A5 defines a C++ class that includes the functionality to track the number of queries made of an object. For clarity, most other functionality has been omitted. Object instantiation for three variables is also presented, and Figure A5 shows sample memory allocations for these objects. This discussion is relevant for Java and C# code, the key difference being that, from the C#/Java application programmer perspective, this is a reference.

Discussed briefly in Chapters 2 and 3, functions are named blocks of code that are laid out in the code section of program memory. Functions defined in classes, often called methods, are defined in class scope. Thus, the query() function defined for the hitCount class is really named hitCount::query(). A query() function defined in a dataStore class would be named dataStore::query(), etc. Class scope allows many different classes to define methods with the same name, such as query(). To identify the appropriate function, class methods must be invoked through an object instantiated from that class. But how does the hitCount::query() method invoked in line #A of Example A5 know that it should update the hit count of object a? Likewise, how does the hitCount::query() method invoked in #B of Example A5 know that it should update the hit count of object b? Etc.

To control access to encapsulated data members, the compiler translates the method invocation a.query() to hitCount::query(&a). That is, the compiler passes in an implicit parameter — the address of the object a. When the data member count is incremented in the method query(), it is the data member of a, namely a.count++. Similarly, when the compiler translates the invocation b.query(), it again passes in an implicit parameter — the address of the object b. When count is now incremented, it is b.count++. The implicit parameter so passed is called the this pointer; the this pointer is the address of the object through which a class method is invoked.

The this pointer may be used to disambiguate references. What does that mean? In a class method, to clearly note association, formal parameters often carry the same name as the associated data field. One cannot use the same name in one scope to reference different memory locations.

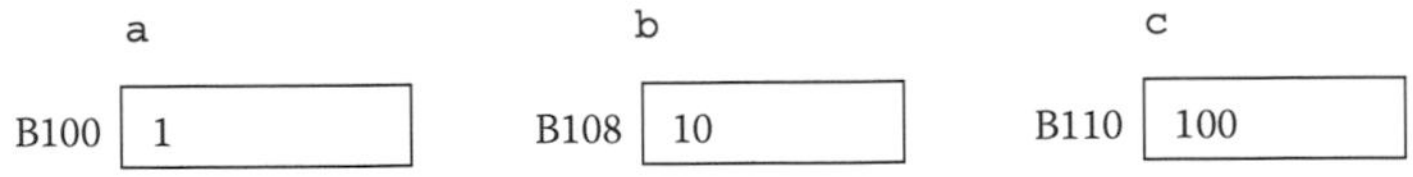

FIGURE A5 Three hitCount objects.

The this pointer clarifies that the field being referenced is a data member of the object through which the function was invoked. Example A5a shows the implementation code for a second method declared in the hitCount class, where this method has a passed parameter with the same name as a data member. Like other C++ pointers, the this pointer must be dereferenced first before accessing any data field of its object. Again the dereferenced pointer must be put is parentheses because field access, ".", has higher precedence than "*". An equivalent, and more readable, syntax is achieved using the -> operator. Thus, "(*this).min" is equivalent to "this->min".

Example A5a: C++ this Pointer Used to Disambiguate

```
// method definition in .cpp file
bool hitCount::threshold(int min)
{       return (min < (*this).min); }
```

A.5 PARAMETER PASSING

Two parameter passing modes are commonly used in modern programming languages: **call by reference** and **call by value**. "Formal parameter" refers to the parameter as named in the function definition while "actual argument" refers to the value or variable passed for a specific function invocation. Call by value encompasses both pass by value (when a value is passed into a function) and return by value (when a value is returned from a function). Similarly, call by reference encompasses both pass by reference and return by reference. What is the difference between the two parameter passing modes? Memory use. C++ and C# support both modes. Java supports only call by value, which is the default parameter passing mode for both C++ and C#.

Call by value is considered a secure but inefficient means of passing data in and out of functions. For pass by value, the formal parameter is allocated its own local memory (in the **stack frame** associated with the function), which then is initialized with the value of the passed parameter. Hence, one can pass a **literal** value, a **constant** value, or a **variable**. In all cases, the value is copied; the original data is unaffected. In return by value, a temporary of the appropriate type is allocated memory in the function stack frame. The return value is then copied into this location when the function returns to the point of call. Copying data incurs a significant overhead if the passed or returned value is large. Nonetheless, for primitive (built-in) types, call by value guarantees that data outside the function will not be affected by actions on the passed values. We consider call by value with respect to objects in Appendix C.

Call by reference is considered to be an efficient but insecure means of passing data in and out of functions. Instead of providing local memory into which the passed (or returned) data values are copied, call by reference establishes aliases. One cannot use literal values or constant values with call by reference. For pass by reference, the formal parameter is aliased with the actual argument. In return by reference, the function returns the address of the variable so returned. Call by reference is often used as an alternative to call by value when data objects are large and the overhead of local memory allocation and initialization should be avoided. To ensure that passed values do not change, while retaining the efficiency of passing by reference, C++ design guidelines recommend passing by const reference. As shown in Chapter 4 and Appendix B, copy constructors and overloaded assignment operators typically illustrate this approach.

Example A6 contrasts pass by value and pass by reference with the corresponding memory diagrams illustrated in Figure A6. Since pass by value allocates a local copy (p) for the passed parameter (safe), the function's action of incrementing p has no impact on the actual argument: after the function call, the value of safe is the same as before the call. In contrast, pass by reference aliases the formal parameter with the actual argument. Thus, a change to q is a change to the actual argument insecure.

Example A6: Pass by Value and Pass by Reference (C++)

```
// C++ code: parameter passing
// formal parameter: p
void passByValue(int         p)                    {        p++;    }

// formal parameter: q
void passByReference(int&   q)          {        q++;    }

const int     noMemory = 22;
int           safe = 100;
int           insecure = 100;
// #A
passByValue(11);              // actual parameter: literal '11'
// #B
passByValue(noMemory);        // actual parameter: noMemory
// #C
passByValue(safe);            // actual parameter: safe
// #D
passByReference(insecure); // actual parameter: insecure
// #E
cout << safe << insecure << endl;        // outputs 100 101
```

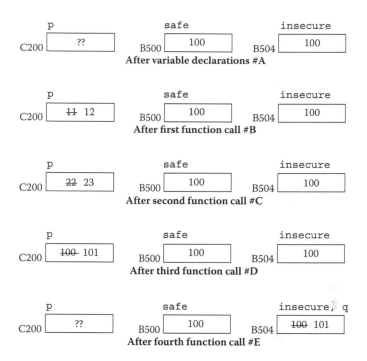

FIGURE A6   Local memory holds copied value for PassByValue.

Example A7 contrasts return by value and return by reference. Figure A7 presents the corresponding memory diagrams. In return by value, the value returned is copied into the temporary allocated on the function stack frame. Since the value is copied, one can return a literal value, a value held in a constant, or a value held in a variable (regardless of where that variable resides). Programmers must be careful when returning by reference since doing so establishes an alias. Literal values and constant values cannot be returned by reference because there is no memory associated with such values.

Example A7: Return by Value and Return by Reference (C++)

```
// C++ code: parameter passing
int returnByValue1()
{    // ok to return literal: value copied
     return 42;
}

int returnByValue2()
{    const int      noMemory = 43;
```

```
      // ok to return const: value copied
      return noMemory;
}

int returnByValue3()
{     int      stackMemory = 44;
      // ok to return local variable: value copied
      return stackMemory;
}

int& returnByReference()
{     int      stackMemory = 66;
      // NOT ok to return (address of local variable)
      return stackMemory;
}

int           hitch = returnByValue1();        // #A
int           hiker = returnByValue2();        // #B
int           guide = returnByValue3();        // #C
int&          riskyAlias = returnByReference();  // #D
...
riskyAlias++;          // What data is incremented?  // #E
```

Aliases are problematic when the scope of the alias exceeds that of the memory. Consider the runtime stack. Each stack frame contains data necessary for entering function scope and exiting function scope, including

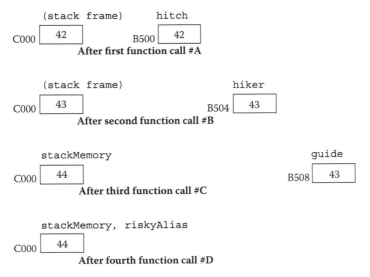

#E **No stack frames in scope:** `riskyAlias` not associated with valid memory

FIGURE A7   Stack frames go out of scope.

memory for local variables. What happens if a reference to a local variable is returned from a function call, as in statement #E of Example A7? The caller then holds an address to memory in a stack frame. However, stack frames are popped off the runtime stack as part of the routine return from a function call! The caller would then be left with a handle to memory that will be reassigned, again establishing an unseen vulnerability for data corruption. Guidelines mandate that one should not return local variables by reference.

Even without knowledge of stack frames, a programmer should remember that local variables go out of scope when a function is exited. When returning a reference, programmers must ensure that the address returned is currently valid, and will remain valid after function scope is exited. Aliases to heap memory should be more stable. Nonetheless, in C++, as shown in Appendix B, one must track ownership of heap memory so memory leaks do not occur.

Appendix B: Heap Memory and Aliases

THIS APPENDIX REVIEWS THE USE OF HEAP MEMORY in C++, C#, and Java. We contrast stack and heap allocation as well as explicit and implicit deallocation. We examine class design responsibilities when heap memory is allocated internal to an object. This appendix augments material presented in Chapters 4 and 5. Readers are not expected to have experience with either C or C++, but those without such exposure should first read Appendix A.

B.1 HEAP VERSUS STACK ALLOCATION

Chapter 4 provided an overview of a program memory, distinguishing between the runtime stack and the heap. The runtime stack is used to hold data as it comes into scope via function calls. When a function is invoked, the stack frame associated with the function is pushed onto the runtime stack. When a function terminates, its scope is exited, and its stack frame popped off the runtime stack. A stack frame holds all variables local to the function, whether allocated by declaration, pass by value, or return by value. The memory used in stack frames is determined by the compiler and hence is viewed as static allocation.

In contrast, memory allocated on the heap is termed dynamic allocation because memory requests are made at runtime through a call to the new operator. The size of memory requested need not be specified until runtime. Dynamic memory deallocation is more complex. As examined in Chapter 4, different languages provide different schemes. C++ uses explicit deallocation: conceptually, each allocation request (call to new operator) must be matched with a corresponding deallocation request (call to delete operator). C# and Java use implicit deallocation, that is, garbage collection.

Stack allocation and deallocation is easy and lossless. The compiler takes care of the generation and manipulation of stack frames, and supporting hardware make such processing very efficient. However, stack memory allocation is rigid since memory allocation size must be known at compile-time. Heap allocation incurs the runtime overhead of invoking the allocator via the call to new. Heap deallocation is complex, and often imprecise. However, heap memory usage provides more flexibility: memory requirements need not be known until runtime, and thus can vary from one run to another (without re-compiling code). These contrasting characteristics of memory management may be summed up as efficient versus flexible, secure versus vulnerable, and lossless versus leaky.

C# and Java allocate objects only on the heap. As shown in Example B1, one must call the new operator to allocate an object. Object declarations in C# and Java are merely declarations of references. If an object declaration is not combined with initialization (as is the case for #A in Example B1), C#/Java references are zeroed out. Since the C#/Java programmer must always call the new operator, and thus specify a constructor, there are no hidden assumptions about which constructor is triggered. In Example B1, statement #B invokes the **no-argument** (often default, compiler-provided) constructor, statement #C invokes an overloaded constructor that takes a passed integer value.

Example B1: Object Definition (Allocation)

```
// C#/Java object definition: objects are references
//    variables zeroed out if not initialized
myType        objA;            // #A objA zeroed out
myType        objB = new myType();        // #B no-arg constructor
myType        objC = new myType(42); // #C constructor takes int

// C++ object definition: by default, stack allocation
myType        objD;            // #D default constructor invoked
myType        objE(42);        // #E constructor that takes int

// C++ object definition: specification of heap allocation
myType*       objPtr1;                // #F objPtr1 not zeroed
myType*       objPtr2 = new myType;   // #G call to allocator
....

// must deallocate C++ heap object when no longer used
delete        objPtr2;               // #H heap memory released
```

C++ allocates objects on the stack, by default. C++ allocates heap objects in the same manner as Java and C#, via a call to the new operator. C++ programmers commonly use pointers, rather than references, to hold the addresses of heap-allocated memory. As noted in statement #F of Example B1, C++ does not zero out pointers. Otherwise, the process of initializing the pointer variable is much the same as that in C#/Java: a call to the new operator results in the allocation of heap memory and the return of that address. In Example B1, a C# no-argument constructor is called to initialize objB, whereas a C# constructor that takes an integer value is called to initialize objC. Two similar C++ constructors are involved in the declarations of objD and objE, but it may not be as evident in C++ that constructors are invoked.

A C++ programmer must remember to deallocate all heap objects before their handles (the pointer variables that contain their addresses) go out of scope. Otherwise, access to the heap memory will be lost; that is, a memory leak will occur. Figure B1 provides memory diagrams corresponding to Example B1.

All caveats discussed in Appendix A relative to pointers apply here because C++ heap objects require the use of pointers. The uninitialized

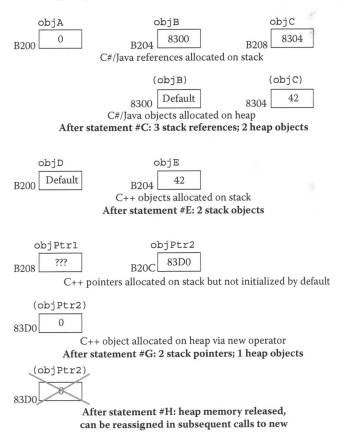

FIGURE B1   Memory diagrams for Example B1.

C++ pointer, objPtr1 (statement #B), will not be zeroed out. Whatever bit string resides in the memory associated with the pointer will then be interpreted as an address. If subsequent code statements dereference objPtr1, what happens? Possibilities include: a runtime exception because the memory address is reserved for the operating system; alteration of memory not owned, thus leading to data corruption; alteration of memory that is subsequently overwritten with valid data so that no ill effect persists. Without proper initialization, it is hard to predict behavior. Without a language construct to enforce consistency, programmers must rely on convention. C++ design guidelines always stress the necessity of initializing and, when memory is released, zeroing out pointers. Why? Programmers can then interpret a nonzero value as a legal address.

Care must also be taken when initializing objects. OOP provides the means to define a class initialization routine via a special function called a constructor. Constructors bear the same name as their class and return no value (not even void). When stack objects are declared in C++, the compiler automatically patches in a call to the **default constructor**.

An object definition is a two-step process: memory is allocated and then a constructor fires to initialize data fields and put the object into an initial, valid state. In C# and Java, because one must explicitly invoke the new operator, one must explicitly identify the constructor to invoke. Constructors may be overloaded. That is, a class may define more than one constructor. Each constructor bears the name of the class, and returns no value, but is distinguished by the number, type, and order of formal parameters.

The terms default constructor and no-argument constructor are interchanged and often confused. Default constructor is an older, C++ term and refers to the constructor provided by the compiler if the class designer does not define any constructors. The default constructor never takes any arguments. How could the compiler decide what arguments to pass? Java and newer languages refer to the no-argument constructor as the constructor (defined or default) that takes no arguments. When requesting the allocation of heap objects, whether in C++ or C#/Java, the constructor must be explicitly invoked, and thus, it is trivial to invoke a constructor other than the default (or no-argument) constructor. Details become a bit trickier, as we see below, for the stack allocation of C++ arrays.

An array of objects is allocated and initialized in two (or three) steps in C# and Java. First, a reference to an array is declared. Then, this reference is initialized to hold the address of an array of references, that is, the programmer specifies the size of the array, indicating how many references will be housed in the array. These two steps are combined into one statement, #A in Example B2. Lastly, the array of references is initialized to hold the addresses of the individually allocated objects. In the body of the for-loop, statement #B in Example B2, a specific constructor may be invoked to initialize each object as it is allocated on the heap with a call to the new operator.

Example B2: Array Allocation: C# versus C++

```
// C# and Java object arrays: array of references
// #A an array of 100 references allocated
myType[]            db = new myType[100];

// #B each C#/Java reference individually initialized
//      to hold address of heap-allocated object
for (int j = 0; j < db.Length; j++)
        db[j] = new myType(j);

// #C   C++: array of objects allocated on stack
//      default constructor implicitly invoked for each object
// PROBLEM IF CLASS myType DOES NOT HAVE NO-ARGUMENT CONSTRUCTOR
myType      db[100];

// #D may overwrite default C++ initialization
for (int j = 0; j < 100; j++)
{       myType          local(j);      // non-default constructor
        db[j] = local;                 // #D.2
}

// #E C++: if myType provides only constructors with arguments
//      => must use pointers
myType*      db[100];
for (int j = 0; j < 100; j++)
        db[j] = new myType(j);
```

C++ object arrays are allocated, by default, on the stack. In the array declaration of statement #C in Example B2, the syntax suggests that the compiler has no choice but to patch in calls to the no-argument constructor for each object initialization. Why? There is no means to specify any other constructor in the array variable declaration. Nonetheless, one can overwrite the default initialization, as shown in #D2. However, if a class does not provide a public constructor that takes no arguments, one cannot even allocate an array of objects on the stack in C++. What can a programmer do then? (1) Use a container from the STL as an alternative to an array. (2) Allocate an array of pointers and then allocate objects individually on the heap, as shown in statement #E, just as is done in Java and C#. Figure B2 correlates to Example B2.

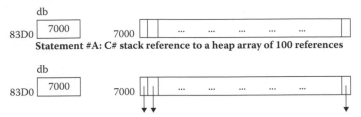

Statement #A: C# stack reference to a heap array of 100 references

Statement #B: C# heap array of 100 references initialized to hold objects' addresses

FIGURE B2   Memory diagrams for Example B2.

B.2 OWNERSHIP

C++ programmers must track and deallocate heap memory. When should a programmer deallocate? Match every new to a delete is a simplistic mantra that is difficult to follow in the midst of function calls and aliases. We provide examples next of pointer usage with respect to memory ownership. The first function in Example B3 calls the new operator to allocate a single integer on the heap. When this function executes at runtime, the address of the heap integer so allocated is returned (and assigned to the local pointer variable heapInt). In the unlikely event that there is insufficient memory available to allocate one integer, the new operator will throw an exception. Unless specified, a failed memory request does not return a zero. Programmers must specify a "nothrow" form of the new operator so that zero is returned to indicate a failed memory allocation request. For more detail on secure coding, see Robert Seacord's (2013) book.

Example B3: C++ Memory Management

```
// C++ code: allocation, transfer and deallocation of heap memory
void matchNewDelete1()
{    int*    heapInt = new int;
    ...
    delete heapInt;
}

void matchNewDelete2()
{    int*    heapIntA = new int[100];
    ...
    delete[] heapIntA;
}

int* transferOwnershipOut(int threshold)
{    int*    heapInt = new int;
    *heapInt = threshold;
```

```
        ...
        return heapInt;
}

void assumeOwnership(int*& ptrPassedByRef)
{    int*   heapInt = ptrPassedByRef;
     ptrPassedByRef = 0;           // no longer owner
     *heapInt = 999;
     ...
     delete heapInt;
     return;
}

int* assumeThenTransfer(int*& ptrPassedByRef)
{    int*   heapInt = ptrPassedByRef;
     ptrPassedByRef = 0;           // no longer owner
     ...
     return heapInt;
}
....
matchNewDelete1();                    // call #1
matchNewDelete2();                    // call #2

int* myPtr = transferOwnershipOut(33);     // call #3
*myPtr = 21;

assumeOwnership(myPtr);                // call #4
if (myPtr)    cout << *myPtr << endl; // is there output?

myPtr = transferOwnershipOut(55);               // call #5
int*   yourPtr = assumeThenTransfer(myPtr);     // call #6
if (myPtr)   cout << *myPtr << endl;
if (yourPtr) cout << *yourPtr << endl;
```

The second function in Example B3 calls the new[] operator to allocate an array of 100 integers on the heap. When this function executes at runtime, the address of the first element of the array of 100 heap integers is returned (and assigned to the pointer variable heapIntA). All array elements must be allocated contiguously. Thus, requests for large arrays are more likely to fail because of insufficient heap memory. Hence, if large amounts of heap data may be requested, and failure is possible, exceptions or the "nothrow" version of the new operator should be employed to avoid runtime error.

Calls to the new and new[] operators execute similarly in C#/Java. Most modern languages provide the means to explicitly allocate dynamic memory. C++ requires explicit deallocation as well. C++ supports the delete operator, which takes a passed pointer and releases (to the allocator) the heap memory associated with that pointer. Released heap memory may be reassigned in subsequent calls to the new operator. Since pointers are typed in C++, the delete operator can infer the size of the allocated memory being released. For arrays, the delete[] operator should be invoked. In C++, every new should be matched with a delete, and every new[] should be matched with a delete[]. Aliases, transfer of ownership, parameter passing, etc. make such a simplistic design guideline difficult to follow, especially without adequate documentation.

As noted in Chapter 4, Java and C# provide implicit deallocation. That is, programmers may request memory from the heap, via the new operator but do not need to invoke a delete operator (none is provided in Java) to deallocate such memory. Garbage collection reclaims allocated but "dead" memory from the heap. Garbage collection frees the programmer from the headaches of tracking memory but has its own drawbacks. Program execution must be suspended for the garbage collector to run; garbage collection is not perfect (not all dead memory is reclaimed); and, while waiting to be collected, dead blocks of memory, interspersed among free blocks, fragment the heap. Although a **fragmented** heap negatively impacts performance, many programmers do not attempt to track ownership, minimize the use of temporaries, or share data to decrease the amount of data allocated but left to linger until the garbage collector runs. C++ programmers must be more conscious of the use of heap memory because, in C++, heap memory must be explicitly deallocated. Nonetheless, we recommend that all programmers consciously consider program memory usage to design safer and cleaner code.

Example B3 illustrates appropriate management of heap memory. Functions are used to isolate memory allocation and to clearly identify when that memory is released or the responsibility to do so (ownership) is passed. Figure B3 provides the corresponding memory diagrams. When heap memory is allocated and then deallocated in the same scope, as in the first two functions, it is easy to verify that no memory leaks. Note that array allocation requires that the delete[] operator be used. If the delete operator is used to deallocate an array, there is a memory leak because only the first array element would be deallocated. In our example, that would be a leak of 99 integers.

The last two functions in Example B3 assume the ownership of the heap memory passed into the function (via a pointer passed by reference). The int pointer passed by reference into each function is zeroed out. Why? Upon assumption of memory, the function must indicate that the caller no longer owns the memory. By zeroing out the pointer passed by reference, the function records its assumption of ownership. Upon return from

heapInt
C300 | 7800 | (heapInt)
7800 | ??? |

Call to function matchNewDelete: heap object allocated (then deallocated)

heapInt
C300 | 7A00 | (heapInt)
7A00 | ??? |

Call to function matchNewDelete2: heap object allocated (then deallocated)

heapInt
C300 | 7B00 | (heapInt)
7B00 | ~~33~~ 21 | myPtr
B000 | 7B00 |

**Call to function transferOwnershipOut: caller assumes ownership
heap object allocated, initialized (and then address passed out)**

heapInt
C300 | 7B00 | (heapInt)
7B00 | ~~21~~ 999 | myPtr
B000 | ~~7B00~~ 0 |

**Call to function assumeOwnership: address passed in
passed pointer zeroed out, data value updated indirectly (then deallocated)**

heapInt
C300 | 7C00 | (heapInt)
7C00 | 55 | myPtr
B000 | 7C00 |

**Call to function transferOwnershipOut: caller assumes ownership
heap object allocated, initialized (and then address passed out)**

heapInt
C300 | 7C00 | myPtr
B000 | ~~7C00~~ 0 | yourPtr
B004 | 7C00 |

**Call to function assumeThenTransfer: address passed in
passed pointer zeroed out (and then address passed out)**

FIGURE B3   Memory diagrams for Example B3.

the function call, the caller now has a pointer variable that points to nothing because the caller has released its ownership of heap memory.

It is crucial to track ownership. If ownership is transferred, the pointer
that releases ownership must be nulled or zeroed out. Recall a null pointer
indicates that it does not contain a valid address.

B.2.1 Internal (Object) Heap Memory

We continue our examination of memory ownership by considering class
designs that allocate heap memory internally. That is, an object contains
a pointer (reference) as a data member and that pointer holds the address
of heap memory. When is that memory transferred or deallocated? We

cover various scenarios. Our discussion is applicable only to C++ because C# and Java do not explicitly deallocate heap memory. Yet, C#/Java programmers may improve performance (and the efficacy of garbage collection) by tracking ownership and zeroing out references when appropriate.

The names of the two variables in Example B4 suggest that one variable leaks but the other does not. In the context of stack allocated objects, this distinction does not make sense. Both objects are allocated memory in the stack frame associated with strangeFn(). This frame is popped off the runtime stack when the function exits, so where is the memory leak? Not on the stack. Could there be a memory leak from the heap? There is no explicit call to the new operator in the function of Example B4.

Example B4 C++ Application Code Obscures Leak

```
// application code uses hiddenLeak and noLeak objects
//      NO CALLS to NEW => calls to DELETE inappropriate
void strangeFn()
{       hiddenLeak    objA;
        noLeak        objB;

        cout << "I am following design guidelines" << endl;
}
```

The internal structure of either type of object declared in Example B4 is unknown but appropriate class design is assumed. Perhaps that assumption is not warranted. The hiddenLeak class in Example B5 allocates heap memory in the constructor, and thus invokes the new operator. However, the class code does not contain evidence of any call to a matching delete. We have found the problem. How do we correct it? C++ provides a special function called the destructor.

Example B5: C++ Class Design Must Address Memory

```
// IMPROPERLY DESIGNED: heap memory allocated in constructor
//      NO DEALLOCATION: no delete[] to match new[]
class hiddenLeak{
   private:
        int*    heapData;
        int     size;
   public:
        hiddenLeak(unsigned s = 100)
        { size = s;            heapData = new int[size]; }
        ...
};
```

A destructor is a special class function that bears the same name as the class, preceded by the special character "~." Like constructors, the destructor returns no value, not even void. Unlike constructors, the destructor cannot be overloaded: each class has only one destructor and it takes no arguments. The application programmer does not invoke the destructor. The C++ compiler automatically patches in a call to the destructor when a stack object goes out of scope, or when a heap object is deallocated via the `delete` (or `delete[]`) operator. Essentially, the destructor is a cleanup routine: it performs any actions, such as deallocating heap memory, that must be executed before an object goes out of scope.

Although some C++ design guidelines suggest that class designers should always define a destructor, many class designs meet expectations without a destructor. When is a destructor required? When an object allocates heap memory. The class designs in Example B5 and Example B6 appear similar, except that the `noLeak` class provides a destructor: now there is a matching delete for the new call in the constructor!

Example B6: C++ Destructor Deallocates Heap Memory

```
// Heap memory:
//     allocated in constructor; deallocated in destructor
class noLeak{
   private:
       int*  heapData;
       int   size;
       ...
   public:
       noLeak(unsigned s = 100)
       { size = s;             heapData = new int[size]; }

       // destructor deallocates heapData
       ~noLeak() {delete[] heapData;}
       ...
};
```

When the (stack) objects go out of scope in Example B4, the `noLeak` destructor will be implicitly invoked and the heap memory allocated internal to `objB` will be deallocated. There is no `hiddenLeak` destructor to invoke. Hence, the heap memory allocated internal to `objA` will remain allocated but unused: the pointer (handle) that provides access to that memory, `objA.heapData`, goes out of scope when `objA` goes out of scope. Memory leaks can be prevented with destructors. C++ class design also requires an explicit decision about the extent to which copying is supported. We examine such details next.

B.3 COPYING

C# and Java offer a measure of security when manipulating references. A declared but undefined (that is, uninitialized) reference will be zeroed out, thus preventing any inappropriate manipulation of memory. However, a design vulnerability arises when passing objects by value. Example B7 rewrites the class from Example A5 in C#, and provides sample application code that passes a hitCount object by value. Figure B4 traces corresponding memory modifications. Pass by value is not necessarily secure for objects in C# or Java, as it can lead to data modification. After the execution of the function call is statement #D of Example B7, the object a has an internal count of 2 rather than 1. Why?

Example B7: C# Pass by Value (Objects Are References)

```
public class hitCount
{       private int  count;
        private int  min;
        ...
        public hitCount()    { count = 0;    min = 0;}
        public void query()  { count++;}
        ...
}


// parameter passed by value == object reference passed
//       => address copied into local reference (p)
//       => both p and actual argument 'point' to same heap memory
void someFunction(hitCount p)
{       ...
        p.query();
        return;
}


...
// application code
hitCount    a = new hitCount();
hitCount    b = new hitCount();
hitCount    c = new hitCount();    // #A: 3 heap objects

a.query();             // #B equivalent to hitCount::query(B100)

for (int k = 0; k < 10; k++)
     b.query();        // #C equivalent to hitCount::query(B108)

for (int k = 0; k < 100; k++)
     c.query();        // #D equivalent to hitCount::query(B110)

someFunction(a);       // #E pass by value not secure for objects
```

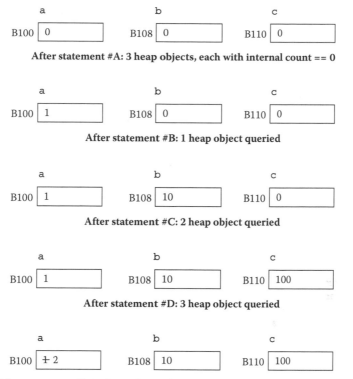

After statement #A: 3 heap objects, each with internal count == 0

After statement #B: 1 heap object queried

After statement #C: 2 heap object queried

After statement #D: 3 heap object queried

After statement #E: 1st heap object altered via embedded query in function call

FIGURE B4   Three hitCount objects.

C#/Java object declarations are references allocated on the stack. The actual object is allocated on the heap, via a call to the new operator. Thus, when the programmer manipulates an object, the programmer is manipulating a reference (an address that the compiler automatically dereferences). Hence, when an object is passed (by value) in C#/Java, really a reference (the heap address of the object) is passed. If a mutator is then called using this reference within the function, the aliased object does change state. In someFunction, the formal parameter p has the same value as the actual argument, a: both contain the address (B100) of the hitCount object allocated on the heap. Thus, when p.query() fires in someFunction, count++ modifies the memory of the object at location B100, that is, object a.

If rewritten in C++, this code would be secure. Why? C++ passes an object, not a reference, and the C++ compiler automatically provides a default "copy constructor." A copy constructor is an overloaded constructor that is invoked upon call by value. It constructs a new object and copies the values from the original object (the formal parameter or the return temporary in the stack frame) to the new object. However, we could easily construct an example that would be problematic in C++, and will do so, subsequently. First, we review the mechanics of copying—an endeavor that is more complicated with objects, aliases, and heap memory than with built-in types.

B.3.1 Shallow versus Deep Copying

Often, programmers assume that copying occurs "automatically," just like variable initialization. For built-in types, that is true. Whenever copying is necessary for assignment, or for call by value, the compiler usually patches in code for a bitwise copy. Hence, the bit string that resides in one variable (whether it is the right-hand side of the assignment statement or the actual argument in a function call) is copied into the memory of another variable (the left-hand side of assignment, or the formal parameter, respectively). This form of copying is called **shallow copying** because only the first-level data (the bit string accessed directly in memory) is manipulated. Shallow copying may produce aliases when the values copied are addresses, as in Example B1 and thus is not always sufficient.

Deep copying is a layered copying process that is often necessary for objects. Deeping copying yields a true copy because values that are addresses are not copied directly: the values in the addressed memory are copied instead. Figure B5 illustrates the memory layout of two distinct objects, where each object has a handle (pointer or reference) to heap memory. What is the result of the assignment objA = objB, if only a bitwise copy is employed? objA loses access to its heap memory because it takes on the address value from objB. Now the two different objects share the same memory, as sketched in Figure B6. In addition to the memory leak at location 8104, objA can now change data associated with objB, without, necessarily, the awareness of objB.

FIGURE B5   Two objects with differently valued memory references.

FIGURE B6   Shallow copy: `objA = objB`.

To have individual memory allocation, such that the heap memory associated with `objA` becomes identical in size and value to the heap memory associated with `objB`, as shown in Figure B7, more work is required. The class designer must acknowledge (and document) the need to support deep copying. C#/Java programmers must design and support a cloneable interface, which places some responsibility on the application programmer. C++ class designers must implement an overloaded assignment operator: an established procedure that we outline next.

B.3.2 Copying Heap Memory

Memory ownership concerns arise when copying data from heap memory. Why? Copying an address value establishes an alias: two references (or pointers) hold the same address. Aliases provide value when deliberately

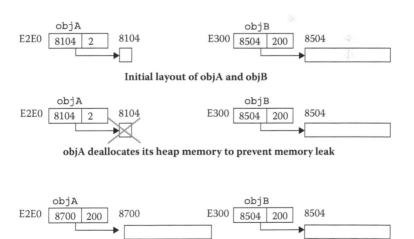

FIGURE B7   Deep copy: `objA = objB`.

used to avoid data redundancy or integrity problems. Aliases are problematic when not tracked. If two different pointers (references) hold the same address to a heap object and each pointer assumes that it owns this heap data, then either pointer can manipulate this data, including deallocating it, without regard to any other "owner." In C++, with a properly defined destructor, but without properly defined copying, if objB were to go out of scope before objA, then objA would continue to point to memory that it no longer owned. Premature deallocation, data corruption, and memory leaks are all undesirable side-effects of unforeseen aliasing.

Figure B7 illustrates properly defined deep copying: the value of every nonpointer field is copied directly from one object to another; in lieu of copying pointer values, additional heap memory is allocated, and then the data values indirectly accessed via the source pointer are copied. After a deep copy, the two objects have the same sized heap memory, with the same data values, but they do not share the same memory space. Subsequently, if one object modifies its heap data, the heap data of the second object will be unaffected. As importantly, if objB were to go out of scope before objA, there would be no negative impact on objA because objA would continue to point to memory that it solely owned.

Copying in C++ is more onerous for the class designer but less so for the application programmer. The compiler automatically provides a default assignment operator and a default copy constructor. Both simply implement bitwise copying. Hence, to avoid shallow copying, the C++ designer must redefine (overload) the assignment operator and the copy constructor.

To correctly manage internally allocated heap memory, a C++ class designer must define the destructor and either suppress or define the copy constructor and the overloaded assignment operator. In C++11, a class designer may also employ move semantics, see Appendix B. Example B8 displays a C++ class with properly managed internal memory. A destructor, copy constructor, and overloaded assignment operator have all been defined. Objects thus allocate heap memory internally but no memory leaks and no unintended aliasing occur with call by value or assignment.

Example B8: C++: Deep Copying Supported

```
// good MemoryManagement: destructor deallocates heap memory
// SUPPORTS deep copy for call by value via copy constructor
// SUPPORTS deep copy for assignment via overloaded assignment
class goodMM{
```

```
    private:
        int* heapData;
        int  size;
    public:
        goodMM(unsigned s = 100)
        { size = s;  heapData = new int[size]; }

        // DEEP copying supported: copy constructor
        goodMM(const goodMM&);
        // DEEP copying supported: overloaded assignment operator
        void operator=(const goodMM&);

        // destructor deallocates heapData
        ~ goodMM() {delete[] heapData;}
        ...
};

// .cpp file: implementation details
// copy constructor: new memory allocated, old values copied
goodMM:: goodMM(const goodMM& x)
{    size = x.size;
     heapData = new int[size];
     for (int j=0; j < size; j++)
         heapData[j] = x.heapData[j];
}

// overloaded assignment operator
// delete old memory, heap memory of left-hand side object of =
// allocate new heap memory for right-hand side object of =
// copy old values from rhs to lhs
void goodMM::operator=(const goodMM& rhs)
{    if (this !=&rhs)       // avoid self-assignment
     {    delete[] heapData;
          size = rhs.size;
          heapData = new int[size];
          for (int j=0; j < size; j++)
               heapData[j] = rhs.heapData[j];
     }
     return;
}
```

Example B9 also displays a C++ class with properly managed internal memory: copying is suppressed. A destructor is defined, but the copy constructor and overloaded assignment operator are declared as private. No implementation need be defined for these private, suppressed functions. The application programmer can allocate objects but cannot copy from one object to another (via call by value or assignment). Objects thus allocate heap memory internally, but no memory leaks and no unintended aliasing occur because call by value and assignment are not supported.

Example B9: C++: Copying Suppressed

```
//       copy constructor and overloaded= declared private
class copySuppress{
   private:
        int*  heapData;
        int   size;

        // copying suppressed
        copySuppress(const copySuppress&);

        // assignment suppressed
        void operator=(const copySuppress&);
   public:
        copySuppress(unsigned s = 100)
        { size = s;              heapData = new int[size]; }

        // destructor deallocates heapData
        ~copySuppress() {delete[] heapData;}
        ...
};

// .cpp file: no need to define suppressed, private methods
```

In Example B8, note that both the overloaded assignment operator and the copy constructor take a goodMM object passed by const reference. The passed parameter provides the source data for copying. By convention, it is passed by reference to avoid the overhead of allocating and initializing a local copy. It is passed by const reference for security: any attempt to alter the formal parameter in the body of the function would cause a compilation error. The two function bodies are also similar: both copy nonpointer data directly; allocate new data on the heap of the same size as that which the source object holds; and then copy the data values from the source heap memory.

The copy constructor is invoked when the construction of a new object is warranted. Without an existing object, there is no "old" heap memory to deallocate. The assignment operator differs: it is invoked through an existing object. Hence, to prevent a memory leak, it must deallocate the "old" heap memory associated with the object through which it was invoked.

Example B10 demonstrates application code that declares objects from the two classes defined in Examples B8 and B9. As expected, any attempt to copy copySuppress objects will trigger a compilation error. Why? When assignment is attempted in statement #B, the compiler looks up assignment and finds that it is declared private in the copySuppress class. Hence, external access is invalid and the compiler complains. When pass by value is attempted in statement #C, the compiler searches for the copy constructor and finds that it is declared private in the copySuppress class. Hence, external access is invalid and the compiler again complains.

Consider next the assignment b = a; in statement #A of Example B10. b is the object through which the function operator= is invoked. The assignment b = a; is thus equivalent to goodMM.operator=(&b,a). a is the explicitly passed parameter; &b is the implicitly passed this pointer. What if the assignment statement were 'b = b;'? Such clear cases of self-assignment are usually optimized away by a modern compiler. However, not all cases of self-assignment are evident due to aliases. Thus, the this pointer is used to check for self-assignment in a C++ overloaded assignment operator.

Example B10: C++ Memory Handled Appropriately

```
// function that passes parameters using call by value
//     copy constructor provides deep copy: NO ALIASING
//     data (from address held in pointer) copied
//     => local parameter altered; passed parameter safe
void noLeakyFn(goodMM x)
{
    ...
    x.chgState();
    return;        // destructor invoked for local object
}


// application code allocates goodMM and copySuppress objects
//     assignment or call by value preserves object integrity
goodMM        a(20);
goodMM        b(200);
copySuppress  c(20);
copySuppress  d(200);

b = a;        // #A b's 200 ints deallocated
d = c;        // compiler error #B

noLeakyFn(b);// b's state secure
noLeakyFn(d);// compiler error #C
```

B.3.3 C++11 Move Semantics

The appropriate choice of deep or shallow copying is essential for designing correct software. As we have seen, unintended aliases can lead to data corruption (in any language) as well as premature deallocation in C++. Deep copying prevents such aliasing but is much more expensive than shallow copying, especially for large objects. Can one avoid this expense? Yes, by stealing! C++11 offers the ability to do so through "move semantics."

The key idea behind move semantics is to avoid the overhead of a constructor/destructor pairing when a temporary is generated and used without long-term persistence. Consider returning a C++ object by value: the copy constructor is invoked to copy the (stack) object into the temporary returned. With deep copying, this process may be expensive. In any case, the cost is not warranted: when the function is exited, the (stack) object goes out of scope so there is no danger of its heap memory being corrupted or prematurely deallocated. Yet, a shallow copy will not suffice as it establishes an alias to stack memory just before the (stack) object goes out of scope and its destructor is invoked. The move constructor assumes (or steals) the data content of the source object, thus avoiding a call to the new operator and the copying of data values.

Similar inefficiencies arise when using deep copying for assignment. Consider the assignment statement c = a + b. When a and b are types for which the "+" operator is overloaded, a temporary of the same type will be returned from the operator+ method. Immediately, the temporary will be assigned to c. Again, a shallow copy establishes an unseen alias that may lead to data corruption, while a deep copy is inefficient. The move assignment operator acquires the memory of the temporary, thus preventing data corruption and achieving efficiency.

As shown in Example B11, the move constructor and move assignment operator are distinguished from the standard copy constructor and assignment operator by "&&." Also note that the passed parameter (source object) cannot be "const" because it must release ownership of its memory.

Example B11: C++: Move Semantics

```
// copying avoided: assume data of rvalue reference
//        move constructor
//        move assignment operator
class copyAcquire{
  private:
      int*       heapData;
      int        size;

public:
      copyAcquire(unsigned s = 100)
      {    size = s;    heapData = new int[size]; }

      // (deep) copy constructor
      copyAcquire(const copyAcquire& a)
      {          ...          }
```

```
    // copying avoided via move constructor &&
    //       source object c yields ownership
    copyAcquire(copyAcquire&& c)
       : size {c.size}, heapData {c.heapData}
    {
       c.size = 0; c.heapData = nullptr;
    }

    // assignment with deep copy
    copyAcquire& operator=(const copyAcquire& a)
    {        ...       }

    // move assignment && exchanges ownership
    copyAcquire& operator=(copyAcquire&& c)
    {        swap(size, c.size);
             swap(heapData, c.heapData);

                     return *this;
    }

    // destructor deallocates heapData
    ~copyAcquire() { delete[] heapData; }
    ...
};
```

How do move semantics work? The move constructor steals the memory from the source object (passed parameter) and sets its heap pointer to null. The move assignment operator swaps its existing heap memory with that of the passed parameter. Whenever a move constructor or a move assignment operator fires, its passed parameter is an expiring temporary and thus is able to release its memory.

Verifying the legitimacy of a move constructor versus a copy constructor call is not the class designer's responsibility. The compiler distinguishes between references that permit assignment (*lvalues*, as in the left-hand side of an assignment statement) and those that do not (*rvalues*, as in the right-hand side of an assignment statement). Thus, the compiler may transfer (rather than copy) memory if the source value is an rvalue and its class supports move semantics.

When using C++11, a class designer need not support move semantics. A move constructor and a move assignment operator should be defined when deep copying is needed but may be expensive. In which case, the class designer should also define a copy constructor and an overloaded assignment operator for standard deep copying. The compiler resolves which constructor or assignment operator should be called, based on whether the object triggering the call is an rvalue or an lvalue.

With respect to copy semantics, C++11 also offers a syntactical means to suppress copying: the "delete"-ing of the copy constructor and the over-loaded assignment operator. Example B12 presents a C++11 revision of Example B9: a C++ class that suppresses copying.

Example B12: C++11: DELETE Copy Constructor, Assignment Operator

```
// copying suppressed:
//    copy constructor and operator= "delete"d
class copySuppress{
    private:
        int*      heapData;
        int       size;
    public:
        // copying suppressed
        copySuppress(const copySuppress&) = delete;
        copySuppress(copySuppress&&) = delete;

        // assignment suppressed
        void operator=(const copySuppress&) = delete;
        void operator=(copySuppress&&) = delete;

        copySuppress(unsigned s = 100)
        {    size = s;      heapData = new int[size]; }

        // destructor deallocates heapData
        ~copySuppress() { delete[] heapData; }
        …
};

// .cpp file: no need to define deleted methods
```

Appendix C: Function Pointers

C.1 C++ FUNCTION POINTERS

As noted in Chapter 2, software development became more abstract as programming languages became more sophisticated. By freeing software development from machine-level details, software could be designed and implemented to run on a variety of platforms. Programmers no longer accessed memory locations directly but manipulated data values via variable names. Control flow no longer centered on explicit goto statements but centered on function calls and the appropriate use of control constructs. Software design stressed functional decomposition. Modern programming languages thus streamlined software development by removing dependencies on hardware and memory assignment.

Why then return to the question of manipulating memory? *Memory management is essential to constructing safe software. Efficient memory management is essential to producing efficient software.* One of the hallmarks of C, the industry forerunner of modern software development, was the provision of high-level constructs (control structures, composite data, etc.) alongside the means (the pointer) to access memory. The pointer construct allows programmers to hold addresses.

Appendix A reviewed the pointer construct, the means to store a memory address in a variable and thus directly access memory (and indirectly access the value held in that memory). In this appendix, we examine the function pointer, embedded function pointers, and then discuss language support for dynamic function invocation (covered thoroughly in Chapter 7).

In theory, and in C, as an address holder, a pointer can hold the address of any type of memory. C provides a void pointer type that can hold the address of any memory location: data type is irrelevant to void pointers. Pointers are typed in C and C++ to provide a bit more safety. A typed pointer can hold only a memory address that is associated with a compatible type: an int pointer can hold only the address of an int variable; a minMaxRec pointer can hold only the address of a minMaxRec object; etc. The pointer construct is a powerful programming construct. Pointers give software developers the means to access memory indirectly. *Control over memory location can thus be retained in the program without tying the code directly to specific hardware locations.*

Recall that a function is an isolated set of programming statements, possibly associated with local variable(s) and/or passed data and potentially returning data. This set of programming statements is laid out in the code section of program memory function and thus is associated with an address. *The function name then is a symbolic representation of the function address.*

A function call or invocation is an instruction mandating a jump to the function so named. The compiler usually translates a function call directly into a JUMP statement. In other words, a function invocation can be perceived as a circular goto statement where the target destination is the named function, and control returns to the point of call after the function executes. Although function calls are more readable and maintainable than JUMP statements, we stress here that, relative to control flow, a function name is really the same as an address. Fortunately, the compiler handles the many details necessary to ensure correct processing, such as setting up the stack frame or activation record to hold the program counter so that control automatically jumps back to point of call when a function ends.

A pointer is simply a variable that holds an address. Since a function is (the symbolic representation of) an address, a pointer can hold the address of a function. This type of pointer is called a function pointer. Formally, a function pointer is typed to hold the address of function. The function signature and its return type define the function type. There is no conversion between different function types. Example C1 illustrates the declaration and initialization of differently typed function pointers, the general form of a function pointer declaration, as well as a type definition (typedef) that supports readability by defining a function pointer type for reuse.

Example C1: C++ Function Pointers

```
// sample function forward declarations
void FN();          // function takes no parms, returns nothing
int  iFN();         // function takes no parms, returns int
void FNi(int);      // function takes int parm, returns nothing
int  iFNi(int);     // function takes int parm, returns int
```

```
// function pointer declarations
//   corresponding to above "function types"
void (*FP)();
int  (*iFP)();
void (*FPi)(int);
int  (*iFPi)(int);

// generic form of function pointer declaration
return_type   (*FPname)(fnParmList);

// typedef to define 'function pointer' type => readable code
typedef       bool (*boolFP)();

// functions return bool, take no argument: same function type!
bool done()  {     ...      }
bool active() {    ...      }

// function pointer declaration using defined function type
boolFP        fP1 = done;
boolFP        fP2 = active;
```

Function pointers add a layer of indirection to control flow and thus provide the means to design flexible execution paths. A programmer can use a function pointer to dynamically (at runtime) select a function to execute. How? Change the (function) address held in the (function) pointer at runtime. Example C2 illustrates sample function invocations via function pointers as well as a couple of invalid calls.

Example C2: C++ Function Invocation via Function Pointers

```
// function invocation through pointer
(*iFP)();             // OK call after dereferencing
iFP();                // OK call without dereferencing
FPi(22);              // OK correct parameter list
FPi(22.3);            // compiler ERROR bad argument, no casting
int check = iFP();    // OK return value used
iFP();                // OK return value discarded
int err = FPi(22);    // compiler ERROR: no return value
```

To call a function, one dereferences a function pointer. Since the function pointer can hold the address of any function that matches its type, *calling a function through a function pointer causes the postponement of function selection until runtime.* By breaking the one-to-one correspondence between function invocation and function selection, significant flexibility is achieved: the value of the function pointer will determine what function is invoked, and, like any variable, the value of a function pointer can be changed when code executes.

How should a function be selected? The programmer can design selection criteria to be evaluated at runtime, and whose changing values drive the choice of different functions. Data values can be resident in memory, calculated from other data values, supplied by the user, or read from a file. To design viable control paths, one must carefully consider the value of the data that drives the initialization of the function pointer, the choice of external files that yields the data, etc.

C.2 DESIGN EXAMPLE: LIBRARY INVENTORY

To illustrate the design flexibility achieved using function pointers and to prepare the reader for understanding the complexity of polymorphism, as covered in Chapter 7, we walk through an iterative design of a system with significant potential for longevity, reuse, and extension. We choose an inventory system because inventories track many different types of items, but manipulate them relatively uniformly, whether for sales or classification. Thus, (sub)type is a significant factor in design but a common interface unites all subtypes.

Our example tracks the design of a library catalog (Dingle, 2002), which may initially hold books, DVDs, CDs, reference materials, etc. Consider a library resource as the basic entity. Then view each particular item (book, DVD, etc.) as a subtype. In processing items, the library system must provide much functionality: check out, renew, replace, report lost, etc. Our design example focuses solely on the renewal process but the concepts covered apply to other functionality as well.

The basic renewal process is similar for all items; extra details may vary according to subtype. Our design goal is to construct the renewal function in an extensible manner. That is, renewals should be processed uniformly, regardless of what (sub)type of library item is being renewed. Consequently, the inventory system that should not break with the addition of a new subtype, such as eBooks.

C.2.1 Pass #1: Non-OO Code

Example C3 illustrates the first pass of our design, using function pointers directly. The code is not OO. More importantly, it is not extensible. A switch statement is used to initialize the function pointers. Whenever a new subtype of library item is added to the system inventory, this switch statement would have to be modified.

Example C3: Library Inventory: Pass #1 (C-Style Code)

```
// subtype specific renewal actions isolated in functions
void    BkRenew()     {        ...        }
void    DVDRenew()    {        ...        }
...
enum ItemType{BOOK, DVD, ...};   // structured but not OO design

ItemType      what;
void          (*RenewFP)();      // function pointer

// external initialization of function pointer
switch(what){
        case        BOOK:      RenewFP = &BkRenew;     break;
        case        DVD:       RenewFP = &DVDRenew;    break;
        ...
        case        REFERENCE:     RenewFP = 0;
}

// call general renewal routine, pass function pointer
//    general routine performs tasks common to all subtypes
// function pointer holds address of specific renewal routine
// classic CALLBACK design
//    specific renewal called via passed function pointer
...
if (RenewFP) RenewItem(RenewFP);

// general renewal routine
void RenewItem(void (*FP)())
{       // actions common to all subtypes          // #A
        ...
        // subtype specific actions invoked through FP
        (*FP)();
}
```

This first pass at designing a flexible and extensible inventory system has significant drawbacks. The application programmer is left with the responsibility to track type. Even with the use of an enumerated type (enums) to improve readability, this design is essentially hard coding, and is also error-prone. There is no association between subtype and functionality. The application programmer sets the value of the function pointer. Thus, the function pointer could easily be initialized with an incorrect function address.

Our initial design, shown in Example C3, is tedious, error-prone, and not extensible. The function pointer is not controlled and could easily be set to an incorrect value. Furthermore, every library process (checkout, return, replace, etc.) that depends on subtype to select an appropriate function must use a similar switch statement to initialize function pointers correctly. What happens if a new subtype is added? Each of these multiple switch statements must be updated with the option of initializing the function pointer to hold the address of the appropriate function for the new subtype. Clearly, maintenance is then tedious. Why is it error-prone? It is usually not a trivial task to find all relevant switch statements, especially if the library system is large and distributed across many modules.

C.2.2 Pass #2: Struct Ties Together Data and Functionality

Our second pass attempts to reduce the software complexity of the initial design by tying together data type and functionality. As shown in Example C4, the LibItem struct defines library item data as well as the renewal function pointer. Functional decomposition is explicit. The pre-ProcessRenewal function collects actions common to all LibraryItem variants (noted in statement #A of Example C3). This function is defined internal to the LibItem data type, ensuring some degree of consistency.

Example C4: Library Inventory: Pass #2 (C-Style Code)

```
// old-style: type overlay
struct LibItem                    // vulnerable: public by default
{       string        title;
        int           loanPeriod;
        ...
        // Function Pointer must be initialized
        void (*Trenew)();

        union {       // subtype overlay
                string          authorBook;
                int             runTimeDVD;
                ...
        } u;
        void preProcessRenewal();              // #A
};

// application C-style code for initializing book
LibItem* book = (LibItem*) malloc(sizeof(LibItem));
book->Trenew = &BkRenew;

// application C-style code for initializing DVD
LibItem* dvd = (LibItem*) malloc(sizeof(LibItem))
dvd->Trenew = &DVDRenew;

// general renewal routine uses embedded function pointer
void RenewItem(LibItem* x)
{       // actions common to all subtypes
        x->preProcessRenewal();     // #A.1
        // type-specific actions invoked via function pointer
        (*x->Trenew)();             // #B
}
```

This second pass retains the primary drawback of the first: the application code still "manually" sets function pointers, resulting in software that is tedious to maintain, error-prone, and not extensible. Since the specialized renewal function is still external, the function pointer is still initialized externally, and thus vulnerable to improper initialization. The application programmer could easily initialize the function pointer of a DVD variable with the book renewal function, or vice versa. There would be no compiler error because all the renewal functions conform to the same function pointer type. Although the function pointer is embedded in the LibItem strut, and thus associated with the LibItem type, its value is not forced to be consistent with the data type variant. Moreoover, the function pointer is public so it can be easily modified, even after an appropriate initialization. Type overlays, as shown via the union construct are not an effective means of distinguishing between various subtypes: data integrity is not assured.

C.2.3 Pass #3: Object Encapsulates Data and Functionality

Shown in Example C5, our third pass exploits the security inherent in the encapsulation provided by the class construct. All data members are private by default and thus not vulnerable to random alteration by the application programmer. Once initialized, the renewal function pointer should not change. Furthermore, the use of a class hierarchy to define subtypes provides an extensible design. If a new LibraryItem subtype is needed, simply design another child class. Additional benefits of inheritance include the centralization of common data and functionality. Each subtype has common publication, loan, and name data. Each subtype inherits the renew function, as defined in the parent class, which then calls the preProcessRenewal function.

Example C5: Library Inventory: Pass #3 (C++ Code)

```
// objects but no substitutability yet
class LibraryItem     // safer: default private
{       string        title;
        Date          publication;
        int           loanPeriod;
        ...
        void preProcessRenewal();
   protected:          // only descendant classes may access
        // Function Pointer: syntax UGLY
        //     necessary to counter scope change
        void (LibraryItem::*FP)();                   // #A
```

```
public:
     LibraryItem(){        FP = 0; …        }
     void renew()
     {     if (FP)
          {          preProcessRenewal();
                     (this->*FP());          // #B
          }
     }
};

class Book: public LibraryItem
{       string author;
        …
        void BookRenew();
  public:
        // constructor sets function pointer
        Book()          {        FP = BookRenew();        …        }
};

class DVD: public LibraryItem
{       int    runningTime;
        …
        void DVDRenew();
  public:
        // set function pointer
        DVD()           {        FP = DVDRenew();        …        }
};
```

Since each variant is now defined via a child class, each specific renewal function can now be encapsulated in the appropriate subtype class definition. Renewal functions are now private, and associated with subtype. Function pointer initialization is no longer the responsibility of the application programmer because the function pointers are embedded in the class construct. The dependency on application programmer has shifted to class designer. The class constructor now initializes the function pointer.

Although this third pass has removed the responsibility for declaring and initializing function pointers from the client, the class designer must still deal with such tedium. The constructor in the LibraryItem base class sets the renewal function pointer to zero, indicating that there is no renewal function associated with LibraryItem. Why? LibraryItem is an incomplete definition of an actual item in the library inventory. Consequently, each descendant class must initialize the function pointer to its own renewal function.

Note that every object instantiated from a particular class has its own individual function pointer data member, *although every renewal function pointer from a particular class is initialized to the same value.* The

`LibraryItem` protected function pointer is initialized in each child class constructor and its value is not subsequently altered! There is thus no need to have multiple function pointers for all `Book` objects: only one renewal function pointer is needed for the `Book` class. Likewise, there is no need to have multiple function pointers for all `DVD` objects: only one renewal function pointer is needed for the `DVD` class and so forth.

The redundancy of extra function pointers, one per object versus one per class as defined in Example C5, quickly increases as additional functions are designed for dynamic invocation. Consider other library processes (checkout, return, replace, etc.) that must be customized for subtypes. Extrapolation of the renewal example for each such routine yields one additional function pointer member in each descendant class of the `LibraryItem` class. Thus, if there were seven library processes, there would be seven function pointer members per descendant class.

What is the net effect of this design with its embedded function pointers? A huge allocation of function pointer data members, seven function pointer data members per object! But we need only one function pointer for each dynamically resolved function in a particular class. That is, we need a table of (here, seven) function pointers per class. Let us call it a virtual function table (vtab)! Clearly, it is easier and safer to use the virtual function construct as supported by OOPL. The compiler is responsible for the construction, initialization, and maintenance of vtabs.

C.2.4 Pass #4: Virtual Functions!

Our fourth pass illustrates the use of virtual functions as the means of achieving the dynamic selection of functions (Example C6). Virtual functions are covered in detail in Chapter 7. This final design of the library renewal process achieves our goal of designing a flexible and extensible inventory system. New subtypes can be easily added, and specialized routines can be easily modified, all without negatively impacting application code.

Example C6: Library Inventory: Pass #4 (C++ Code)

```cpp
// Virtual Functions!!!
class LibraryItem                // safer: default private
{       string          title;
        int             loanPeriod;
        ...
        void preProcessRenewal();
public:
```

```
        LibraryItem();
        …
        // default behavior: no renewal
        virtual void renew(){}
};

class Book: public LibraryItem
{       string author;
        …
public:
        …
        // once virtual, always virtual
        //      use keyword to document
        // override renewal to customize behavior
        virtual void renew();
};

class DVD: public LibraryItem
{       int            runningTime;
        …
public:
        // override renewal to customize behavior
        virtual void renew();
};

// application code
LibraryItem* baseptr;
…
// get address of some LibraryItem object: exact subtype
unknown
//              may change upon different runs of software
//              object initialized by file, file usage can change
baseptr = getLibraryItem();
…
// renew function called depends on
//                      subtype of object held in baseptr
// #2 call virtual function through base pointer
baseptr->renew();
```

Appendix D: Operator Overloading

D.1 ABSTRACTING FUNCTIONALITY

Operator overloading supports the definition of functions that may be invoked via a built-in operator, such as "+". When used in an expression, a symbol (or operator), such as "+", is interpreted by the compiler as a function call. The compiler automatically patches in the operands as parameters to the function call. Using operators, a programmer can represent actions, or operations, in a concise, intuitive, and readable fashion. Since most operators can be applied to multiple types, and each type may have a different implementation of an operator, operators are "overloaded."

Consider addition. This simple operation has at least two obvious implementations: real addition and integer addition, each of which triggers different numerical algorithms. Now introduce strings. What does the statement "x + y" imply, the addition of two numbers or the concatenation of two strings? The type of x and y must be known to correctly infer the appropriate operation. Compilers have overloaded operators for a long time.

Example D1 displays four equivalent invocations of the operation "x + y." From the programmer's perspective, statement #1 uses "operator syntax" for addition while statement #2 uses "function call" syntax (assuming function "add" is defined). Statements #3 and #4 illustrate legal calls using function call syntax but from the compiler's perspective. Statement #3 represents how a C++ compiler translates "x + y" into an invocation of a class method, through the object x. Statement #4 represents how a C++ or a C# compiler translates "x + y" into a call to an overloaded operator that is not invoked through an object.

Which one of the four calls in Example D1 is the most readable? Used with primitive types, operator syntax is the most intuitive means of triggering an operation. Function call syntax is less abstract and does not allow the application programmer to treat a programmer-defined type as a primitive.

Example D1: Syntactical Variants of Operator Invocation

```
x + y;              //#1 operator syntax

add(x,y)            //#2 function call syntax

x.operator+(y)   //#3 OO method call C++ syntax

operator+(x,y)   //#3 OO static method call C# syntax
```

Implicit casting of an operand may impact the choice of what function is invoked via an overloaded symbol. Why? Operand type is evaluated as part of a function signature. If an operand type changes, the function signature changes, and thus, the function invoked may also change. For example, if x is an integer value and y is a real, then y may be truncated to an integer and added to x via integer addition. In contrast, if x is a real and y is an integer value, then y may be promoted to a real and added to x via real addition. Casting offers convenience but causes some difficulty when overloading operators for user-defined types. We explore the impact of type in more detail when we examine mixed-mode arithmetic.

As a design technique, operator overloading has been both heralded for increasing abstraction and dismissed as **syntactical sugar**. C++ fully supports operator overloading, permitting a programmer to overload all but four operators. Java does not support any operator overloading. C# takes the middle ground by supporting limited operator overloading while placing restrictions on the mechanics of such overloading. We examine operator overloading in both C++ and in C#. As always, we strive to highlight design alternatives and the impact of different design choices.

D.1.1 Operator Overloading Overview

An operator is a symbol that represents the application of a function. "x + y" represents the "addition" of x and y; however, the type of x defines addition. Use of an operator in an expression is thus the invocation of a function. The symbol "+" is common and intuitive. Hence, the statement "x + y" is more readable than the statements "add(x,y)" or "x.add(y)." Operator overloading can thus increase abstraction and readability. Table D1

TABLE D1   Types of Operators

Semantic Meaning	Operators	Destructive	Value Returned
Mathematical	+, −, *, /, %	No	Temporary
Relational/comparison	<, < =, = =, ! =, >, > =	No	Boolean
Logical	&&, ||, !	No	Boolean
Shortcut increment/ decrement	++, − −	Yes	Object/Primitive
Access	[], ->, *	No	subObject
Function	()	Possibly	Varies
Stream I/O	<<, >>	No/Yes	Stream
Assignment	=, + =, * =, − =, /=	Yes	Lvalue

delineates the different types of operators commonly available in modern programming languages, identifies values returned from such operations, and denotes whether the operations are destructive, that is, alter the operand. Although counterintuitive, for example, "+" is not destructive: neither operand is altered; "+" returns a temporary object holding the value of the sum.

In OOD, operator overloading enables the client to use a symbol rather than a function call to invoke an operation via an object. If a binary operator is overloaded as a class method, then the function (operation) is invoked through the left operand and the right operand is passed as a parameter. This approach is taken by C++. If a binary operator is overloaded as a global or static class method, then the function (operation) is invoked through the function name (symbol) and both the left and the right operands are passed as parameters. This approach is taken by both C++ and C# as illustrated in Example D1.

Except for assignment, which is implemented by default as a bitwise copy, operators are undefined for user-defined types. Class designers must overload the operator's meaning for the targeted class. The parsing phase of the compiler does not change with the addition of a class-based meaning for an operator: "x + y" is always parsed as a binary operation; the resolution of type, and thus the identification of the specific operation, comes later. The compiler resolves the type of the operands after verifying the legality of the token sequence "x + y." Thus, neither the parity nor the precedence of an operator may change when overloaded. Furthermore, a class designer may not define functions for new symbols. Why? The compiler is written relative to a language standard, and that language's use of symbols as operators, so the set of symbols may not be expanded.

D.2 OVERLOADING C++ OPERATORS

To illustrate overloaded operators, we first sketch the design of a C++ class. We present this design incrementally to highlight the intent and effect of overloading different operators. Subsequently, we examine operator overloading in C#, noting essential language differences. Example D2 lays out a basic sequence class. We assume, but do not show, that this class provides public functionality for insertion, deletion, and query. We focus on functionality provided by overloaded operators that allow the application programmer to treat a sequence object as if it were a primitive type.

D.2.1 Assignment

The Sequence class allocates heap memory. Adhering to fundamental C++ design principles, the class MUST then define a constructor and destructor. If copying is to be supported, the class must also define a copy constructor and an overloaded assignment operator. C++ programmers must explicitly design copy semantics for classes with heap memory. Chapter 4 reviews C++ memory management details. We extend this example to illustrate the benefits of overloading additional operators.

Example D2: C++: Assignment Overloaded for Memory Management

```
//Sequence.h
class Sequence
{   unsigned    capacity;
    unsigned    size
    int*        ptr;

    void        initArray(const Sequence&);
    public:
    Sequence (unsigned x = 100)
    {     size = 0;
          capacity = x;
          ptr = new int[capacity];
          for (int i = 0; i < capacity; i++)
                ptr[i] = 2*i;
    }
    ...
    //dynamic memory allocated
    //need destructor, copy constructor, overloaded =
    ~Sequence() {      delete[]    ptr;              }
```

```
    Sequence(const Sequence&);
    Sequence&              operator=(const Sequence&);
};

//Sequence .cpp
void       Sequence::initArray(const Sequence& source)
{          size = source.size;
    capacity = source.capacity;
    //allocate & initialize new memory
    ptr = new int[capacity];
    for (int i=0; i< size; i++)
          ptr[i] = source.ptr[i];
}


Sequence::Sequence(const Sequence&      copy)
{    initArray(copy);                            }

//reference returned iot support chaining
Sequence&    Sequence::operator=(const Sequence& rhs)
{     if (this != &rhs)        //NOP self-assignment
      {       // deallocate old memory
            delete[]    ptr;
            initArray(rhs);
      }
      return *this;
}
```

D.2.2 Array Access

Our Sequence class contains numeric sequences; this design exercise explores the use of operator overloading as a means to make data access to these encapsulated sequences seem as simple as accessing array elements. Array access is direct and intuitive. "x = A[i]" extracts the i+1st element from the array A and assigns that value to the variable x. To mimic this indexed access for the Sequence class, we overload the [] or index operator, as shown in Example D3. Bounds checking, a safety feature not provided in C++, is provided in the overloaded operator. Access to Sequence data is thus both convenient and safe: the application programmer can manipulate a sequence object as if it were an array, but without concern about over or underflow.

Why is a reference returned from the overloaded []? To identify the location of the indexed element. Recall that an array name is viewed as an address, specifically the address of the first element of the array. The location of each individual array element is calculated as an offset from the base address of the array: the jth element has an offset of (j*ElementSize). In a zero-based array, A[0] is thus the address of the first element, A[1] the address of the second element, etc. A[i] is thus associated with the address of the i+1st element. The compiler automatically deferences the array address so that the programmer manipulates array elements as data rather than as addresses.

Example D3: C++ [] Overloaded for Intuitive Access

```
// intended use:       Sequence      a(SIZE);
//                        ...
//                      a[index] =    b;
// overloaded operator provide bounds checking
//    requires #include cassert
int&       Sequence::operator[](int index)
{      assert(0 <= index) && (index <= capacity));
       return ptr[index];
}
```

Programmers do not typically think of function invocation when they use symbols for arithmetic operations, array access, or input/output. Why not manipulate user-defined types in the same manner as built-in types? *Operator overloading is effective when the design of the overloaded operator supports the application programmer's expectations*, as seen via the overloaded [] operator. What of other operators?

D.2.3 Simple Addition

The addition of two Sequences may be interpreted as the summation of "corresponding" values. Addition is a nondestructive operation: neither operand is altered, a temporary value holding the sum of the two operands is returned. For example, if the first Sequence holds values 1, 14, 10, and the second holds values 2, 6, –3, then the sum of the two Sequences is 3, 20, 7 (but neither of the original Sequences is altered).

We present two versions of overloading "+" in Example D4. Which version is preferred? The second version is slightly "prettier," but its most significant benefit is that it provides bounds checking, via the overloaded [] operator. The first version accesses the ptr array data member directly in statement #D4.1, and thus the array index will not be checked for validity.

Statement #D4.2 invokes the operator[] method that uses the cassert facility to check array bounds at runtime.

Example D4: C++: + Overloaded

```
//version #1: access data members directly, no bounds checking
Sequence  Sequence::operator+(const Sequence& b)
{
      Sequence      local(b);
      for (int i=0; i< size; i++)
          local.ptr[i] += ptr[i];    // #D4.1
      return local;
}


//version #2: bounds checking via previously overloaded []
Sequence  Sequence::operator+(const Sequence& b)
{
      Sequence local(b);
      for (int i=0; i< size; i++)
          local[i] += ptr[i];       //#D4.2
      return local;
}
```

What were our goals in overloading addition? What did the application programmer expect? Does the application programmer make any assumptions about use that are not met by our design? *Compilers do not evaluate design.* Thus, there is no automatic verification of the design effect of overloaded operators. Tracing the application code in Example D5, it becomes evident that the overloaded addition for Sequence "works" when the operands are both of the expected Sequence type.

Statement #D5.1 illustrates the overloading of the [] operator while statement #D5.3 illustrates the addition of a large sequence to a tiny sequence. If Sequence addition should concatenate trailing values to a composite sequence, when two unequal-sized sequences are added, then this addition "works." What if a tiny sequence is added to a large sequence, as done in statement #D5.2? Ouch! Both versions of the overloaded "+" in Example D4 allocate a local object that is initialized (via the copy constructor) by the passed parameter (the second operand of the addition operation). When a smaller sequence is added to a larger sequence, overflow (and, thus data corruption) is possible in our first version. Why? The local sequence object is smaller than the sequence through which the function was invoked, and array bounds are not automatically checked in C++ (statement #D4.1). The second version of overloaded addition does check bounds and thus would yield a runtime error (statement #D4.2). Neither option is attractive.

Example D5: C++: Application Code for Simple Arithmetic

```
// two Sequence objects instantiated:  different capacities
Sequence    tiny(5), large;
...
tiny[0] = data;                       // #D5.1 operator syntax
tiny.operator[](0) = data;            // function call syntax

// addition yields temp which is then assigned to Lvalue
tiny = large + tiny;                  // #D5.2 operator syntax
tiny.operator=(large.operator+(tiny)); //function call syntax

tiny = tiny + large;                  // #D5.3 operator syntax
tiny.operator=(tiny.operator+(large)); //function call syntax
```

In Example D6, we redo the implementation of the overloaded "+" to handle capacity inconsistency. When "+" is invoked, a local Sequence object is constructed, via the copy constructor, as a copy of the larger Sequence object. Then, element by element, values from the smaller Sequence are added to the local Sequence, until every item in the smaller sequence has been used.

Example D6: C++ Overloaded +

```
Sequence     Sequence::operator+(const Sequence& b)
{     //find larger sized operand for local copy
    if (size > b.size)
    {       Sequence        local(*this);
            for (int i=0; i< b.size; i++)
                    local[i] += b[i];
            return local;
    }

    else
    {       Sequence        local(b);
            for (int i=0; i< size; i++)
                    local[i] += ptr[i];
            return local;
    }
}

//overload + to add increment to each element in a Sequence
//          local Sequence allocated because '+' nondestructive
Sequence     Sequence::operator+(int increment)
{
    Sequence local(capacity);
    for (int i=0; i< size; i++)
```

```
            local[i] += increment;
        return local;
}
```

D.2.4 Mixed-Mode Addition

In Example D6, we also provide a second (overloaded) version of the overloaded "+": adding a fixed increment to each element stored in a Sequence. This second version of addition allows mixed-mode arithmetic: the first operand is a Sequence; the second operand is an integer value that will be added to each element in the Sequence represented by the left operand. Again, "+" is not destructive. The Sequence operand is not altered: "+" generates a temporary Sequence object that holds the result of addition.

The application code in Example D7 uses the updated version of the overloaded "+" operators. Once we support the ability to "add" an increment to each element in a sequence via the "+" operator, the application programmer can compile statements such as "a = b + 8" in Example D7. However, design inconsistencies persist. If "a = b + 8" is legal, then so should "a = 8 + b," since addition is expected to be commutative. Yet, "8 + b" does not compile because the left operand of the "+" operation is a literal value, 8, not an object. Hence, there is no object, no this pointer, through which to evaluate the call. "8.operator+(b)" is not a legal call. When mixed-mode arithmetic is supported, the client has no intuition to always use the object as the left operand in an expression.

Example D7: C++ Application Code for Arithmetic and Assignment

```
Sequence             a(200), b(200);
Sequence             x;
...
a = b + 8;   //# D7.1 ok
             //same as a = b.operator+(8);
a = 8 + b;   //# D7.2 COMPILATION ERROR even though
             //# D7.2 conceptually same as #A
             //same as a = 8.operator+(b);
x = a + b;   //# D7.3 ok, ' = ' overloaded; no leaks

a = a + b;   //# D7.4 same as #C7.3 except different Lvalue

//application programmer then reasonably expects:
a += b;      //# D7.5 COMPILATION ERROR: '+=' not overloaded

x = x + 1;   //# D7.6 ok, conceptually same as #C7.1
```

```
x += 1;      //# D7.7 COMPILATION ERROR if'+=' not overloaded

x++;         //# D7.8 COMPILATION ERROR if'++' not overloaded
```

Another compilation error occurs if shortcut assignment operators are used. Statement "a = a + b" compiles but "a += b" does not. Why? In C++, "+=" is treated as a distinct operation, not as a composite of addition followed by assignment. The operator "+=" is not overloaded so when the C++ compiler tries to resolve the call, it searches for, and does not find, a "operator+=" function in the Sequence class. C# does not have this problem with short-cut assignment because "+=" is parsed as a combination of the two operators "+" and "=". Hence, once the "+" operator is overloaded, the operator "+=" can be processed because assignment in C# is always defined.

We have overloaded "+" for two operands of type Sequence as well as for mixed-mode arithmetic. If "+" and "=" are supported, then support for "+=" may be assumed by the client. Example D8 shows the overloading of "+=" to support shortcut assignment. However, if mixed-mode "+" is supported and "+=" is supported, then maybe "++" should be supported.

Support for simple incrementation is commonly assumed. Since "x = x + 1" is legal, it is reasonable to expect that "x += 1" compiles. Likewise, an application programmer might expect "x++" to compile. However, the post-increment operator would have to be overloaded to support this statement. Otherwise, when the compiler tries to resolve the statement "x++," it searches for, and does not find, a "operator++" function in the Sequence class, and consequently generates an error.

Example D8: C++ Shortcut Assignment

```
//overloaded += (shortcut for addition AND assignment)
//    a += b is destructive //same as a = a + b
//    += invoked through object a => object a altered
Sequence&            Sequence::operator+=(Sequence& b)
{
     for (int i=0; (i< b.size) && (i< size); i++)
            ptr[i] += b[i];

     if (b.size > size)
            for (int i= size; i< capacity && i< b.size; i++)
                   ptr[i] += b[i];
     return *this;
}
```

Even with fairly intuitive operations, such as addition, operator over-loading in C++ may present design challenges. Why? When using tools, such as compilers, programmers expect consistent use, compatible with their experience and knowledge. Our initial design did not address implicit assumptions about the broad use of addition. An experienced program-mer expects a += b to be supported if a = a + b is supported. Also, if a = a + 1 is a valid statement, then, for consistency, a++ and ++a should also be valid. Even if one cannot remember the formal name, commutativity, one expects that "a + b" yields the same value as "b + a."

How does one design around the impasse of invoking a class method through a literal? Recall that operation "a + b" is translated as the function call "a.operator+(b)," which is equivalent to "Sequence::operator+(&a, b)" from the compiler's perspective. Hence, the a.operator+(b) call works when a is an object: b can be either an object or an integer because two versions of the overloaded operator+ are defined in the Sequence class, as shown in Example D6 (the first method takes a Sequence object as a parameter, the second takes an int). However, the a.operator+(b) call does not work when a is a literal: "7.operator+(b)" is not a valid invocation of a class method and we cannot turn it into one. *Class designers cannot rewrite the compiler.*

To support overloading binary operators when the left operand is not an object, use global functions. Global functions are not invoked through an object, and thus do not pass a this pointer as an implicit parameter. Both operands must be passed as parameters. The provision of a global function can then meet commutative expectations. "7 + a" will compile if a global function operator+(int,Sequence) is defined. If the operation is commutative, as in this example, one need not implement much new code. The global function simply forwards the call to the class method, reversing the order of the operands, as shown in Example D9.

Example D9: C++: Commutative Operation => Forward Call

```
//Addition COMMUTATIVE: a + b == b + a
//Global function to accommodate "7 + a" invocation
//    REUSE class method!!
//    pass call "7 + a" to "a + 7", that is "a.operator+(7)"
Sequence      operator+(int inc, const Sequence& b)
{     //forward call: b.operator+(inc)
      return b + inc;
}
```

D.2.5 Incrementation

Overloading "++" in C++ is a bit tricky because "++" is a placeholder for two different functions: pre-increment and post-increment. With pre-increment, the updated object state is returned to the caller. With post-increment, the object state is updated internally, but the original state of the object is returned to the caller. In this manner, pre- and post-increment mimic the application of these operators with primitives. Example D10 displays standard code for illustrating the use of pre- and post-increment on integers.

Example D10: C++: Pre- and Post-Increment

```
int         x = 10, y = 14;

//Pre increment: cout receives updated value: x + 1
//Post increment: cout passed original value: y

cout << ++x << y++ << endl;              //11 and 14 output
```

Conceptually, both functions have the same function signature (function name: operator++), and the same number of parameters (the implicit this pointer). The compiler uses the placement of the "++" symbol before or after the object to determine whether pre- or post-increment is appropriate. The C++ compiler must then be able to distinguish between two different class methods for incrementation. Hence, the class designer must define two operator++ functions: one for pre-increment; one for post-increment. By convention, a dummy int is placed in the parameter list for post-increment, forcing a distinction between the two functions. This dummy int is ignored in the implementation of operator++.

Example D11 illustrates the design of pre- and post-increment for an intuitive example: a Clock. Note that a private utility function, tick(), is defined. For pre-increment, tick() is called and then the function returns the object, which has just now been "incremented." For post-increment, a copy of the incoming object is stored, tick() is called and then the function returns the copy of the incoming object: the current, incremented object is not returned. This design technique of storing object state is also used for the post-decrement operator.

Example D11: C++ Pre- and Post-Increment for Clock Class

```
// overloading ++: how to distinguish between pre & post?
//       => C++ compiler inserts a dummy int for post call
```

```
// operator++()              —  pre-increment
// operator--()              —  pre-decrement

// operator++(int)           —  post-increment
// operator--(int)           —  post-decrement

//       => no work for application programmer
// =>class designer constructs appropriate function signature

// GOAL: APPLICATION CODE THAT SHOULD BE SUPPORTED
Clock          a(12,30,true), b(3,45,false);
cout << ++a << b++ << endl;
// cout << a.operator++() << b.operator++(1) << endl;

//Clock.h
class Clock
{       int   hour, min;
        bool AM;
        Clock tick();            // private utility function
  public:
        Clock(int, int, bool);
        Clock operator++();
        Clock operator++(int);
};

//Clock.cpp
Clock   Clock::operator++()   {     return      tick();     }
Clock   Clock::operator++(int x)
{
   Clock       oldState = *this;
   tick();

   return      *oldState;
}

Clock   Clock::tick()
{
   ++min;
   if (min == 60)                    { ++hour;  min = 0;    }
   if (hour == 13)                   hour = 1;
   if (hour == 12 && min == 0)       AM = !AM;
   return      *this;
}
```

D.3 LANGUAGE DIFFERENCES

Operator overloading can effectively increase abstraction and code readability, and thus promotes software maintainability. Yet operator overloading is not universally endorsed. Many view operator overloading merely
as **syntactical sugar**. That is, operator overloading just makes code look

prettier; no computational benefit accrues. Not surprisingly then, different languages provide different levels of support for operator overloading.

C++ fully supports operator overloading. In C++, one can overload all operators except: ".", ".*", "::", and "?:". Design difficulties associated with operator overloading in C++ include inconsistent support of programmer expectations as well as violation of encapsulation through the **friend** construct.

Java does not support any operator overloading, possibly in response to deficiencies evident in C++, or perhaps because the specification of a complete and consistent conceptual framework is not trivial. C# partially supports operator overloading. In C#, one can overload the binary arithmetic operators (and thereby, the shortcut assignment operators "automatically"), pre- and post-increment and decrement, some logical operators as well as the comparison operators. All operators overloaded in C# are static methods.

D.4 OVERLOADING C# OPERATORS

C# supports limited operator overloading. All operators overloaded in C# are static methods, as shown in Example D12. Every function that implements an overloaded operator in C# must process all operands as parameters. An overloaded unary operator passes one parameter; an overloaded binary operator passes both operands as parameters. Since C# overloaded operators must be static class methods, there is no this pointer representing the left operand when the operator is applied. C# overloaded operators are thus not invoked through the left operand.

Example D12: C# Overloaded Operators: Static Class Methods

```
// static class method     =>   assess to all private data
//     =>   both operands passed (no implicit this parameter)
class TypeA
{ // addition non-destructive
  public static TypeA operator+(TypeA a, TypeA b)
  {…}  // must return a new TypeA object

  public static TypeA operator+(TypeA a, int b)
  {…}  // must return a new TypeA object

  public static TypeA operator+(int b, TypeA a)
  {…}  // must return a new TypeA object

  //+= automatically overloaded =>    a += b; supported
}
```

D.4.1 Assignment and Increment

The assignment operator may not be overloaded in C#. In a class design, the Cloneable interface must be implemented, and Clone() invoked by the client to make a deep copy of an object. Yet, in C#, overloaded arithmetic operators cause assignment overload. For example, if "+" is overloaded, then "+=" is "automatically" overloaded. Why? By the language standard, C# compilers treat "+=" as two distinct operations: addition followed by assignment. Thus, if one overloads "+", the compiler will translate the operation "+=" into two calls: a call to the overloaded "+" operator, followed by a call to the assignment operator. Since "=" is defined for all types (as a bitwise copy), "+=" is thereby "automatically" overloaded. In contrast, C++ compilers process shortcut assignment operators as distinct operations. In C++, overloading "+=" is required for design consistency if "+" is overloaded and "=" is supported.

C# compilers' treatment of assignment also affects the design of overloaded pre- and post-increment and decrement operators. Recall that the C++ class designer had to overload two versions of operator++: the pre-increment that directly incremented the target object; and, the post-increment that saved the state of the current (target) object, incremented the target object, and returned a copy of the saved object. In this manner, the application programmer could invoke the post-increment operator while still manipulating the object in its state prior to incrementation. A similar process is required for pre- and post-decrement.

In C#, the class designer may define only one overloaded version of the increment (decrement) operator. This version is invoked whether the client uses pre- or post-increment (decrement). Why? The C# compiler takes the value returned from the pre- or post-increment (decrement) operator and assigns it to the operand as a separate process. For pre-increment, the returned value is assigned to (that is, replaces) the operand before the next operation. For post-increment, the returned value is assigned to (that is, replaces) the operand after the next operation.

Example D13 presents two common implementations of the overloaded operator++. The first version, #D13.1, directly and immediately alters the state of the operand. This version would thus yield the same results for pre- and post-incrementation: the separate assignment of the returned value would be redundant for post increment. The second version, #D13.2, makes a copy of the operand and increments this copy. Upon completion of the post-increment and the manipulation of the object, the compiler would then assign this copy to the original operand.

Example D13: Design Confusion: C# Overloaded Operator++

```
// only one increment definition
//    => used for both pre & post increment
//    => ??DESIGN??: destructive OR non-destructive??

    // version #1: directly modify operand
    public static TypeA operator++(TypeA operand)   // #D13.1
    {   operand.data++;                     // state change for operand
        return operand
    }

    // version #2: construct copy, modify and return copy
    public static TypeA operator+(TypeA operand)    // #D13.2
    {   TypeA separateCopy = new TypeA();
        separateCopy.data = operand.data + 1;  //operand untouched
        return separateCopy;
    }
```

Which version is correct? The second version allows the returned copy to be used "prior" to incrementation, as is appropriate for post increment. Unfortunately, there are no means to enforce design. Without distinct versions of the overloaded operator++ (one for pre and one for post), confusion often results. With a singular implementation for increment, there is no obvious difference between pre- and post-increment in C#. Given that many blog postings are not correct, and that it is difficult to dig through the language standard, design is not obvious.

D.4.2 Relational Operators

Relational operators in C# must be overloaded in pairs. Thus, if one overloads "<", one must overload ">", etc. The compiler will generate an error if the class designer fails to do so. C# thus enforces conceptual expectations from the application programmer's perspective. If the concept of "not equal" is meaningful, then so must be the concept of "equal."

Is mixed-mode arithmetic a design problem in C#? C# overloads operators using static class methods. Hence, for a binary operation both operands must be passed. If an operation supports mixed-mode arithmetic, then the C# class would define 3 overloaded functions, taking parameters: (type, type), (type, int), (int, type). Refer back to Example D12. Unlike C++, there is no difficulty in supporting mixed-mode operations because overloaded operators are not invoked through the left operand. Thus, it is okay if the left operand is not an object of the appropriate type (such as a literal).

D.5 OVERLOADING STREAM OPERATORS

In C++, the stream operators "<<" and ">>" may be overloaded but not as class methods. Why? The left operand is an IO stream and the C++ utility classes cannot be opened up to add overloaded functions for user-defined types. This difficulty is the same as that encountered with mixed-mode arithmetic. When the call "7.operator+(x)" could not be supported via class methods, we defined a global function. However, because addition is usually commutative, the implementation of this global function was simple: the operands of the call were inverted and the call was passed back to the class method. In this manner, the global function had no need to access the private data of the operands.

Supporting the stream operators is not so easy. Although global functions can be easily defined, operator>>(cin, object) and operator<<(cout, object), these functions must have access to the object's private data members. But how? Class designers should not make private data members public just to accommodate overloaded stream operators. Public data members violate the principles of encapsulation and information hiding, making every object vulnerable to uncontrolled state changes. The answer is **friends**.

C++ provides a means to control external access to private data and functionality: the "friend" construct. Using the reserved word "friend," a class designer may select which external functions, and/or classes, that are privileged with private access. If methodA is declared a friend of class TypeY, then the code in the function body of methodA may access the private data and functionality of class TypeY. Declaring an external class a friend is bolder than identifying a single function: if class TypeX is declared a friend of class TypeY, then all functions in class TypeX have access to all private methods and data members of class TypeY.

Friend declarations may be placed anywhere in a C++ class header file. Software developers often adhere to one of two approaches for declaring friends: place in the public section to emphasize communication with the application programmer; place in the private section to avoid cluttering the public interface. Placement of friend declarations makes no difference to the compiler but, for code readability, class designers should be consistent. In either case, documentation should note external support for overloaded operator(s). Example D14 provides sample code for overloading the stream operators for the Clock class to output hour and minute. The global function that overloads the input operator must be declared a friend, as illustrated in Example D15.

> **Example D14: C++ Overloading the Stream Operators: Friends**
>
> ```
> ostream& operator<<(ostream& out, const Clock& c)
> {     out << c.hour << ':' << c.min;
>       ...
>       return     out;
> }
>
> // in application code,   cin >> object;        cout << object;
> // more abstract than     object.input() or     object.display()
> Clock       classEnd(1, 55, true);
> cout << classEnd++ << ++classEnd << classEnd;
> ```

The friend construct is controversial. *Critics observe that the friend construct violates encapsulation, exposes private data to external functions, and increases coupling.* Java enthusiasts note that Java is more OO than C++ because it does not support the friend construct. *C++ enthusiasts emphasize that class designer controls access because friends must be explicitly denoted.* For software maintainability, the class designer should document all friendships, typically in the implementation invariant.

The friend relationship is not transferable or assumable. Other restrictions on the friend construct ameliorate its violation of encapsulation. A friend relationship is not transitive. If A is a friend of B and B is a friend of C, A is not automatically a friend of C. C must explicitly declare A as a friend. The friend relationship cannot be inherited. If A is a friend of Parent, A is not a friend of Child, unless the Child also declares A as a friend. It is not symmetric. If A is a friend of B, B is not friend of A, unless class A also declares B as a friend. The friend construct is necessary in C++ to support mixed-mode operations and the stream operators.

D.6 TYPE CONVERSION

Data types promote safe and consistent manipulation of memory. Casting is the action of converting the value of one type to the equivalent value of another type. Most everyone is familiar with casting an integer to real, as when 3 is represented as 3.0. Implicit casting or type conversion is an action undertaken automatically by the compiler, without direction from the programmer. Explicit casting or type conversion is an action undertaken when so directed by the programmer. Both implicit and explicit type conversion are shown in Example D15.

Example D15: C++ Overloading Type Conversion

```
int             i;
float           f;
f = i;                  //implicit conversion
f = (float) i;          //explicit conversion, C-style
f = float (i);          //explicit conversion, functional style

//   int => Clock object
//          handled via overloaded constructor: Clock(int)
//          constructor creates Clock object, returns nothing
//   Clock object => int
//          function returns type (converted value)
//          non-destructive: Clock object state not changed
//overload type conversion: operator othertype();
//          operator int();

//goal: overload type conversion operator
Clock        myTime(10, 10, 1);
Clock        convertTime(1604);
int          i;
...
i = (int)myTime;             //time converted to int value
                             //same as myTime.operator int(i);
```

While type conversion is supported for primitives, class designers may support comparable type conversion by overloaded the "()" operator. Consider Example D16, which demonstrates overloading the type conversion of a Clock object to an integer value.

Example D16: C++ Converting Clock Object to Int Value

```
class Clock
{            int             hour, min
             Clock tick();
  public:
             Clock(int, int, int);
             Clock(int);                     //convert constructor
             int     operator int();         //conversion operator

             Clock operator++();
             Clock operator++(int);
             friend ostream& operator<<(ostream&, const Clock&);
};

Clock::Clock(int time)             //convert constructor
```

```
{     int     holder = time % 2400;
      hour = holder/100;
      if (13 <= hour && hour <= 23) hour -= 12;
      min = holder - (hour*100);
      ...
}

int  Clock::operator int()          //conversion operator
{     int  time = hour;
      if (time == 12)  time = 0;
      ...

      time *= 100;     time += min;
      return     time;

}
```

Example D17 presents an overview of the Sequence class, supporting a broad range of overloaded C++ operators. Example D18 presents a
comparable design in C#. Both examples focus on the interface supported,
that is, the range of operators overloaded for the application programmer.
Note language differences. C# class designers may overload fewer operators; C++ must deal with accessibility issues.

Within the context of language support, the design evaluation of any
operator overloading must answer the question: is the conceptual framework so defined sufficient? For this example, one might ask if the relational operators ("<", ">") should be supported. Since Sequences are not
ordered, "no" is a reasonable response. However, the notion of equality,
and thus inequality, is relevant.

Example D17: C++ Sequence Class

```
//Sequence.h
class Sequence
{     unsigned        capacity;
      unsigned        size
      int*            ptr;

      void            initArray(const Sequence&);
public:
      Sequence (unsigned x = 100);
      ~Sequence()     {       delete[]       ptr;                    }

      //memory management functionality required for copying
      Sequence(const Sequence&);
      Sequence&       operator=(const Sequence&);

      int&    operator[](int);

      Sequence        operator+(const Sequence&);
      Sequence        operator+(int);
```

```
        Sequence&        operator+=(Sequence& b);
        Sequence         operator++()
        Sequence         operator++(int)

        Sequence         operator-(const Sequence&);
        Sequence         operator-(int);
        Sequence&        operator-=(Sequence& b);
        Sequence         operator--()
        Sequence         operator--(int)

        bool             operator==(const Sequence&);
        bool             operator!=(const Sequence&);
};


//operators with global scope: forward call to class methods

Sequence    operator+(int, const Sequence&);
Sequence    operator-(int, const Sequence&);
```

Example D18: C# Sequence Class

```
public class Sequence
{    private    unsigned            capacity;
     private    unsigned            size
     private    int[]               ptr;

     public Sequence (unsigned x = 100) { … }

     public static Sequence operator+(Sequence, Sequence) {…}
     public static Sequence operator+(int, Sequence) {…}
     public static Sequence operator+(Sequence, int) {…}

     public static Sequence operator-(Sequence, Sequence) {…}
     public static Sequence operator-(int, Sequence) {…}
     public static Sequence operator-(Sequence, int) {…}

     public static bool     operator==(Sequence, Sequence) {…}
     public static bool     operator!=(Sequence, Sequence) {…}

     public static Sequence operator++(Sequence)   {…}
     public static Sequence operator--(Sequence)   {…}
};
```

All C++ operators are inherited EXCEPT the assignment operator. Every C++ class that supports dynamically allocated data should overload its own assignment operator. Technically, overloaded operators can be virtual (see Chapter 7) since they are functions after all. However, the syntax of using virtual functions obviates any abstraction benefits associated with overloaded operators. Additionally, if a child class extends the parent class then the child class should overload any operator(s) that manipulate child class data members.

D.7 DESIGN PRINCIPLES FOR OPERATOR OVERLOADING

A thorough design addresses expectations of the application programmer. Problems arise when the expectations of the application programmer exceed the overloaded functionality provided by the class. What does the application programmer expects once addition is overloaded? Addition has a broad conceptual framework. What operators are associated with addition? Operator overloading strives to increase the level of abstraction, allowing the application programmer to treat user-defined types as built-in types. To manipulate a user-defined type as if it were a primitive type, a client assumes all operators associated with a process, such as addition, to be supported.

In short, the class designer must evaluate the conceptual framework provided by the set of operators overloaded within a class. All related operators should be overloaded, if meaningful for the class design. If "<" is overloaded, then ">" should be overloaded, etc. C# enforces some of this last design expectation. C++ does not. Table D2 delineates common operators and notes associations between similar operators.

When overloading operators, the class designer should distinguish between destructive and nondestructive operators. Why? Adhering to the principles of OO design, a class should control the state of all instantiated objects. Destructive operators should be under the purview of the class. If one invokes an operation through an object and the operation is destructive (such as + =), then the state of the object is altered. Simple addition is not destructive: a temporary object holds the sum.

For C++ class designers, a recommended guideline is to define all destructive operations as nonstatic (regular) class methods. Non-destructive operators need not be so restricted. An exception is the input stream operator ">>". This operator must be overloaded as a global

TABLE D2 Operators in Conceptual Framework

Operator	Related Operators	Associated Operations
+		+ =, ++, − =, − −
*	/	* =, /=
<<	>>	
<	>	< =, > =
= =	! =	
&&	||	!

TABLE D3   C++ Operators

Class Method Only (Destructive)	Global Method Only (Access Private Data)	Either (Nondestructive)
[]	<<	+, −, *, /, %
()	>>	<, >
=, + =, − =, * =, /=, %=		< =, > =
->		= =, ! =
++, − −		||, &&
!		

function even though, by accepting input, it alters state. We cover this operator in a later section. Table D3 delineates C++ operators and how they should be overloaded.

In C++, one may overload operators as nonstatic class methods or global (outside class scope) methods. The former invokes the function through the left operand and passes the left operand through the implicit `this` pointer. Thus, the `this` pointer holds the address of the left operand and the number of parameters passed is one less than the parity of the operation. When an operator is overloaded as a global function, both operands must be passed as parameters.

Example D18 provides a thorough overview of the `Sequence` class, as implemented in C#. Syntactical differences aside, the overloaded operators are conceptually the same as those defined in Example D17, which provides the corresponding C++ version. Table D4 enumerates the operators that may be overloaded in C#, including parenthetically, the shortcut assignment operators implied by the overloaded arithmetic, logical, and shift operators.

Are we done yet with addition? Does our `Sequence` class design support a reasonably complete conceptual framework for addition? What about subtraction? If "+" is supported, it may be reasonable to expect support for "−". Here we go again! With "−", one must consider "−=", "−−" as well as mixed-mode arithmetic. *Operator overloading can be a complex design problem.* Class designers must strive to provide a coherent set of overloaded operators for consistent manipulation of objects.

TABLE D4   C# Operators

Relational (Pairwise)	Arithmetic (=> Assignment)	Increment	Logical (=> Assignment)	Shift/Bit (=> Assignment)
= =, ! =	+, −, *, /, %	++	&, |, !	~
<, >	(/=, % =)	−−	true, false	<<, >>
< =, > =	(+ =, − =, * =)		(& =, | =, ! =)	(<< =, >> =)

D.8 OVERLOADING FOR MEMORY MANAGEMENT IN C++

We close this appendix by reviewing overloaded operators with respect to memory allocation. This advanced material is relevant primarily to applications that must closely manage memory. Such applications would be written in C++.

D.8.1 Transparency

C and C++ provide efficiency at the cost of safety. Memory leaks in C and C++ have been problematic. Although garbage collected languages, such as C# and Java, cannot resolve all memory leaks because garbage collection is not a perfect process, they do reduce the incidence of leaks. A classic memory leak, as noted in Example D19, is allocating heap memory, via a call to the new operator, but not invoking the corresponding delete operator before the handles goes out of scope.

Example D19: C++ Classic Memory Leak: No Delete

```
{       //enter scope
        Type* local = new Type();        //heap object
        ...
        //leave scope WITHOUT transferring ownership
        //leave scope WITHOUT deallocating heap object
}
```

Compilers cannot generate a call to new to match a call to delete. Where would the compiler place such a call? Given aliasing and transferring ownership, it is difficult to determine scope. By restricting scope, however, a design solution can "force" the generation of a missing delete. The wrapped pointer is such a design. The idea is to encapsulate memory management responsibilities. The class constructor "automatically" allocates heap memory via a call to new, AND the destructor "automatically" deallocates this heap memory via a call to delete. Called the **smart pointer**, this design is shown in Example D20. For more details, see Stroustrup (2000).

Example D20: C++ Classic Memory Leak Avoided

```
// SMART POINTERS: pointer wrapped in class
// constructor & destructor manage heap memory
// object (wrapped pointer) goes out of scope
//      => destructor invoked, leak averted

{  //enter scope
```

```
    Type* local = new Type();   // heap object
    SmartPtr   s(local);        // wrap object
    ...
    local->Typefn();            // #D20.1
    s->Typefn();                // #D20.2: compilation error
    // leave scope WITHOUT transferring ownership
    // leave scope WITHOUT deallocating heap object
    //   DESTRUCTOR for s called => heap object deallocated
}
```

In a confined scope, a **smart pointer** can solve the problem of memory leaks if an application programmer forgets to deallocate. However, the wrapped pointer makes the data type private and thus inaccessible. In Example D20, no call to any Type functionality could be made via the s object. Statement #D20.1 compiles; statement #D20.2 does not. Operator overloading overcomes this limitation of smart pointers. How? We overload the access operators, as shown in Example D21. Subsequently, any call to a function in the embedded pointer's interface is supported.

Example D21: Overload C++ Access Operators

```
//OVERLOAD ACCESS OPERATORS -> *
//      to make access of wrapped object transparent
class SmartPtr
{       Type* ptr;
  public:
        SmartPtr(Type* p): ptr(p)  {}
        ~SmartPtr()           { delete ptr; }

        //overload to provide transparency
        Type* operator->() { return ptr; }
        Type& operator*()  { return *ptr; }
};

//   application code, wrapper transparent
{   Type* local = new Type();   // heap object
    Type  local2;               // stack object
    SmartPtr        s(local);   // wrap heap object
    ...
    local->Typefn();
    s->Typefn();        //"s.operator->" yields ptr
    local2 = *local;
    local2 = *s;        //"s.operator*" yields *ptr
    // any problems?: local may still think it owns heap memory
}
```

We make one additional change to our **smart pointer** class. Since aliases easily lead to data corruption, we modify the smart pointer constructor so that it assumes ownership of the memory passed in via the pointer. Example D22 shows this simple but effective modification of Example D21.

Smart pointers add a layer of indirection to support memory management. Overloading access operators "->" and "*" allows a smart pointer to be used in the same manner as the object that it wraps. Operator overloading thus effectively echoes the interface of a private data member.

Example D22: Overload C++ Access Operators and Assume Memory Ownership

```
class SmartPtr2      //assume ownership of wrapped pointer
{        Type* ptr;
   public:
         SmartPtr2(Type*& p): ptr(p) { p = 0;}
         ~SmartPtr2()            {    delete     ptr; }
         Type* operator->()      {    return ptr; }
         Type& operator*()       {    return *ptr; }
};

//   leak AND data corruption averted
{   Type* local = new Type();   // heap object
    SmartPtr2   s(local);        // wrap heap object

    ...
    // local null after wrapped in smart pointer
    //       where documented??   Problems?
    //   DESTRUCTOR for s called => heap object deallocated
}
```

Through the STL, C++98 provided the `auto_ptr` template class that embodied a smart pointer. C++11 deprecates `auto_ptr`, replacing it with three generic types: `unique_ptr` wraps a "raw" pointer and assumes sole ownership; `shared_ptr` models shared ownership via a reference count—the last `shared_ptr` going out of scope deallocates the owned pointer; `weak_ptr` provides access but cannot prevent deallocation. This refinement distinguishes the utility of a smart pointer (a simple wrapper, a reference counter, a secondary reference). The notion of an encapsulated pointer, as a means to safeguard memory management, and avoid "raw" pointers, remains. For more details, see Josuttis (2012).

D.8.2 Optimization

Memory management is overhead. Calls to the heap manager do not advance the state of any computation. A call to the new operator requires the allocator to search through the free list for an available memory block. When the heap is fragmented, the allocator spends more time looking for a free block. A call to delete requires the heap manager to return the released memory block to the free list, and, possibly, coalesce adjacent free blocks.

In applications that demand high performance, it may be desirable to avoid the overhead of calls to the heap manager, especially if many pieces of dynamic data quickly go in and out of scope. One optimization technique is to localize the allocation and deallocation processes so as to avoid this overhead. Three basic steps do so: (1) request a large block of memory; (2) retain this block of memory as a local pool of memory; and (3) manage this pool directly within the class. Calls to the heap manager are thus avoided until the local pool of memory is exhausted or the memory pool is no longer needed. In C++, one can overload the new and delete operators to achieve this customization. We only outline this optimization technique. For more details, see Bulka and Mayhem (1999).

To maintain its own local pool of memory, a C++ class must implement an allocator within the overloaded new operator and a deallocator within the overloaded delete operator. The first call to the new operator triggers a (layered) call to the *real* new operator: heap memory is allocated and its address passed back to the overloaded new operator. The overloaded operator then "allocates" a smaller piece of memory and passes its address back to the caller. Subsequent object calls to new are passed to the overloaded class method new, which can now service the call directly from the local pool of memory held by the class. For each such call, the overloaded new operator passes back a pointer allocated from the local pool rather than passing on the call to the heap manager.

A mirror process for delete is handled by the overloaded class delete method. Each object call to delete triggers a local deallocation, circumventing the heap manager, and thus reducing overhead. If the local pool of memory is exhausted by successive calls to new, without corresponding calls to delete, the new operator can again call the heap manager and replenish its local pool of memory. When the local pool is no longer needed, the delete operator calls the heap via the standard delete to return the allocated memory.

Index

Printed and bound by CPI Group (UK) Ltd, Croydon, CR0 4YY

24/10/2024

01778283-0015